Scripting Addiction

Scripting Addiction

THE POLITICS OF THERAPEUTIC TALK AND AMERICAN SOBRIETY

E. Summerson Carr

PRINCETON UNIVERSITY PRESS
PRINCETON AND OXFORD

Copyright © 2011 by Princeton University Press
Published by Princeton University Press, 41 William Street, Princeton, New Jersey 08540
In the United Kingdom: Princeton University Press, 6 Oxford Street, Woodstock, Oxfordshire OX20 1TW

press.princeton.edu

All Rights Reserved

Library of Congress Cataloging-in-Publication Data

Carr, E. Summerson, 1969–
  Scripting addiction : the politics of therapeutic talk and American sobriety / E. Summerson Carr.
    p. cm.
  Includes bibliographical references and indexes.
  ISBN 978-0-691-14449-8 (hardcover : alk. paper) — ISBN 978-0-691-14450-4 (pbk. : alk. paper) 1. Medical anthropology. 2. Drug abuse—Treatment. 3. Culture—Semiotic models. 4. Culture and communication. 5. Language and culture. I. Title.
  GN296.C37 2011
  362.29—dc22

2010016928

British Library Cataloging-in-Publication Data is available

This book has been composed in Sabon

Printed on acid-free paper. ∞

Printed in the United States of America

10 9 8 7 6 5 4 3

*For fostering my love of language and
learning, I dedicate this book to:
my mother, Lynda Elliott Conway,
my father, Franklyn J. Carr III,
and my stepfather, F. Merlin Bumpus*

Contents

List of Illustrations   ix

Acknowledgments   xi

INTRODUCTION
Considering the Politics of Therapeutic Language   1

CHAPTER ONE
Identifying Icons and the Policies of Personhood   23

CHAPTER TWO
Taking Them In and Talking It Out   49

CHAPTER THREE
Clinographies of Addiction   85

CHAPTER FOUR
Addicted Indexes and Metalinguistic Fixes   121

CHAPTER FIVE
Therapeutic Scenes on an Administrative Stage   151

CHAPTER SIX
Flipping the Script   190

CONCLUSION   224

Notes   239

References   279

Index   317

Illustrations

Figures

Figure I.1. Fresh Beginnings, the Homeless Family Consortium (HFC), and funding/partnering agencies	9
Figure 1.1. President Clinton signs the Personal Responsibility and Work Opportunity Reconciliation Act of 1996, "ending welfare as we kn[e]w it."	24
Figure 2.1. Urie Bronfenbrenner's influential ecological model	58
Figure 2.2. Ann Hartman's ecomap	59
Figure 2.3. Gregory Bateson's and Margaret Mead's genogram	60
Figure 2.4. "Emotional relationship codes" from the genogram software GenoPro	61
Figure 2.5. The potential consequences of an HFC agency assessment	77
Figure 3.1. "Denial," as pictured in "My Ego" by Mary K. Bryant	90
Figure 3.2. The topographical model of the addicted subject	93
Figure 3.3. Criteria for Substance Dependence as designated by the *DSM-IV*	99
Figure 4.1. "How to Sabotage Your Treatment"	128
Figure 5.1. Framing frames: The work of HFC wordsmiths	163
Figure 6.1. "Flip the Script in 2008"	220

Tables

Table 4.1. Interpreting and Anchoring Deictics	142
Table 5.1. Taxonomy of Collective (Meta)Linguistic Crises	159

Acknowledgments

DURING THE THREE-AND-A-HALF YEARS I CONDUCTED THIS STUDY I HAD the privilege to observe and participate in the daily encounters, negotiations, and rituals that entwine two groups of people in the contemporary United States: those who, in the world of social services, are commonly known as "clients" or "consumers," and those whose areas of training and expertise fall under the broad professional category of "social work," including chemical dependency counselors, family counselors, shelter managers, case managers, domestic violence advocates, clinical supervisors, program administrators, recreation therapists, and therapeutic child care workers. My deepest gratitude is to the clients and professional practitioners affiliated with the program that I call "Fresh Beginnings." They have shared with me their ideas and perspectives, which I have worked hard to honor in this book, and have been my most remarkable teachers.

Since completing the research for this book, I have had the opportunity to teach in one of the oldest and most distinguished schools of social work in the country while at the University of Chicago. At the School of Social Service Administration, my lessons in social work and social service provision have continued, thanks to an intellectually diverse and dynamic set of colleagues, and terrific students. I am especially grateful for Michael Sosin's contributions to this project, including reading early drafts of chapters and, more generally, for the support he has given me. This book has also benefited enormously from my engagements with colleagues in the Department of Anthropology. I owe special thanks to Michael Silverstein and Susan Gal, whose work I admired long before I arrived here, and who have warmly engaged me and thoughtfully responded to my work ever since.

On the wider campus I have been lucky to help coordinate the US Locations workshop alongside Jessica Cattelino and Joseph Masco, and the Medicine, Body, Practice workshop with Judith Farquhar, Ray Fogelson and Jean Comaroff. I have learned much from them, and from the student participants in these workshops. This project continued to evolve during my interactions with members of the Michigagoan faculty seminar, as well as with colleagues working on the anthropology of addiction, as convened by Eugene Raihkel and Will Garriott.

The book itself has benefited enormously from members of my writing group—Hussein Agrama, Amahl Bishara, Hilary Parsons Dick, Paja Faudree, and Robin Shoaps—all of whom have also done much to sustain me as a junior faculty member. Offering specific and helpful comments on various elements of the project at its different stages were Julie Chu, Jennifer Cole, Robert Fairbanks, William Garriott, Colleen Grogan, Judith Irvine, Barbara Johnstone, Tanya Luhrmann, Bruce Mannheim, Joseph Masco, Susan Philips, Douglas Rogers, William Sites, Noa Vaisman, Jim Wilce, and Sarah Womack. Shunsuke Nozawa helped prepare the book's index. Greg Matoesian also deserves special thanks. I feel very lucky to have gotten to know Paul Brodwin, who has been a most generous interlocutor over the last couple of years, and has helped me to think through important aspects of this project.

This project first emerged from my work in the unique Joint Doctoral Program in Anthropology and Social Work at the University of Michigan. There I was fortunate to work with Beth Glover Reed, who, as an expert in the field, first interested me in the study of women's addiction treatment. Janet Hart was also an early supporter of my research, as was my first doctoral adviser, the late Sharon Stephens. Webb Keane played an especially important role in the development of this work, and I owe him special thanks. I am also grateful to David Tucker, Lorraine Gutierrez, Mayer Zald, Janet Finn, Charles Garvin, Mieko Yoshihama, Anne Herrmann, Edith Lewis, Skip Rappaport, and Elizabeth Wingrove. Had it not been for my stimulating undergraduate work with William Deal at Case Western Reserve University and with Jennifer Robertson at the University of Michigan, who later served as a dissertation committee member, I likely would have not pursued graduate studies in Anthropology. The research represented in this book was made possible by generous funding from University of Michigan's Rackham Graduate School, as well as the Department of Anthropology, the School of Social Work, the Mary Malcomson Raphael Fellowship fund, and the Women's Studies Program. The Gender and Mental Health Pre-Doctoral Training Program, funded by the National Institute of Mental Health, administered by the Institute of Women and Gender at the University of Michigan, and led by Susan Nolen-Hoeksema, also provided especially critical support.

Young academics are especially bolstered by moral support, and so, in addition to my appreciation of those named above, I am thankful for the stimulating companionship of other friends and colleagues, including Alice Ritscherle, Ashley, Ben, and Zander Pryor, Diane Miller, Giorgio Bertellini, Jessica Cattelino, Noah Zatz, Rob Fairbanks, Sarah Gehlert, Susan Philips, Stanley McCracken, and Stanislav Voskov. My lovely mother, Lynda Elliott Conway, has been a great support throughout this project, and I am proud to add another book to her ever-expanding library.

I suspect it is very rare to work with a doctoral student who is as smart, patient, and willing to help as Yvonne (Eevie) Smith. She read every word in this book more than once, did critical background research, and offered helpful editorial suggestions. Yvonne is very much in the lines below, and I am eager to read the lines she herself will soon write and publish.

Finally, it is with immeasurable gratitude that I thank my husband, Daniel B. Listoe. A scholar of literature, Daniel has given me many new and beautiful ways to look at the lessons of language that were first offered by the women at Fresh Beginnings. I will never forget the patience he has exercised and the support he has given—whether in the form of editorial comments on a key segment of text or in the way of necessary and wonderful distraction. It helps to be so very happy when one is writing a book.

Scripting Addiction

INTRODUCTION

Considering the Politics of Therapeutic Language

IMAGINE YOU ARE AN EXILE IN A FOREIGN LAND AND HAVE BEEN DIAGNOSED with what the natives consider to be an incurable, if treatable, disease. This disease is characterized by the inability to use language to express what you think and how you feel. You are now being treated by local specialists who work to rehabilitate your relationship to language. Through a complex set of traditional ceremonial practices, the specialists teach you how to use words, phrases, and, eventually, entire plotted narratives that reference and reveal your inner states. This rigorous pedagogical program, which you have been told is therapeutic, is also the specialists' means of evaluating you. So, as you engage in rituals of speaking, the specialists judge the extent to which your utterances match your inner states or—in native terms—how "honest, open, and willing" you are as a speaker and as a person. *Honesty*, *openness*, and *willingness* are of the highest cultural value; they are the indigenous markers of individual integrity, morality, and health. This is true according to both the specialists and the broader society that has ordained them as such. And, as indicated by your ritual treatment, these values are thought to manifest in and through the local tongue.

Imagine, too, that aside from your diagnosed troubles the society in which you now live has deprived you of many of the things normally provided to adult persons: a home or shelter; the means to clothe, feed, and care for yourself; a way to travel from place to place; a meaningful vocation; and even a kin network on which you can rely. Now suppose that the specialists are empowered to help you access these things but can also keep them out of your reach. Since the specialists' evaluative powers are linked with the capacity to distribute basic goods and resources, your ritual performance—that is, the way you speak in the course of your treatment—has far-reaching material and symbolic consequences. For instance, if you have children, they may be taken away to be cared for by others. Or, if you have been sleeping under broadleaf trees or in strange men's houses, you may be granted a home of your own with a well-made roof and a lock on the door.

As an initiate of these loaded rites of passage, perhaps you have come to believe—like the natives—in the reality of your "disease." In this case, you also depend on the specialists to determine how much more you will suffer, which they will discern as you try to speak in the ways they have taught you. For, as ritual formulas, the mantras you have learned from the specialists can transform as well as condemn you in the eyes of the locals. It all depends on how you use these efficacious ways of speaking, which the specialists will evaluate and oversee but can never totally control. Indeed, how will they ever really know if you have truly "gone native" and been transformed by their treatment? And, what are the stakes, not to mention the possibilities, of doing so?

Welcome to the world of mainstream American addiction treatment, where disease is conceived as so many illegible signs that can only be read by the sober.

Treating Talk and Talking Treatment

This book is based on more than three years of following an interconnected group of professional practitioners[1] and drug-using clients through a network of social service agencies in a Midwestern city that was (and still is) suffering the effects of economic downturn, disinvestment, and welfare state retrenchment. The ethnography focuses on "Fresh Beginnings"—an outpatient drug treatment program at the center of this social service network—and the associations and negotiations between therapists and clients there. As suggested above, these everyday interactions were semiotic entanglements: clients worked to effectively represent themselves and their problems, and therapists worked to *script*, or set the terms of these representations. Because of the institutionalized ties between Fresh Beginnings therapists and other social service professionals, a variety of resources—from temporary housing, transportation vouchers, and job training to medical care, legal protection, and therapeutic acknowledgment—hung in the balance of these intensive verbal transactions.

Scripting is an especially important, if poorly understood, element of American social work, a multidisciplinary field in which people's symbolic interactions have far-reaching material consequences.[2] While the coercive and controlling nature of social work and welfare practices has been well documented, *Scripting Addiction* illustrates that social service professionals talk about people and problems in ways that resonate with broader cultural narratives, and thereby appeal to powerful, institutional audiences who can help them to help others. After all, addiction counselors, case workers, and shelter managers—like the ones portrayed in this book—do not simply evaluate clients' words as signs of personal progress (or lack thereof); they also use those evaluations as the basis for exonerating or damning reports to parole officers, calls to child protective service workers who can take children into state custody or return them to their homes, or consultations with welfare workers who may provide or withhold the means to consistently feed, clothe, and house a family.

Therefore, clients in drug treatment understandably try to anticipate and control how their words will be taken up by their counselors and case managers. Many, no doubt, do this by investing precisely in the rituals of speaking that comprise their treatment, whether during shelter intakes, clinical assessments, or individual and group therapy sessions. Yet, at Fresh Beginnings, other clients worked to manage their institutional fate by practicing what they called "flipping the script"—that is, formally replicating prescribed ways of speaking about themselves and their problems without investing in the *content* of those scripts. For instance, in a Tuesday morning therapy group, Nikki, a twenty-nine-year old program veteran, compellingly recited a confessional tale of triumph over crack cocaine, weaving autobiographical threads through the well-rehearsed plot of denial, downward spiral, rock bottom, and willful recovery. Just hours later, Nikki poured her nephew's urine into a drug-screen vial marked with her own initials. This ethnography traces the meaning of and continuity in such seemingly disparate acts.

If social service professionals rely on client talk in meeting their dual charge to evaluate people and distribute resources, and if clients leverage material and symbolic resources with their words, it is because their work is, in essence, *semiotic* work. In other words, both clients and professional practitioners use language to achieve a variety of ends, including the production of personhood endowed with the qualities valued by larger American society. In fact, the mission of Fresh Beginnings—as inscribed in its very own mission statement—was to endow people with "lasting sobriety and self-sufficiency." And while both these goals obviously entailed managing material goods and resources, this book shows how and explains why sobriety and self-sufficiency are so closely associated with a specific way of speaking. Indeed, at Fresh Beginnings, therapy was focused on reconfiguring clients' relationship with language rather than simply, or even primarily, reconfiguring their relationship to drugs.

The talking cure has a long history in the United States, where the presupposing, denotative functions of language are systematically privileged by speakers (Duranti 1988; Irvine 1989; Rosaldo 1982; Silverstein 1979, 1996, 2001, 2003a; Woolard 1998); that is, the linguistic regularities characteristic of what Benjamin Whorf called "Standard Average European" are maintained by users' folk theories, which posit that words primarily function to name what's "out there" in the world (see Silverstein

1996). As a number of clinical ethnographies have suggested, the privileging of the presupposing functions of language is particularly prevalent in contemporary clinical settings and situations, where people are supposed to reference and release inner denotata when they speak (e.g., Capps and Ochs 1995; Desjarlais 1996, 1997; Wilce 1998, 2003; see also Crapanzano 1992). More generally, Americans tend to evaluate a person's integrity and health by determining if his or her words correspond with what he or she already "truly" thinks or feels.[3]

As an ethnography of the United States, *Scripting Addiction* shows how treatment programs, like Fresh Beginnings, are central sites where cultural ideologies of language are *distilled*—that is, reproduced in pure and potent form. Specifically, this book focuses on the distillation of what I call the *ideology of inner reference*, an ideology that presumes that (1) "healthy" language refers to preexisting phenomena, and (2) the phenomena to which it refers are internal to speakers.[4] Through the ethnography of clinical assessments, case conferences, and group therapy sessions, the pages that follow show that both the depth of clinical pathology and progress in recovery are linguistically measured, as drug users' representations of themselves and their troubles are held against the cultural and clinical ideal of perfectly transparent and exhaustive—or sober—inner reference. For, as we will see, Fresh Beginning therapists determined the sobriety of their clients by evaluating the sobriety of their speech, namely, how perfectly they matched spoken signs to "inner states," without exaggeration, flourish, or fancy (cf. Keane 2002, 2007).[5]

The ideology of inner reference is particularly potent in the field of mainstream American drug treatment, which has long theorized and treated addiction as a semiotic malady.[6] In line with a well-established stream of clinical theory, crystallized in the idea of addicted denial, Fresh Beginnings therapists averred that addicts suffer from the inability to read their inner states and render them in words. Accordingly, during group and individual therapy, therapists provided detailed guidelines about the formal components of "healthy" referential talk, and carefully monitored their clients' linguistic practices. Words that *did* things like persuade, pronounce, or protest—what J. L. Austin (1962) famously called "performatives"—were eschewed by program therapists, who urged their clients to confine their use of language to simple and sober denotation.[7] Thus, *Scripting Addiction* shows that the familiar prelude, "Hi, my name is X and I am an addict," and the structured tale that follows are not the natural outpourings of the addicted character in recovery, nor are they the inevitable manifestation of a cultural compulsion to confess. Instead, these narratives are the hard-won products of a clinical discipline that demands a totally unmediated language, one that appears to transparently refer to and reveal the inner thoughts, feelings, and memories of its speakers.

One might simply argue that mainstream American addiction treatment produces "addicts" by urging people to name and talk about themselves as such. *Scripting Addiction* instead explains why professional practitioners devote themselves to producing *a way of speaking,* which presumably allows access to the inner states of speakers, including states of addiction. Proceeding from the premise that addiction is a culturally mediated affliction—meaning that both the constitution and classification of any relationship between self and substance is inherently context-specific—this book makes the broad argument that we cannot fully understand the project of person-making until we understand the politics of language.

By ethnographically demonstrating the idea that how one speaks in a clinical setting is both thoroughly cultural and inherently political, the book builds upon the rich anthropological work on semiotic ideology (e.g., Bauman and Briggs 2003; Brenneis 1984; Briggs 1998; Gal 1992; 1998; Gal and Irvine 1995; Hanks 1996a; Hill 1985, 2000, Irvine and Gal 2000; Keane 2002, 2007; Kroskrity 1998, 2000; Mertz 1998; Philips 1998 Silverstein 1979, 1985, 1996, 2004; Woolard 1998; Woolard and Schieffelin 1994). Whereas other studies have addressed the role of language and narrative in socializing people to both treatment milieus and "healthy" identities (e.g., Bezdek and Spicer 2006; Borden 1992; Bruner 1990; Cain 1991; Capps and Ochs 1995; Ferrara 1994; Laird 1994; Mancini 2007; Ochs and Capps 2002; Riessman 1990, 1992, 2003; Swora 2001; White and Epston 1990; Wahlstrom 2006; Wilce 1998, 2003, 2008; Wilcox 1998), this book is distinctive in its concerted, critical attention to the political as well as the cultural dimensions of therapeutic talk. Indeed, the chapters that follow investigate the cultural negotiations and contestations at play within frames that are often understood to be simply therapeutic.

Scripting Addiction demonstrates that the rituals of speaking that characterize mainstream American addiction treatment are political in three primary senses. First, by prescribing talk that can only reference the inner states of speakers, addiction counselors effectively, if not intentionally, enervate clients' institutional critiques and discourage social commentary. Second, the rituals of speaking that produce this highly personalized talk not only affect how social service professionals evaluate people and problems, but also impact how basic goods and services are distributed. Third, *Scripting Addiction* documents the skillful and sometimes surprising ways that clients manage to leverage material and symbolic resources with their words. After all, script flippers like Nikki, effectively suggest that every script, however prescribed or however prescriptive, is open to the purposeful engagements of skilled speakers and actors.

TEXT AND TERRITORY

It is late autumn of 1997. Six of us are spread across the front porch of one of the many three-bedroom frame houses that line Cliff Street. Fallen leaves crunch underfoot of passersby who determinedly ignore our measuring eyes. Nonetheless, their quickened strides suggest that our collective stare shrinks the gap of the postage-stamp lawn and makes the short walk past the porch feel very long indeed.

Over time, the neighbors have come to believe that the women talking, smoking, and staring on this porch are the residents of a "halfway house or *home* or something like that." A few have watched more carefully through curtained living room windows, witnessing women and children piling into the two white vans that arrive toward the end of every weekday. And, those who live next door know that on weekends, the purplish gray house is unusually dark and quiet. Even the swings out back—which generate tiny shouts of glee throughout the week—sag in abandonment.

The women on the porch have their own theories about the people who pass by, and why they so studiously avoid interaction. Sometimes, when the staff and kids are out of earshot, and the banter on the porch has lulled, Marion playfully heckles an attractive, blond neighborhood man whom she calls "Plaid." Or, Nikki bounds off her stoop to ask a startled young woman walking by for a light. (When refused, Nikki laughs and calls out: "I know you *got* one. I *seen* you smoke before.") Most of the women on the porch clearly disapprove of this type of entertainment, scolding: "Just leave the poor things alone." Others flip through hand-me-down magazines, make lists of the week's errands, and find other ways to ignore the latest antics. Regardless, the fun is over before long, as the women extinguish their cigarettes in an old Folgers can and file back up the narrow, dingy staircase to a second-story room where their afternoon therapy sessions are held.

If the passersby don't know what to make of the house on Cliff Street and its transient occupants, it is not just because this middle-class, residential neighborhood is an unusual location for an outpatient drug treatment program,[8] especially one designed specifically for homeless women. It is also, undoubtedly, because the program is an example of a relatively new form of social service delivery. Indeed, the Fresh Beginnings program was born of a formal collaborative of previously independent, community-based social service agencies in a county hit hard by de-industrialization and beset by a well-documented lack of affordable housing.[9] By the late 1980s these agencies, which had focused the bulk of their energies on suicide prevention, teen runaways, and drug overdoses during the 1970s, found that the majority of those calling their "crisis hotlines" were families and individuals with reports, rendered in voices trembling with cold or fright, that they had no place to sleep and nothing to eat. Shifting focus accordingly, each agency independently scrambled to provide shelter and support services to the swelling number of families with children, not to mention adult individuals, who met newly established minimum federal standards of homelessness[10]—whether "doubled-up" in friends' or relatives' houses because of an eviction, a foreclosure, or a domestic incident, or members of the far smaller group of "chronically homeless" in the county.[11]

In light of these jointly recognized exigencies, five of the local agencies serving the county's one thousand newly homeless families banded together to establish what would soon be called the "Homeless Family Consortium" (HFC). From its beginnings in the early 1990s, HFC acknowledged that its members were a rather motley crew characterized by radically different ideological proclivities—from the explicitly feminist orientation of the domestic violence shelter to the mandatory Bible Study groups held at St. Thomas's Shelter. The most critical of these divisions involved each agency's understanding of the etiology of homelessness.

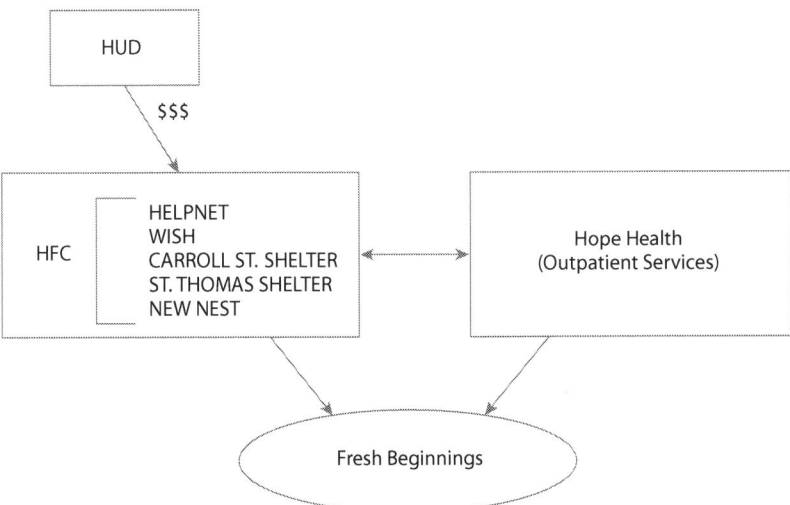

Figure I.1. Fresh Beginnings, the Homeless Family Consortium (HFC), and funding/partnering agencies.

Whereas some agencies claimed that the women smoking on the Cliff Street porch had behaved their way into homelessness by doing drugs and bearing children out of wedlock, other agencies entered the consortium with their eyes squarely focused on the political economic correlates of homelessness, which, they argued, propelled women to behave as they otherwise would not.[12] Not surprisingly, their interventions and interactions with clients varied accordingly.

Regardless of how they defined the widely acknowledged problem of homelessness in the county and envisioned appropriate solutions, all HFC agencies agreed that competing for increasingly scarce federal and state resources was disadvantageous both to their respective institutional health and the well-being of their shared client population. By the mid-1990s, prominent sources of federal funding were already clearly promoting "wrap-around" service delivery, in which collaborating, community-based service agencies would provide unique and well-defined services and thereby eliminate costly "service duplication" (Clark et al. 1996; Malysiak 1997, 1998). "Wrap-around" rhetoric, with its operating frames of "family empowerment," "individualized services," and "community integration" held sway, more generally, in the decidedly devolving political climate. Expertly deploying the language of wrap-around in their grant application to the National Office of Housing and Urban Development (HUD), HFC was awarded a multimillion dollar grant to coordinate transportation between agencies and set up an interagency computer network to track and monitor their shared client base. Most significantly, the grant allowed HFC to contract with a large, local Catholic hospital with extensive psychiatric and substance abuse services, called "Hope Health," and establish an intensive outpatient drug treatment program that would serve eligible clients from any of the collaborating agencies. Indeed, if HFC agencies were primarily bound by the common goal of garnering shrinking federal funds, they also shared the conviction that many of their clients were beset by drug and alcohol problems that warranted the development of an outpatient drug treatment program designed specifically for their joint clientele.

Two and a half years after receiving the funding, Fresh Beginnings was still HFC's most distinguished achievement despite the formidable problems that had characterized the program's development and daily administration. Therapists and program administrators touted the program's specialized services—including on-site child care and transportation—which other treatment programs lacked. They also lauded the program's commitment to "gender-sensitive"[13] and "culturally-sensitive"[14] service provision, which they argued was essential in treating homeless women. From the program's inception, administrators asserted that whereas traditional drug treatment approached their clients as generic addicts with homogeneous needs, their innovative program would recognize that homeless women addicts had *special* needs that could only be answered with correspondingly specialized services. And although HFC professionals differed in how they conceptualized exactly what was special about their clients' needs, and therefore how they aligned themselves with the treatment program's mission of "sobriety and self-sufficiency," they all found that the twin terms of "chemical dependency" and "economic dependency" were particularly efficacious in the American political climate of the mid-1990s, haunted as it was by that troubling figure known as the "welfare dependent."

Identifying Icons and the Policies of Personhood

Opening in the White House Rose Garden where President Bill Clinton is "ending welfare as we know it" and proceeding to a day-long staff retreat on Cliff Street, chapter 1 shows how HFC professionals adopted and adapted discourses of dependency to paint a portrait of "the client" on which their treatment program, in turn, could symbolically depend. The chapter does not simply draw a parallel between neoliberal reformers' casting of characters on national policy stages (such as Clinton's supporting cast of "welfare mothers" who joined him in the Rose Garden) and the program development strategies employed by Fresh Beginnings professionals. Making use of data gathered at the retreat as well as program meeting minutes and grant applications, chapter 1 also examines the semiotic processes by which such politico-therapeutic discourses are registered in practice and thereby reproduced in institutional settings (see Agha 1998, 2007; Mehan 1996; Matoesian 2008; Silverstein 2003b, 2004, 2006).[15]

More generally, chapter 1 highlights the possibilities and dangers of casting political and economic issues of poverty and homelessness as essentially therapeutic concerns. In this sense, the chapter finds inspiration in Nancy Fraser and Linda Gordon's (1994) brilliant demonstration of how the political and economic meanings of the term "dependency" have been collapsed into an all-encompassing psychological register, so that dependence of the poor on the state for a (less than) living wage, for instance, is effectively recast as the pathological manifestation of inherently dependent psyches.[16] While Fraser and Gordon discuss the highly gendered terms of "welfare dependency" and "co-dependency," the study of Fresh Beginnings allows us to consider how cultural ideas about economic dependency and contemporary discourses of addiction or "chemical dependency" are entwined. Indeed, *Scripting Addiction* not only demonstrates that therapeutic language is inherently political; it also highlights how contemporary American political language mobilizes a strikingly therapeutic lexicon.[17]

Taking Them In and Talking It Out

If passersby on Cliff Street recognized the women on the porch to be "homeless women" or "drug users"—if they recognized them at all—the professional practitioners affiliated with the Fresh Beginnings program generally identified their clients as "consumers" in expectation that they would come to inhabit this label and act accordingly.[18] And, regardless of their individual inclinations toward the program's dual goals of imparting "sobriety and self-sufficiency," Fresh Beginnings clients shared very practical stakes in meeting professionals' expectations. After all, the vast majority of incoming clients did not voluntarily attend the program. In some cases, clients had been required to attend drug treatment to meet the terms of parole officers or child welfare workers, who were in regular contact with program therapists. In all cases, Fresh Beginnings clients' subsidized housing, shelter, and ancillary services such as child care, tutoring, and legal advocacy services—as provided by the five HFC agencies—contractually hinged on their therapeutic success on Cliff Street.

Indeed, the Fresh Beginnings program was designed to address drug-using homeless women's "special needs" through a system of coordinated care. Each client was to meet regularly with her designated HFC case manager, whose role it was to address pragmatic issues relating to housing, employment, or education, as well as with a clinical team comprised of family counselors and chemical dependency (or simply "CD") therapists. And while the scheduling of regular case conferences between therapists and case managers was commonly plagued by case overload and rampant staff turnover, all professionals worked hard to coordinate care, which also meant coordinating their evaluations of each client's progress.

Thus, Fresh Beginnings clients found that they were held to the discerning terms of their "treatment contracts"—which were drawn up by chemical dependency therapists Laura and Susan—far beyond the treatment program. And although it was immediately clear that therapists evaluated their therapeutic progress based on what they said in therapy sessions, clients also soon discovered that many other professional practitioners could eventually be party to the words they spoke on Cliff Street. Accordingly, chapter 2 not only documents the institutional pathways by which clients entered into the Fresh Beginnings program, but it also highlights how professional texts about these clients were generated and traveled with them, affecting the flow of resources, services, and sanctions. The chapter begins by focusing on the very first encounters between clients and HFC case managers, which occurred during agency intake interviews. Describing professionals' work of procuring verbal evidence of clients' drug use and translating it into institutionally legible texts, such as case notes and program referrals, chapter 2 then follows a cadre of HFC clients to the Fresh Beginnings program, where they engaged in another round of interviews known as "clinical assessments."

In addition, chapter 2 underscores clients' efforts to control how professional talk and texts about them traveled. Rather than seeing assessment reports and referrals as so much baggage, this chapter takes the perspective of clients and professionals who understand that these institutional texts carry the people represented in them as much as the other way around. Finally, in carefully examining program intakes and clinical assessments as linguistic interactions, chapter 2 also explores the epistemologies of language that commonly underlie interviewing, which have profound implications for ethnographic research as well as clinical practice (see also Briggs 1986, 2007; Carr 2010).

Clinographies of Addiction

Once admitted to Fresh Beginnings, one's economic as well as therapeutic well-being was tied to the adoption of a particular way of speaking—a fact hardly lost on the women who attended the program. As five of the six women smoking on the porch that autumn afternoon reached the second-story therapy room, they entered into a ritual space where "sobriety" and "self-sufficiency" were generated—at least ideally—in words. Arming themselves with mugs of instant coffee and pastel colored tissue boxes, clients settled into donated couches arranged around an empty, swiveling office chair. As the therapist took the central seat, the unpredictable cadence of multidirectional banter, hushed sympathies about children, lovers, or johns, and the occasional exasperated guffaw segued quickly into the daily regimen of group therapy. Fresh Beginnings clients took turns weaving the day's designated theme (e.g., shame, codependency, responsibility) into personalized narratives of early trauma, accelerated denial, rock bottom, and willful recovery as an attentive therapist looked on.

The women on Cliff Street dutifully engaged in these rituals of speaking precisely because American addiction specialists have long theorized addiction as a disease of denial—which afflicts the ability to read and render inner states in words—and accordingly prescribed the language of inner reference.[19] Indeed, whether one enters a clinician-led group therapy session, such as the one described above, within the formal drug treatment system, which consists of approximately 13,600 federal, state, and local programs that see about 1.1 million clients annually (N-SSAT 2007),[20] or visits one of the approximately 65,000 Alcoholics Anonymous (AA) or Narcotics Anonymous (NA) groups across the U.S., one discovers that drug rehabilitation commonly revolves around rehabilitating the drug user's relationship with language. Following linear plotlines that proceed from a denoted dirty past to an anticipated clean future, recovery narratives are the means by which millions of drug using Americans have practiced self-insight in their efforts to get sober. And for many thousands of practitioners, recovery narratives are also the very measure of this insight, and therefore the most highly valued signs of their professional efficacy.[21]

This is especially true of those who espouse the "disease concept" of addiction, which has been popularized through AA and institutionalized by the Minnesota Model—a counseling approach developed in the 1940s and 1950s (Cook 2006).[22] Premised on the idea that addiction is an incurable, if treatable, disease that specifically afflicts drug users' insight, the Minnesota Model combines psycho-education, whose goal is to build self-awareness, with group counseling, which is designed to confront denial (Chiauzzi and Liljegren 1993:305). At the time that HFC administrators were envisioning their treatment program and inscribing that vision on paper to HUD, more than 90 percent of professional treatment programs adhered to the basic principles and practices of the Minnesota Model (Spicer 1993; see also Morgenstern 2000; Weisner and Greenfield 1995). And even though those involved in the founding of Fresh Beginnings insisted that their program would be unique in its clinical orientation as well as its program design, just a glance at the weekly schedule betrayed the new program's debt to the Minnesota Model, with a weekly psycho-educational group, individual counseling session, and trip to a local AA meeting interspersed in a solid slate of group therapy sessions devoted to talk.

Although the disease concept of addiction has been recently challenged, particularly by an innovative new approach to addiction treatment called Motivational Interviewing, many of its ideas about denial, insight, and the language of recovery are widely shared among addiction specialists and practitioners across otherwise distinctive theoretical orientations (e.g., Carroll 1980; Chafetz 1997 [1959]; Davidson 1977b; Doweiko 1996; El Rasheed 2001; Fewell and Bissell 1978; Flores 1988, 2004; Hazelden 1975; Johnson 1980; Kauffman 1994; Kearney 1996; Keller et al. 1995; Krystal and Raskin 1970; Mandell et al. 2007; Morgan 2006; O'Dwyer 2004; Peterson, Nisenholz, and Robinson 2003; Rinn et al. 2002; Rosenfeld 1994; Rasmussen 2000; Razlog et al. 2007; Speranza et al. 2004; Sifneos 1996; Spiegel and Fewell 2004; Taylor et al. 1990;

Tiebout 1953; Troisi et al. 1998; Wallace 1978; Walters 1994; Wurmser 1974, 1985, 1992, 1995). Chapter 3 charts this rich terrain of clinical theory, with an eye on how program therapists made use of well-established and widely held ideas about addicted denial in the course of their everyday practice. For, at Fresh Beginnings, denial—along with anger and shame—was theorized as a kind of psychic residue that settled, in layers, atop the innermost region of the self, preventing a sober accounting of its contents. Making use of the documents therapists accrued during the course of their professional training, as well as the psychoeducational materials they distributed to clients and the explanations they offered in ethnographic interviews, chapter 3 examines how Laura and Susan envisioned the subjectivity of their clients. Titled "Clinographies of Addiction," this chapter not only describes the topographical model of addicted subjectivity recognized in the Cliff Street therapy rooms; it also introduces the linguistic methods therapists used to excavate it.

Although addiction was theorized at Fresh Beginnings as an incurable disease, chapter 3 works to shed light on the broader questions of just why and in what sense so many Americans invest in the idea that talking cures. After all, the sobriety of mind, body, and spirit are valued far beyond the domain of mainstream American addiction treatment, as is the idea that one can demonstrate this sobriety by clearly reading and cleanly relaying inner states, as thinkers from Augustine to Weber have suggested.[23] Thus, in ethnographically examining how these enduring cultural values and ideas were distilled on Cliff Street, chapter 3 follows clients from the front porch and into the group therapy room where therapists impart what it means to speak like, and therefore *be,* a healthy and valuable American person as well as a recovering addict.

Addicted Indexes and Metalinguistic Fixes

Thursdays were especially trying days on the front porch of Fresh Beginnings. For, on Thursdays, the porch accommodated clients who waited, sometimes for more than an hour, for the chronically tardy program van to pick them up and transport them to a local AA meeting. Aside from the wait, many clients resented these required weekly trips, especially after the many hours of the week that they had already devoted to talk, even if in the relatively intimate setting of Fresh Beginnings. Some, like their therapist Laura, expressed philosophical critiques of AA, preferring its "sister institution"—Women for Sobriety (WFS)—and its foundational motto, "We are the author of the script by which we live our lives," over AA's injunction to "admit we are powerless over alcohol." And because clients who had recently relapsed or otherwise broken program rules were commonly required to attend ninety AA meetings in ninety days (otherwise known as "90/90s"), the regular Thursday meeting felt particularly punishing to some. So, in addition to waiting, smoking, and grumbling on the porch, clients sometimes devised creative ways to dodge AA and therefore circumvent yet another round of talk.

The hybridization of self-help and formal modes of social service is clearly symptomatic of late-twentieth-century (post) welfare state politics (Cruikshank 1999; Fairbanks 2009; Maskovsky 2001; Schull 2006). However, Fresh Beginnings' integration of AA's disease concept (with its emphasis on denial), WFS's "Thirteen Affirmations" (which indicate that recovering addicts can clearly think and therefore behave in sober ways), and attempted applications of dialectical behavior therapy[24] also suggest significant *clinical hybridity* as well. Consider therapists' prolific use of the therapeutic slogan "secrets keep us sick," which combines the psychodynamic presumption that inner states can be dangerously cystic unless they are put into words, with the cognitive behavioral idea that the very recitation of such a catchy semantic package may just compel the speaker to think and act accordingly. (Stuart Smalley's mirror incantations—"*I'm Good Enough, I'm Smart Enough, and, Doggone It, People Like Me*"— are cogent pop-cultural exemplars of the practically reinforcing, if conceptually contradictory, relationship between the semantic content and pragmatic force of such therapeutic statements). And, indeed, when it came to applications of formal clinical theory, Fresh Beginnings therapists were generally inclined to heed "whatever works" in practice—a motto indicative of the pragmatic and eclectic orientation common among many professional practitioners of psychotherapy (Ball et al. 2002; Ford 1996; Taleff 1997).[25]

Although Fresh Beginnings was characterized by a clinical heterodoxy, whereby ideas from different clinical traditions were creatively combined to meet particular demands of practice, therapists' theories about language and its proper uses were orthodox, and often explicitly so. In the therapy room, around the staff table, and in many conversations with a curious ethnographer, therapists delineated the ingredients of "healthy" talk. For example, program therapists not only reminded quiet clients that "secrets keep us sick," they also urged critical clients to "share your experience, not your opinion," and periodically scrawled across the dry erase board "D-E-N-I-A-L = Don't Even Notice I Am Lying," for all clients to see. Furthermore, on the east wall of the therapy room, therapists posted complex rules of speaking, which explicitly forbade interruption, repetition, or giving advice; required eye contact between speakers and listeners; and demanded that emotions be "owned" by those who expressed them. Thus, not only was there a lot of *talk* at Fresh Beginnings; the program also played host to a copious amount of *talk about talk,* all of which concertedly delineated the principles of inner reference.

The prolific use of therapeutic metalanguage is the focus of chapter 4, "Addicted Indexes and Metalinguistic Fixes." The chapter works to solve an interesting puzzle: given American language ideology, which systematically privileges the use of language to reference preexisting psychic and social facts, why do therapists have to work so hard to produce, protect, and patrol such highly naturalized—or commonsensical—ideas about language? I call such work "metalinguistic labor" (see also Carr 2006), demonstrating that whereas therapeutic interventions seem to elicit inner signs that are always already there, awaiting cathartic escape in language, Fresh Beginnings therapy was instead an exercise in linguistic purification—one that required the labor of therapists, the cooperation of clients, and the use of particular semiotic processes for producing a perfectly clean and sober language.

If therapists worked hard to produce the language of inner reference, it is most obviously because they were dedicated to producing healthy speakers. Nevertheless, chapter 4 shows that by formally restricting talk to the reference of already existing inner states, therapists effectively—if not intentionally—insulated themselves and their young program from clients' critiques and challenges. For instance, a client's comment that therapists favored white clients could be swiftly robbed of its critical efficacy once it was taken up as a sign of the commentator's therapeutically troubling "inability to trust." Thus, chapter 4 not only suggests that mainstream American addiction treatment is a *normative* site, where broader cultural ideas about language are practiced and policed; the chapter also demonstrates that programs like Fresh Beginnings are *normalizing* sites where people learn to represent themselves in a manner that supports existing institutional and cultural orders.

Therapeutic Scenes on an Administrative Stage

Rhonda was one of those clients clearly not amused by Nikki's and Marion's antics on the porch of the treatment program. She generally kept to herself and was outside the circle of friends formed by many Fresh Beginnings clients, whose relationships were sometimes forged well before they began their treatment (whether in grade school or Sunday School classes or on the street) and often outlasted their stints in treatment. Accordingly, Rhonda quickly became a prime suspect in the series of petty thefts from the client-run "Clothes Closet"—a secondhand clothing shop set up in the basement of the treatment program. Whether she was actually the one who made off with highly coveted items, including the brightly colored toddler gear, which had been most fortuitously donated by the Disney Store, remained unclear.

Furthermore, Rhonda participated only in the most perfunctory way in bimonthly Client Advisory Committee meetings, a semiformal mechanism designed to garner clients' feedback about program administration and development. She also seemed decidedly uninterested in the regular reports from the first generation of "client representatives," who had been elected by their peers to attend Fresh Beginnings advisory board meetings, where program policies were officially debated and developed by the professionals affiliated with the treatment program. I was therefore a bit taken aback when, after the first client representatives "retired" from their post, Rhonda enthusiastically volunteered to take the position. With no one else willing to volunteer or intervene, Rhonda became, if only for a short time, the sole "client representative." This meant that twice a month, alongside program administrators, therapists, clinical supervisors, and shelter managers, Rhonda would attend advisory board meetings, held several miles away from Cliff Street, and even farther away from the subsidized apartment that she had just landed with the significant support of her HFC case manager.

If I was somewhat puzzled by Rhonda's sudden interest in administrative affairs, my surprise multiplied when a placid and poised Rhonda entered the boardroom for her first board meeting as if she had done so many times before. Indeed, she had never seemed more at home. As members took their seats around a makeshift conglomerate of institutional folding tables, the HFC director called for a round of introductions in acknowledgment of the brand new board member. In classic institutional fashion, the professionals took turns identifying themselves by name and organizational role and function, with friendly smiles but little personal embellishment. All the board members explicitly directed their introductions to Rhonda, who nodded and returned smiles until the circling discourse made its way to her seat. Finally, it was Rhonda's turn to identify herself. Without hesitation and with seemingly unimpeachable confidence, the newest board member announced, "Hi, my name is Rhonda, and I am a recovering crack addict." As in an AA pair structure, her professional audience responded, "Hi Rhonda," before proceeding with the rest of their business.

Chapter 5, titled "Therapeutic Scenes on an Administrative Stage," takes this scene as its point of departure, exploring why modes of self-representation operant *inside* the therapy room affected how clients spoke *outside* the therapy room as well. Considering a range of analytic possibilities, including the possibility that Rhonda actually adopted the addict identity that she put into words, I bring to bear Louis Althusser's (1971) and Judith Butler's (1993, 1997) work to theorize Rhonda's boardroom confession as an instance of what I call "anticipatory interpellation": a process of anticipating how a powerful audience expects one to speak and beckoning that audience to address one accordingly (see also Carr 2009). Comparing Rhonda's boardroom career to that of another client representative—who adopted the explicitly instrumentalist lingo of professional board members, which I also describe in some detail—chapter 5 is a parable about the unexpected political gains as well as the strategic quagmires of speaking "like an addict." More generally, in demonstrating that scripts adhere to roles (i.e., "client," "counselor," "administrator") regardless of the institutional stages on which they are performed (i.e., therapy room, boardroom, shelter), this chapter explicitly theorizes the relationship of ways of speaking, speakers, and contexts of speech, delineating a highly consequential taxonomy of possibilities for "doing things with words" (cf. Austin 1962).

Flipping the Script

One cold evening in March, Nikki and I met in a Bob's Big Boy, located on a busy strip of suburban boulevard, for the final chapter of her oral history interview. I hardly recognized her as she made her way through the crowded restaurant to the smoking section where I was sitting. Gaunt, eyes ablaze, and sporting recently cropped, slightly dreadlocked hair stuffed into an old baseball cap, she demanded a hug and I happily obliged. Catching both her hands in mine as we broke our embrace, I confessed, "I've really missed you," to which she responded with a noncommittal silence.

Aside from a brief telephone conversation to schedule our meeting, I had not seen nor talked to Nikki since her treatment had been terminated several months earlier by her new therapist, Lizzy, for "failure to comply." We settled into the sticky vinyl booth, still smiling in reunion, when Nikki asked, "I look horrible, don't I?" In uncomfortable reply, I hedged, "You're a little thin . . . you changed your hair." Taking off her cap, as if to give me a chance to survey the damage, she offered, "It was just breakin' off in my hand . . . cocaine will do that to you. You know I've been back out, right?" I nodded slowly, exchanging a long and loaded stare; "Yeah, I sorta figured."

"You should really eat . . . can you eat?" I queried, reminding her of our deal—a $25 stipend in exchange for her tale, plus all she could eat at the restaurant of her choosing. "I should eat some salad . . . order me a black coffee with lots of sugar," Nikki charged as she pulled herself up and headed toward the salad bar. I fiddled with my tape recorder, ordered Nikki's coffee, and watched as she critically perused the pickings. Returning with a plate piled high with cottage cheese, pasta salad, shaved carrots, and canned beets, she asked with some eagerness, "You ready?" This was not the first time I sensed that Nikki enjoyed these recorded events, a chance to do what she did most brilliantly: talk.

"Ok, so let me remind you of where we left off," I rejoined, needing no interview notes to get back on cue. Indeed, Nikki's previous two interviews had stuck in my memory like glue, filled as they were with illustrative scenes and riveting anecdotes that gave ample evidence of Nikki's talents as a narrator. Spun while still a client at Fresh Beginnings, Nikki's first oral history interview oscillated between tales told seemingly to elicit shock (often prefaced with "you can't imagine" or "you wouldn't believe") and moving accounts of surviving life's many blows. The second chapter of her oral history, told while she was on probation from the program after hospital nurses revealed to program therapists that Nikki's newborn baby had tested positive for cocaine, was highly confessional, laden with clinical explanations, and replete with the kind of religious sentiment characteristic of mainstream, American addiction treatment. Now, seeking to start where we had left off, I reminded her of a touching anecdote she told me at the end of her second interview about a recovering alcoholic "John"-turned-lover who "transformed" her life by lovingly encouraging her to seek treatment. Her response to my query was unnerving but highly instructive:

1 I: So that's where we left off [in our last interview].
2 N: (long pause . . . laughter). Oh my. (laughter).
3 I: What? . . . *What*?
4 N: I told you *that* (laughter).
5 I: Yeah (giggle) . . . don't you remember?
6 N: You knew that didn't happen, right? (laughter). Please tell me
7 I: What?
8 N: Oh, poor ol' Summerson (sigh). *Girl*, don't you know, I flipped a *script* on you?!

Titled, simply, "Flipping the Script," chapter 6 not only demonstrates how script flipping troubled therapeutic practices at Fresh Beginnings; it also analyzes how, in performing acts of inner reference, clients challenged an ideology of language that enjoys prominence far beyond the therapy rooms on Cliff Street. After all, script flippers demanded that their analysts—whether anthropologist or therapist[26]—consider their narratives as effectual, context-sensitive social actions, with histories and futures of their own, rather than transparent reports on the contents of their psyches. For example, as the comparison of Nikki's interviews confirmed, her position in the program (as active and in "good standing" to "on probation" to "terminated") influenced the way she relayed life events. Wanting to convince me of her newly found faith in recovery, perhaps hoping I would relay it to program therapists who could reinstate her, her second interview was highly personalized, fervent, confessional, and clinically provocative. After termination, however, Nikki had "nothing to lose," at least from an institutional point of view, and confessed that her previous confessions were decidedly flipped (line 8). In this sense, Nikki's oral history interview keenly illustrates the need for analyses that carefully gauge the specific conditions of all linguistic performance (see also Carr 2010b). Thus, in creating evidentiary crises for social service professionals and ethnographer alike—who are unable to readily distinguish flipped scripts from "followed" ones—script flipping evinces both the possibilities and limits of language as a means of detecting or denoting inner states. It also raises critical questions about a therapeutic program and attendant set of institutional practices premised on this cultural ideal.

While one might legitimately blame the "poor ol'" anthropologist (line 8) for her naiveté, as Nikki does above, chapter 6 focuses on script flipping as a kind of expertise. More specifically, this chapter proposes that script flippers were ethnographers of language in their own right, in that they constantly strove to decipher the conditions in which they spoke so that they might linguistically maneuver within them. Working with script flippers' and therapists' descriptions of the practice, the chapter pursues the question of how one learns to flip a script and, in doing so, engages the current thinking on *metalinguistic awareness*—that is, the knowledge people have about the language they speak (e.g., Briggs 1986; Jakobson 1980; Lucy 1993; Silverstein 1993, 2001; Kroskrity 2000). I will demonstrate, in particular, that flipping the script was enabled by an acute awareness of referential speech as a creative, pragmatic, and potentially efficacious mode of social action. Accordingly, chapter 6 suggests that metalinguistic awareness has more to do with the analytical and rhetorical skills accrued in practice than with any inherent quality of a speech act, event, or speaker.

Finally, chapter 6 substantiates the claim that people can act politically by strategically reproducing—rather than simply resisting—ideologies of language. For in perfectly performing inner reference and therefore the role of the "good client," those who flipped scripts also directed the flow of the basic resources, sanctions, and services. Indeed, careful ethnography explains that Nikki would say and do most anything to keep the state from taking her children, including convincing her therapists not to make the call that would have set this process in motion. Ethnography can also show that clients bound to treatment contracts that required them to attend ninety AA meetings in ninety days, sometimes flipped feminist scripts in order to keep the irregular shifts at their menial jobs, as new welfare laws mandate. Thus, *Scripting Addiction* follows flipped scripts through the institutional and social terrains that so often punish and penalize in order to gauge the rewards of this linguistic practice—whether in the form of real resources gained or tragic losses avoided.

Only then can a politics, which is too often misdiagnosed as pathology, be recognized.

METHOD AND MEANING IN THE ANTHROPOLOGY OF THE U.S.

Ever since Bronislaw Malinowski (1922), the father of anthropological fieldwork, asked his readers to "imagine" arriving in the Trobriand Islands just as he first did, ethnographers have worked to demonstrate knowledge of native practices based on their experience of *being there*. As practitioners of an interpretive rather than positivist science, anthropologists rely on readers to trust that we have not only witnessed what we describe, but also that we have tried to see it all through the eyes of those we represent, even when our interpretations diverge from those of our informants.

Ethnographic representation is somewhat complicated when one works in a culture with which the majority of one's readers are already familiar, even if they have not experienced firsthand the institutions, people, or practices described. In such cases, the ethnographer urges readers to reflect on the practices and ideas that they commonly take for granted, showing what is exotic and strange in the familiar and intimate, rather than the other way around. Furthermore, the native anthropologist who studies professional practices commonly collaborates and contends with large and diverse communities of scholars who are focused on the study of the very same field (e.g., Brodwin 2008; Dumit 2004; Gal 1995b; Garriott 2008; Gremillion 2003; Luhrmann 2001; Martin 1987, 1994; Masco 2006; Rapp 1988, 1990; Saunders 2009; Young 1995). In cases such as these, the ethnographer's challenge is to demonstrate both the specificity and the cultural continuity of practices, concepts, and interactions that can be overlooked in larger-scale studies, and thereby contribute uniquely to the broader scholarly endeavor.

Considering the experiential and interpretive nature of ethnographic fieldwork, it is understandable that audiences commonly demand to know just how the ethnographer was situated in the field. Accordingly, the nature of my position and interactions at Fresh Beginnings during three and a half years of fieldwork will unfold in the pages that follow. By way of welcome, suffice it to say that I learned my very first lessons in linguistic anthropology from the clients and professionals at Fresh Beginnings, well before I decided to make the subfield a scholarly focus or to engage in the ethnographic study of addiction treatment. For it was as a student intern—working to accrue the field hours required to earn my MSW and trying to help the young treatment program establish its practices and policies, particularly in relation to client participation in program governance—that I first realized that the program's therapeutic regimen was predicated on talk. Waiting outside the closed door of the therapy room, where I convened weekly Client Advisory Committee meetings, I listened to the muffled cadence of therapy sessions that lasted up to three hours. Other days, I smoked cigarettes with clients on the building's front porch, where therapeutic talk frequently spilled over, sometimes in the form of critical commentary. And while I generally steered clear of group therapy in an ultimately futile effort to segregate my policy-oriented projects from therapists' clinical activities, I regularly attended "special" group sessions such as those celebrating a client's birthday, sobriety anniversary, or advancement to the next treatment phase. Even more frequently, I found myself witness to impromptu therapeutic exchanges between therapists and clients—clients who spent a good portion of their waking weekdays talking about themselves on Cliff Street.

These early experiences not only provided the first of many lessons I learned on Cliff Street and further fueled my interest in pursuing graduate training in anthropology. They were also the way I gained access to places and people described in this book. Furthermore, once my job shifted from influencing program policy and practices as a fledgling social worker to describing and analyzing them as an ethnographer, I also became responsible for representing the sometimes conflicting and always fascinating perspectives of those I studied, whether professional practitioners or clients. To that end, the pages that follow quote verbatim from the dozens of recorded interviews I conducted during the course of my fieldwork. I also make use of data collected over countless hours of participant observation, including the informal conversations I had on the front porch, in the therapy room, or around the boardroom table. The trust I established with the professional practitioners affiliated with Fresh Beginnings is demonstrated by the scores of program documents— including meeting minutes, grant applications, e-mails to colleagues, letters to clients and supervisors, training materials, and group therapy plans and worksheets—that they gave me to aid my efforts to understand and analyze their practices. The trust I established with the clients of Fresh Beginnings is demonstrated by the fact that they taught me that the discourse contained in these institutional documents could be "flipped" to their advantage. And whether it indexed a growing intimacy between us, or simply a pragmatic investment in teaching me about the semiotic and political quagmires entailed in being a Fresh Beginnings client, Nikki's suggestion that she had flipped my very own professional text — namely, the ethnographic interview—was simply invaluable. For at that moment I understood that my charge as an ethnographer was to account for the complexities of speech events, however much I, myself, was implicated or involved in them.

Considering the meaningful investments of the staff and clients of Fresh Beginnings, which yielded such multidimensional data, my responsibility is to elucidate the perspectives of the professional practitioners and clients affiliated with the Fresh Beginnings program, without conceding my own. As Marilyn Strathern (1988) once wrote, the goal of ethnographic description is to set up parallel worlds in writing, which both describes informants' ways of setting up the world as they do and indicates the ethnographer's interests in construing the world as she does, keeping these perspectives analytically distinct.

So whereas an anthropologist may initially wonder what the ethnography of an addiction treatment program can offer the study of language use and ideology, and a professional practitioner may doubt that linguistic anthropology can shed much light on the politics and practices of the many such programs across the U.S. where she might find herself at work, my intention in *Scripting Addiction* is to demonstrate that mainstream American addiction treatment is a particularly illuminating site, where dominant cultural ideas about language are put into concerted practice. In drawing attention to the labors needed to sustain even the most naturalized linguistic ideologies, as well as the surprising strategies deployed to trump them, the book also shows why one must understand the politics of language in order to appreciate the complex stakes of clinical interventions.

That said, *Scripting Addiction* is not a prescriptive book but instead a descriptive and analytical one. And although I firmly believe that careful descriptive analysis is an essential building block of any successful intervention, it is beyond the scope of this text to prescribe what addiction programs should be like or, for that matter, how social service board meetings should be run, shelter intakes conducted, or mechanisms for client participation instituted. Although each of these important professional practices is described and analyzed in the following chapters, sometimes quite critically, I leave the important work of revising, revamping, or improving upon these practices to the many others devoted to this important work—some of whom I hope will be influenced by this book. In the concluding chapter, I describe some existing attempts to do just that, as well as the broader implications of this book, both for students of culture and language, and for professional social work students. Indeed, *Scripting Addiction*'s most practical hope is to suggest that these two bodies of students have much to learn from each other. For as Fresh Beginnings professionals and clients poignantly demonstrate, both administrative practices and therapeutic ideas are thoroughly cultural and inexorably political. And, in the end, *Scripting Addiction* will remind the reader that culture and politics are always subject to change.

CHAPTER ONE

Identifying Icons and the Policies of Personhood

INTRODUCTION: POLITICS AS USUAL

ON A SUNNY AUGUST MORNING IN 1996, FLANKED BY TWO BROADLY smiling, casually dressed African American women,[1] President Bill Clinton "ended welfare as we kn[e]w it" with a resolved stroke of his pen. Though the blossoming scene of the White House Rose Garden and the beaming smiles of the chosen cast of characters suggested that America's poor and downtrodden had finally found their way under the sun, the "end of welfare" was terribly unseasonable. Despite the New Democratic[2] promise to dismantle the federal AFDC program only if and when the state could guarantee affordable health care, a living wage, and a "dignified and meaningful community service job," none of these conditions had (or have yet) been met.[3] Additionally, with the minimum wage set at $4.75 an hour, an average of 33 percent of poor families' income devoted to child care, and a myriad of federally funded social programs decidedly devolving, the forecast for the first generation of the country's poorest finding themselves without social security since 1935 was very gray indeed.

However, in light of the coming elections and the tremendous unpopularity of welfare (even among welfare recipients, as Clinton's script would have it),[4] these threatening conditions were widely overlooked. After all, the problem of welfare, as politicians and their constituents left and right charged, was that poor people like those gathered in the Rose Garden that day came to *depend* on it, even if it was substantially shy of a living wage. Notably, poor people's "dependence" was cast as not only—nor even primarily—economic in nature. Dependence had weaseled its way down into the impoverished psyche and then proliferated, through intergenerational and (sub)cultural transmission. What Oscar Lewis had deemed a "culture of poverty" in a widely read 1966 *Scientific American* article had degenerated into an even more troubling "culture of dependency"—with culture understood as "values" and "beliefs" cleansed of their political economic correlates.[5] As George W. Bush put it in his 1999 book, *A Charge to Keep*, "people became less interested in pulling themselves up by their bootstraps and more interested in pulling down a monthly government check. A culture of dependency was born" (1999:229–230). And although Clinton—whose "charge" on welfare

Figure 1.1. President Clinton signs the Personal Responsibility and Work Opportunity Reconciliation Act of 1996, "ending welfare as we kn[e]w it."

was happily kept by his successor—blamed an antiquated welfare system for "trapping" recipients in a culture not of their own choosing, when discussing problems of poverty he also implicated a "cycle of dependency that keeps dragging people down."[6]

In these quasi-anthropological terms, welfare state retrenchment found its powerful poetics. Indeed, when Clinton signed into law the Personal Responsibility and Work Opportunity Reconciliation Act (PRWORA), which would establish lifetime limits, work requirements, and a number of conditions concerning both out-of-wedlock and teen parenting, he successfully performed a profound act of government retrenchment cast as moral cure: if poor people are afflicted with dependence, even the most menial and lowest paying "work opportunity" would provide a much needed dose of "personal responsibility." Accordingly, before putting pen to paper, President Clinton turned to the former welfare recipients beside him—who did much to authenticate his morality play—and commented, "They, too, have worked their way from welfare to independence and we're honored to have them here."[7]

Nancy Fraser and Linda Gordon (1994) observe that American debates about poverty have long been framed in the terms of "dependency." Drawing on Raymond Williams's (1983) insight that particular *keywords* become focal points in political contests, and abiding by Foucault's genealogical method, Fraser and Gordon trace "dependency" across economic, socio-legal, political, and moral registers. As they "contextualize discursive shifts in relation to broad institutional and socio-structural shifts" (1994:311), Fraser and Gordon find that in post-industrial society, all adult "dependency"—save perhaps the economic dependence of a new wave of upper-middle-class housewives on their wage earning husbands—has been swathed in the rhetorical garb of individual pathology and moral failing.

Fraser and Gordon further argue that the discursive development of "dependency" has involved over-determined figures they call *icons*, which "condense multiple and often contradictory meanings" (1994:311). More pointedly, Fraser and Gordon note that icons dissimulate the political economic bases of social problems by personifying them. For instance, the iconic figure of the welfare dependent—itself a composite of other socially abhorrent historical figures—*typifies* deep and persistent cultural anxieties about race, gender, and citizenship while appearing simply a token of a naturally existing type. Accordingly, icons of dependency quite literally stand for the social contract gone awry (ibid.). Providing the rhetorical support for powerful political agendas, such as the one formally codified in the Rose Garden that August morning, icons buttress what I call *policies of personhood*—that is, policies that appear to respond to (rather than imagine or produce) particular *types* of people.

Policies of personhood are not just dramatized on grand, national stages, directed by presidential players with far-reaching plots in mind. As political scientist Michael Lipsky (1980) has cogently argued, policy is commonly made on the ground by "street-level bureaucrats"—teachers, police officers, social workers, and others charged with implementing policy mandates and therefore determining their efficacy. This chapter demonstrates how a diverse group of social service professionals builds icons and sustains policies of personhood through their everyday rhetorical practices. So while Fraser and Gordon are interested in *doxa*— the commonsense beliefs that escape the analytical scrutiny of those who feel they are merely an audience to political spectacles—this chapter focuses on the practices and beliefs of those most intricately involved in policy and person making (cf. Douglas and Ney 1998).

Notably, this focus requires a kind of analysis not readily afforded by the Foucaultian genealogy that Fraser and Gordon adopt and adapt. While a genealogy does the invaluable work of helping us to understand "broad discursive shifts"—as Fraser and Gordon do so well—it does much less to elucidate the everyday semiotic processes involved in the establishment and sustenance of powerful iconic figures.[8] Indeed, if the ambitious analyses that Foucault inspired help us identify kinship patterns that connect our current-day icons ("welfare queens") to their equally troubling ancestors ("the pauper," "the native," "the slave"), we are nonetheless left with a critical question: What are the everyday ways of speaking and interacting that sustain the discourses and icons of dependency? And why might the very same people who express outrage at the sexism and racism of welfare reform discourse, or are themselves the subjects of it, engage closely related story lines, especially ones that involve the feminized and racialized themes of dependency?

To answer these questions, this chapter calls upon another analyst who specifically attended to the powers of the icon. In laying out his tripartite theory of the sign, American Pragmatist philosopher and father of semiotics Charles S. Peirce defined the icon as that which gains its significance in resemblance to its object. Iconic signs differ from their indexical brethren, which gain their meaning in a contiguous relation to their object (as in the case of smoke and fire) and also from symbols, which have an arbitrary (that is, *conventional*) relationship with that which they represent. However, the highly contingent and conventional nature of icons—as signs of semblance—was not lost on Peirce, who argued that since anything may resemble anything else, iconic signs are necessarily "motivated." In other words, icons are the product of the analogic practices of language users as they selectively establish relationships of likeness (Peirce 1955). Icons, then, gain their meaning not because they naturally resemble some unmediated thing in the world but instead because a community of speakers collectively designates that one kind of thing *is like* and therefore can come to *stand for* another. Drawing on the conversations of social service professionals and clients at Fresh Beginnings, as they work to establish and sustain program policy during troubling institutional times, this chapter illustrates the "motivated" processes by which icons come to realize their powerful political effects.

The policy stage in focus here is a daylong retreat in which a range of program participants—from administrators and clinical supervisors to therapists and case managers—work together to rebuild the Fresh Beginnings program, which had recently suffered a series of institutional blows and troubles. While we witness professionals discussing and sometimes debating the program mission, organizational structure, staff communication, and even interagency transportation, we will see that it is not until they reconstruct an iconic image of the Fresh Beginnings client that they are able to restructure the program.

Considering the timing of the event, only two and a half years after that fateful day in the White House Rose Garden, perhaps it is no surprise that the image the retreat participants built of the client highlights her *dependency*— both economic and chemical. And although the icon at Fresh Beginnings, like her counterpart in the Rose Garden, certainly functioned to redirect analytical energy from political and institutional analyses to moral and psychological evaluations, the point here is not to draw a simple parallel. Rather, I argue that the linguistic exchanges between retreat participants were *motivated* in two related senses. Primarily, and most obviously, professionals were desperately intent to (re)establish a strong foundation for their faltering program, and, for reasons elaborated below, they used a particular image of the client as an institutional support. However, Fresh Beginnings professionals did not simply borrow the dominant discourse of dependency, wholesale, nor adopt already established icons of dependency. Instead, through their extended and often arduous linguistic exchanges, retreat participants interactively established relations of likeness—work that was, in the Peircean sense, *motivated*. Indeed, it was largely through their semiotic labor that Fresh Beginnings professionals were able to forge an icon of dependency on which they themselves could depend.

MISSIONS OF STRUCTURE

It is a damp, heavy morning in March 1999. Affiliates of the Fresh Beginnings program—from agency case managers and program administrators to the newly hired therapist and her clinical supervisors—are climbing a narrow staircase to a stuffy second-story room on Cliff Street. The smell of stale Folgers and recently copied paper fills the two small adjoining rooms that, along with a dingy and rarely working bathroom, comprise the "administrative side" of the building. Usually it is here where supervisors tackle their paperwork, place important phone calls to other Homeless Family Consortium professionals, or conduct weekly meetings with child care staff who cajole, cuddle, and chase homeless children throughout the more expansive space of the affiliated "Kiddie Care" center downstairs.

The gathering staff, most of whom have commuted to Cliff Street from other HFC agency sites, peer into the smaller of the two upstairs rooms. Crammed with donated stuffed animals and other ragtag playthings, the cramped space has most recently served as a venue for "child therapy" as well as the after-school program run by Fresh Beginnings' two family therapists (Ella and Joe). Indeed, both upstairs rooms have taken on rotating purposes over the three and a half years of Fresh Beginnings' institutional life. Administrators' desks accommodate stacks of therapeutic pamphlets and giant teddy bears; child therapy sessions regularly relocate to the swing-set out back to allow space for an impromptu meeting of administrators in crisis.

This eclectic and sometimes chaotic environment stands in marked contrast to the cloistered therapy rooms on the other side of the building.

28 • Chapter 1

Mirror-like, another set of stairs leads Fresh Beginnings clients to the L-shaped "group room" graced with cushy couches and pastel colored tissue boxes, to the chemical dependency (CD) therapists' office where individual sessions proceed behind a carefully sealed door, and to a relatively large bathroom where urine is "dropped" for screening. This architectural dichotomy is clinched by the lack of a direct passageway from the therapeutic to the administrative side of the building, leaving institutional travelers to cut through the first floor Kiddie Care Center, often amid the protests of its already overwhelmed staff.

Today, however, tired footsteps land only on one set of the Cliff Street stairs. Outdated FAX machines and desktop computers have been crammed into corners to make room for three long fold-out tables arranged in a giant "U" formation. Still, there is not enough space at the table for everyone, so latecomers drag folding chairs from across the hall and settle around the perimeter of the room, creating a nest-like effect. Warm greetings sporadically interrupt the steady murmur of packed-in neighbors who express muted incredulity about the lack of parking on Cliff Street, a largely student-populated, residential area in which the Fresh Beginnings program and its people cannot help but stand out conspicuously. Unread program documents are used as fans and eyes dart around, perhaps planning escape routes through the maze of human and metal chair legs for bathroom and cigarette breaks to come.

We have been called on this day to gather for a "retreat," a rosy label for a day-long meeting of official stock taking and strategic program planning. The timing of the retreat is no accident.[9] After a bumpy three and a half years of institutional life, Fresh Beginnings has now found itself in a state of upheaval, suffering the exodus of the entire disgruntled staff at the child care center downstairs, the loss of two child and family therapists, and the forced resignation of the sole remaining CD therapist, Laura. Widely disliked by HFC staff, but adored by many of those she treated, Laura was followed by all but two of the clients, leaving a program that was designed to accommodate ten to twelve families with a record low census.

By special invitation, the two remaining clients will join the group today for a designated period, causing quiet discomfort among some of the professionals present. In response to carefully posed suggestions that clients are not well equipped to participate in administrative labor, Marne, the talented but embattled director of the HFC collaborative and the convener of the retreat, has cast her invitation as a sign of Fresh Beginnings' continued dedication to "consumer participation."[10] In the program's start-up funding application to the Office of Housing and Urban Development, administrators emphasized their progressive dedication to "participant involvement in [HFC] decision-making" and "shared responsibility for program success." Yet despite the powerful rhetorical resonance of "responsible involvement," establishing mechanisms for such participation had proved both challenging and controversial in the past, rendering Marne's invitation a loaded gesture.

The range of invited participants was indeed intended to reflect—and therefore *effect*—inclusive collaboration. However, the negativity in the air is at least partially attributable to the fact that these sorts of events, which seemingly offer everyone an opportunity to contribute, tend to take on a rather superficial quality. In the face of those who dole out needed services from housing to therapy, it is unlikely that clients, for instance, would be inclined to complain as vociferously or pointedly as they otherwise might. Line workers' comments, too, are carefully edited as their bosses either nod emphatically or remain expressionless in a telling non-response. And though administrators generally acknowledge and sometimes work to sort through clients' and line workers' comments and contributions, all are aware that decisions are ultimately made by Marne, Leif (the commanding director of HELPNET—HFC's largest and most comprehensive service provider), and Charles (the lead man at Hope Health). (Marne reports to Leif and is, in theory, equally responsible to Charles; she also serves as the perennial fall guy as she relays upper-level decisions to HFC staff members with the not-always-accurate, and often rankling, pronoun "we".) Today few in the room seem to buy Marne's suggestion that the retreat will be a marketplace of ideas, each with potentially valuable purchasing power.

Although Marne has advertised the day's event as a "fresh" start for a "Fresher Beginnings," she cannot be unaware that many in the room feel she is largely responsible for the troubling events that precipitated the retreat. On the staff-side front stoop during the short breaks between retreat activities, a smart, attractive Marne nervously chain-smokes and smiles broadly, working to gain the sympathies of her detractors. But now, in the cramped, unglamorous second-story room on Cliff Street, the pressure of such scrutiny is etched on Marne's furrowed face as she issues a strained, if still enthusiastic, welcome. Not without unforgiving irony, she is interrupted by a tape recorder microphone wire that tangles around her neck as it is awkwardly toted across the crowded room. As if the pressure of the retreat itself was not enough, Marne's ordeal is further complicated by the fact that the resident ethnographer is now flanked by other program "evaluators." HFC has chosen this time to undergo a formal evaluation and Fresh Beginnings has been identified as a nexus of collaborative activity. So not only do her overworked and unimpressed colleagues, bosses, and underlings take critical mental notes as she reviews the formidable retreat agenda more like a cheerleader than a program director; now her inaugurating words are also captured on tape, which can and will be reviewed.

Readjusting her blond coiffed hair and regaining composure, Marne distributes the program's three-year-old mission statement for the group's review. ("It seemed like a logical place to start," Marne later explained, "I needed to make sure everyone was still on the same page.") Around the table, tired eyes scan the familiar statement and fall back on Marne who concedes, "So, um . . . this is feeling very formal and structured." Unwilling to entertain the ensuing silence, Marne boldly asks for a "volunteer" to read the mission statement aloud. Diane, the tirelessly sympathetic clinical consultant, complies:

1 [Fresh Beginnings]' mission is to provide individually designed,
2 family focused services to homeless women with children who are experiencing
3 alcohol and other drug problems. [Fresh Beginnings] maintains a multiagency
4 commitment to achieving lasting sobriety and self-sufficiency.

The group falls into a collective shrug. Apparently there is little reason to redirect their program's mission away from "individual design" and "family focus," nor to complicate a straightforward portrait of client population and "problems." No one even bothers to comment on the fact that in committing itself "to achieving lasting sobriety and self-sufficiency" (line 4), the statement portrays the program as if it were a recovering homeless addict itself—a significant oversight indeed. It seems that a misguided mission is not what has landed us in the retreat room this morning, and, finally, an impatient Leif clips, "It looks fine to me," to which the group swiftly joins in semi-automatic assent.

"Structure" and "Practice"

While having failed to spark a creative redirection of mission, Marne's comment that "this is feeling very [. . .] structured" may well be more than simple concession: at Fresh Beginnings formal programmatic appraisals were not uncommonly articulated in terms of "structure" and the dangers of having too much or too little of it. Here, the term "structure" carries negative connotations, expressing Marne's worries that the retreat is already failing at its work of collaborative recreation—that is, the "structured feeling" of the proceedings will not allow for the creativity and spontaneity that programmatic revision requires (cf. Stinchcombe 1965).

Such anti-structure sentiment was commonly expressed in the earliest days of Fresh Beginnings. According to the program's founding narrative, "traditional" drug treatment programs—with their rigid treatment protocols and one-size-fits-all approach to service delivery—were incapable of serving homeless women, whose daily lives had been rendered radically unpredictable in a political economy that defied and excluded them. Expecting homeless women to drop off the kids with packed lunches at day care and drive themselves to midday, ninety-minute therapy group sessions where they would "share" their problems with middle-class counterparts was both impractical and "insensitive." By contrast, the young Fresh Beginnings touted its dedication to respond to the *individual* needs of clients, as the mission statement indicates above (line 1). Therapy schedules were to accommodate the unpredictable demands of clients' need to find housing or employment; treatment approaches were to be "sensitive" to clients' "culture" and "gender;" and the provision of support services—such as on-site child care and transportation—were to offer clients the very best chance of making it to Cliff Street regularly. Administrators' preference for loosely structured programming was even codified in the funding application to HUD, which listed at the very top of "fundamental principles" that "services and policies will be open-ended, flexible, and individualized, not defined by 'rules' for participation."

However, while "structure" was once collectively cast as a vestige of addiction treatment's "traditionalism" and a hindrance to both clinical and institutional success, as the program encountered more and more problems around service coordination and interagency collaboration, administrators and therapists alike began to worry much more about the liabilities of "open-ended, individualized, and flexible" policies than the encumbrances of structured "rules of participation." Indeed, Leif's clipped response above indicates the widely shared opinion that although the program's mission was pointed in the right direction, the foundation of the program was structurally unsound.

Particularly troubling was client transportation, the support service that emblematized Fresh Beginnings' sensitive response to its target population. From the outset, staff and administrators agreed that the program would need to provide each Fresh Beginnings client with transportation between Cliff Street and the dozen different HFC-affiliated shelters and transitional housing sites, scattered throughout the county, where a client could be living at any given time. However, such "individualized," door-to-door service, when multiplied by ten to twelve clients and their children, was a practical quagmire that defied the best efforts of five consecutive transportation coordinators, two working vans, and the bevy of "paraprofessional" drivers.

It was not unusual for the white vans—half-filled with exasperated clients—to arrive at Cliff Street forty-five minutes after therapy sessions were scheduled to begin. Clients' children were sometimes delivered to the wrong after-school program, and occasionally a Fresh Beginnings

32 • Chapter 1

family was stranded altogether. Administrators, therapists, and drivers argued about who was to blame during an especially cantankerous series of meetings. In the meantime, frustrated therapists systematically documented the vans' erratic arrival and departure times to show administrators that a "structured schedule" (lines 3–4, below) was a practical necessity. For instance, in July 1998, a clearly irritated therapist sent an e-mail to the new transportation coordinator that read:

1 We still do not have an effective means of communicating with the van drivers
2 consistently and the vans are arriving later and more sporadically than ever before.
3 It sends a negative message to our clients when we do not have a reliable structured
4 schedule to offer them as they work on their recovery.

The problem of the van's performance, according to the therapist, is one of unreliable structure, a problem that clearly belongs to a professional "we" (line 3). Yet, as if the ineffectual communication among relevant staff (line 1) was not troubling enough, the therapist charges that the sporadic and late vans "send a negative message" (line 3) to clients as well. Notably the e-mail reverses the program's founding logic: here, clients need a reliable structure rather than flexible service if they are to successfully "work on their recovery" (line 4). Due to missives such as this, in which administrative failings were discursively entangled with therapeutic ones, transportation readily became a powerful indication of the young program's faltering.

CD therapists did not simply worry about the kind of "message" that transportation failings sent to Fresh Beginnings clients; they also fretted about just what those clients would do with the message once they received it. Across HFC, practitioners were aware that some clients seized upon transportation problems to explain away their frequent absences on Cliff Street. However, fewer were willing to admit that what had once been referred to by clients as "the hook"—a firm mandate that required clients to attend daily therapy sessions in order to keep their HFC-provided housing or shelter—was being flexed and bent at will. In a concerned letter to her clinical supervisor, therapist Laura explained:

1 In an effort to be flexible and non-traditional, [Fresh Beginnings] has adopted more
2 fluid boundaries than are present in traditional therapeutic settings.
3 This appeared to be very effective as long as the clients believed that their transitional
4 housing depended upon their active participation in this intensive outpatient program.
5 As some clients recognized that their housing was not contingent upon their active
6 participation in this program, commitment to treatment began to disintegrate, and
7 there has been an increase in the numbers of times and variety of ways clients have
8 tested the boundaries.

In line with social work scholarship that highlights the therapeutic importance of firm boundaries between professionals and clients,[11] Laura now expresses her concerns about *program structure* in terms of "fluid" and highly crossable "boundaries" (lines 2, 8). More specifically, she asserts that without a "believ[able]" hook (lines 3–4), clients would "test" (line 8) the already fluid boundaries of their therapeutic setting or perhaps step outside them altogether.

Acknowledging that clients' tests had grown in frequency and variety, Laura is again clear that such trials derive from a program without adequate structure populated by clients who are in desperate therapeutic need of it. Less explicitly, Laura implicates what was perhaps the most troubling gap in the young program's infrastructure: "case coordination." On paper, the model of case coordination seemed simple enough: each Fresh Beginnings client would work with a case manager at the HFC agency with which she was affiliated as well as a CD therapist and family therapist at Cliff Street. Case managers would assist clients in securing permanent housing, gainful employment, government assistance, or educational opportunities—the practical stuff of self-sufficiency.[12] Therapists, on the other hand, were to delve deeper in search of the psychological hindrances to both sobriety and self-sufficiency. In theory, case managers and therapists were to meet monthly to discuss each case, working together to develop a coordinated "case plan" based on each client's agreed-upon needs.

In practice, however, this neatly delineated model of case coordination proved both enormously time-consuming, as therapists met with a bevy of case managers at five different HFC agencies, and ideologically messy, as the needs of the clients were bitterly debated. For instance, a case manager might urge a client to leave the transitional housing program to take a much coveted and rare Section Eight housing voucher[13] while a CD therapist insisted such a step was therapeutically premature; or a therapist might demand that a veteran client, found to be abusing prescription medicine, be "terminated" from an HFC shelter while a case manager balked, citing the client's successes in finding employment or enrolling in school. It was not unusual for supervisors and consultants to be called to mediate therapist–case manager standoffs. Meanwhile, such dramatic staff conflict gave clients, so inclined, the perfect chance to "triangulate"—that is, selectively play upon each staff member's well-advertised philosophical stakes to further their own agenda.

As clients succeeded at forging triangles, staff saw their problems of coordinating cases as a failure to realize structure—of any shape—at all. Indeed, in an interview with a HELPNET case manager, she stated unequivocally, "If you are going to talk about the *structure* of the program, you have to *talk about* the issues of *conflict* between the case manager and the therapist." At the retreat Marne summarized these long-brewing conflicts as follows:

```
1  Marne:  See when the rubber hits the road, you have sort of day to day problems,
2          which are really challenges for the . . . consumer and the treatment team to
3          figure out what is really best for that person at that point in time . . .
4          Uhm, and they have been working on developing self-sufficiency and taking
5          control back over their lives and, uhm, are in a position now that they could
6          make a pretty long trip down to Kentucky to see relatives . . . but that also
7          means that everything that you can associate with it from moonshine to a
8  Angie:  Oh god! And, uh, and . . . mint juleps! (laughter, group)
9  Marne:  Anyway, so then the question is, so you can see where the case managers
10         may be saying you know, you know: "we're glad to see this person ready to
11         take those steps" and the treatment team saying, "my god, they're going to
12         feel terrible when they get back!" or "will they get back?" and so on.
13         And as they get invested in wanting to do stuff over here or wanting to
14         do stuff over there, it becomes this tugging, consumers end up in the
15         middle of it as we try to negotiate which goals are the most important goals.
```

Relying upon a thinly veiled example, derived from an actual incident that had occurred months earlier, Marne articulates a perspective carefully pitched between the two opposing stances that she narratively orchestrates. Placing her analytical vision (line 9) between *"tugging"* parties (line 14), she effectively exonerates both the embattled treatment team and the frustrated case managers, suggesting that their competing goals are equally sound in relation to their traveling client. At the same time, the Kentucky trip evokes a typical quagmire; that is, "self-sufficiency"—in the form of "taking *control*" (lines 4–5) is potentially consistent and contiguous with failed sobriety—in the form of moonshine and mint juleps (lines 7–8). Therefore, the answer of "what is really best" (line 3) can hardly be found in the program's dually focused mission statement.

Yeheskel Hasenfeld (1972, 1983, 1992) argues that human service organizations, as "people processing" entities, are characterized by ambiguous, if highly ideological, goals. Taking human beings as their "raw material," such organizations invest the persons being processed with available cultural values and social identities so as to create "reference points" in coping with the moral components of decision making (Hasenfeld and English 1974: 8; see also Hasenfeld 2009a). Such a perspective resonates with Mary Douglas's (1986) assertion that by affording its members a set of "natural" analogies with which to explore the world, institutions justify the "naturalness" of instituted rules, roles, and protocols so as to protect their otherwise fragile form. Indeed, as Marne speaks of the "rubber hit[ting] the road" (line 1), it becomes all the clearer that the program's mission statement is read by participants as an abstract structure that fails to accurately capture or control actual practice.

Retreat participants had yet to determine that the most "natural," or productive, reference point is not the practitioners who tug but instead the client who stands "in the middle" (lines 14–15). Yet while Marne's question of whether the client will "get back" from Kentucky is left unanswered (line 12), the group would soon "figure out what is best" for the program and its people (line 3) by figuring out an analogy. In the motivated work of building an icon, the analytic energies of practitioners would be redirected from their own unstructured professional dynamics to the drug-induced psychodynamics of the unstructured client.

"A Forty Ounce and a Joint"

It is 11:20 AM, minutes before an indigestion-inspiring "working lunch," and the room is heavy with consternation. Despite entreaties to "look forward" toward a brighter organizational future, the morning's discussion has raised distressing institutional memories of staff conflict, communicative snafus, and resources spread too thin. Even Marne, whose energy usually seems double that of her colleagues, slumps a bit in her chair, dejected perhaps that her Kentucky tale has failed to produce a collective response to the dilemma it raised. The group falls into exasperated silence.

The two clients present had remained virtually silent all morning, discreetly exchanging disapproving glances and producing the occasional furtive sigh as they listened to administrators "ramble." Seemingly startled that the professionals had now also fallen into silence, Nikki scans the room, smirks as she discovers her neighbor's doodles, takes a quick deep breath, and fires:

```
1  Nikki:  Well, I think what you people are failing to realize: we're recovering women.
2          Our lives have been centered around getting and using drugs and, basically,
3          this recovery thing is that we are learning to live our lives over again.
4  Group:  Yes/Hm-hmm/hmm-hmm (simultaneous)
5  Nikki:  That means we are learning to make friends without using drugs;
6          we are learning to get up in the morning, wash our face and brush our teeth
7          without.
8  Group:  Yes/hm-hmm/That's right.
9  Nikki:  Some of us had to get a 40 ounce before we got out of bed;
10         some of us had to smoke a joint; whatever it was before we could even go to
11         the bathroom and wash our faces and get our acts together, you know.
12         So, I mean, so basically what recovery is supposed to be teachin', teaching us
13         how to live our lives without using drugs.
```

36 • Chapter 1

14 Leif: That's right!
15 Angie: You got it!
16 Nikki: And give us some kind of support.

Clearly, Nikki's portraiture is more effective than the unmoving mission statement, the meandering tales of institutional failure, and the thinly veiled finger pointing that characterized the retreat to that point. As Nikki purportedly renders an (auto)biographical sketch of "recovering women" (line 1), the slumping professionals suddenly sit up in their seats, start to nod steadily, and join in a chorus of enthusiastic agreement (line 4). Nikki, the consummate script-flipper,[14] tells her audience what they want and, perhaps, *need* to hear. Indeed, her parable serves as a distinctive pivot, as the clinical supervisor declares, almost triumphantly, "You got it!" (line 15), as the fictionalized women trade in their beer bottles and joints for "this recovery thing" (line 3) and learn how to "live [their] lives" in line with therapeutic pedagogy (line 13).

Toward what does Nikki's discursive pivot turn and why is her anecdote met with such approval? What is the relation between Marne's Kentucky traveler who stands stubbornly in the middle of the tugging staff and Nikki's client-student who orchestrates such harmony among retreat participants?

As Michael Silverstein (2003a:23) notes, political discourse—whether national or institutional—develops via chains of analogies, as people seek to solve conceptual problems until happening upon what must be semiotically *realized* (line 1):

> Such thought-about but unfocused narrative relations, if seized upon by a pregnant captioning label or image, suddenly makes the whole analogical series take on a definitive identity—in fact retrospectively a necessary identity that we now recognize as so many examples of one underlying principle, conceptually implicit, even immanent.

Nikki "seizes upon" Marne's narrative, fleshes out the character contained therein, and helps give her a "definitive identity." She also regrounds the causal logic of Marne's account, which had suggested that the failures of programmatic structure (i.e., uncoordinated case coordination) *resulted in* troubling actions on the part of clients (i.e., moonshining in the "middle" of fighting staff). Nikki instead begins with the image of the dysfunctional, drug-using client and ends with a program that, if it is functioning properly, is "supposed . . . to give us some sort of support" (lines 12–16). In the end Nikki's chiding forces the retreat participants to see that their exhausting morning stemmed from their "failure to *realize*" (line 1) that administrative riddles are far easier to solve by focusing on the "pregnant image" (ibid.) of the fictionalized client rather than the institutional conflicts of tugging staff.

As we will see below, the client that Nikki identifies effectively releases retreat participants from their reflexive musing about administrative failings and staffing snafus, dramatically refocusing attention from institutional problems to the problematic client much in need of their "support" (line 16). Rather than seeing the image of the beer-guzzling, joint-smoking client as a menace, they adopt her as an opportunity. Precisely because Nikki's figure *centers* her life on "getting and using drugs" (line 2), they determine that Fresh Beginnings should provide an alternative structure that, according to Nikki as well as to the professionals whose scripts she flips, addicts definitively lack.

Dependable Analogues and Independent Icons

With the program's icon brought to center stage, thanks to Marne's and Nikki's collaboration, retreat participants spent the afternoon further characterizing her, and therefore *themselves*, in motivated ways. Notably they did so in the highly resonant terms of "dependency."

```
 1 Marne:  Um, so if there was a way to really structure the [program],
 2         so that underlying that, there would be some beginning of structuring,
 3         building new relationships and helping them bridge kind of . . . because
 4         really what . . . the goal, I think underlying goal of this program is to get
 5         women not only to be sober, but to be able to function independently . . .
 6 Angie:  Uh-hm.
 7 Marne:  . . . without drugs . . .
 8 Angie:  Exactly.
 9 Marne:  . . . to be good participators.
10 Angie:  Right.
11 Marne:  To be able to use the external resources, ah, that exist in the community when
12         they need them.
13 Angie:  Uh-hm.
14 Marne:  And if there was a way to really figure out how to build some of that testing
15         the world . . . or testing the waters, I think the people would say. And I think
16         that's really important. I think when you come up with that, I think we need
17         to move from a dependency model [Voices: "Uh-hm, Uh-hm."] to an
18         independency model.
19 Leif:   Yes!
```

While Marne's narrative now results in an "independency model" with her colleagues' effusive encouragement and punctuating praise (lines 17–19), it is important to recognize where she begins. Namely, she imagines that in order to "really structure" the program (line 1), a client who is not yet able to "function independently" (line 5) must "underl[ie]" it (line 2; cf. Silverstein 2003a:23). With the help of Fresh Beginnings, Marne further offers, women become independent not only by achieving sobriety (line 5) but also by becoming self-sufficient, participating in an idealized community of already existing resources (lines 9–12). In short, Marne's "*participators*" (line 9) bring the program's mission statement to life.

Indeed, bolstered by Nikki's foundational work, Marne's *personal* portrait of the client results in a clear *institutional* picture. Marne can now speak of the program as a "bridge" (line 3) that provides passage for economically and chemically dependent *clients* who start on one bank to emerge as independent *participators* (line 9) on the other. To the extent that she effectively elides economic and psychological (in)dependence, Marne seems to simply channel the neoliberal discourses that accompany and justify welfare state retrenchment. To be sure, Marne's evocation of the program as a bridge seems politically, personally, and professionally motivated. However, her mobilization of the client icon was motivated in a Peircean sense as well. After all, retreat participants engaged in unfocused, abstract talk about mission, structure, and flexibility for many arduous hours, until suddenly "the whole analogical series [took] on a definitive identity" (Silverstein 2003a:23) and found "underlying" principle (lines 2, 4). So when Marne speaks of an "independency model" (line 18) she seems *at once* to refer to an institution that instills such independence, a community of independent actors, and the newly independent class of client-participators (line 9).

For the remainder of the afternoon, retreat participants talk in terms of resemblance rather than causality or contiguity; the awkward stops and starts of abstract and disjointed discourse disappear. Now they almost effortlessly build on one another's comments, like narrative scaffolding. Consider how Cecelia—a longtime advisory board member and manager of family services at WISH, HFC's domestic violence shelter—develops Marne's calls for an "independency model" (line 18):

```
 1 Cecelia: And I think if we really think about [it], the program is designed to eliminate
 2          the barriers that have traditionally kept women
 3 Marne:   Uh-hm
 4 Cecelia: from being successful in treatment. But we have tried to create support
 5          around those things. I think as they move through the program,
 6          you need to start taking those things away.
 7 Marne:   Like the transportation, like the child care, like whatever else that we give
 8          them. And that that is seen as a privilege like you said, that maybe that can
 9          be connected with a positive.
10 Angie:   Yes.
```

Identifying Icons • 39

11 Cecelia: You know, like: "Oh, look, you're responsible enough now to drive
12   your*self* here or to take a bus here, and so you get a celebration in group,
13   because you move *up* a phase, and you get a bus pass," or whatever ...

In line with the program's foundational documents, Cecelia describes Fresh Beginnings as a program in which traditional "barriers" (line 2) are replaced by sensitive "support" (line 4), qualified by Marne as "transportation, child care and whatever else we give them" (lines 7–8). Yet, intriguingly, Cecelia's emphasis is not that unsupported clients need supportive resources but, instead, that "you *need* to start taking those things away" (line 6) as clients "move through the program" (line 5).[15] In strikingly Clintonian terms, she goes on to rehearse (as if for a future performance for an audience of clients) the framing of resource removal in terms of personal responsibility (line 11–13). Not only should "taking things away" be "seen as a privilege" (lines 6–8) and "connected with a positive" (line 9); Cecelia further suggests that resource removal should be *used to define* the newly responsible client, who is honored by a celebration and armed with a bus pass (lines 12–13).

As Cecelia and Marne continue, they clinch the analogic relationship between the more or less dependent client and their program as more or less dependent on shrinking federal dollars:

14 Cecelia: And part of building into this structure, if I *grow* in the program, um, one of
15   the things I need to ask about is the child care that will be taking place after
16   I am done with the basics, you know.
17 Nikki: I ...
18 Cecelia: And so that I can *hook* into that. Because I'm not always going to have
19   services here. And that also leaves room for the new people, because that's ...
20 Marne: Uh-hm.
21 Cecelia: ... been an ongoing ...
22 Marne: Uh-hm.
23 Cecelia: ... problem of the *buildup*.
24 Marne: Exactly.
25 Cecelia: And if there is some woman who is like "Where are the resources?"
26   There again is that *dependency*.

Note that Cecelia directly references the "problem of *buildup*" (line 23)—that is the problem of low supply and high demand for program resources like child care. As Marne and Cecelia collaboratively extol the virtues of the client "I" (lines 14, 15, 18) who "hooks" into *external* resources (line 18), and thereby "leaves room for the new people" (line 19), they betray that it will be the client—at least to the extent that she is figured as independent of the program—who solves "the ongoing problem of buildup" (lines 21–23). Intriguingly, it is *also* the imagined client who, when exhibiting "*dependency*" (line 26) in her request for program resources (line 25), takes the blame for the program's diminished supply of them.

Considering that this conversation falls on the heels of the exodus of the entire child care staff, as well as ongoing transportation problems, we can see that Cecelia's and Marne's semiotic practice allows the program to discursively funnel the institutional and political economic problem of the dearth of resources to the therapeutically compromising overprovision of them. The policies of personhood at Fresh Beginnings had finally found their poetic form, and the politics of welfare state retrenchment and institutional conflict were discursively erased.

. . .

The professionals affiliated with Fresh Beginnings were critical of welfare reform, and many extremely so. Through their work in HFC, they had become intimately acquainted with the dire circumstances that led people to seek government aid and openly balked at Clinton's claims to know what poor people wanted and needed. Very few would suggest that the federal welfare system either produced dependent people—as Clinton would have it—or fed their dependent nature. Most immediately, all worried tremendously about the havoc that PRWORA would wreak on the families that made up their caseloads, particularly at a time when HFC resources were more thinly stretched than ever.

Despite this critical stance, the language of dependency clearly took root at Fresh Beginnings, particularly at moments of institutional crises, such as those that precipitated the March retreat. Moreover, the program *depended* on the language of dependence, as well as on the iconic client that they fashioned to embody it. As the preceding pages have demonstrated, the client icon was developed through ongoing talk—among case managers, administrators, therapists, and clients themselves—about "her" qualities and potentials. Through this linguistic labor, they were able to collaboratively establish that it was not the program that lacked "structure" but instead the clients that it determined to help.

In the end the client icon also helped the program sustain an image of itself as a kind of "marketplace" serving those who could choose and purchase institutional "goods" and move out, satiated, into a larger marketplace world. Of course, the institution-as-marketplace, itself, has a long ideological history in the United States. According to this vision, institutions are sites in which ideas are traded, purchased, or discarded in a more or less agentive teleology toward rational form. However, institutions may rely less upon such "rational" exchanges than they do upon concerted processes of *naturalization*— the process in which social distinctions are rendered "natural" and therefore protected from institutional players' critical appraisals. Just as Clinton's Rose Garden staging worked to justify welfare state retrenchment as a moral response to demoralized "welfare dependents," the client icon helped Fresh Beginnings "sustain the view of nature that is complementary to itself" (Douglas 1986:112).

Teetering Tales of the Unstructured Client

Unless solicited by a nosy ethnographer or framed by an event, like the retreat that was specifically aimed at programmatic analysis, Fresh Beginnings professionals did not generally render administrative problems in terms of "structure." Much more commonly, HFC staff most often spoke of structure in psychosocial terms, and specifically in reference to the relative health of the clients with whom they worked. Indeed, if there was one thing on which members of the HFC collaborative could agree, it was that their clients lacked "structure," although their respective understandings of this lacuna varied in significant ways.

For instance, laying the foundation for Nikki's portrait at the March retreat, CD therapists asserted that their clients' lives centered solely on their addiction to drugs and were otherwise unstructured. In an interview with me, several months before the retreat, therapist Laura explained,

1 L: What happens at the point in someone's life, when they are homeless, and
2   chemically dependent . . .
3 I: Umhm.
4 L: is that their world revolves around how to get the next drug.
5 I: Umhm.
6 L: And that's a very . . . cunning survival head space.
7 I: Ok.
8 L: Because you're engaged in illegal activity, you're having to get money illegally,
9   you're trying to juggle being a mom and a partner, whatever, to, to make this
10   happen. And so it's like constant head work to do it.
11 I: Ok, ok.
12 L: But there's no *structure* to it.
13 I: Oh, uh-huh.
14 L: It's very much at an instinctual survival level and, on the one hand, that's a very
15   risky unsafe way to live but when you're in it—
16   It's like Maslow's hierarchy of needs gone totally awry (chuckle) . . .
17   When you're in it, it's the only thing that makes sense, ya know.
18   That drug has become more important than food and shelter.

As Laura traces the constant revolutions of active addiction, she is careful to distinguish the drug-driven thoughts and actions of addicts from any *structure* (line 12) that might organize and legitimate them. She even goes so far as to say—quite counterintuitively—that while the juggling addict lives on an "instinctual survival level" (line 14), she nevertheless flips Maslow's triangle (line 16), leaving it to teeter on its precarious tip. Drugs become more important than food and shelter (line 18), explaining addicts' homelessness, at least implicitly.

As vehement supporters of the "social drift" thesis (see Fisher and Breakley 1991; Cohen and Koegel 1996), which posits that homelessness both precedes and precipitates problems like addiction, most of Laura's HFC colleagues would object to her final statement above (lines 17–18). In fact, at the center of the ideological conflict between case managers and therapists was the question of which professional and institutional province—housing or CD treatment—corresponded with the most prominent and pressing problem of their shared client base, homelessness or chemical dependency. Not surprisingly, then, in contrast to therapists, HFC case managers focused on the circumstances of homelessness when they spoke of structure—or, more precisely, their clients' lack thereof. Some described structure as an external guide, a socioeconomically organized matrix comprised of home, school, work, and family, which allowed middle-class people to move easily, and productively, through life. These staff members reasoned that without a home, and usually without a (legitimate, day) job and a solid education, their clients were thrown into a chaotic spree that had no evident "structure" to it.[16]

Other case managers went further to draw a causal relationship between the more or less generous provisions of the social structure and psychological structure of individual clients. In other words, HFC case managers sometimes understood their clients, who had been deprived of the accoutrements of normal middle-class life, as lacking structure *themselves*. For example, when asked to describe the intake process at the HFC shelter that she managed, Deanna explained:

1 D: They were assessed on an individual basis, but the common issues are
2   credit problems, domestic violence, substance abuse, mental illness, you know.
3   All those usual issues; a lot of the moms were teen parents and, you know,
4   they dropped out of school in tenth grade and, you know, their education kind of
5   like, their *life* had stopped then and they had gone through, you know . . .
6   a *series* of things
7 I: Uh-huh.
8 D: Like probably about half the women were teen moms when they became
9   pregnant, but when they came to us, they were a little bit older.
10 I: Ok.
11 D: But along with all those other of issues, there was a lack of *skills*, you know.
12   Like *life skills*. Like how to do a budget, like how to prepare for your

13	child, you know, like how to do an array of common things that they
14	would have learned growing up, but they didn't.
15	They just didn't have any structure. They have *no structure*.
16 I:	Alright ...
17 D:	... so then there was *that* to deal with as well.

As Deanna recites the "*series* of things" clients had gone through (lines 5–6), she suggests that clients lack critical *life skills* (line 12), because their "li[ves] had stopped" (line 5), leaving them mired in a daunting morass of social problems (i.e., credit problems, teenage pregnancy, truncated education, and domestic violence). In my many conversations with Deanna over the years, I know that she linked these problems to a socioeconomic system unforgiving of the poor, African American women who made up the bulk of her caseload.

However, Deanna also rhetorically slides from the acknowledgement that many of her clients lacked "basic life skills ... that they would have learned growing up but they didn't" (lines 12–14) to the idea that "they just didn't have any structure" (line 15). Thus, rather than assessing her clients for the skills they lacked and determining which services and resources might be provided accordingly, the case manager implies that her first line of work was to build infrastructure—not in the program but in the person.

"Time's Up!"

HFC case workers and CD therapists commonly saw their work as building psychic structure for their Fresh Beginnings clients, structure that administrators later used to prop up their programs. When these programs began to reveal structural weaknesses, administrators, like Marne, began supervising their employees' structuring practices more carefully. Considering the recent departure of all four program therapists and most of the clients, it is no surprise that administrators carefully inspected the Cliff Street therapy room as the institutional venue where structure was inadequately transmitted to clients.[17]

Program administrators from both HFC and Hope Health considered the management of therapeutic *time* particularly important in the instillation of structure at Fresh Beginnings. Accordingly the final activities at the March retreat involved four "breakout" groups, two of which were devoted to reestablishing treatment temporalities. The first group was charged with addressing the "phase structure" of Fresh Beginnings treatment. According to official program documents, treatment was to be divided into "four phases" meant to stimulate the movement from incoming client to outgoing consumer. Considering there had been only one recognized program "graduate," who had moved through all four phases and out into an imagined world of external resources, the existing implementation of the treatment phase structure was marked at the retreat as especially problematic.

Yet, interestingly, Marne tied clients' failure to move through the phases of treatment to the departed CD therapists' mismanagement of *daily units* of therapeutic time. Accordingly, the second breakout group at the retreat was charged with rethinking a daily therapy schedule, including the number and length of group therapy sessions. Since its inception, Fresh Beginnings had promised to provide five or six group therapy sessions over four days every week, in addition to individual therapy sessions and transportation to and from community AA meetings. On the one hand, this program schedule was part of an effort to flexibly accommodate clients—who were inevitably looking for housing and employment, and not infrequently dealing with an array of legal and bureaucratic matters—while attending treatment. On the other hand, the therapy session was considered a critical "time out" of the ongoing flow of clients' busy days so that dual mission of "lasting sobriety and self-sufficiency" could be processed and practiced in a concerted way. As therapist Laura herself once put it, "We worked really hard to start on time, 'cause that was part of the structure. And it was kinda like a simple boundary, like: 'with all the stuff you been doin', stuff outside here, now it's time to start *group*.' And *my role* was to maintain structure and boundaries and safety."

Yet, over many months preceding Laura's ignominious resignation, HFC and Hope Health administrators alike worried that therapy sessions at Fresh Beginnings far exceeded a standard ninety-minute session, evincing a lack of proper therapeutic structure. Rumors swirled that both individual and group sessions sometimes lasted more than three hours, which my research substantiated. And, quite unlike Cecelia's articulated vision of taking precious resources away as clients moved through treatment, it appeared that advanced clients received more and more of their CD therapists' time and attention. Thus, at the retreat, talk of client "dependency" and institutional "buildup" segued into talk about the length of the departed therapists' group therapy sessions. Marne offered:

1 M: I've been observing, and what I'm observing is that they . . . every *day*
2   they have therapy and just talk and there's no . . . it doesn't seem like that there's
3   very much education, very much . . . *structure*. All the things that they talk about,
4   and we want better *goals*. I don't know how much people were working on that.
5   I don't know about what actually *happened* all day.

Using the "day" as her unit of analysis (lines 1, 5), Marne implies that clients had been languishing in Laura's inchoate therapy sessions comprised of "just talk" (line 2). Opposing this directionless talking with

Identifying Icons • 45

"*structure*" (line 3), Marne further suggests that "all the things they talk about" are incompatible with the "better *goals*" (lines 3–4) that have just been discussed by retreat participants. It is now clear that the mission of "economic self-sufficiency and lasting sobriety" requires that structure "happen[s]" (line 5) during the course of each and every day of chemical dependency treatment.

Laura was keenly aware that Marne, her administrative supervisor, and her clinical supervisor at Hope Health worried about the temporal structure of her therapy groups. Almost as if in direct response to Marne's comments above, Laura defended her approach to the bitter end. In the last of five recorded interviews with me, conducted soon after she left the program, she asserted:

1 L: We worked diligently to structure groups according to the *purpose* of the group
2   because if you don't do that, it turns into constant bitch sessions.
3 I: Right, right.
4 L: And so . . . in trying to structure the safety of the group, we would talk about
5   the purpose of the group, whether it was educational or creative or whatever.
6   For example, like a purpose of the group would be . . . to learn these models
7   and we made it clear that if you're in crisis and that really has to be dealt with
8   now, we'll deal with it now.
9 I: Ok.
10 L: So there was flexibility, but we made it real clear that you would get the most out
11   of this if you learn this model first . . .
12 I: Ok.
13 L: But you're not gonna have to walk out of here bleeding and so (chuckle)
14   because this population had a lot of crisis that was *real*, it was not attention-
15   seeking behavior, which is what a lot of clinicians think these things are . . .
16 I: Right, right
17 L: So that was a big part of my responsibility to monitor the time so that if
18   something big and painful was being opened, that we start putting it back
19   together in advance of the group ending . . .
20   I can't tell you how it gets under my skin that therapist: "TIME IS UP!" (laughter)
21   Ya know, "do something about your bloody guts," ya know (chuckles)
22 I: Right, right, yeah.
23 L: . . . I mean that, to me, that is not *practice*.

Laura suggests that the stated "*purpose*" of the groups, rather than any artificial temporal marker, was what provided the "structure" of the therapy groups she ran on Cliff Street (lines 1, 4). She links structure to client "safety" as well as to therapeutic "purpose" (line 4), emphasizing the importance of education and the "models" transmitted therein (lines 6, 11). However, Laura also implies the need to balance "structure" and

46 • Chapter 1

"flexibility" (line 10). She adds that striking this balance is particularly important since the "real crises" of clients inevitably "bleed" (line 13–14) into the time reserved for a group's designated purpose.

Laura also criticizes the clinicians who mistake clients' *real* crises as "attention-seeking" (lines 14–15) and impose their own *artificial* temporal structures, declaring that "Time is up!" to their bleeding clients (line 20). In line with the program's framing of itself to HUD, she is careful to point out not only her "flexibility" (line 10) but also her sensitivity to a particular "population" of clients (line 14). And although Laura acknowledges the importance of structure, in the end she adds an important qualifier— that the unyielding imposition of external structure is simply "not *practice*" (line 23).

Essentially, Laura's and Marne's dilemma is the same: how to reconcile structure and practice, a problem that, as we have seen, had profound implications for the institution as well as the client. Yet having employed the bleeding client rather than the bridge crossing one as the pivot around which therapeutic time was structured, Laura threatens to throw programmatic time back into the inchoate, goalless days when the purpose was to mop up the spilling guts of languishing clients rather than to turn clean consumers out into the world.

Conclusions: The Slippery Slopes of Structurelessness

Considering her own appeals to the notion of boundaries in her memos about transportation and staff communication, it is ironic that Laura herself was ultimately accused, by memo recipients, of exercising poor boundaries herself. As Laura's conflict with case managers mounted, administrators from both HELPNET and Hope Health became involved as well, expressing concern with Laura's less-than-bounded practice. An addendum to her last performance evaluation read,[18]

1 [Laura Brown] is a valued employee possessing a wealth of sophisticated
2 competence in the area of chemical dependency treatment, and the potential
3 for significant contributions to the Health System and its clientele over time.
4 However, there seems to be a serious danger that her service delivery may be
5 comprised by difficulties working collaboratively with other professionals
6 and, under certain stressful conditions, by a pattern of clinical and
7 professional boundary lapses.

Here, acknowledgment of Laura's "sophisticated competence in the area of chemical dependency treatment" (lines 1–2) is accompanied by the suggestion of a "serious danger" (line 4) of "clinical and professional boundary lapses" (lines 6–7). The addendum makes clear that Laura's relationships are plagued by poor boundaries and implies that these difficulties may well be deep-seated. Note that Laura's lapses are portrayed as both "pattern[ed]" and as being precipitated by "certain stressful conditions" (line 6), indicating that her actions stem from a characterological tendency that is simply revealed in times of crisis.

Laura's clinical supervisors became concerned not only with *how long* she met with her clients but with *where* she met with them as well. In fact, Laura's supervisors regarded her fairly frequent visits and telephone calls to crises-laden clients in their homes or shelter the most problematic aspect of her practice. In line with traditional chemical dependency philosophy, Hope Health supervisors argued that driving with clients, visiting with them or their families outside the group room, or placing nightly phone calls were violations of the appropriate boundaries of the client-therapist relationship.[19] Of course, Laura had largely learned these practices from HFC case managers, who regularly visited or called clients' dwellings as an expected part of their job.

In the end, Laura's resignation was accepted in light of a long list of documented "boundary lapses." And though I think Laura was partially right when she suggested that she served as scapegoat for an unstable institution, the question of why she was targeted can be more precisely explained by following the lines of analysis introduced in this chapter; namely, when the program and its clients were imagined to need "flexibility," Laura's flexible therapeutic approach was deemed unproblematic, even when it veered from her Hope Health supervisors' sense of professional ethics. Yet when the program found itself suffering from "structural problems," it needed a vision of a client and a therapeutic approach to provide a solid foundation. In other words, as retreat participants pieced together that March afternoon, a well-structured program needed a well-structured client. So when the lead CD therapist maintains her flexible approach to "achieving lasting sobriety and self-sufficiency," in line with the program's mission statement, she slips down the slope of structurelessness, right along with her bleeding client.

. . .

The great Erving Goffman once posited that institutions have "semipermeable membranes" (Goffman 1961; Emmet and Morgan 1982) through which only select features of social life and identity are articulated, and often epitomized, while others are erased (cf. Morgan 1986; Young 1989). One might imagine that the client icon slipped out of the Rose Garden and into Fresh Beginnings, based on a perfunctory reading of the comments of the retreat participants. Indeed, endowed with highly recognizable and compelling needs, problems, and proclivities, the client icon clearly integrated ideals and values from the broader cultural and political environment, particularly in relation to cultural ideologies of personhood. As the American welfare reform discourse of the last decades of the twentieth century so relentlessly demonstrated, the "healthy" individual is one who is psychologically as well as economically independent. And, as I explore in later chapters, American clinical discourse commonly casts addiction in the terms of "chemical dependence" and pathologizes it accordingly.

This chapter has suggested certain limitations to a vision of institutions that focuses on membranes and filters rather than the active practices of filtering. As Batteau (2000) has pointed out, and as this chapter illustrates, institutions are poetic, not simply osmotic. They imagine people in ways that suit their own institutional proclivities. And if institutional poetry makes use of all sorts of signs, icons—and the analogic practices that build and sustain them—may play a particularly important role in its creative success. This was certainly the case at Fresh Beginnings. Through their *motivated* labor, retreat participants built an image of the dependent client on which the Fresh Beginnings program, in turn, could depend. This client icon was not a simple product of professionals' political motivations—after all, Nikki did a healthy share of the work. The iconic image of the dependent client was also motivated in a Peircean sense, as professionals struggled to establish the relations of likeness that could provide the necessary support for their faltering program. Indeed, it was not simply through osmosis, nor through genealogical descent, that the discourse of dependency—and its oh-so-familiar personifying icon—found yet another problematic home in the Fresh Beginnings program.

The following chapter tracks clients as they become part of the institutional poetry of Fresh Beginnings, demonstrating that they didn't just "lose" some attributes and identities for the sake of having others highlighted and worked upon. Through an examination of intake interviews and clinical assessments, we will see how the very tools meant to determine who clients are and why they suffer are also the tools of client-making.

CHAPTER TWO

Taking Them In and Talking It Out

Introduction: "Who's There?"

Shelly said that if I had twenty more minutes of tape she would list all the eviction notices she had collected over the years. Much to the delight of her friends at the Alano Club, where she attended AA meetings and worked as a cashier, Shelly had a lot of "war stories"—almost always involving drugs and usually costarring her husband, Jack, who was locked up again, "this time for a good long while." These stories reached back forty years to her days in grade school, where she said she "never did really learn to read and write like I shoulda." Although her daughters' first years had been tough by all accounts, the two preteen girls were now plied with all the classes, counselors, activities, and affection that Shelly could afford. She could fill an entire ashtray with cigarette butts as she talked about her dedicated regimen of raising them. Although Shelly had a severe case of asthma, it didn't put a dent in her two-packs-a-day smoking habit. Once I accompanied her to the emergency room when her cache of inhalers wouldn't do the trick. When Shelly's friend from the club showed up to drive her home and, discreetly aiming the crown of his head in my direction, quietly queried whether I was her "case worker," Shelly narrowed her dark brown eyes and retorted: "No, you *fuck*; she's my *friend*."

. . .

Yolanda also had a lot of war stories. She wore one on her body: seventeen scars from a nearly life-ending knife attack. Though her early years in foster care certainly weren't easy, and her twenty-three-year marriage was hardly perfect, things got really bad when her husband died. Soon thereafter Yolanda, who had worked as a nurse's aid for more than ten years, began having serious trouble lifting patients due to a stress injury to her right arm, not to mention the fact that she was sometimes so depressed that she "couldn't make it out of bed [her]self." Disability checks were hardly enough to cover the mortgage payments on the spacious but quickly dilapidating house where she and her husband had lived for many years. Once unemployed, Yolanda began to rely on friends and acquaintances to bring cartons of milk along with the drugs and alcohol they used in her house, which was considered the most comfortable and safest place in the neighborhood to socialize. Yet it was during this time that Yolanda met the man who would later attack her, and began to drink and smoke cocaine now and then with her visitors. So seldom did she smoke, however, that during Yolanda's first assessment interview Fresh Beginnings therapists made the rare determination that she did not warrant their treatment. Yolanda tried again a few months later and eventually became one of Fresh Beginnings most dedicated clients.

. . .

I could never quite figure out how old Mabel was until one day she proudly announced that it was her sixtieth birthday. Though her maxim-filled stories suggested that she had survived at least six decades, Mabel's silky skin and wardrobe of Tommy Hilfiger jogging suits, which she shared with her seventeen year old "daughter" (who was, technically, her granddaughter) indicated otherwise. Sometimes the seventeen year old would make Mabel cry—like the time the young woman stole fifty dollars "plain out of [her] pocketbook." "She's doin' like I done now," Mabel later bemoaned, "we run like blood *and* water." Mabel had a way with words. Her adages could lighten the grimmest conversations or turn cheap talk into a tearful dirge. Perhaps for this reason people always said that Mabel had a "spiritual way about her." Once a longtime drinker, and later a convert to crack cocaine, the now devoutly sober Mabel told me once: "I got me *two* Big Books now." And though she continued to have trouble paying bills, argued regularly and sometimes violently with her family, neighbors, and Child Protective Services workers, and complained that the psychotropics the doctor prescribed made her "skin crawl clear on out the door," Fresh Beginnings staff considered her the only "successful" graduate of the program—success measured by consecutive months of sustained sobriety.

. . .

By the time Shelly, Yolanda, and Mabel reached the doors of the Fresh Beginnings building on Cliff Street, they had already accrued plenty of experience telling social service professionals about themselves and their lives, if not in the particulars detailed above. For as they sought entrance into one of the various HFC agencies with which Fresh Beginnings was affiliated, they were greeted by case workers and shelter managers armed with a long list of questions—about finances, romantic relationships, prescription and illicit drug use, family history, legal history, educational history, employment history, and mental and physical health—that most Americans would characterize as private.[1] Indeed, the "assessment" (sometimes also called the "intake interview" or simply the "intake") was every client's first necessary step in entering any of the HFC agencies, whether they engaged with those agencies for several hours or several years.[2] And though assessors' questions differed in line with the particular foci of their respective programs, all clients-to-be quickly learned that HFC social workers invariably considered "I got evicted" or "I didn't have money to buy my kids food" a grossly insufficient answer to their tightly paired questions: *who* are you and why are you *here*?

Some HFC agencies required that their workers adhere to already scheduled and standardized questions when conducting assessments. In these cases, assessors dutifully read questions directly from required agency forms and systematically converted the verbal responses of assessees into carefully printed prose. However, most HFC assessors exercised considerable individual discretion in conducting their inquiry, not having assessment forms (or at least not knowing where to locate them!) with which to work, or rather loosely following their guidelines (cf. Freidson 1986; Lipsky 1980; Sosin 1986, 2009). A few assessors prided themselves on an acquired talent for efficiently garnering crucial information while conducting what seemed a relatively casual conversation with those they were assessing.[3] Yet, without exception, HFC assessments included a range of open-ended questions aimed at eliciting narrative responses. Assessors sought social facts in biographical form (i.e., "How long have you been homeless" or, more simply, "what brings you here today?") and, to a lesser extent, assessees' attendant interpretations and reactions (i.e., "How are you feeling about that?"; "What finally caused you to leave him?"; or "What do you think are the reasons that caused you to be homeless?").

To the layperson, assessments might seem to play an obvious functional role in social service organizations serving the poor and homeless—that is, to determine assessees' immediate needs and distribute available services and resources accordingly. To the ethnographic observer, social work assessments appear to be power-laden, goal-driven exchanges in which clients and professional practitioners transform symbolic representations— such as descriptions of personal histories or inner states—into material resources—such as shelter, food, and bus passes. To the HFC caseworkers and shelter managers who actually conducted them, assessments were an opportunity to elicit incoming clients' "stories." And although some HFC assessors glossed these stories as "social histories" and others understood them as autobiographical, they all highlighted the symbolic nature of their work, characterizing assessments in primarily metalinguistic rather than distributional terms.

From the perspective of many of those who inhabited the position of "storyteller," assessments at HFC agencies were puzzling and often maddening interrogations, curiously removed from their immediate material concerns. For instance, when Yolanda arrived at WISH, she found that her assessors were not just interested in her fresh scars and how to assure that her attacker's harassing relatives would not learn of her whereabouts; they also wanted to know about her painful twelve-year tenure in foster care, her work history, and her age when she first took a sip of alcohol. When landing at HELPNET, Mabel was not only asked about her credit, her criminal record, and her housing history before she was admitted to the shelter; she was also soon faced with directed inquires about whether she had been the victim of childhood sexual abuse or had been diagnosed with a mental illness. To her puzzlement, Shelly's assessors not only asked her what drugs she had tried, when she first tried them, how regularly she used them and in what quantities; they also wanted detailed accounts of family members' drug use. And although they were aware that incoming clients sometimes resisted and resented what they took to be unnecessary questions, HFC assessors saw their job as eliciting the infinitely complex details of people's lives—whether articulated as a "war story," a confessional account, or a bare-boned list of clipped responses—and translating them into institutionally legible texts.

Indeed, soon-to-be-clients such as Mabel, Shelly, and Yolanda understood that HFC assessments were not simply verbal exchanges between two parties; they watched as assessors transcribed their spoken responses into various kinds of written texts—whether neatly filling out preprinted forms or scrawling notes on an empty page of a notebook—and worried over how their words were represented in professional writing. For if admitted to an HFC program, these notes became the prologue of a growing "case file." And because they were not authorized to read, write, or edit these files, Mabel, Shelly, and Yolanda learned that the only way to control what was written about them was to carefully manage their verbal exchanges with HFC social service professionals (cf. Floersch 2000, 2002; Margolin 1997; Tice 1998).[4]

Managing how they were represented in writing was crucial from the incoming clients' perspective not simply because HFC assessment was a way of generating locally legible texts about who they were and why they suffered.[5] Assessment texts *traveled*, generating a wide range of professional responses as they went. For instance, Mabel, Shelly, and Yolanda might find that their answers to HFC assessors' questions were transcribed in such a way as to land them in group therapy or parenting classes, to assign them a child welfare worker with the power to take their children away, or to connect them with a court advocate who would hold their hands through a traumatic domestic violence hearing. Each seemingly obscure question an assessor asked corresponded to a set of possibilities about what would happen to the people who responded. And as these responses were transformed into texts that traveled, soon-to-be-clients like Mabel, Shelly, and Yolanda packed their proverbial bags for what was a long trip through a complex network of clinical and juridical institutions. Ultimately some found the trip rewarding, but others wished they had never encountered the agent of their travels, namely, the HFC agency assessor.

One particularly common route for an assessment text to travel was from the HFC shelters to therapists' offices on Cliff Street. Indeed, depending on the narrative yields of assessors' work at HFC agencies, some incoming clients found themselves telling stories to a second set of assessors: the chemical dependency therapists at Fresh Beginnings. If, according to therapists, these clients met criteria for substance dependence, they were faced with a dilemma: spend four out of five weekdays at Fresh Beginnings, complying with program requirements and therapists' recommendations, *and* receive the housing and other services HFC offered. Or, decline to become a Fresh Beginnings client and pack the family's bags and leave the shelter or subsidized apartment.

Attending to HFC professionals' and clients' reflections on assessment and intake practices, this chapter follows Fresh Beginnings clients-to-be—like Yolanda, Mabel, and Shelly—through the assessment process beginning at the HFC shelters through to their first encounters with program therapists. I approach assessment encounters as ritual events, where value-laden texts about people are produced so that those people can be professionally assisted. These texts include documents such as case files or assessment forms, as well as the impressions and interpretations passed between professionals consulting or decompressing at the water cooler. In approaching the assessment as a practice of *representation* as well as evaluation, this chapter illustrates and elaborates the critical semiotic processes involved in turning people into clients (cf. Hasenfeld 1983, 1992; 2009a; Hall et al. 2003, 2006; Lipsky, Prottas, and Spenser 1994, 2001; Sandfort 2009).[6]

Whereas the previous chapter portrayed professional practitioners at a program retreat—with a bit of crucial aid from Nikki—building the client icon by drawing on broader cultural discourses of structure and dependency and establishing analogic chains, here we will see another kind of discursive process at play. Assessments, after all, are dialogic and collaborative routines that actively engage clients in "telling their story."[7] Through the assessment process, the successful assessee identified herself and her problems in ways that *helped professional practitioners help her* in the dim light of an ever shrinking and decentralized cache of resources and services with which to do so. Indeed, HFC assessees learned that if they were to gain the services and resources they wanted and needed, and avoid a variety of censures and sanctions, they had to verbally represent themselves as particular kinds of people.[8]

Although each assessment interaction can be analytically isolated as a site where texts about people and problems are produced, both assessors and assessees were acutely aware that these texts would be introduced to new contexts and read by others. Indeed, edited chapters of assessees' "stories" traveled far beyond the network of HFC agencies and programs, as professionals placed phone calls, wrote letters or e-mails, and sent portions of files to other professionals, all the while doing their best to guard what was left of the client's confidentiality. Accordingly, the assessment process will be theorized in the analytical terms of entextualization—that is, "the rendering of a given instance of discourse as text, detachable from its local context" (Urban 1996:21; see also Bauman and Briggs 1990, 1992; Briggs 2007; Collins 1996; Gal 2005; Hanks 1996b; Kuipers 1989; Mehan 1996; Mertz 1996; Philips 2010; Shoaps 2002; Silverstein 2004, 2005, 2006; Silverstein and Urban 1996; Spitulnik 1996; Urban 1992)—and contextualization, the accommodation of those texts to new contextual surroundings.

With the understanding that assessment texts traveled, both clients and case workers worked to manipulate the content of those texts—for instance, plotting a history of drug use so that it might be read by therapists, child welfare workers, or parole officers as more or less problematic. The assessment process at HFC was not just about the writing of people as clients and cases but also about the ongoing process of co-editing. Yet, as Silverstein and Urban note, people work to manipulate not only the content of texts that implicate them but also the local "metadiscourse about texts and the entextualization process" (1996:9). In fact, case workers and clients alike seemed to understand that the "content" of any text emerges as readers come to understandings of just what kind of text it is. Thus, the first puzzle this chapter seeks to solve is why HFC assessors so often described the assessment interview as a "storytelling" event. For it was in these metadiscursive terms that they elicited narrative material from assessees and inscribed it in efforts to control future interpretations of it.

Finally, and most generally, this chapter is about the dynamics of interviews and the ideologies of language that underlie them. And although the chapter focuses on social work interviewing, social scientists may find that they share HFC assessors' assumptions about the ideal yield, if not the goal or function, of interviews. As Charles Briggs has noted

(1986; 2007; see also Carr 2010b), language ideologies are built into the technology of the interview, as are assumptions about the kind of knowledge people (or interviewees) contain and how it can be accessed. By examining HFC assessors' and clients' reflections on the intake interview as a process of eliciting, translating, categorizing, and representing human experience, we may decipher the widely shared ideological assumptions about language and personhood that interviewing—whether in social work or social science—so often entails.

SHELTER ASSESSMENTS AND THE NEED(S) TO KNOW

Social work assessments are complex professional technologies that entail a number of linguistic and metalinguistic processes. This complexity is captured by Hepworth, Rooney, and Larsen's textbook definition of assessment, which many HFC assessors would have encountered in their social work training. In *Direct Social Work Practice: Theory and Skills*, Hepworth, Rooney, and Larsen (2002:197) begin by relaying that "the word *assessment* can be defined in several ways" and continue,

1 First, it refers to a process occurring between practitioner and client in which
2 information is gathered, analyzed, and synthesized to provide a concise picture of the
3 client and his or her needs and strengths . . .
4 A second use of the term refers to a process whereby potential clients interact with
5 practitioners and organizations to determine if their needs and wants can be
6 appropriately dealt with by the organization . . .
7 Finally, assessment refers to the written products that result from these processes.

In the highly functional terms of "process" and "product," Hepworth, Rooney, and Larsen lay out three ways that assessment is used and understood within the world of social work. First, the authors describe assessment as a process of *portraiture*, involving an encyclopedic gathering, analyzing, and synthesizing of information, which results in "a concise picture of the client" (lines 2–3). Second, the authors define assessment as a goal-driven, institutionally oriented, and highly practical *interaction* among three parties: practitioners, clients, and organizations (lines 4–5). Finally, Hepworth, Rooney, and Larsen note how the first two processes sediment as *text* or "written product" (line 7). How these three generic castings of assessment—as portraiture, interaction, and text—are correlated in theory or practice remains unclear in this definition.

When discussing their assessment work, HFC shelter and case managers were likely to appeal to Hepworth, Rooney, and Larsen's first definition, emphasizing the breadth of information they gathered in drawing

56 • Chapter 2

an effective and evocative picture of the client. For instance, when asked to describe the intake process at HELPNET, Trudy—a newly promoted shelter manager—stated:

1 T: Well, the first thing that I do is I *meet* with clients the first day that they come and
2   I do an *intake* interview with them. So, I sit down with them and it usually takes,
3   uhm, up to like *two* hours.
4 I: Wow.
5 T: I get them to tell me their story . . . of how they became homeless and all and
6   what's going on with them. I get a lot of information from them, like, about their kids,
7   and I ask about things that will, like, help, like substance abuse, like legal
8   involvement, housing history, education and employment history, credit, income.
9   You know, I just get really a *broad range* of information.

Curiously, even though Trudy explicitly lists the categories into which her bevy of questions fall (i.e., lines 7–8), employs active verbs suggestive of a survey or examination (i.e., lines 6, 7, 9), and emphasizes the significant time demands of her inquiry (line 3), she does not characterize the intake interview as an interrogatory event. Instead, she employs the somewhat unusual construction: "I get them to tell me their story" (line 5). She thereby suggests both that assessees' "stories" are already formed and awaiting expression, and that her role is simply to elicit them. Indeed, some HFC assessors insisted that intake interviews were purely autobiographical despite the obviously interlocutory way they emerged.[9]

Though clearly following along a particular plot line (i.e., "how they became homeless"), the "stories" Trudy elicits seem, at first, to allow narrators a large degree of creative freedom in telling about "what's going on with them" (line 6). However, as Trudy goes on to delineate the "*broad range* of information" (line 9) she "asks about" and "gets" (lines 6, 7, 9)—including information about "substance abuse . . . legal involvement, housing history, education and employment history, credit, income" (lines 7–9)—it becomes clear that her categorical questions provide the thematic foci, and therefore the narrative structure, of assessees' reports. Following up on Trudy's indication that her questions were functionally organized as "things that will, like, help" (line 7), I asked, "So the goal of assessment is to link people with services?" She responded, rather adamantly, "It can be, yeah. But it really is to *know* what you're really dealing with, *know* what their challenges are, *why* they behave the way they do." In other words, according to Trudy, assessments are first and foremost a process of taking inventory of the assessee as a person rather than determining the external resources they may want or need.

This way of understanding the work of assessment was not particular to Trudy or to HELPNET, where she worked. Consider my exchange with Cassie, who was employed by HFC's domestic violence shelter WISH:

1 I: So the assessment is a tool staff uses to figure out what services a client needs?
2 C: Well, ye-, no. Really, it's more about finding out what their *experience* has been.
3   These women come in with really horrific histories of victimization, and that
4   is our first chance to really find out about them: who they are, where they've been.
5 I: Uh-huh.
6 C: So it's not really about services; it's really about *them*.

Much like Trudy, Cassie describes the assessment as a process of "find[ing] out" about people and experience (lines 2, 4) rather than "figuring out" what services might be needed, as I rather insistently offer (e.g., line 1). Emphasizing the historical epistemology of WISH's assessment, Cassie elaborates that by soliciting verbal accounts from her clients-to-be, she can connect identities ("who they are") with experiential trajectories ("where they've been") (line 4). And although the homeless shelter manager Trudy "gets stories" (line 5) focused on homelessness, and domestic violence, advocate Cassie "finds out" (p. 56, line 5) about "histories of victimization" (line 3), neither assessor explicitly connects these narrative acquisitions with their respective institutional categories and foci. They instead cast assessees' answers to their directed questions as relatively unmediated and curiously non-utilitarian autobiographical representations.

A Piece of the PIE

While Trudy's and Cassie's descriptions of the assessment process may seem inconsistent with the work of case management, which according to the then current entry in the *Encyclopedia of Social Work* is properly focused on "ensuring the timely and adequate delivery of appropriate services" (1995:335),[10] their responses are consistent with the professional process of portraiture that Hepworth, Rooney, and Larson describe above. More generally, both assessors clearly demonstrate allegiance to social work's professional commitment to *naturalistic* portraiture, that is, the picturing of *people* in their *environment*. The "Person-In-Environment" perspective (otherwise known as "PIE")—which Hartman (1988) suggests has professionally distinguished American social work from its very beginnings (cf. Kemp 2001; Saari 2004)— views clients as intrinsically embedded in nested spheres of interpersonal and social context (Hollis 1964; Weik 1981; Germain and Gitterman 1980; Hartman 1988; Meyer 1983a, 1983b; Saleebey 1992, 2002; Kemp, Whittaker, and Tracy 1997).

Consider again, then, the "broad range of information" that Trudy elicits from client-storytellers in relation to these well-known portrayals

58 • Chapter 2

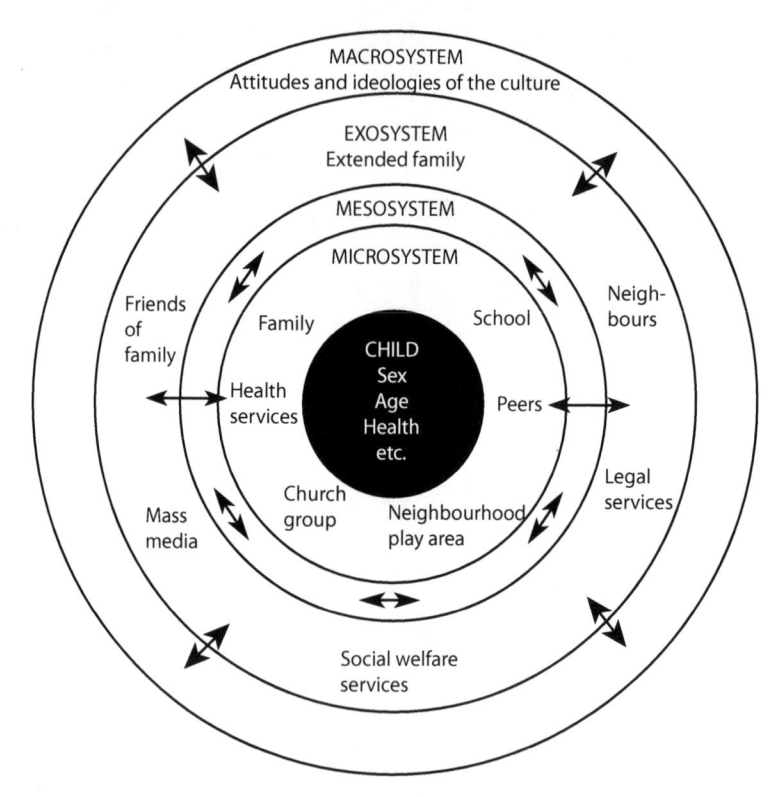

Figure 2.1. Urie Bronfenbrenner's influential ecological model (1979) (from Dockrell and Messer 1999:139).

of PIE as Person (smack dab)-In-(the middle of a more or less orderly)-Environment (see Figures 2.1 and 2.2).

Needless to say, the person-in-environment perspective lends itself to an ambitious—and some would argue *ambiguous* (cf. Abbott 1988, 1995; Brodkin 1990; Hasenfeld 1983, 1992, 2009b; Meyer 1983b, 1976)—project, in which social workers are called upon to ascertain vast spheres of social activity, to understand both the immediate and more remote contexts of clients' lives, and to trace the life histories and social trajectories of people and problems immediately in front of them. It is a daunting professional charge to which the professional anthropologist might readily relate. Indeed, as a student of both anthropology and social work, I was taught in two separate classrooms, across a large swath of campus, how to do the genealogical work of connecting person and environment, with a particular attention to kin. Just as anthropologists learn how to produce kinship charts, Trudy and Cassie had learned to

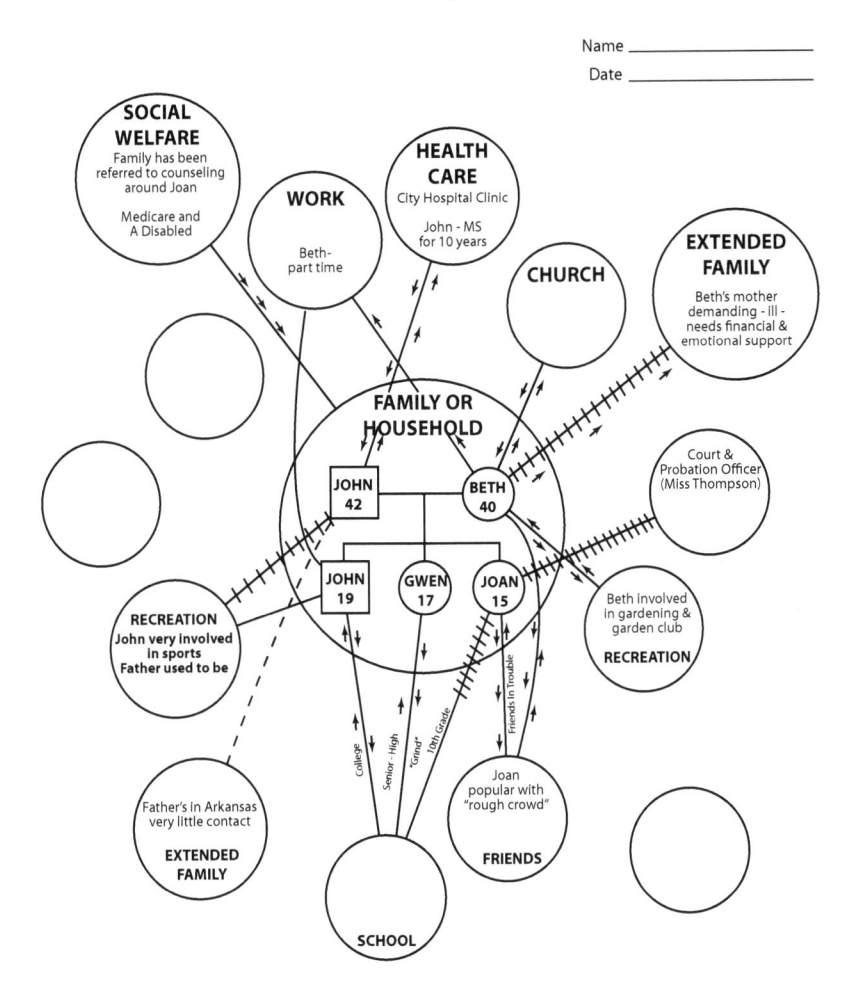

Figure 2.2. Ann Hartman's ecomap, developed in 1978 to give a "holistic" depiction of "the relations between a person and different variables in his or her environment" (Meyer 1995:264–265). Copyrighted material reprinted with permission from the National Association of Social Workers, Inc.

produce "genograms"—graphical maps that display family relationships in order to "provide a quick gestalt of complex family patterns and a rich source of hypotheses about how a clinical problem may be connected to a family context and the evolution of both problem and context over time" (McGoldrick and Gerson 1985:1) (Figure 2.3).

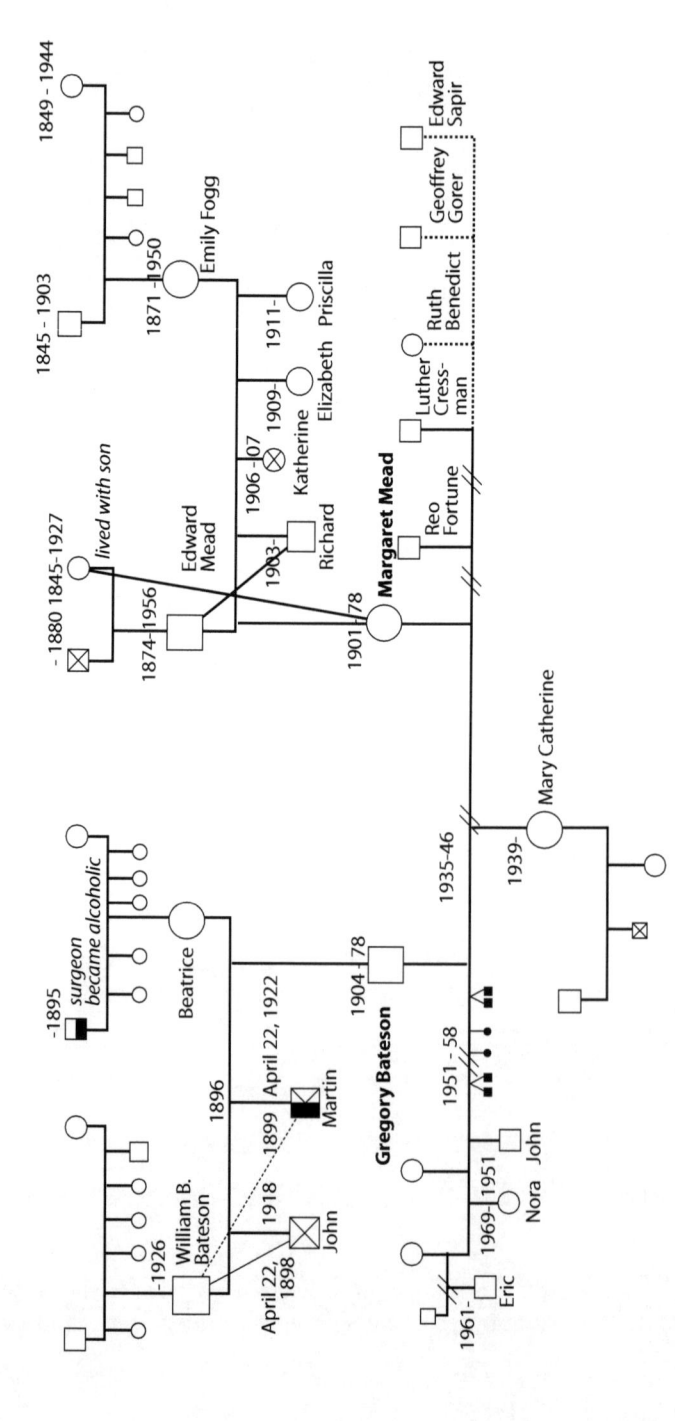

Figure 2.3. Gregory Bateson's and Margaret Mead's genogram (from McGoldrick and Gerson 1985:55).

So, at some point early in their careers at HFC, Mabel, Shelly, and Yolanda would likely have sat through long sessions with HFC assessors who posed questions about family relations (many of which had been answered before). They then watched as seasoned case managers and fresh-faced student interns rendered their responses about divorces, deaths, abortions, adoptions, family frictions, and intimacies into maps meant to "give a picture of where family members have been and the direction in which they need to go" (Visher and Visher 1988:33).[11] During supervision sessions, seasoned case managers cued and corrected interns as they worked to elaborate their genograms, connecting carefully penciled circles (i.e., mothers, sisters, aunts, etc.) and squares (i.e., fathers, step-brothers, sons) with squiggly lines to represent "fused-hostile" relations, arrows with dashed lines to indicate "neglect" or x's to represent "manipulation," and orb-like chains meant to show who was still "in love."(Figure 2.4)[12]

As indicated in both Bronfenbrenner's and Hartman's ecological diagrams, the familial was considered the primary and most consequential "environment" of each "person" that HFC assessed. So when I asked

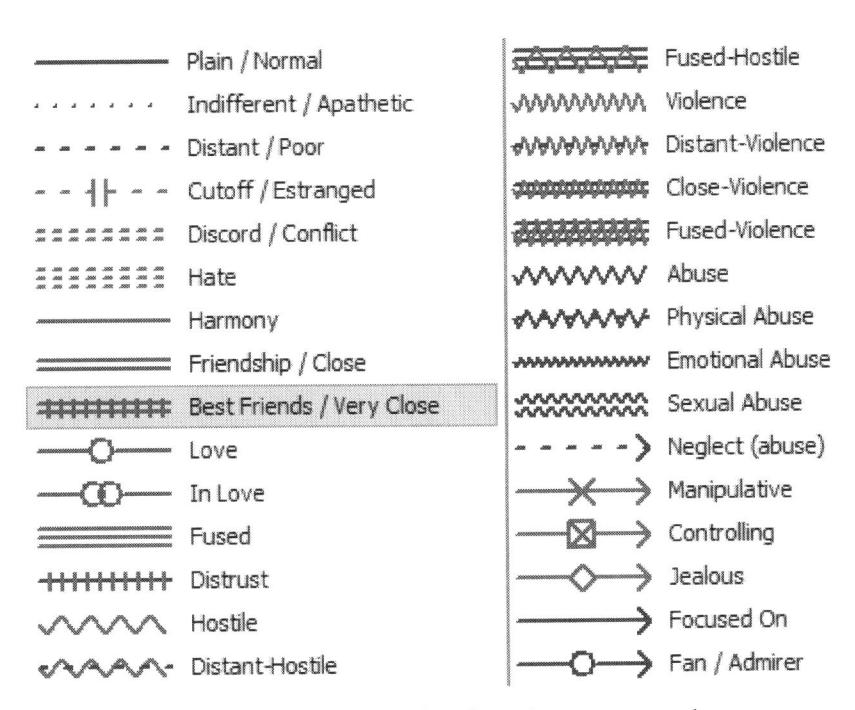

————	Plain / Normal	≠≠≠≠≠	Fused-Hostile
· · · · · · ·	Indifferent / Apathetic	∿∿∿∿∿∿	Violence
– – – – – –	Distant / Poor	∿∿∿∿∿∿	Distant-Violence
– – ⊦ – –	Cutoff / Estranged	∿∿∿∿∿∿	Close-Violence
≈≈≈≈≈≈≈	Discord / Conflict	∿∿∿∿∿∿	Fused-Violence
≡≡≡≡≡≡≡	Hate	∿∿∿∿∿	Abuse
————	Harmony	∿∿∿∿∿	Physical Abuse
════════	Friendship / Close	∼∼∼∼∼∼	Emotional Abuse
++++++++	Best Friends / Very Close	∿∿∿∿∿	Sexual Abuse
——○——	Love	– – – – –>	Neglect (abuse)
——∞——	In Love	——✕——>	Manipulative
════════	Fused	——⊠——>	Controlling
+++++++++	Distrust	——◇——>	Jealous
∧∧∧∧	Hostile	————>	Focused On
∿∿∿∿	Distant-Hostile	——○——>	Fan / Admirer

Figure 2.4. "Emotional relationship codes" from the genogram software GenoPro

Deanna, a case manager who worked with Trudy at HELPNET, why case managers conducted one or even two follow-up assessments if a person was admitted to a HELPNET program, she explained: "The follow-ups give us a window onto family dynamics, which are incredibly important in helping us understand these women. There are *patterns* that we can see, and we can *use* to explain a lot of things." And though one might assume that assessors were most pressingly interested in understanding assessees' *current* familial relationships, Trudy clearly indicated otherwise. Describing the purpose of the follow-up assessments, she noted that they were "more in depth about childhood history of *trauma* and domestic violence and that kind of stuff. [We] *really* try to find out what it was like for them growing up: Did they, uhm, were they *involved* in any kind of child abuse or neglect when they were a *child?* Have they experienced any *incest* or anything like that?" And while Trudy added that the follow-up assessment was like a "*social history*," it was clearly a history plotted along the lines of familial trauma and victimization.

My own oral history interviews with Fresh Beginnings clients indicated that child abuse and neglect was a tragically prevalent feature of clients' reported histories. However, it certainly did not seem commensurate with "what it was like for them growing up." Factory closings, community violence, and poverty, for instance, as well as hopscotch, vegetable gardens, and more or less glowing grade school report cards were also important chapters of most HFC assessees' "social histories." In their pursuit of information they thought would be institutionally legible and useful, HFC assessors commonly took these parts of clients' histories for granted while still holding onto the idea that they came to know both a woman and her "story" through the assessment process.

Translating Trauma

Across HFC, the assessment was a process of classifying assessees' statements into preexisting institutional, clinical, and social categories, and, in so doing, designating roles into which assessees could be institutionally recruited (cf. Agha 1993; Silverstein 1998, 2004, 2005, 2006).[13] Aside from the possibility that incoming clients might manipulate historical narratives to convince their assessors of pressing crises or past traumas or both so they would be *taken in*, their words were *taken up* as evidence of predefined problems as HFC professionals completed their assessment reports.

If HFC assessors generally did not acknowledge the categorizing tasks involved in the assessment process—as indicated by their repeated references to "getting stories," discovering "experience," and "finding out who [people] are and where they've been"—they did suggest that conducting assessments required honed translational skills on the part of the assessor. For instance, struck by her attention to child abuse and neglect as a defining feature of clients' lives, I followed up with Trudy, asking about the prevalence of sexual trauma in her assessed clientele. She responded:

1 T: As far as the women, the *moms* in our shelter, it's, uh, unbelievably high,
2   like 90 percent have had some sort of sexual assault or incest, and damn near 100
3   percent domestic violence . . .
4 I: Hm-mm
5 T: Or they have had at least one or two relationships that *we* would call,
6   classify as domestic violence.
7   *They* don't . . . necessarily call it that, but if you ask them, if you ask them:
8   "Have you had a domestic violence relationship?" they might say no.
9   But if you ask them later on questions about the relationship, they might tell you:
10   "Oh, he used to come over and kick the door in, or he broke this of mine, or he
11   *shoved* me," or something.
12   *They* don't necessarily think of that as domestic violence, necessarily . . .
13 I: Yeah.
14 T: So you *really* have to ask more questions, you can't just use our terminology.

Trudy begins by identifying a translational predicament, one in which there is a semantic gap between what "*they* call" and "*we* would call" (lines 5–7) domestic violence. Her proposed solution is an intriguing one. First, she reflects that by asking targeted questions that solicit seemingly spontaneous narrative responses (lines 9–10) she compels assessees to articulate particular acts (i.e., shoving, breaking belongings, kicking the door) that "*we* would call [and] classify" (lines 5–6) as domestic violence. In other words, Trudy comes to understand the assessee as a victim of domestic violence not because the assessee names her experience as such. Instead, and in response to a series of pointed questions, the assessee describes an encounter of "shoving," "kicking the door in," or "breaking" that the *assessor* can document as domestic violence on her assessment form.[14]

Second, although Trudy explicitly outlines the semantic distinction between what "*they* call" and "*we* call" domestic violence, she points to more troubling and fundamental divisions: that is, between what clients *think* is domestic violence, what they can *name* as domestic violence, and what *really is* domestic violence, the latter of which she seems to conflate with her own classification. It is important to note that the reality of the assessed client's experience *as* an experience of domestic violence is never in question. The idea that assessors had the names that referenced clients' experiences, and that clients had the experiences that assessors could name, coexisted with the idea that the assessment was a chance for clients to tell "their story" in an unmediated way.

Finally, when Trudy warns "you can't just use our terminology" (line 14) and implies that it will take awhile before her incoming clients will find the real names to reference their problems, she arguably betrays that assessment was not purely or even primarily a process of discovering "who the client is" as some of her colleagues suggest above. And if, as Trudy implies, assessment is better thought of as a process of "making people up" to fit preexisting social service classifications (cf. Hacking 1991, 1999), note that this may have more to do with an acknowledgment of corresponding institutional trajectories of help. Indeed, the savvy Trudy undertook her assessment work with acute awareness of how categories like "domestic violence" correspond to institutional trajectories of help. So when Trudy says "you really have to ask more questions," it is with an understanding that those classified as survivors of domestic violence could receive benefits and services—such as legal aid, support groups, and perhaps even a specialized case worker, called "an advocate"—that other HELPNET assessees would not.

Narrative Impositions

In undertaking this potentially unwieldy work of assessing people and their environment, HFC assessors had a number of well-established methodological options—at least in theory.[15] Scores of formal instruments have been developed to assess everything from mental illness to suicide risk to "readiness for change" and have been tested on a wide range of populations, including homeless people (e.g., Aiemagno 1996; Mercer-McFadden and Drake 1992; Sacks et al. 2003). By the mid-1990s, for instance, there were approximately 210 published assessment instruments for use with adults, from the "hardiness scale" and "compulsiveness index" to the "social support behaviors scale"; 74 published instruments for use with couples and families on topics like "boundaries," cohesiveness, marital conflict or abuse, and parent-child relationships; and 49 published instruments for use with children covering matters such as self-concept, loneliness, and self-esteem (see Fischer 1994; Schutte and Malouff 1995). These are in addition to the institution-specific assessment guides followed by some HFC assessors, not to mention the individuals who developed their very own method and style of gathering information so as to formulate it into "a coherent picture of the client and his or her circumstances" (Hepworth, Rooney, and Larsen 2002:187).

However, working in the thick of welfare reform, this range of assessment tools had increasingly little utility for HFC assessors. For while they steadfastly strived to gather a "*broad* range of information" (line 9), these professionals found that the actual pertinence of that information had substantially narrowed. As a veteran case manager named Elinor put it:

```
 1 E:  Before the big push for welfare reform, before welfare reform actually was
 2     implemented, you know, we were able to work with people on a lot of things to get
 3     them ready for jobs, you know. If they had been sexually abused and they just
 4     couldn't do anything until that was addressed or their mental illness or substance
 5     abuse, or they can't read. You know, all sorts of stuff that they were able to work
 6     on, so that they could be a success.
 7 I:  Ok. Ok.
 8 E:  And, you know, after, you know, welfare reform, now everybody has to work,
 9     they have to have a job. So now it's not like, "let's assess where someone is" and
10     then, you know, send them to training. Or you know, "do they need to go to literacy
11     or training or whatever, or a basic math, or high school completion."
12     It is like, "how do I help them find a job?" So that has changed a lot.
```

Recalling the multidisciplinary demands of her work before "the end of welfare as [she knew] it," Elinor suggests that assessment is no longer a particularly useful tool in her work, at least as a "process whereby potential clients interact with practitioners and organizations to determine if their needs and wants can be appropriately dealt with by the organization" (Hepworth, Rooney, and Larson 2002:187). Thanks to fifteen years of welfare state retrenchment, veteran HFC employees like Elinor were operating with fewer and fewer funded services and resources with which "to work with people on a lot of things" (line 2). Rather than abiding by the classic social work mantra of meeting the client "where [she] is" (line 9) as they were trained,[16] welfare reform had reset assessors' compass from an exploration of the past and person to the new, unforgiving policies of "welfare to work." Regardless of clients' past traumas (line 3), present problems (lines 4–5), or lack of skills (lines 9–10), "a job" was the ultimate destination of every assessment Elinor conducted (line 9).

As forecasted in the White House Rose Garden that fateful August afternoon, welfare reform was not generally inconsistent with the painting of personal portraits. As suggested in chapter 1, it was arguably *dependent* on it. Yet, beyond the question of how the structural forces of welfare state retrenchment shaped the actual telling of the assessee's story, those forces certainly did much to determine how assessment texts traveled and what effect they had. Across HFC, professional practitioners and clients alike were now charged with turning assessment "stories" and "social histories" into work-oriented texts, which would be read by discerning state welfare workers or hesitant employers of the thankless, minimum-wage jobs into which HFC clients would be funneled.

URINE OR YOU'RE OUT

If assessors like Trudy and Cassie were insistent that the assessment was "not really about services; it's really about *them*" (line 6), they understood that assessees may not appreciate or cooperate with this epistemological presumption. When pushed, assessors conceded that what clients-to-be said during an intake interview was contingent upon the dire circumstances of its articulation; that is, they recognized that assessees' words pointed as much to the immediate interaction as they did to personal pasts. A case manager at the Carroll Crisis Shelter, for instance, suggested that "all [incoming clients] are worried about is 'where am I going to sleep tonight?' and they will tell you *anything* or agree to anything basically at that point just to get into the shelter" (see also Loeske 1992:79). And though Trudy idealizes the assessment as a tool for eliciting clients' stories, she later added that her first encounters with clients are "*somewhat* superficial" because they were invariably "in *crisis*." After all, assessors needed some way to explain why it was so often the case that the "broad range of information" they gathered during their initial assessments turned out to be inaccurate or incomplete. This was especially true when the information elicited had to do with drugs.

Assessments at each of the HFC agencies included questions concerning incoming clients' drug and alcohol use. There were clear utilitarian aspects of this line of questioning: each and every HFC agency officially disallowed clients to use or possess drugs or alcohol while receiving shelter or transitional housing services. Enforcement of this policy was especially strict in HFC shelters, where staff worried about drugs being sold or exchanged for other goods. Shelter staff, therefore, had a particular institutional stake in identifying clients who used drugs and alcohol at all, regardless of whether they considered a particular individual's drug or alcohol use problematic—which they frequently did not.[17]

Whereas the "social histories" that HFC assessors worked to gather may be said to have diagnostic elements, the drug-specific portions of the assessment had a clear and discrete diagnostic function: to determine whether drugs were circulating in assessees' bodies. With the exception of WISH, recent use was detected through a tandem process that involved a special set of questions and urinalyses (called "drops" or "screens").[18] Many HFC case and shelter managers expressed particular discomfort with this part of the assessment process: Elinor told me that "it feels pretty invasive"; Deanna reported, "it's *embarrassing*"; and HFC's domestic violence program, WISH, eschewed drug tests altogether on the grounds that it violated women's privacy and was therefore potentially "re-traumatizing."

However, the majority of HFC agencies and assessors approached urinalyses as a necessary evil in light of their impression that most assessees were not inclined to verbally share the "story" of their drug use. When I asked her if assessees readily disclosed their drug and alcohol intake, Trudy explained:

1 T: Hm-mm, yeah. They may not. They may sugar coat it *a little bit*.
2 But they usually will *say*, you know, "I smoke weed" or "I *used to* drink a lot" or "I
3 drink," like, uhm . . .
4 I usually tell them, you know: "We're going to do a drug screen today;
5 it's not going to *keep* you *out* of the shelter if the drug screen is *positive*.
6 But it will *shape* the services that you receive while you're here.
7 So you might as well go ahead and *tell me* about it 'cause we're going to do a drug
8 screen anyway." So, so I just *encourage* people to just go and, and tell me.

Trudy gives a sense of both the stakes and semiotics of HFC drug screening: assessees "sugar coat" their drug use (line 1) largely because they understand its institutional consequences, to which Trudy, in turn, applies her own sugary coating.[19] Indeed, although it is true that people were not "ke[pt] out of the shelter" (line 5) if they relayed signs of drug use during their assessment, "shap[ing] services" (line 6) meant that they would be referred to Fresh Beginnings therapists for further battery of assessments and obliged to follow whatever the resulting recommendations were. And, if assessees refused, they would then, indeed, be kept out of the shelter (line 5).

Trudy's comments above are interesting in another regard. She relays the high value of *verbal* revelation of drug use, figuring the drug screen as a prod for clients to "go ahead and *tell*" (line 7) rather than as a revelatory instrument in its own right. One might think that with the knowledge that people in crisis will "tell you anything to get into the shelter," assessors might take some measure of comfort in the belief that the body does not lie. However, HFC assessors maintained no such illusions and commonly devalued the utility as well as the morality of the urine-based drug tests as an evidential instrument (cf. Butler 1993). In fact, veteran assessors such as Trudy, Deanna, and Elinor were acutely aware that there were numerous ways that one could beat a "drop." Although they would make people leave their jacket, purse, and kids outside the bathroom—as any one of these could serve as a carrier of contraband urine—they did not doubt that, as one young case manager named Robin put it, "people *can* like have it in their bra or something . . . I mean we don't *search* them." Besides, once beyond the watchful eye of case and shelter managers, assessees could dilute urine with water or salt, which was known to be enough to chemically cloud the lab results.[20]

Furthermore, many HFC assessees were able to *discursively* manage the results if not the actual process of their drug tests. While Trudy laughed at the frequency with which "people tell me that they can't pee: 'I don't have to pee,'" her sense of humor seemed to slowly dissipate when she relayed:

1 T: I've heard every story in the book. I mean, I had a woman tell me that her husband
2 was blowing smoke in her face while she was sleeping, you know.
3 I mean, I've heard it all, but (laughter) . . .
4 And I had a woman tell me that it was her nine-year-old daughter's pee!
5 So I am like, "You mean you're telling me that your nine-year-old daughter is
6 positive for cocaine?" [And she says,] "Well, yeah," and so I said,
7 "Well you know that I'll have to call Protective Services then."
8 [And she says,] "Ok." And you know she actually let me call Protective Services
9 rather than telling me the truth!

While such strategies commonly produced incredulity and dismay in HFC assessors, in the end they were highly effective. By claiming the positive test results belong to her nine-year-old daughter, the woman in question redirects her doubting assessor's attention from Fresh Beginnings therapists to child welfare workers, who are also highly unlikely to believe such a tale (and, in fact, are far more likely to intervene if it is corroborated that the mother is using cocaine).[21] After all, if Trudy disbelieves that her assessee has not used cocaine, she cannot currently prove otherwise. And by the time the woman takes the test again, the "evidence" has likely been cleansed away.[22] As central parts of assessment texts, urinalyses had limited shelf lives, which clients commonly accounted for when working to discern just who would read them, and when.

To the extent that assessees generated such professional double binds, they also generated further assessments. Indeed, most HFC professionals did not just stop at one drug test. Follow-up drug tests were used not so much to monitor clients' progress but rather to accumulate enough evidence to feel confident in drawing categorical conclusions about new clients' drug use. Assessors were responsible for writing up all the evidence they had garnered—whether verbal or bodily in origin—in reports to their supervisors, appropriate referrals to HFC and other social service programs, and case notes that would become the crucial prologue of a client's file.

Ultimately, however, drug tests made assessors' responsibility for rendering a "concise picture of the client" *more* rather than less difficult. In fact, as texts, urinalysis tended to exacerbate rather than resolve professional practitioners' evidentiary crises. For as the case above so poignantly demonstrates, drug tests betrayed the basic inefficacy of verbal assessment strategies as truth-detecting devices. For these reasons, assessors often grew frustrated with the inconclusive evidence that assessees gave them, both in word and from body. Consider, for instance, Robin's agitated account:

```
1  R:  There is a drug screen done, and people are told: "We will not kick you out of the
2      program if your drug screen is positive, but you'll have to have another assessment
3      done, and whatever [the therapist's] recommendations are, that will be part of your
4      contract in our program as well." We require that from the consumer, and they're
5      told that from the very beginning and it's in writing and they sign something that
6      says you know, that, "I know that I'm, you know, taking a drug screen and I know
7      that if it comes back positive I'll have to go for a further assessment and I know that
8      whatever the assessor recommends, I will have to do if I want to stay in the
9      [HELPNET] program."
10 I:  Ok.
11 R:  So they know that; it doesn't mean they're real cooperative.
12     But they do know that.
```

Here, we have a far less "sugar-coated" description of the stakes of assessments, as the therapeutic metalanguage of storytelling and sharing gives way to a kind of institutional legalese (lines 3–9). Although program contracts were rarely discussed—that is, until they were broken—all incoming HFC clients signed papers that elaborated institutional rules and policies, delineated various behavioral expectations, and laid out the grounds for termination of services.

Notably, in describing the standard process by which clients are referred to Fresh Beginnings, first by citing what "people are *told*" (lines 1, 5) and then by stressing what is *written* and signed (line 5), Robin emphasizes what clients consequently *know* (lines 6, 7, 11, 13) about drug use policies and procedures. Furthermore, she points to a discernable gap between clients' thorough knowledge of institutional norms and rules and assessors' implied *lack* of knowledge, which requires them to augment their initial narrative assessments with follow-up drug screens. Indeed, HFC assessments were sometimes recognized as intensive and power-laden negotiations even if they were usually idealized as "storytelling" events. In fact, the very institution of drug screens was premised on assessors' quiet acknowledgment that assessees' narratives did not always lend access to the "person" or their "environment" as they ideally should.

In the end, while HFC assessors had the power to give and withhold resources according to their elicitations and evaluations of assessees' answers, the assessees also had a valuable resource: anecdotes, confessions, admissions, and affirmations that counted as the knowledge that assessors wanted and needed in order to do their job. And, as we will see in the next chapter, Fresh Beginnings therapists had an effective way to erase the difference between what clients supposedly *knew* versus what HFC programs *wanted to know*. Therefore, clients who were referred to the treatment program would have to learn new ways to control the production, reception, and future travels of the professional texts generated about them.

Shelly's Shock

According to most assessors within the HFC system, they eventually detected enough signs of drug use in approximately half their clients to warrant a referral to Fresh Beginnings. And, as dirty drops, client-circulated rumors, or other "telltale" signs of drug use accumulated during their tenure with HFC, some clients—especially those with limited experience in social service systems—found that their range of narrative maneuver was substantially truncated. Therefore, by the time most clients encountered a second set of assessors at Fresh Beginnings, they often spent less energy editing or evading questions, or discursively packaging urine results, and were more likely to exhibit outright resistance. The encounter between Shelly, a client at the Carroll Crisis Shelter, and Susan, the younger and less active of Fresh Beginnings two CD therapists, is an emblematic case in point.

Shelly entered the facility with her husband, Jack, and one of her two young daughters after being evicted from a second consecutive apartment for failure to pay rent and outstaying the subsequent welcome of Jack's mother in a nearby trailer park. An experienced polydrug user, with a particular penchant for crack cocaine, Shelly temporarily convinced her assessor at the Carroll Street Shelter that she only "drank sometimes" and tried marijuana once or twice, feeling that she was in danger of rejection if she detailed her substantial drug use. Shelly "borrowed" urine to pass the obligatory, but unsupervised, drug test. Several weeks later, when Shelly and her husband were caught sneaking out of the shelter at night only to return obviously high and seriously inebriated, the shelter manager demanded another test on the spot. "Of course, I failed it," Shelly later snickered, "he was standing right outside the door." With all expecting the results to come back positive, the shelter manager informed Shelly that if she did not comply with a further assessment at Fresh Beginnings, as well as the recommendations of her clinical assessors, she would be "terminated"[23] immediately from Carroll Street with her family in tow.

Still high and horribly hung over the next morning, Shelly eased her way off her cot only to be greeted by Susan, one of Fresh Beginnings' therapists. Susan had a quiet, calm, and patient demeanor, though her substantial height, wire-rimmed glasses, and highbrowed head crowned with long jet black braids rendered her presence formidable, which Shelly may or may not have noticed as she stumbled and swore her way to a corner table where the assessment would be conducted. Although case managers and therapists alike agreed that such on-site assessments were ideal, especially in cases where it was unlikely that the client—owing to lingering inebriation, lack of transportation, or sheer defiance—would make it across town to Cliff Street, the other substantial demands of their job did not always allow therapists to make the journey to the five different HFC sites. Nonetheless, Fresh Beginnings therapists tried hard to make the trip, reasoning that by going to the shelters where clients had more or less settled in with their families, they could establish rapport and increase the likelihood of compliance with their recommendations.

However, on the day in question, Susan found that establishing rapport with Shelly would be a challenge. Shelly described the encounter as follows:

1 S: They were asking me all these questions.
2 I was like, I done *been* through this before.
3 I've said everything I'm going to say, you know, and here we go *again*:
4 This is my god damned story, alright?
5 I: Uh-huh.
6 S: And now you are trying to *stick* me in some other program, you know, and [Jack]
7 was on his way to jail, *again*.
8 I didn't know what was going to happen to me and [my daughter] if we got kicked
9 out of [the shelter] and I was *real* pissed off that there is another one of these
10 women in my face, all up in my business.
11 I: Yeah.
12 S: I said to myself, "Don't say *anything*, don't say a *word*." But then I did too!
13 I: You *did*?
14 S: *You know I did*! I cussed that woman out *so bad* (laughter) . . .
15 I: (Laughter)
16 S: She didn't know what hit her. Poor woman (laughter).

After only two weeks in the HFC system, Shelly is already aggravated by "these women in [her] face" and "all up in her business" (lines 9–10) with their repetitive questions (lines 1–2). Nonetheless, like her assessors, Shelly uses the metalanguage of "story" to characterize her responses, though her exasperation with the storytelling process is palpable. At first, she considers resisting with silence, warning herself: "Don't say *anything*. Don't say a *word*" (line 12). However, Shelly ultimately decides that her words can be used to wound her assessor rather than simply expose herself. Rather than keeping another "god damned story" (line 4) locked in silence, Shelly directs her words as weapons as she "cussed that woman out so bad . . . she didn't know what hit her" (lines 14, 16).

In cussing out her new therapist, Shelly elects to index the irritating circumstances of the assessment rather than referring to what she has cordoned off as her private "business" (line 8). But the practical limits of Shelly's decision are clear if we follow her words through institutional space. Although Shelly represents herself as the victor in this discursive battle, laughing with a seeming mix of sympathy and satisfaction at the "poor" assessor who didn't know what "hit" her (line 14), she does not mention how she, herself, was ultimately "hit" by Susan's assessment report. Indeed, that assessment report assured Shelly's admission to the program, reading "opioid dependency, cocaine dependency, major depression, personality disorder with borderline features, borderline intellectual functioning: referred to [Fresh Beginnings] for intensive outpatient treatment." Shelly's performance clearly fell flat as Susan agglomerated her incoming client's linguistic maneuvers as signs of illness and need, and inscribed it as such, writing the first notes in a case record that would be circulated and distributed in ways over which Shelly would have little subsequent control.

Adding insult to injury, Susan did not act as if she had been at all offended by the verbal assault. She later described Shelly's behavior during the assessment not as offensive but as "understandable," explaining that "aggression and hostility is part of her disease; I knew that." And whether Susan believed that Shelly was really the person she assessed her to be, she was certain of one thing: her assessment would assure that Shelly and her family could stay in the Carroll Street Shelter as long as she showed up four times a week for addiction treatment on Cliff Street. There Shelly would find that Fresh Beginnings therapists had a cache of unique theories and methods that would require much subtler acts of verbal resistance if she was to effectively direct the texts that were generated about her.

Disclosing Drugs

According to Fresh Beginnings therapists and some of their clients, drug use was particularly rampant at the one HFC program that did not conduct drug tests: WISH, the domestic violence shelter. Consistent rumors of drug use at WISH occasionally blossomed into therapeutic "panics" on Cliff Street, if not at the shelter itself. Fresh Beginnings therapists and some stalwart clients—not to mention less than stalwart clients who nevertheless wanted to appeal to one of these two groups—targeted WISH's anti-testing policy as "naïve" and causally linked undetected drug use with unexamined urine.

Yet WISH administrators maintained that urinalysis was invasive and even potentially re-traumatizing.[24] And although they never said so, I assumed that the politics of domestic violence intervention, which legally and ideologically motivate social service professionals to privilege victims as "truth tellers," also rendered drug tests a particularly dubious evidential instrument. In lieu of drug tests, administrators appealed to workers to cultivate trust with clients, trust that many at WISH glossed in the terms of empowered sisterhood despite the clear power differentials between assessor and assessee. Therefore, WISH resolved to enforce its drug policy—which, like other HFC agencies, prohibited clients from using or possessing drugs while staying at the shelter—by obtaining verbal rather than bodily evidence. An experienced assessor at WISH, Cassie, explained:

1 C: Um, actually it is just kind of like a questionnaire.
2 And, and you go through a list of different alcohol and drugs and ask, you know,
3 if they ever tried it and what age they were.
4 If they ever started using it regularly and how much they're using now.
5 I think, *how much*, [and] if they have used in the last twenty-four hours.

Considering WISH's alleged problems with the presence of drug use at the shelter, their adherence to a historical epistemology is particularly striking.[25] With the use of a preprinted questionnaire, Cassie works to decipher the client's problematic past, asking questions about initial experimentation with specific drugs (line 2), past use (line 3), habitual behavior (line 4), and the quantities ingested (line 5). And though one would think it was most critical, from an institutional standpoint, to learn whether clients had used in the "last twenty-four hours" (line 5), Cassie seems unsure if this question is actually on her questionnaire (line 5). Indeed, as Cassie describes it, the *practical present* of clients' drug use seems almost an afterthought. This may be because drug assessments were particularly loaded at WISH, where assessors knew that texts about HFC clients' drug use might enter into court documents, influencing judges or juries about cases in which the drug user was also the victim of violence.

WISH clients' reasons for crafting texts about their drug histories were at least as complicated as their assessors'. While many WISH clients shared their assessors' worry that admission of drug use might affect their treatment as a victim, others used Cassie's questionnaire as an opportunity to obtain therapeutic services or other resources they wanted or, sometimes in desperation, felt they needed. For example, during an interview conducted six months after she was discharged from the Fresh Beginnings program, Yolanda recollected her assessment interview with Cassie at WISH:

1 Y: They asked me, did I . . . did . . . did I use drugs and drink and stuff?
2 I told them I *did* drink. I didn't tell them about using drugs.
3 I: Uh-hm.

4 Y: And then when I saw these happy faces and people were trying to help me so much,
5   I'm like, *what the fuck?* "Yes, I smoke crack, too. Yeah, put me on that list there, so . . .
6 I: Uh-hm.
7 Y: Naturally when I said that, you know . . . I think it was [Cassie] I told that.
8   You know, that . . . I had smoked and I had drank and I was on a death sentence on
9   my own.
10 I: Hm-hmm.
11 Y: And then you know as . . . as a part of the [WISH] thing, you know, you have to go . . .
12   You have to clean up that shit. You know what I'm saying?
13 I: Right, right. You can't stay there . . .
14 Y: Right.
15 I: . . . if you're using.
16 Y: Exactly, you know.

Yolanda describes in stutters how she first edited her answers to Cassie's drug-specific questions so as to obscure evidence of her crack habit (lines 1–2).[26] In doing so, she indicates her awareness of the cultural and clinical line drawn between drinking and drugging—especially when the latter involves crack cocaine. Suggesting she had a crisis of conscience in response to people who "were trying to help [her] so much" (line 4), Yolanda shifts the course of her narrative. She declares *"what the fuck"* and reports that she also smokes cocaine (line 5).

Although Cassie is the "happy face" who, most immediately, seems to inspire the late disclosure, Yolanda's repeated use of the plural pronoun (lines 1, 2, 4) indicates her awareness that it was not just Cassie who evaluated her words. And while she suggests that her admission flowed "naturally" (line 7) from the happy helpers to their helpful referral to treatment at Fresh Beginnings, Yolanda's reference to "that list there" (line 5) and to WISH's drug policy (lines 10–11) reframes her disclosure as a strategic decision within an intricate institutional system. Clearly, Yolanda was well aware that she would "have to go to" treatment to "clean up that shit" (lines 11–12) if she wanted to stay in the WISH shelter. As a woman without a home and with the family of her violent ex-boyfriend stalking and threatening her, one might reasonably guess that those stakes were simply too high. Therefore, she eventually disclosed her cocaine habit, figuring it might come to light another way.

Other interpretive possibilities are raised by the fact that—soon after Yolanda's confession to Cassie—Fresh Beginnings therapists determined that if Yolanda was on a "death sentence" (line 8), it was unrelated to drugs. Indeed, Yolanda, by her own contrite responses, failed to meet clinical criteria for substance dependence or abuse during her first assessment on Cliff Street.[27] In fact, she was admitted to the program only after she convinced Cassie to make another referral several weeks later and give the assessment process with Laura a "second try."

How do we make sense of this chain of events? Did Yolanda fool Fresh Beginnings therapists during the first round of assessments, keeping her drug habit well under wraps and evading their interrogatory efforts? That is, did she "fake negative" on her first drug assessment? This explanation seems unlikely considering that she had reportedly "come clean" to Cassie just days before and that Fresh Beginnings was armed with far more discriminating means of detecting drug problems—as explored at some length in the following chapter. Indeed, an alternative explanation is just as likely, if not far more so; Yolanda's drug use was, in fact, sporadic and non-problematic, even by the discerning standards of the program's CD therapists. After failing to convince her Fresh Beginnings assessors of her drug-induced "death sentence" the first time around, Yolanda exaggerated (rather than minimized) her habits in order to *gain entrance* into the treatment program. In other words, Yolanda "faked positive" on the second set of tests rather than "faking negative" on the first.[28]

Notably, the question of *why* Yolanda would "fake positive" to gain entrance to Fresh Beginnings, not to mention *whether* she actually did, is one not easily answered by the technology of the interview, whether wielded by social scientists or social service professionals. After all, taken on their own, my own ethnographic interviews with Yolanda do not answer these questions any more definitively than Yolanda's four (plus) assessment interviews at Fresh Beginnings and WISH. In light of what Charles Briggs, drawing on Gubrium and Holstein (1997), calls the widely held belief in the "magical ability of interviews to reveal interior spaces" (2007:557), I had to account for the epistemological premises of HFC interviews, while strategically deviating from them, in collecting and representing my own data. Although some HFC assessors may have believed that Yolanda's truth would eventually emerge if they conducted enough interviews, I determined that other sources of data and means of collecting it were in order. This work would include accounting for the complex stakes of HFC assessments—both as practice and product—and learning about how Fresh Beginnings clients, like Yolanda, theorized the interviewing process and "the complex pragmatics that make [interviews] work" (ibid.:555; see also Carr 2010b).

READING THE FUTURES OF IMMEDIATE ASSESSMENTS

This chapter has examined HFC assessments as processes of *entextualization*—that is, "the rendering of a given instance of discourse as text, detachable from its local context" (Urban 1996:21; see also Bauman and Briggs 1990, 1992; Briggs 2007; Collins 1996; Gal 2005; Mehan 1996; Mertz 1996; Silverstein 2005; Silverstein and Urban 1996; Spitulnik

1996; Urban 1992). Though each assessment interaction can be isolated as a ritual site where texts about people and problems are produced, both assessors and assessees were acutely aware that these texts would be "recontextualized"—that is, introduced to new contexts and read by others. So when HFC assessors sent drug-plotted assessment texts to Fresh Beginnings therapists, they knew they would be read according to therapists' norms (described at length in the following chapter) and would be subject to only partially predictable and controllable configurations of power and authority. They therefore worked to inculcate "a metadiscourse about texts and the entextualization process" (Silverstein and Urban 1996:9), suggesting that assessments were "stories" that needy clients told to those responsible for knowing them well and crafting happier endings. Thus one way to understand HFC assessors' glossing of assessment interviewing as "storytelling" is as an attempt to telegraph to future readers their intimate knowledge of the person and problems they passed along. If successfully positioning themselves as the knowers and keepers of clients' full and true stories, they might continue to exercise influence about how those people and the problems they represented were treated by other professionals who did not know them so well.

Whereas HFC assessors repeatedly appealed to the metalinguistic terms of personal "storytelling" when describing the assessment process, incoming clients generally described assessments as institutional texts, as indicated by Yolanda's reference above to "that list there" (line 5). In other words, they appealed to Hepworth, Rooney, and Larsen's definition of assessment as "the written products that result from processes" of portraiture and interaction (2002:189). Cued by assessors' pencils and forms, assessees quickly learned that the stakes of assessment questions went far beyond the immediate interaction, as their responses were documented in letters, lists, and case files. Assessees with previous experience in similar social service settings also knew that the management of the assessment interview, as a linguistic event, was all the more important precisely because assessment texts would and could circulate—both within and outside the HFC system—in ways they could not control after they verbally rendered their final response. Thus each incoming client was faced with a daunting predicament: it was one thing to be "drawn" by a questioning assessor; it was quite another to wonder where the assessor's "concise picture" would land and how it would be viewed and used once it got there. "[Trudy] seemed real nice," one client told me, "but I'm thinkin' the whole time: *'why* you wanna know this stuff and *who* you gonna tell?'" (Figure 2.5).

Indeed, tracing the paths by which HFC assessment texts commonly traveled gets us closer to the question of why clients would be inclined to carefully manage their exchanges with assessors. In review: HFC assess-

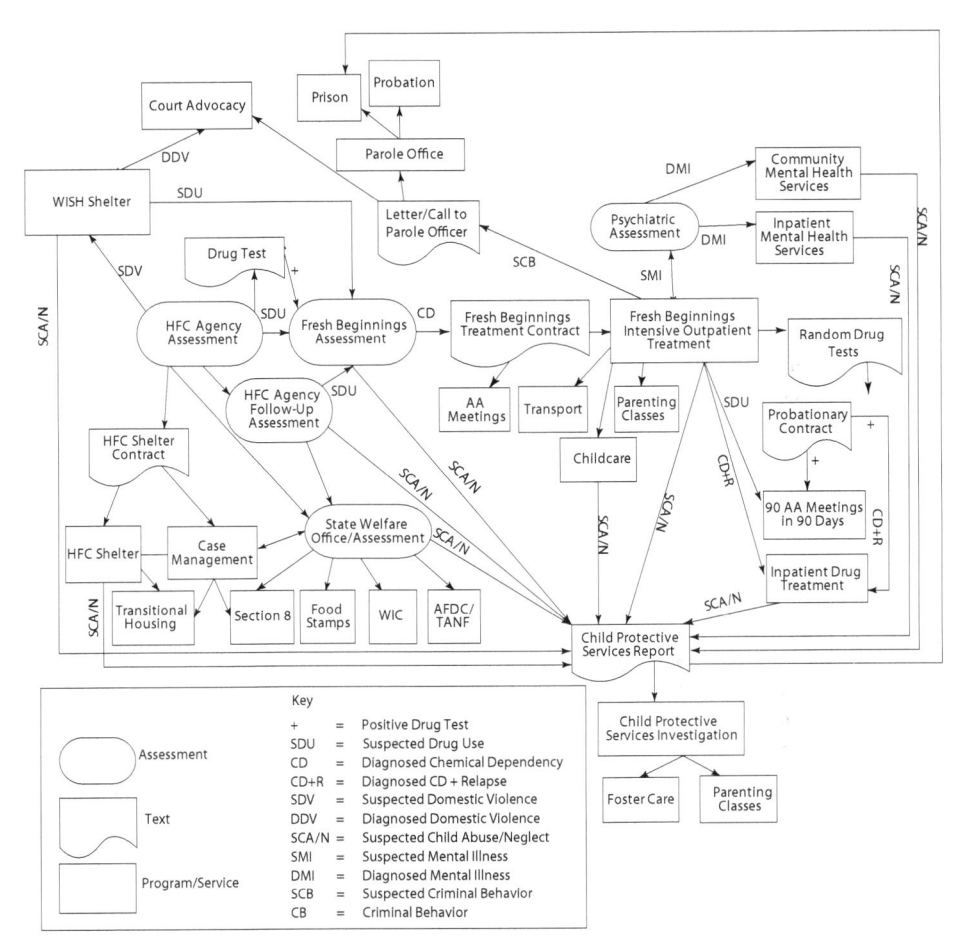

Figure 2.5. The potentialities of an HFC agency assessment

ments, if yielding evidence of drug use, traveled to Cliff Street in the form of case managers' referrals. These referrals generated a second set of assessment questions, which themselves yielded a variety of texts, including a case file to which chapters would be added throughout each client's treatment tenure. Clients determined to be "substance dependent" by the Fresh Beginnings assessment were then tethered to the rules and regulations of the Fresh Beginnings program, which themselves were documented in "contract" form. Indeed, in addition to their contracts at the shelter, all clients admitted to Fresh Beginnings signed "treatment contracts" detailing everything from the logistical requirements of treatment (e.g., timeliness, previous permission for missed sessions) as well as more substantive demands (e.g., sustained sobriety, weekly attendance at AA).

In addition to these general injunctions, treatment contracts were commonly "individualized" so that a client may face additional mandates such as complying with prescribed psychiatric medications or refraining from interactions with a drug-supplying friend or relative.

Of course, one might suggest—as Fresh Beginnings therapists often did—that clients exercised choice in deciding whether to abide by such therapeutic directives. However, the stakes of these "choices" were enormously high considering that clients' shelter or transitional housing, as provided by one of the HFC-affiliated programs, was contingent upon the successful completion of treatment at Fresh Beginnings. Referred to by some clients as "the hook," the formal policy linking treatment and housing characterized every client's tenure at Fresh Beginnings.

Furthermore, because most inpatient facilities in the state did not allow women to bring their children along, "going inpatient" not only significantly disrupted one's own daily life but also translated into separation from one's children and the need for alternative child care arrangements. Since all Fresh Beginnings clients were homeless and could not generally rely upon kin networks with the capacity to feed additional mouths, such "alternatives" sometimes fell into state or institutional purview. However, this is not the only, nor the most common, way that Fresh Beginnings clients encountered Child Protective Services (CPS). In fact, a substantial part of therapists' communicative work fell outside the HFC collaborative itself, as phone calls were placed to parole officers or child welfare workers who shared professional interests in clients' therapeutic progress. And whereas therapists' calls to parole officers or trips to court were largely discretionary, their ties with CPS were formalized by a legal "duty to report."[29] Indeed, like other social service professionals in the U.S., Fresh Beginnings therapists were legally bound to report to the state all suspected cases of child abuse or neglect.

Fresh Beginnings therapists took their duty to report very seriously. In a conversation with me after she left the program, Laura estimated that she made an average of one CPS report a month, totaling approximately thirty-six reports during her tenure.[30] And although Laura also expressed some discomfort with the legal requirements of her job (line 7, below), her tendency, much like her colleague Susan, was to couch her duties to the state in the psychological terms of addiction and recovery. For example, modeling a conversation she might have with one of her clients, Laura offered:

1 L: "If you have relapsed, you have to *share*."
2 I: Ok.
3 L: "That doesn't mean you get kicked out of the shelter, it doesn't mean . . . (chuckle)
4   but it's something that they have to know. . . if you're using in the shelter . . .

5   they have to know that it's a *safety* issue.
6 I: Ok.
7 L: And if there's child abuse I *have* to report it to the state.
8 I: Ok, how?
9 L: 'Cuz that's *the law* . . . and unfortunately I did that a lot.
10 I made more child abuse reports in the three years I was at [Fresh Beginnings] than
11 I did the whole rest of my career.

Naturalizing the institutional stakes of disclosure, Laura begins her imagined conversation by stating that, "if you have relapsed, you have to *share*" (line 1)—a proposition that swallows up the institutional need to "know" in the therapeutic need to "share." Notice that Laura's addressee shifts from the fictional client, to whom she explains the stakes of "sharing" a relapse while exhorting her to do so (lines 1, 4, 5), to me as her interviewer, for whom she reserves her metacommentary about the necessary burdens of the duty to report (lines 4, 7, 9–10).[31] Interestingly, she uses the pronoun "I" only in the latter case, demonstrating the highly euphemistic ways she spoke to clients about the authority the state had invested in her.

Indeed, when Laura turns to an explicit discussion of CPS reporting, she is careful to qualify that her reports are an "unfortunate" response to *the law* (line 9) rather than a volitional or discretionary act on her part. Laura also discursively manages her involvement in *institution-specific* sanctions, as she artfully suggests to her client-addressee that it is "they" at HFC shelters, rather than "she" at Fresh Beginnings, who needs to "know" about relapses (line 4). And, in suggesting that the "issue" of relapse is really a "*safety* issue" (line 5), Laura leaves unclear whether the key referent is the safety of the using client or the safety of her institutional surroundings.

Selectively indexing features of the duty-to-report in her explanation of it (Irvine and Gal 2000), Laura provides a good example of the highly poetic and pragmatic language that characterized the administration of the Fresh Beginnings program. Indeed, Laura's language—which is itself an instrument with which she frames her own power and professionalism in the course of our interview—is clearly "context-creating." After all, she both delineates and substantially softens the high stakes of her duty to report. Consider, for instance, the way Laura counsels her client-addressee, with a reassuring chuckle, that a relapse "doesn't mean you will get kicked out of the shelter" (line 3). Although it is true that a client's relapse did not usually result in immediate or automatic discharge from an HFC shelter, it did translate into an additional set of rules and regulations (e.g., curfews, daily drug tests) inscribed in "probationary contracts" which, if not followed, often resulted in termination of HFC services.

Yolanda's Confession and Mabel's Cake

No matter how therapists rendered it, almost all Fresh Beginnings clients were acquainted in some way with the powers of Child Protective Services.[32] Either through their own or their friends', relatives', or neighbors' unfortunate encounters, clients knew that if their talk or other behavior included anything that therapists could construe as abuse or neglect—potentially including a relapse[33]—CPS workers would be called with a (dutiful) "report" and an investigation could ensue. And, while most Fresh Beginnings clients would agree with Laura's statement to me once that "losing custody of their children is probably one of the paramount fears and *dreads* that these women felt," they also knew that a negative report from Laura or Susan could result in return to a jail cell, eviction from HELPNET's transitional housing program, or termination of other HFC support services.

In light of the widespread knowledge of the hefty stakes of treatment at Fresh Beginnings, Yolanda's actions—whether an intentional "false positive" or confessional admission to "happy faces"—may seem all the more puzzling. Clearly, in light of the ways that therapists could package and send the potentially damaging information they gleaned from clients, clients worked to hide or underplay their drug-related problems rather than advertise and exaggerate them.

In figuring out why Yolanda "faked positive" into the program, one might argue that she felt relatively immune to the institutional powers that regularly entangled her fellow clients. Her two sons were grown, and, aside from the recent attack that landed her at WISH, Yolanda was financially stable relative to her peers at Fresh Beginnings. Though she had precious little money from the sale of her large home, she was bolstered by monthly disability checks for her stress injury. Indeed, soon after she left the WISH shelter, she was able to pay for a one-bedroom apartment, even in the high-rent county where she lived. Yolanda had no serious trouble with the law, and was certainly educated and experienced enough to find another job in health care if her chronically injured arm would allow. And although at the time Yolanda decided to tell Cassie about her drug use she was receiving critical legal counsel and emotional support from her case advocates at WISH as she prepared for court hearings with her attackers, she would have been able to continue to receive these services once she "failed" to meet Fresh Beginnings' criteria for substance abuse or dependence. So, why did Yolanda confess a drug problem that the therapists at Fresh Beginnings first determined she did not have?

If my own encyclopedic assessments of Yolanda's circumstances were still inconclusive, consulting with her fellow clients eventually helped solve the riddle of her "false positive." These clients suggested that the powerful networks that connected Fresh Beginnings therapists to parole officers, case managers, CPS workers, and judges were potentially as promising and rewarding as they were threatening and punishing. Consider, for instance, Mabel's contributions to this small group interview with three former Fresh Beginnings clients:[34]

```
1  M: I don't know what kind of power this, uh, [Laurie] have, influence she have with
2     the law. But if you in trouble, she can keep you from going to jail if you
3  B: (laughing)
4  M: I serio-, but I'm tellin' you. She did it before,
5     She done did it with other people like servin' cake.
6  B: (laughing harder)
7  M: Why you —? [to B who is still laughing]. She have did it with other peoples that
8     was in the recovery . . . She One girl had to go to um, court, and uh and she was gonna
9     go to jail, and [Laurie] went with her and [Laurie] went with her and told them that
10    she was in recovery, so um, the judge told 'em that she wasn't gonna let her go to
11    jail if she just stayed in recovery, um she'll be OK.
12    I don't know how she do it.
```

While Mabel's animated rendition of "Laurie's "power" and "influence with the *law*" (lines 1–2) produced the appreciative laughter of her peers (lines 3 and 6), those interested in the recent developments of the therapeutic state may nod in sober appreciation. As a veteran client at Fresh Beginnings, Mabel had indeed witnessed ways that therapists could keep clients *out of* legal trouble. And though all veteran clients knew an unimpressed Laura could use her "power" and "influence with the law" (lines 1–2) in damaging and punitive ways, they were also aware that if impressed with a client's therapeutic efforts, she could cajole judges as effortlessly as she could "serv[e] cake" (line 5).

Although Mabel expresses impressed incredulity of how easily Laura handled the judge, she does not mention the ways that the "girl . . . who was gonna go to jail" (lines 8–9) handled Laura. Indeed, if clients were successful in managing interactions, like assessments, with HFC case workers and therapists, they could render professional authority a resource rather than a threat. As Mabel indicates, Laura and Susan, as well as the case managers at Fresh Beginnings, were experienced and authoritative advocates within systems—like the court system that determined whether or not one would go to jail or the housing authorities that decided where you were on the list for a Section Eight apartment—that were extremely difficult for clients to manage on their own. In the end, Mabel helped me to determine that while Yolanda was appreciative of the legal aid and emotional support WISH gave her, traumatized by her recent attack, and bored by a life robbed of work and normal social interaction, she "faked positive" into the Fresh Beginnings program in pursuit of a resource: concerted therapeutic attention on four days of each week, along with the other resources that attention generally entailed.

Of course, the fact that clients approached interviews as strategic opportunities certainly does not preclude that some of the information they told HFC assessors and CD therapists at Fresh Beginnings, or the local ethnographer, was true or accurate. After all, we can certainly all think of times that we feel we both tell the truth and strategically manage our audience's reception of that truth. We may also then be wise to acknowledge that the line between where truth ends and strategy begins is an impossible one to draw. Indeed, Yolanda points to the highly complex things that people do with words, especially when navigating highly treacherous political situations—situations which interviewers, whether social scientists or social service professionals, should certainly take into account. Ultimately HFC clients, like Yolanda, teach us to "think of interviews not [only] as events that take place in a particular spatio-temporal location but as dimensions of [a] larger set of practices of knowledge production" (Briggs 2007:566).

Conclusions: Getting Serious

As we will see in the following chapter, Yolanda, Shelly, and Mabel encountered a whole new "set of practices of knowledge production" (ibid.) when they entered the Fresh Beginnings program as clients. For if HFC assessors reflexively struggled with "stories"—along with the various flourishes, fancies, and narrative strategies entailed in that genre—Fresh Beginnings therapists recognized only two linguistic properties in their assessee's words: truth and its denial. Thus, once they were admitted to the Fresh Beginnings program, Yolanda, Shelly, and Mabel became speakers and actors in a new semiotic economy that valued the verbal revelation of inner states rather than the production of personal stories per se. And if they were to be successful in the program, make use of its extensive resources, and avoid discomfiting sanctions, they had to learn the language ideology of addiction treatment and calibrate the ways they talked about themselves and their problems accordingly.

Indeed, every HFC client referred to Fresh Beginnings for an assessment was met by both a therapist and an epistemology which posited that the only sign of addiction could very well be the absence of symptoms. Thus, according to Laura, she and fellow therapist Susan were prepared for a long fact-finding mission:

1 L: Virtually none of the women came willingly and said, "I need help . . . *Help* me."
2 I: Ok.
3 L: You can't depend on the women to volunteer themselves, after all.
4   So it was mostly that there was *suspected* use and the case manager would get in
5   touch with me. That's how I would get the information.
6   Clients' response to me at that point was to say, "*yes*, I do use this many days a
7   week," and some of them would just deny everything.

Because they believed that clients would not "volunteer themselves" (line 1–3), therapists readily translated case managers' suspicions into clients' unspoken pleas for therapeutic *help* (line 1), whether or not these pleas were actually rendered by clients themselves. In relying upon case managers' suspicions, Laura and Susan worked in line with much of the literature on addiction assessment, which suggests that although the "clinical interview forms the cornerstone of the chemical dependency assessment," because the assessee "may either consciously or unconsciously distort the information he or she provides, other sources of data should also be used in the evaluation of a person suspected to be addicted to chemicals" (Doweiko 1996:325). Likewise, Fresh Beginnings therapists assumed deception when conducting assessments, and therefore they "gather[ed] collateral information" from "as many sources as possible" (ibid.: 318–319).

Considering the fractured nature of most incoming clients' social networks in relation to the connectedness of their newly established institutional one, HFC case managers were the most obvious source of such collateral information. Yet, although Laura at first contrasts the unreliability of clients who "deny everything" with the relative dependability of case managers' suspicions, as she continues, she makes the need for her more disciplined intervention between the two parties all the more evident:

8 L: Sometimes, though, there were actually doubts, 'cuz I would get *one story* from
9   the case managers that didn't match the story I was gettin' from the woman.
10 And so in those situations, we had sort of a need for continuing evaluation.
11 Most case managers tend to *buy* into the client's story, whatever it is, so when they
12 *do* suspect something, it's time to get *serious* and find out what is really going on.

In characterizing HFC assessors' reports as "stor[ies]" (line 8), the same generic term she applies to assessees' verbal renderings, Laura demotes the products of case managers' labors. Unlike case managers' use of the term to denote a full, intimate, personal account, the therapist highlights the fictional and fluctuating nature of "stories," suggesting their futility as truth-detecting mediums. Laura also suggests that stories have a seductive quality, proposing that whereas case managers "tend to buy into a client's story, whatever it is" (line 11), Fresh Beginnings therapists were equipped to "find out what is really going on" (line 12), presumably based on their more sophisticated methods of doing so. So even if HFC assessors sometimes had the wherewithal to "suspect something" (line 12), Laura implies her superior assessment techniques allowed her to "get *serious*" (line 12) and produce a decidedly nonfictional account.

Addiction specialist Ronald Paolino wrote a passage that perfectly underscores what Laura meant by "getting serious" and anticipates what would happen next to soon-to-be Fresh Beginnings clients such as Yolanda, Shelly, and Mabel:

> The experienced substance-abuse treatment provider will not fall into the trap common among inexperienced health care providers attempting to treat addicts—taking the patient at face value. Health care workers such as physicians and nurses rely heavily on a patient's self-report of complaints and history, assuming the person to be a reliable historian without hidden or devious motives. The prevailing notion is that with the exception of patients seeking evidence for undisclosed medico-legal litigation or prescribed medications to maintain a drug habit, patients who seek treatment do so because they want to and they tell the truth. The treatment provider must be aware that this is *not* true for abusers. (1991:220)

Along these lines we will see that when Laura said that it was time to "get *serious*" (line 12) with HFC clients, she meant that she was prepared to both encounter and dismantle the hardy denial that she had been taught was a central, pathological part of the addicted psyche. Chapter 3 explores denial as the conceptual lynchpin of both the theory of language and the theory of subjectivity that would come to define the next stop on Yolanda's, Shelly's, and Mabel's journey through the institutional network they had only begun to talk their way through.

CHAPTER THREE

Clinographies of Addiction

> *cli·nog·ra·phy* (noun)
> 1. In medicine: Graphic representation of the signs and symptoms exhibited by a patient.
>
> *cli·no·graph* (noun)
> 1. In mining, construction, etc.: An instrument that records the deviation of boreholes and the like from the vertical.
> 2. In drafting: A pair of straightedges hinged together so as to be adjustable to any angle.

INTRODUCTION: REALIGNMENTS WITH THE REAL

In a 1989 interview with Jacques Derrida, conducted eight years after he was accused by the Czechoslovakian government of trafficking drugs, the French philosopher and father of deconstruction put forward one of his most spirited and overtly political attacks on logocentrism—that is, the assumption that Truth is independent of its representation. In working to reverse the logocentric privileging of the spoken word as the primary expression, and therefore presence, of Truth over writing as secondary, derivative, and dependent upon speech for its meaning, Derrida enlisted the figure of the addict as a stand-in for the maverick writer whom he had so long championed. He found that the two had much in common. Both the addict and the writer, Derrida suggested, are culturally condemned for a passivity of spirit: they dare to seek external sources of inspiration rather than relying upon internal powers of will. Additionally both the addict and writer have a proclivity to repeat and reproduce acts, often with blatant disregard for authentic representation of something other than the acts themselves (i.e., words and drugs are valued in terms of their immediate effects rather than their sources). Finally, Derrida's addict, like his writer, resists integration into the very institutions that confer value and, as a result, remains not only outside authority but also outside Truth. Indeed, Derrida charges that the addict is considered problematic precisely because she cuts ties with the world and escapes into simulacrum; "We do not object to the drug user's pleasure per se, but to a pleasure taken in an experience without truth" (1992:236). In opposition to the Platonic subject who gains his authenticity through his productive interactions in the life of the community, the drug addict purportedly "produces nothing, nothing true or real" (ibid.) and instead takes in, injects, and inhales, epitomizing the unproductive citizen.[1]

Although Derrida's 1989 comments to his student, Jean-Luc Nancy, were clearly polemical, eliciting critical attention to the intersecting semiotic and material economies that figure the addict/writer as incapable of legitimate production, the interview is keenly diagnostic of a cultural and clinical conviction: the belief that drug users have very tenuous ties to reality. While some worry that the addict cannot see and participate in the world as it is, as Derrida indicates above, it is the concern that addicts do not recognize *themselves* that drives the discourse of addiction. One need only peruse the clinical literature on addiction treatment, published in the latter half of the twentieth century, to find that "addiction is a disease of denial" (Paolino 1991:219) and, moreover, that "client denial *distinguishes* addiction" (Rasmussen 2000:114, emphasis added; see also Alcoholics Anonymous 1939; Chafetz 1959; Davidson 1977b; Denzin 1993; Doweiko 1996; Fewell and Bissell 1978; Flores 1988; Hazelden 1975; Johnson 1980; Kauffman 1994; Kearney 1996; Lemanski 2001; Morgan 2006; O'Dwyer 2004; Peterson, Nisenholz, and Robinson 2003; Rinn et al. 2002; Rosenfeld 1994; Spiegel and Fewell 2004; Tiebout 1953; Wallace 1978; Walters 1994; Wurmser 1978, 1985, 1987, 1992).

Indeed, despite their general abjuration of many fundamental psychoanalytic concepts, American addiction specialists have long agreed with Virginia Davidson's statement that "denial of entire segments of reality, especially behavior concerning drug usage is typical [of the addict]" (1977a:165; also see 1977b). And, significantly, this agreement cuts across distinctive theoretical orientations.[2] For instance, casting their textbook overview of addiction in distinctly behavioral terms, David McDowell and Henry Spitz nonetheless devote significant attention to denial, defining it not only as a "primitive psychological mechanism for dealing with reality," but also as a "focused delusional system" in which the addict avoids the realities that are "obvious to everyone else" (1999: 121; see also Rothschild 1995:193). Terrence Gorski identifies twelve types of denial that can be addressed with "traditional cognitive therapy" (2000:2) and Erikson-inspired John Lovern writes, "[the denial] system allows a chemically dependent person to become more and more out of touch with reality, while somehow hanging onto the ability to convincingly appear competent, rational, and right" (1991:11–12). Ever since the publication of the "Big Book" (Alcoholics Anonymous 1939), those who espouse the "disease concept" of addiction also indicate that denial is its chief symptom. And, in a foundational paper, Morris E. Chafetz simply claimed that "denial constitutes the main method which alcoholics use in dealing with life" (1997 [1959]:319). So if it is true, as Freud suggested in 1926, that there is "an intimate connection between special forms of defense and particular illnesses" (1959:163–164), denial has long enjoyed the privileged status as American addiction's special defense.

Denial and Its Discontents (A Brief History)

As is well known, Freud believed there is a group of ego operations (or "defenses") that function to ward off threats to the integrity of the individual psyche. In 1924, Freud began using the term *Verleugnung*—which has been translated as disavowal as well as denial—and elaborated upon it in his 1938 essay, "An Outline of Psycho-analysis." However, Freud never distinguished denial from other closely related defenses and therefore cannot be said to have developed a theory of denial (LaPlanche and Pontalis 1973:118). This work would be left to his daughter, Anna, who delineated two kinds of denial defenses: "denial in fantasy," in which daydreams are used to substitute or reverse painful realities, and "denial in word and act," which requires collaboration with an audience who responds to a performance contrary to social facts. Anna Freud stressed that whereas denial is a normal feature of children's psychic development, it is pathological in adults because, in order to maintain a state of denial, the individual ego must sacrifice both its synthesizing function and its capacity to recognize and critically test reality (1937; see also Altschul 1968). Nonetheless, most psychoanalysts hold that denial, like all defense mechanisms, can be adaptive, helping the denier to hold painful realities at bay so they can function in the here and now, or maladaptive and even psychotic, constricting normal adult development (e.g., Bond and Vaillant 1986; Dorpat 1987; Kaplan and Sadock 1981, Kübler-Ross 1969; Rothschild 1995; Russell 1993).

Of the ego defenses that contemporary Americans have inherited from Freudian thought, denial has proven to be the most illustrious, as demonstrated by the frequency with which laypeople "diagnose" friends, relatives, co-workers, and politicians with cases of denial. The elasticity of denial as a clinical concept—bemoaned by clinical historians and practicing clinicians alike (e.g., Altschul 1968; Fine 1979; Janis 1983; Laplanche and Pontalis 1973; Trunnel and Holt 1974)—may explain its prolific cultural uses. In addition to Anna Freud's bifurcation of denial into fantasy and word/act, types of denial proliferated in the latter half of the twentieth century. For instance, Breznitz (1983) named seven kinds of denial (denial of personal relevance, denial of vulnerability, denial of responsibility, denial of affect, denial of affect relevance, denial of threatening information, and denial of information). And whereas both Freud and his daughter drew a clear line between denial as defensive against external reality (or "idea") and repression as defensive against internal reality (or "affect"), this once key distinction is routinely ignored in both clinical practice and scholarship, much to some commentators' dismay (LaPlanche and Pontalis 1973; A. Freud 1937; Miller 1976; Vaillant 1971; Kaplan and Sadock 1981). For instance, Bond defines denial as "the automatic refusal to acknowledge painful or disturbing aspects of *inner or outer* reality" (1986:138, emphasis added; see also Dorpat 1983; Hauser 1986; Waelder 1951). And, strikingly, despite Anna Freud's charming portraits of denial in fantasy as a childhood "achievement," psychoanalysts now even debate whether an adaptive form of denial exists at all (see Breznitz 1983; Dorpat 1987; Sperling 1958), thereby further loosening the term's definition.

Nowhere has the elasticity of the concept of denial been more evident than in American addiction treatment. As Edward Kaufman unapologetically notes,

> The word "denial" has many more meanings in the field of substance abuse than was intended by its original psychoanalytical usage. Each meaning or definition of denial makes a valuable contribution to the understanding of psychotherapy with SAs [Substance Abusers]. Generally in the field of chemical dependence, "denial" is applied to the denial of obvious reality, as well as to a whole range of behaviors and statements that have a denying quality (1994:49).

Indeed, among addiction specialists, denial is thought to manifest in an astonishing number of acts: drug-induced blackouts (e.g. Lovern 1991:11), "selective recall of events" (e.g., Flores 1988:284; Kaufman 1992:52), verbal negation that one "has a problem" (e.g., Peterson et al. 2003:5; Rothschild 1995:193), reluctance to recognize "even the most obvious psycho-dynamic aspects of their behavior" (Kaufman 1994:52), and refutation that one's life problems are directly correlated with drinking and drugging—which some have called "complex thinking quandary" (Michels et al 1999; Wallace 1995; Whitfield 1982). Some also use the term "denial" to connote the refusal to identify as an addict (Paolino 1991:219), not to mention abdication of one's identity altogether (Wurmser 1995:82). The prolific Leon Wurmser even suggested that drug use itself is, "in the final analysis, only a pharmacologically reinforced denial—an attempt to get rid of feelings and thus of undesirable inner and outer reality" (1992:93; also see Kaufman 1994:47).

According to clinical literature on addiction treatment, the objects that addicts deny are as diverse as the actual forms denial takes. "Addicted patients deny many things: the fact of their drug (and alcohol) use, the amount of drug used, the awareness of the concomitants of drug use, and the damaging effects of drug use" (Derby 1992:118). It seems that addicted denial comes in many patterns as well. For instance, addiction specialist and originator of "Denial Management Counseling" Terrence Gorski (2000:54) identifies "Big Five Denial Patterns" along with their typical expression in what he calls "self-talk":

1. Avoidance ("I'll talk about anything but the problem!");
2. Absolute Denial ("No not me!");
3. Minimizing ("It's Not That Bad!");
4. Rationalizing: ("I Have A Good Reason!");
5. Blaming ("It's Not My Fault!")

According to Gorski, there are "Small Seven Denial Patterns" as well:

6. Comparing ("Because others are worse than me I don't have a problem");
7. Manipulating ("I'll Only Recover If You Do What I Want!");
8. Scaring Myself Into Recovery ("Being afraid of the consequences of drinking and drugging will keep me sober!");
9. Compliance ("I'll say anything you want to hear if you leave me alone!");
10. Flight Into Health ("Feeling better means that I am better!");
11. Strategic Hopelessness ("Since nothing will work I don't have to try!");
12. The Democratic Disease State ("I have the right to drink and drug myself to death!").

In fact, addicted denial is commonly thought to come in so many forms, patterns, and guises that Edward Kaufman issued the rare but well-warranted "note of caution" in his 1994 book *Psychotherapy with Addicted Persons*:

> One note of caution needs to be sounded about the use of "denial" as a label. Denial has become so widely acknowledged as a hallmark of alcoholism or drug abuse that to deny substance abuse is frequently considered diagnostic of the disease. Obviously, however, some individuals who deny that they are alcoholics or drug addicts do so only because they have been wrongly accused, not because they are SAs [Substance Abusers]. Caution would also be utilized in not over-labeling a multitude of substance abuse behaviors as "denials." (1994:54)[3]

Examining the concept of denial as it was articulated in clinical training materials, diagnostic practices, and therapeutic interactions at Fresh Beginnings, this chapter delineates the reasons why this warning is heeded so infrequently. Specifically, I show that although denial is most explicitly considered a psychological defense, the concept—when mobilized in practice—also serves to defend institutional and clinical authority. And while Derrida did not address the dynamics of institutionalized rehabilitative practices, as this chapter does, he helps us understand the concept of denial as a central strategy in the broader project of bringing the addict back in line with authority, reality, and Truth.

Look before You Leap

Cultural historians and other commentators interested in American addiction have commonly deemed it a "disease of the will" (Keller 1972; Levine 1978; Rush 1805; Valverde 1998).[4] However, like many of their colleagues and in line with the clinical scholarship on drug use and abuse, Fresh Beginnings therapists instead approached addiction as a *disease of insight* and treated it accordingly. As Fresh Beginnings therapists counseled their clients: "Our immediate purpose [in group therapy] is to discover and identify in order to see clearly who I am and what needs to change. Acceptance of *what is* precedes change." In other words, clients were to look (at themselves) before they leapt (into sobriety).

Furthermore, Fresh Beginnings therapists did not think of their clients as weak-willed but rather as problematically strong-willed, a characterization that has much clinical support. For instance, consider Leon Wurmser's explanation of the "psychophobia" typical of addicts: "the disregard for the importance of introspection of any kind and *its resolute self-righteous avoidance* —in fact, not rarely a disdain for any approach to it" (1985:82, emphasis added). Notably, the willfulness of addicts also interested a prominent anthropologist, who suggested that the alcoholic epitomizes the fundamental "epistemological error" of the Occident—that is, the fallacy of mind over matter. Indeed, Gregory Bateson (1971) claimed that it is the addict's hyperactive will—which relentlessly tries to control the intake of alcohol—that is "corrected" in AA, where the first step is to see that he is, in fact, powerless over the bottle.[5]

Fresh Beginnings clients themselves were introduced to the idea that they were problematically willful when therapists distributed this cartoon in group therapy, offering it as fodder for reflection and discussion (Figure 3.1).

Clearly the portrayed problem is not that "My Ego" lacks a strong will; despite his buckling knees, dramatic trembling, and sinking feet, he

Figure 3.1. "Denial," as pictured in Mary K. Bryant's (1986) "My Ego."

believes that he can "handle" a colossal boulder that has evidently rolled downhill. Significantly the cartoon's punch line is not that "My Ego" cannot *do* what he *willed*. Instead, even after having been crushed into the ground, he cannot *see* "WHY" he could not do it. With growing clinical sophistication, client consumers of this cartoon would learn to explain that "My Ego" has a problem—or boulder—that is much bigger than he thought it was and there is no conceivable way to "handle it" on his own.

Accordingly, at Fresh Beginnings, the primary goal of treatment was not to encourage clients to willfully act but instead to *see* their inner states, including what they willed. Consider this document that Laura and Susan received from their clinical supervisors at Hope Health. Called "Group Therapy," it was intended to orient new clients to the main goals, assumptions, and techniques of their treatment:

1 The purpose of this paper is to discuss the assumptions and techniques we are using in
2 conducting group therapy. To begin with, let's look at some of the similarities within
3 the group. In addition to chemical dependency we all have two things in common.
4 First, before we came to the point of seeking outside help, we each tried our own
5 *Do It Yourself* program in an effort to change ourselves or someone else.
6 The second similarity is that we all failed.
7 A basic assumption of group therapy is that a major reason for this failure is that our
8 most determined efforts can't change what we can't see, and there is a great deal we are
9 not seeing clearly. (emphasis in the original)

After establishing the need for institutional intervention, considering the failures of the "Do It Yourself" program (lines 4–6), the document summarizes the predicament of "My Ego" (though, as far as I know, the two documents did not circulate in tandem). In short, it is not because of a lack of "determined efforts" (line 8) that addicts fail but rather because we can't "change what we can't see" (line 6). Put differently, it is not the addict's "*will* but his *sight*" that fails him (notice, by the way, that "My Ego" has been given ears but no eyes by his artist). And while the document suggests to its readers that "there is a great deal we are not seeing clearly," through the course of therapy clients would learn that they suffer from extreme far-sightedness—an inability to see that which is closest to them. In this vein, the document continues:

10 For this reason our *goal* in group therapy is: TO DISCOVER OURSELVES AND
11 OTHERS AS FEELING PERSONS AND TO IDENTIFY THE DEFENSES
12 THAT PREVENT THIS DISCOVERY. (emphasis in the original)

Group therapy, in other words, aims not only to help addicts "discover [them]selves" (line 11); it is also designed to help participants identify what blocked that discovery in the first place, namely, denial and its defensive brethren (line 11). Indeed, Fresh Beginnings therapists claimed that once denial had been recognized by the denier, it became more porous and penetrable and, with continued treatment, eventually disintegrated.[6]

Thus, according to Hope Health clinicians as well as the therapists they supervised on Cliff Street, recovery is not simply a matter of quitting drugs in a willful manner, as the common therapeutic term "dry drunk" suggests.[7] Instead, recovery is a matter of coming to terms with, or *discovering*, one's true inner self that is purportedly denied in active addiction.

Denial and the Constitution of Addicted Subjectivity

American addiction specialists regularly borrow the terminology of mechanical engineering and the building trades when defining and describing addicted denial. For instance, Robert Kearney (1996:15), author of *Within the Wall of Denial: Conquering Addictive Behaviors*, portrays denial as "a stone wall," and in his book *Pathways to Reality,* John Lovern (1991:11) describes denial as "a nearly *impenetrable fortress"* (emphasis added). Topographical terms such as "layer," "strata," or "level" are particularly prevalent in discussions of addicted denial (e.g., Denzin 1993:76–83; Gorski 2001; Kaufman 1994:53; Kearney 1996:12–26; Wurmser 1985:89). Indeed, as Kauffman succinctly explains, denial "work[s] within a topographical model, serving to keep painful affects out of the conscious mind, and pushing them down into and keeping them in the unconscious mind. Thus, the defenses can be seen as functioning horizontally" (1994:47).

Fresh Beginnings therapists, as well as their supervisors and clinical consultants, adopted the common view that denial is a horizontal layer or barrier that prevents the addict from recognizing her inner truths. In therapists' files of treatment literature—accumulated over the course of their training at Hope Health, in their Masters of Counseling and Social Work programs, and in the various continuing education courses they attended—was a document titled, "DENIAL: SOME FACTS TO REMEMBER." In line with the literature cited above, the document describes denial as "a buffer against unacceptable reality [that] people use to protect themselves from something threatening by blocking their awareness." In a Wednesday morning psychoeducational group,[8] Laura and Susan distributed this very document so that clients could read for themselves an emphatic warning that was also frequently issued verbally: "Denial allows us to avoid pain or shame, thus, in a sense, preserving our self-worth and dignity. But we must remember that denial is *a major barrier to recovery"* (emphasis in the original).

In examining clinical documents such as this, as well as interactions between clinical professionals and clients, this chapter explains how Fresh Beginnings modeled addicted subjectivity in topographical terms.[9]

More specifically, the pages that follow show that therapists assembled a tubular model of addicted subjectivity in which layers of denial were topped by a thin if formidable layer of anger, which itself covered over a dense stratum of shame (Figure 3.2). According to therapists, these layers—residues of drugs as well as the trauma and suffering that induced their use—prevented addicts from recognizing their inner truths. They therefore understood their work—particularly in the early stages of treat-

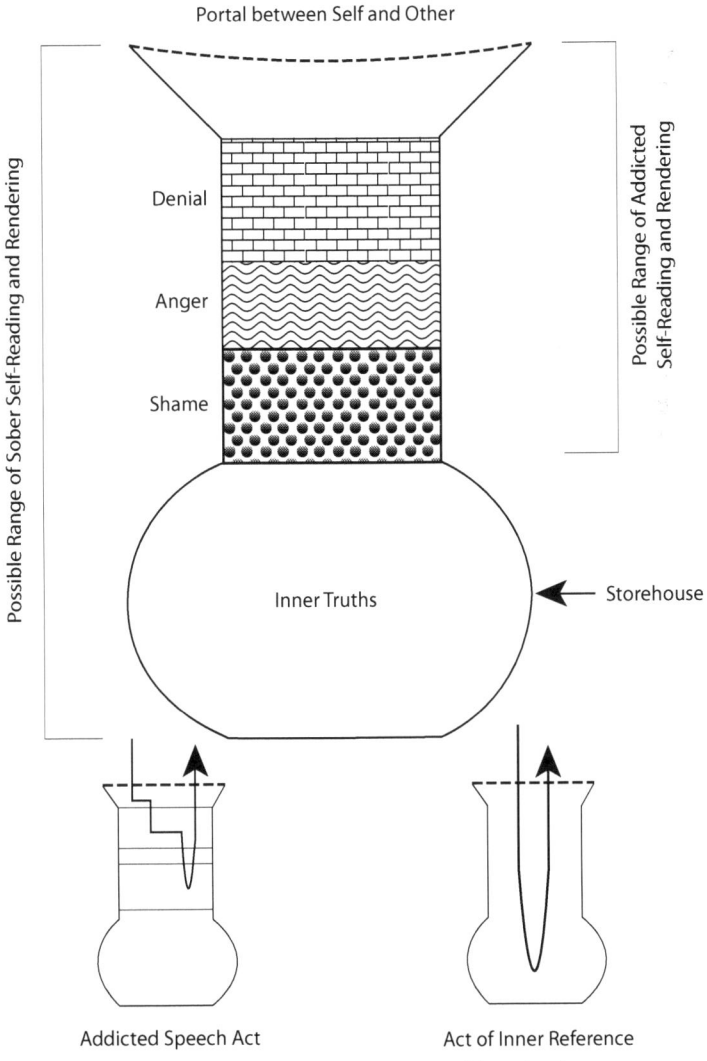

Figure 3.2. The topographical model of the addicted subject.

ment—as a matter of detecting, penetrating, and disintegrating what they claimed to be the very real layers of denial, anger, and shame that comprised the addicted subject.

As trained adherents to a set of professional norms that privilege the instrumental change of *what is* over its historical and practical constitution, Fresh Beginnings therapists did not so much understand themselves as building a model of addicted subjectivity as they believed they were excavating psychic structure, molded by a pre-institutional set of drug and drug-related experiences.[10] They consistently framed their theories and practical interventions as necessary responses to the realities of addicted subjectivity, already constituted as such. Notably therapists employed verbs such as "pierce," "get underneath," and "clean" to describe their therapeutic work on clients' psyches.[11] And, much like miners, Laura and Susan not only dug down to retrieve precious goods, they also took careful measure of the dangerous layers they worked their way through.

In both mining and measuring, language was the primary instrument of Fresh Beginnings therapists' labors. After all, teaching clients to read and speak what they once denied and buried was the primary objective of treatment at Fresh Beginnings, as it is much more broadly in the world of mainstream American addiction treatment. As therapist Susan once succinctly put it, "We teach them to be true to themselves, to come to the truth, *their* truth . . . and share it with others." With this ambitious goal in mind, therapists engaged their clients in an intensive therapeutic project that they called "taking inventory."

As this chapter will illustrate, taking inventory involved boring down through internal layers of denial, anger, and shame toward the innermost storehouse of the self, taking stock of and verbally relaying all that was encountered along the way, with special attention to that which could be felicitously associated with drug use. Much like the examination of conscience in the confession of sins, the exercise of taking inventory was grounded in the belief that one must verbally account for past actions and experiences, along with attendant desires, thoughts, and feelings, if one hoped for catharsis if not absolution. Indeed, at Fresh Beginnings, taking inventory was not a simple process of accounting. Rather, therapists suggested that by reading and rendering themselves aloud, stock takers could also *clear away* the pathological layers of the addicted psyche, allowing for deeper, more direct, and purer internal access. Accordingly, successful clients learned to use language as a means of inner reference: matching spoken signs to innermost signifieds, which were thought to be already there and awaiting expression.

In determining the relative depth, thoroughness, and transparency of clients' inventories, Fresh Beginnings therapists not only evaluated clients' therapeutic progress but also, and by extension, gauged their own diagnostic efficacy and expertise. Specifically, with clients' symbolic productions as their primary material evidence, therapists focused their analytic attention on deciphering how cleanly and clearly each client referenced her inner states during both group and individual therapy sessions. Whereas in an addicted state, a client's stock taking might bounce off the first layer of denial or become mired in the hoary grounds of anger or shame, a properly recovering client could conduct her inventory unobstructed, reaching straight down and verbally rendering the deepest stuff of the self, thereby demonstrating accurate insight. Therefore, every word a client uttered on Cliff Street had diagnostic, if not necessarily therapeutic, value.

Acknowledging that the most addicted clients could "look good, sound good, and say all the right stuff," as Laura once put it, Fresh Beginnings therapists needed a way to carefully measure—like a miner's clinograph—any deviations from speech as clean inner referential rendering. Accordingly, what follows is an ethnographic illustration of "clinographies of addiction"—that is, the constitution of the addicted subject and the measurement of her recovery by specific semiotic means and measures. The clinographic qualities of therapists' work are first illustrated by a discussion of diagnostic practices, which significantly differed from the assessment procedures described in the previous chapter. Whereas social service professionals at HFC recognized, if sometimes begrudgingly, the many strategic and highly social things that assessed clients did with words, therapists at Fresh Beginnings were already at work identifying and clearing the way for an unobstructed linguistic channel to clients' inner truths. And although therapists aimed for exactitude in identifying inner states, they understood their work to be primarily aesthetic and intuitive rather than objective and technical.

The Science of Addiction and the Art of Its Detection

> The art of treating addiction is to overcome the enormous denial and resistance, whether it be passive or active, that most alcoholics and addicts possess
> —Phillip Flores, "Psychoanalytic Considerations of the Etiology of Compulsive Drug Use"

In 1988 addiction specialist Phillip Flores called addiction treatment "an art," suggesting that overcoming addicts' denial requires substantial creativity on the part of clinicians. This idea would be quite familiar to Laura and Susan, who were well-versed in literature that was written by medical doctors and Ph.D.s in social work, psychology, nursing, or other members of the multidisciplinary field of addiction studies, such as the text cited above. In their studies of these texts, Laura and Susan learned that while "the art of treating addiction" begins with a set of general assumptions—for instance, that addicts "possess . . . enormous denial and resistance"—their day-to-day work would require creative improvisation.

Certainly many who currently work and write in the field of addiction treatment would be wary of Flores's humanist terms, insisting instead that addiction treatment should be considered a scientific and empirical rather than creative or intuitive endeavor. This attitude is reflected in the *Journal of Substance Abuse Treatment* article "Taboo Topics in Addiction Treatment: An Empirical Review of Clinical Folklore," in which Chiauzzi and Liljegren (1993) critically aver: "Perhaps more than any other discipline, the treatment of addicted people relies more on faith than science, more on personal experience than empirical findings" (303). The naming of this professional "taboo" marks a tension that had been growing since the rapid expansion and organization of the field in the 1970s, with the institution of the National Institute for Alcohol Abuse and Alcoholism (NIAAA) and the National Institute on Drug Abuse (NIDA), which aims to "lead the Nation in bringing the power of science to bear on drug abuse and addiction" (National Institute on Drug Abuse 1997).[12] In other words, when Chiauzzi and Liljegren distinguish "faith and personal experience" from "science and empirical finding" they are indexing—intentionally or not—a tension-filled gap between the relative expertise of addiction researchers and scholars, on the one hand, and addiction practitioners, on the other. Although a number of contemporary American clinical fields suffer from this sort of crisis of expertise, it is particularly pronounced in the addiction treatment field. For, at about the time the research for this book was in progress, an estimated 58 percent of practitioners had "personal experience" with addiction (NAADAC 1994)—like Laura did—and approximately 20 percent had only a high school diploma or less (Mulvey et al. 2003).

As highly educated practitioners, Laura and Susan were likely aware of one particular point of tension between scholars and practitioners: the underutilization of established diagnostic and assessment instruments, of which there are scores (cf. Carroll and Rounsaville 2002).[13] Indeed, at least theoretically, addiction counselors have their choice among a virtual smorgasbord of instruments, including the Addiction Severity Assessment Tool (ASAT), the Substance Abuse Subtle Screening Inventory 1, 2, and 3 (SASSI), the Drug Abuse Screening Test (DAST), the Addiction Admission Scale (AAS), the Ecological Assessment of Substance-abuse Experiences (EASE), the Recovery Attitude and Treatment Evaluation—Questionnaire I (RAATE-QI), the Drug Use Screening Inventory (DUSI), the Addiction Severity Index (ASI), and—for those who have been particularly naughty—SANTA: the Substance Abuse Need for Treatment among Arrestees.

From the perspective of many addiction researchers, practitioners' failure to use well-validated assessment instruments is nothing less than a professional crisis (ibid.:1337; see also Flynn et al. 1995:214 and Paolino 1991:120). The worries are many. Some claim that without a standardized assessment instrument on which to rely, the determination of an assessee's relationship to drugs depends on the subjective appraisal of the individual assessor (Paolino 1991:220). Aside from these concerns about individual bias, questions of rigor are also implied as "formal structured assessments are likely to be more sensitive than the unstructured clinical interviews used by many clinicians" (Carroll and Rounsaville 2002:1330). And, finally, the seemingly haphazard assessment process apparently threatens to reflect poorly on addiction treatment as a (not quite) professional field. Along these lines, Flynn and colleagues bemoan that "strategies may range from highly structured and comprehensive clinical assessments by trained clinicians to more rudimentary intake screenings by clerical staff to gather administrative information. Accordingly, the information gathered varies considerably not only substantively, but also in specific responses and response categories" (1995:214).[14]

According to Laura and Susan, therapists like themselves did not jettison formal assessment instruments because of their lengthy interview formats in relation to the pressing time demands of treatment work, as Carroll and Rounsaville suggest.[15] Instead, they resisted relying upon these standardized instruments because they understood the diagnosis of addiction to be an experiential, intuitive, and inductive endeavor, rather than a systematic or deductive one. Consider therapist Laura's response to my question of how she determined whether someone met diagnostic criteria for chemical dependency:

1 L: That is such a difficult thing to ascertain.
2 I: Umhm.
3 L: Because it's impossible to have a completely objective assessment.
4 I: Umhm.
5 L: Because it's based on the interviewer's *feeling* at the time (laughter).
6 I: Right.
7 L: The *cues* that are or are not available . . .

Here Laura plainly dismisses the possibility of a "completely objective assessment" (line 3). She goes on to frame her diagnostic work as detective work, which carefully tracks the "cues that are or are not available" (line 7), on the one hand, and her own "feeling at the time" (line 5), on the other. Note that there is no doubt about the existence of the inner facts of the assessee, which remain stably located and theoretically ascertainable (line 1). Rather, Laura suggests that a particular kind of expertise is at stake in diagnostic work, one in which the therapist connects the manifest cues of addiction with the truths buried deep within.

The Inconvenient Formalities of Enacting Diagnostic Expertise

If Fresh Beginnings therapists were not swayed by their professors and continuing education class instructors to use formalized assessment instruments, they were nonetheless obliged to follow Hope Health's assessment guidelines during their initial encounters with HFC clients. They were also responsible for filing copious assessment reports for each client they assessed. These assessments had four basic components.

First, therapists were required to conduct a "biopsychosocial" assessment that, as its moniker suggests, was comprehensive in scope, consisting of questions relating to "family, living environment, friends/associates, legal problems, employment, emotional status, major life changes, medical concerns, nutrition, recreation, spirituality, sexuality, and education and cognitive matters," in that order (cf. Ray and Ksir 1999). Not surprisingly, the guidelines inscribed on the top of the biopsychosocial assessment form clearly instructed therapist assessors to "make sense of the presenting problem" in relation to the assessed client's biological, psychological, and social history—suggesting, if not establishing, an etiology of personal problems. Second, therapists were to assess referred clients for their "degree of their motivation" for entering treatment—a clear instantiation of the "stages of change" model, which was especially revered at the time, and continues to hold influence in the field.[16] This model posits that recovery involves a five-stage process of precontemplation, contemplation, preparation, action, and maintenance (Prochaska and DiClemente 1982; Prochaska, DiClemente, and Norcross 1992). Considering the nonvoluntary nature of treatment at Fresh Beginnings, as described in chapter 2, Laura and Susan became intimately familiar with the category of "pre-contemplation" during the course of their employment there.

Fresh Beginnings assessments also included a psychiatric evaluation known as a "mental status evaluation" which was, notably, the only section of the assessment not explicitly based on self-report. Instead of eliciting a separate set of answers through a specific series of questions, therapists engaged in a meta-analysis of the biopsychosocial portion of the assessment.[17] A separate evaluation form with sections on "appearance" (dress, posture, psychomotor activity, and speech), "emotional reactions" (attitude, mood, and affect), "thought" (form and content), and "general intellectual functioning" indicated that the job of therapists was to skillfully read the "form" of clients' "thought" from their assessees' linguistic and paralinguistic behavior.

Finally, Fresh Beginnings therapists were required to consult the criteria in the *Diagnostic and Statistical Manual of Mental Disorders*, 4th ed. (1994) (*DSM-IV*) to officially diagnose the HFC clients they encountered. The *DSM-IV* lays out the framework with which to diagnose each and every recognized mental illness and disorder, including substance-related disorders.[18] In order to be admitted to Fresh Beginnings, all the clients who had been referred by HFC agencies had to be diagnosed as "substance dependent,"[19] using *DSM-IV* criteria (see Figure 3.3). Although the *DSM-IV* is widely considered the authoritative guide for diagnosing "substance dependence," program therapists were rather begrudging and skeptical executors. When I asked Laura whether she relied upon *DSM-IV* criteria, she replied with a roll of the eyes: "Yeah, I *have* to. Cause that is part of the medical model of the [Hope Health] people who hired me."[20]

Substance dependence is defined as a maladaptive pattern of substance use leading to clinically significant impairment or distress, as manifested by three (or more) of the following, occurring any time in the same 12-month period:

1. Tolerance, as defined by either of the following: (a) A need for markedly increased amounts of the substance to achieve intoxication or the desired effect or (b) Markedly diminished effect with continued use of the same amount of the substance.
2. Withdrawal, as manifested by either of the following: (a) The characteristic withdrawal syndrome for the substance or (b) The same (or closely related) substance is taken to relieve or avoid withdrawal symptoms.
3. The substance is often taken in larger amounts or over a longer period than intended.
4. There is a persistent desire or unsuccessful efforts to cut down or control substance use.
5. A great deal of time is spent in activities necessary to obtain the substance, use the substance, or recover from its effects.
6. Important social, occupational, or recreational activities are given up or reduced because of substance use.
7. The substance use is continued despite knowledge of having a persistent physical or psychological problem that is likely to have been caused or exacerbated by the substance (for example, current cocaine use despite recognition of cocaine-induced depression or continued drinking despite recognition that an ulcer was made worse by alcohol consumption).

Figure 3.3. Criteria for Substance Dependence as designated by the *DSM-IV* (Washington, D.C.: American Psychiatric Association, 1994, 181–183).

Laura's response is consistent with her more general skepticism about standardized instruments and frameworks; she felt they were less sensitive than her own analytical skills which had been honed with on-the-ground experience. Yet it is important to note that she and Susan—like other professionals in their field—exercised substantial discretion in their interpretation of the *DSM-IV* criteria. After all, to be diagnosed as substance dependent, one only had to meet any three of *DSM-IV*'s seven criteria, which, as sociologist Craig Reinarman has keenly observed, "range from vague and context dependent behavioral indicators such as using more of a drug than intended to classic tolerance and withdrawal" (2005:312). Indeed, several of the *DSM-IV* criteria are especially commodious. Take, for instance, criterion 6: "Important social, occupational, or recreational activities are given up or reduced because of substance use," which leaves the assessor to determine exactly which activities are "important." Assessed clients who have limited occupational opportunities, such as the clients at Fresh Beginnings, may readily meet this criterion depending on how assessors choose to make causal links in reported behavior. As Reinarman notes: "what is taken as empirical indicators of an underlying disease of addiction consists of a broad range of behaviors that are interpreted as 'symptoms' only under some circumstances" (2005:308).

Furthermore, while the *DSM-IV* framework explicitly stipulates that assessors must satisfy at least three criteria to substantiate a diagnosis of substance dependence, this stipulation is not regularly followed in practice. In his chapter on assessment, Doweiko unapologetically notes, "Even after the addict reaches [the point of a fully developed disorder], however, one does not always see clearly all elements outlined above in every case. The existence of one symptom of addiction is often taken as evidence by health care professionals that the other symptoms also exist" (1996:317).

However, it is the concept of denial that does most to open the diagnostic gates for individual assessors' interpretive discretion in relation to the *DSM-IV*'s criteria for substance dependence. One may curiously note that, despite addiction specialists' long and concerted attention to denial, it is not included as one of *DSM-IV*'s seven diagnostic building blocks of substance dependence. We might readily explain this omission as an indication that the manual relies heavily on positive evidence. But consider that the omission of denial from *DSM-IV* criteria leaves open the possibility—*in practice*—that the assessee is simply denying the applicability of any or all of the seven criteria. As Peterson, Nisenholz, and Robinson note,

> One of the most frustrating aspects of alcoholism is that the syndrome can be objectively diagnosed by a physician or other trained professional but then,

rather than accepting the diagnosis and asking about recovery strategies, the patient will argue and deny the evidence. In fact, although denial is not a *DSM-IV* criterion, it is such a predictable occurrence that it often is a valid precursor of a diagnosis of alcoholism. (2003:96)

Indeed, as indicated in the psychoanalytic literature as well, the very concept of denial can help transform evidential lacunae into positive knowledge. After all, many believe that "denial is a rather primitive way of dealing with conflict but also perhaps an indication that it exists" (Rothschild 1995:193).

Denial on Arrival

In some ways the assessments conducted by case managers at HFC and therapists at Fresh Beginnings were very much alike. Both adhered to an interview format, eliciting self-reports from assessees; both collected "material evidence" as well, screening for traces of drugs in clients' urine; and both were faced with the same set of clients who—either in word or body—frequently failed to relay what was wanted: truthful accounts of the self, past and present.

There was, however, a fundamental *epistemological* difference between Fresh Beginnings' and HFC's assessments that rendered Laura's and Susan's work quite unlike that of their HFC colleagues; namely, Fresh Beginnings therapists claimed that because of addicts' proclivity for denial, an accurate assessment was not so much a matter of identifying the truth in assessees' intentionally spurious tales. Instead, Laura and Susan assumed that addicted clients were simply *unable* to recognize and articulate their own truths, especially the truth of their addiction. This meant that therapists were prepared to identify and articulate the truth *on behalf of* their denying clients, which would require intuition, creativity, and sometimes—rather ironically—outright illusion and trickery. Accordingly, when asked to describe the assessment process at Fresh Beginnings, Laura responded with this "classic example" (line 1 below):

1 L: This is a classic example of kinda how it went: there was a woman at [WISH] who
2   had used cocaine and alcohol right before she came into the shelter.
3 I: Ok.
4 L: And she couldn't hide the alcohol because it *smells*.
5 I: Right.
6 L: But she denied the cocaine use. And, another woman stayin' at [WISH] who knew
7   her and knew that was an issue for her *identified* her to me in treatment . . .
8   And so I made an *inquiry* to the case managers . . .
9 I: Umhm.

10 L: Saying "you've got somebody in here that one of our clients is *worried* about,
11   but is afraid to come to you about it; so, could I do an evaluation?

Here Laura describes a fascinating taxonomy in which active users hide and deny (lines 4, 6), clients in treatment knowingly worry (lines 7, 10), case managers naïvely smell (line 4), and therapists keenly evaluate (line 11), ultimately identifying the etiology of cocaine and alcohol use (lines 1–2). In so doing, she positions herself in the epistemological life of the institution as closest to the truth of clients' experiences (second only to her well-trained client informant). Laura continued:

12 L: So I interviewed this woman . . .
13 I: Uh, huh.
14 L: She is completely denying to me that she's used cocaine, but she agreed to do a
15   urinanalysis.
16 I: Umhm.
17 L: And it came back *positive* . . .
18   And I'm sitting there with her, with the results showing the *positive* cocaine.
19 I: Umhm.
20 L: And she's like, "*I did not*!" "I *have not* used cocaine!"
21   And so there, to try to help her feel *safer*.
22   I'm like, "Nothing *bad* is gonna happen to you. This is just denial."

Pitting the client's specious protests (line 20) against her own disciplined knowledge—bolstered as it is by a positive urine screen (line 17)—Laura describes a discursive coup in which she can declare, unequivocally, "This is just denial" (line 22). Well assured of her own position relative to the client's still unspoken truth, Laura initially greets the client's denial with empathy, as well as some amusement (line 17). She then provides the denier with assurance, telling her that "nothing bad will happen" (line 22)—a statement reportedly rendered in the name of therapeutic safety (line 21).

Yet, if Laura indeed wanted to make her assessee "feel safer" (line 21), it was specifically so that she would admit what she had putatively denied. When this admission is not forthcoming, Laura shifts strategy, taking a more directive and didactic approach:

23 L: I explained denial. And I suggest perhaps she's *repressing* it . . .
24 I: Umhm.
25 L: Ya know. And she asked me what that *means*, and I explained what [denial] means.
26 I: Ok, what did you say?
27 L: I prefaced it with "A lot of people think denial is lying. And denying is not lying.
28   When we are in a state of denial, it's because we cannot deal with *reality* or the
29   consequences of something that is happening or has happened in our life.
30   And it's not *conscious*, so there's no control over it . . .

31 I: Ok.
32 L: "And if and when it becomes *safe* for us to accept it, then it comes to our
33   consciousness."
34 I: I see.
35 L: And for a lot of people, including a lot of the women that came into my program,
36   they thought, "Oh, that's *bullshit* . . ." (chuckle) "that's just lying."

In familiar clinical terms, Laura's lesson on denial emphasizes its unconscious (line 30), protective (lines 28, 32), and uncontrollable (line 30) qualities. Interestingly, Laura carefully differentiates denial and lying along these very same lines (line 27), implying that whereas lying is a speech act in an Austinian sense—that is, intentional and highly social—denial is a barrier that prevents the recognition of inner intentions before they can be acted out or on at all.[21] Laura is also careful to clearly discriminate between "the state of denial" and *reality* (line 28), which she emphatically insists will emerge into consciousness (and presumably into words) once the denier can accept and deal with it (line 28; lines 32–33). By way of her explication, Laura also substantiates her *own* ties to that reality by her bemused citation of the clients who reject her learned explanation of denial (line 36). When asked, "When you explained these things to her, then what happened?" Laura continued to chuckle and responded: "She continued to deny."

Considering Laura's attempts to create therapeutic "safety," her next move may seem, at first, rather surprising. As she continued to recount the incident, Laura herself conceded that in order to "break through" the client's tenacious denial, she proceeded with the assessment with a "sort of a paradoxical intent." She explained:

37 L: I got this woman sitting in front of me denying that she's ever used cocaine and
38   thinks I'm full of *shit* and I've got these cocaine results from her *urine*
39 I: Ok
40 L: Saying that she used cocaine, so I figured what the *hell*, ya know?
41   This is the last trick in my bag, I'm gonna pull it out.
42   Said, "Well . . . you're tellin' me you haven't used cocaine for six *months*,
43   that you did not use cocaine the night you came in here,"
44 I: Hm-mm.
45 L: "Yet your level shows that you had this much cocaine still circulating in your urine
46   *two days* ago. So either your liver isn't working and your body can't process
47   cocaine that you used six months ago,"
48 I: Umhm.
49 L: "which means you're in *really bad shape* physically or you're repressing."

Here, in the face of a client who thinks her assessor is "full of shit" (line 38), Laura gives her assessee two choices: either admit that she has fallen victim to denial and repression or face liver dysfunction and imminent death. Most striking is not Laura's seeming abandonment of her mission to create "safety" but rather the explicitly theatrical terms she uses to describe her own linguistic actions. Laura reaches down to retrieve the "last trick in [her] bag" and, as if thinking aloud, quickly calculates and decides: "what the *hell* . . . I'm gonna pull it out" (lines 40–41).

It is important to recognize that, for Laura, there is no contradiction between her genuine care for clients and the tricky strategies she uses here, grounded as they both are in her efforts to dismantle denial. And though it may be tempting to point the finger at Laura as an inexperienced, unethical, or even somewhat fanatical therapist, it is important to note that her highly performative actions are well supported by clinical literature on addiction treatment. Even with the recently growing critique of the confrontational models that long characterized addiction treatment, there is still precious little debate that addicts need to be persuaded to enter treatment, partially because they do not recognize their problem in the way their therapist does (see Paolino 1991). [22]

Consider, for instance, the widely known and still commonly exercised family confrontation model, otherwise known as the "intervention"—recently dramatized by the popular series televised by the A&E Channel. Under a therapist's supervision, friends and family are gathered to "confront" an addict, often in emotionally charged terms, and persuade the individual to enter treatment. Suggesting that it is the addict's impoverished insight that must be targeted, Vernon Johnson, father of the intervention, once tellingly noted: "We are most useful as confronters when we are not so much trying to change another person as we are trying to help him see himself more accurately" (as cited in Flores 1988:287). Similarly, Karen Derby provides Laura with much support when she writes, "The therapist must juxtapose the stark contradiction of the reality of the patient's life with the patient's view of that reality. This can be done gently, although technically it is a 'confrontation.' The patient must be helped to examine critically the ways in which he or she continues to act to bring about his or her own destruction ('self'-destruction)" (1992:118).

Furthermore, it is important to note that while Laura did not believe for a minute that her assessee was immediately at risk of dying of liver dysfunction, she *did* believe that the client would ultimately have to choose between denial and death—an idea she introduces in a concretized way in the reported dialogue. As Derby's reference to "self-destruction" implies (ibid.), the equation of denial and death is common among addiction specialists and was routinely made at Fresh Beginnings. For instance, Susan admonished one client who did not show up for treatment on several occasions by writing: "addiction is a disease which is progressive, chronic, and fatal and that denial is part of your disease. If you do not stop using mood altering chemicals, you can expect that your life will continually become unmanageable." Therapists also honored Bobbi—a chronic relapser but skillful confessant—with an award that read: "[Bobbi] continues to appropriately address therapeutic issues and now recognizes that her denial about her addiction made it difficult to admit that her continued use of alcohol would eventually result in her death."[23]

Fresh Beginnings therapists suggested that it was not just clients who needed to be educated about the relationship between death and denial but their professional colleagues in HFC as well. In a "Program Summary," distributed to HFC staff in an attempt to educate them about the structure and logistics of the still relatively new program, therapists devoted far more attention to summarizing the psychodynamics of denial than they did to explaining the referral process, phases of treatment, or daily schedule. The Program Summary begins as follows:

> [Fresh Beginnings] is an intensive outpatient program for chemically dependent homeless mothers. This means that each client in [Fresh Beginnings] is diagnosed as being dependent on one or more substances before she is eligible for admission. The American Medical Journal defines addiction as a *primary*, *chronic* disease with genetic, psychosocial, and environmental factors influencing its development and manifestations. The disease is often *progressive* and *fatal*. It is characterized by impaired control over substance use, preoccupation with the substance(s), use of substances despite adverse consequences, and distortions in thinking, most notably, denial. (Emphasis in the original)[24]

Accordingly, Fresh Beginnings therapists presumed that assessees—like the one in the "classic case" described above—were "dead on arrival." For this reason, therapists prepared themselves to take radical (and heroic) measures to rescue and revive deniers as soon as they encountered them.

It was along these lines that Laura felt justified in laying out for her recalcitrant assessee only two possible answers to her insistent questions: death or denial. Laura further reasoned that the fact that her denying assessee chose death when given these two options simply proves the therapeutic point (line 51, below). Laura continued to reflect upon the encounter:

50 L: And rather than take the opportunity to say "Ok, maybe I'm repressing it,"
51   She decided that she was dying. And so . . .
52 I: She decided she was dying!?
53 L: That her body was not processing it.
54 I: I see . . . hmmm.
55 L: And then she was able to get mad at me because I was so insensitive to her physical
56   well-being and she was just really *pissed* that I was telling her that she's dying.
57   And . . . ya know, she's had enough shit to deal with. She just got beat up, she's in a

58   shelter, and here I am telling her she's dying . . .
59 I: Yeah.
60 L: And so I just had to go with it and said, "Well, while you're getting that checked
61   out and seeking medical attention, why don't you try our program?"

Perhaps in reaction to my stunned question (line 52), Laura implies that her tactics have taken on a life of their own, declaring: "I just had to go with it" (line 60). At the same time, Laura makes the ethical trajectory of her actions clear: she allows the assessee to continue with the misguided premise that she is dying, encourages her to seek medical attention, and, while she is at it, "try" Fresh Beginnings (lines 60–61). In Laura's skillful double voicing, when "the client" suggests that her therapist is "so insensitive" (line 55), Laura simply responds that her means were justified by the therapeutic ends of getting the denier into treatment, thereby saving her from impending death.[25]

Therapist assessors' trained ability to read and categorize incoming clients' words and actions in line with clinical theory, coupled with their institutional authority to recommend various forms of treatment and services, meant that they clearly had the upper hand in these initial encounters with clients. One might imagine that this sometimes angered clients. However, note that in the above report Laura does not *make her client mad* through her verbal manipulations but instead merely incites the anger that she presumes is already lodged in the clients' addicted psyche (see line 55). As we will see below, anger—like denial—was considered a purely intrapsychic property, a leftover layer of drug use rather than a reasonable response to a coercive interaction. So when Laura says that the assessed client was "able to get mad" (line 55), she suggests that therapeutic progress has been made in the course of the arduous interchange. To be more specific, having excavated denial through her self-described assessment "tricks," Laura progresses further down to find a layer of anger. This, too, would have to be clinically mined and clinographically measured, as the following section illustrates.

Before moving on, it is important to underscore the loaded institutional circumstances of clinical assessments at Fresh Beginnings, which serve as an alternative explanation for the assessee's recalcitrance. For instance, as we saw in the previous chapter, many clients at the WISH shelter wisely ascertained that in order to receive shelter services and legal aid, they had to play the blameless victim and that admission of drug use could threaten their status as worthy service recipients (see Bennett and Lawson 1994; Kilpatrick et al. 1997). Yet if Laura acknowledged that her assessee may have good reason to intentionally manipulate the truth, she would also have to recognize how the gendered politics of victimhood and blame played out within her very own "gender-sensitive" program. Arguably, then, Fresh Beginnings therapists had ample reason for erasing the social and strategic indexes of clients' talk, and recognizing only inner truth and its denial.

TAKING STOCK WITH ANGER TALK

At Fresh Beginnings, as tends to be the case in the world of American addiction treatment more broadly, the stated goal of therapy was to attain a thorough and explicit knowledge of oneself. To this end, a posting in the group room instructed: "A more accurate picture of myself is essential to recovery." As we saw above, in order to accurately picture one's self one was obliged to recognize what had blocked this vision in the first place: a thick and formidable layer of denial.

Because recognizing one's denial was the first step in excavating it, it was also the point of departure for a pedagogical program of self-discovery that those in the field of addiction treatment commonly call "taking inventory." Recall that in taking inventory clients were required to look into their inner selves, retrieve, and transparently relay in words what they found there. According to Fresh Beginnings therapists, once stock-taking clients "got underneath" their denial, they were ready to recognize a formidable layer of *feelings*, which they would also have to mine before retrieving inner truths and achieving an "accurate picture" of themselves. Consider how the orienting document, "Group Therapy," discussed this next stage of treatment:

1 In examining [sic] our purpose one of the things that stands out is our emphasis on feelings.
2 We stress feelings for several reasons.
3 First of all, our behavior in the past has been so opposed to our value system that
4 considerable feelings of remorse and self-loathing have been built up.
5 It appears that we have accumulated a pool of negative feelings and walled them off
6 with a variety of masks or *defenses that prevent this discovery.*

Here we have a topographical portrait quite similar to the one depicted at the outset of this chapter (see Figure 3.2)—that is, an addicted subject (here denoted by a collective "we") with a defensive wall (line 5) that prevents the discovery of an "accumulated pool of negative feelings" (line 5). And while Fresh Beginnings therapists directly followed their Hope Health supervisors' lead by "stress[ing] feelings" (line 2) in group therapy, they also had strong support in the clinical literature on addiction for doing so. Indeed, as Quirk (2001) has noted in the *Drug and Alcohol Review*: "[Interest in] emotion pervades current substance abuse perspectives including the genetic-disease, personality-coping, cognitive-behavioral learning, and psychodynamic models of addiction" (95).

The widespread clinical interest in the addict's emotions has a two-pronged conceptual basis. First, as Johnson (1980), Tarter, Alternam, and

Edwards (1984), and Lovern (1991) posit, addicted people initially use drugs to mute out negative feelings but eventually come to ignore their emotions entirely.[26] The document "Group Therapy" cited above echoes this theory, stating plainly: "Most of us are badly out of touch with our feelings." Second, addicts are thought to be unable to articulate, let alone identify, their own emotions, a phenomenon that Rothschild calls "dysfunctional affect management" (cf. Krystal 1979, 1982–1983; and Krystal and Raskin 1970, on "alexithymia"). According to this theory, addicts lack "the ability to tolerate, modulate and express affect in an appropriate and constructive manner" (Rothschild 1992:84).

Notably many addiction specialists closely link the *identification* of feelings to the *verbalization* of feelings and sometimes go so far as to conflate the two.[27] For instance, Krystal and Raskin (1970) famously proposed that addicts fear feelings because they cannot define them, experiencing discomforts that are decidedly "preverbal." So if, as Benveniste (1971) notes, the clinician has access to the inner lives of clients only through discourse, addictionologists extend this principle of therapeutic discourse to clients themselves, suggesting that what is not spoken aloud has yet to be recognized by the speaker.

Accordingly, Fresh Beginnings therapists saw the primary goal of group therapy as getting the "addict [to] learn how to recognize *and label* emotions . . . in an appropriate and constructive manner"(Rothschild 1992: 84, emphasis added). Thus, "taking inventory" was a matter of helping clients both to identify and *express* their feelings—the latter act being the only evidence that the former task had been accomplished. A wide variety of group activities, discussions, and exercises were designed to meet this goal. One long-term client, Keisha, described a common example:

1 K: We would have a meditation period when we'd have, "how do you feel today?"
2   "Not good," "fine," you know, we always, you *usually* say, when people say,
3   "How are you doin'?" then you say, "I'm *fine*," you know, "we're *good*."
4 I: Yeah.
5 K: But, in *group*, we would get more into how we were *really* feelin'.

Here Keisha differentiates what "you *usually* say" (line 2) when people ask "how are you doin'?" (line 3) with demands of the very same question when posed in the therapy rooms on Cliff Street. Unlike in quotidian exchanges of meeting and greeting, in which both question and answer are conventional acknowledgments of oneself in relation to another, clients found that the polite response of "*fine*" did not begin to satisfy their therapists' query. As Keisha explains above, to answer therapists' questions, clients would have to "get more into how [they] were *really* feelin'" (line 5). Indeed, therapists' goal was to circumnavigate the banalities of everyday communication, including its intersubjective quality, so that *real* feelings could be located and released into words.[28]

Fresh Beginnings therapists averred that such exercises required keen concentration on the part of participants, for as Karen Derby once noted, "the [client] may deny feelings moments before they are expressed" (1992:118). Thus "a meditation period" (line 1) was required not because there was anything particularly elusive or slippery about feelings themselves but because client participants were always poised to deny what they might otherwise say. Indeed, the exercise of inventory assumed that feelings—when housed in a sober psyche—were discrete, easily distinguishable from one another, and inherently namable inner facts. The document "Group Therapy" summarized this view:

1 Most of us have ignored our feelings for years in an effort to see the facts.
2 In group therapy *Feelings are Facts*. "How does that make you feel?" is a question
3 asked frequently to help us focus on these facts. (emphasis in original)

Although this document is categorical as well as emphatic in its statement that "Feelings are Facts," once Fresh Beginnings clients began to attend group therapy, they found that—according to their therapists—some feelings were more factual than others. Consider Laura's description of the very same "meditation period" that Keisha describes above:

1   L: I would walk women through this in group
2   I: Ok.
3   L: I would say, "Ok take a second, and get in touch with how you *feel*"...
4   "How do you feel?" (pause)
5   I: Umhm ... hmmp.
6   L: And it was almost always anger (laughter ... pause).
7   And I told them that anger was an *umbrella* feeling for other stuff and ...
8   I: Uh huh.
9   L: I would draw that on the board, and [say], "here's this umbrella and it says *anger*."
10 I: Ok.
11 L: And it was important to get in touch with what's underneath the anger, ya know.
12   Was it *hurt*? Was it *betrayal*? Was it *grief*? Was it *fear*?
13   Because those were the *real* feelings.

Here we see the exactitude with which clients were expected to name their feelings, which Laura offers here in a list of possible but seemingly mutually exclusive emotions (line 12). Yet, unlike *hurt, betrayal, grief,* and *fear*, which can be contained and relayed by verbal signs, anger is portrayed as having no meaning in and of itself; anger is an "umbrella feeling" (line 7), which reaches out and away from the *real* feelings (line 13) that are left "underneath" its protective spread (line 11). Indeed, at Fresh Beginnings, anger had more in common with denial than it did with feelings such as betrayal and grief—a defense that needed to be confronted and undermined if therapeutic progress was to be made.

Notice also how Laura models a topographical subject, and does so not only with her words but also with a portrait drawn on the dry-erase board for all clients to see. Clients thereby learned that they needed to square this strange figure, armed with an internal umbrella, with the injunction to draw "an accurate picture" of themselves. Of course, Laura's lesson on anger suggests that therapists knew what the *real* feelings were (line 13), whether or not the angry client did. And though inventory was explicitly cast as a meditative process in which clients identified their own feelings, we see here that Laura is already setting the terms of the search by differentiating the real feelings from the spurious ones.

Owning Answers

Fresh Beginnings clients described the exercise of taking inventory as an intensively interactive one. According to these accounts, their therapists posed personal questions to which they were to respond with discrete answers, which would then either be accepted or rejected as inadequate, incomplete, or beside the point. In other words, clients implied that their therapists—to a significant degree—had already determined what counted as valuable inner stock.

Fresh Beginnings therapists, on the other hand, maintained that taking inventory was an intensely solo affair. They therefore encouraged their clients to "own" their feelings, as well as the words they used to express them. And, somewhat ironically, therapists regularly engaged clients in intensive, complicated, and sometimes downright confusing dyadic exchanges so as to instantiate the idea that clients were the simple and sole proprietors of their inner stock. For instance, consider Tealie's explanation of how she came to "realize why [she was] so angry" (line 11, below):

1 T: You know, [the therapists] ask me, um, "how do . . . how come I feel so much
2   anger," okay?
3 I: Hm-mm.
4 T: And, ah, I would then be asking them, "Yeah, why *do* I feel so much anger?"
5   It would be coming . . . it would come back to me as a *question*, like
6   "We don't know, how *come* you do, how *come*, *why* you feel so much anger?"
7   You with me?
8 I: Uh-hm.
9 T: "Did *this* happen, *that* happen?" Or *whatever* happened that made . . . you know,
10   that type of thing. Something that would help you *figure* out, you know.
11   So that made me realize why I'm so angry.

Tealie describes a dizzying interrogative circle: therapists' initial question (lines 1–2) is taken up by Tealie and redirected at her therapists in an ostensible request for therapeutic guidance or clarification (line 4). Rather than answering the question by drawing on their definitive theories of anger, as they did on the dry-erase board that summer morning, therapists feigned ignorance (line 6) and returned the question to the one they believed should "own" the answer to it, as well as the anger imputed therein.

Of course, in spinning these feeling questions, therapists did not understand themselves to be *establishing* a topography of feelings, nor imputing an etiology of anger. Rather, therapists insisted that they were helping to *excavate* a layer of anger that was already anchored inside clients like Tealie, if yet to be let out in words. Because anger was considered a pathological residue of past events stored away deep in the memory, therapists averred that the best way to unearth it was to propose possible etiologic connections (see line 9), which might incite Tealie to explore her anger aloud. When Tealie breaks frame to ask, "You with me?" (line 7), she arguably indicates the alien and alienating quality of these interactions with her therapists, a sentiment expressed by many Fresh Beginnings clients, especially when they first entered treatment. However, Tealie also suggests that by the end of the therapeutic exercise, she both recognizes anger and comes to a new understanding of it—that is, as an internal property. So if we are uncertain that the therapists' first question is merely an attribution graced with a question mark (lines 1–2), by the end of the interrogative circling Tealie not only shares therapists' initiating presumption that she is angry but also "realizes" *their* reasons "why" (line 11).

We might guess that Tealie's conclusion about why she was "so angry" may be similar to those her peers expressed in conversations or interviews with me. For instance, Tealie may have been angry because she and her teenage daughter had been put out by an unforgiving landlord, denied a Section Eight, or fired by a racist supervisor. She may have been angry about the 1996 legislation, which would eventually force her to take a minimum wage job at Kentucky Fried Chicken alongside a group of surly and harassing teenagers. She may have been angry about a CPS worker, who didn't return her calls, or the fact that she still hadn't seen her younger kids even though she'd been clean for several months. She might have been angry because her apartment had been broken into *again*, or because her boyfriend used her as a punching bag. There was also the guy on the bus who wouldn't leave her alone, the broken bottle of grape juice she'd saved up to buy that week, and the wicked case of insomnia that led her to relive it all while others at the shelter snored. Instead, Tealie's report to her therapists was characterized by an unsurprising crescendo: "I'm so angry cause of what my mother done put me through . . . all the abuse I suffered as a child."

Although Fresh Beginnings therapists were aware of the many experiences and injustices that would reasonably make their clients angry, they recognized very few as relevant to their clients' drug use and recovery. Thus angry words were generally read as signs that clients had not made much progress in their inventory. Shameful words were another story entirely. Indeed, if Tealie had continued her therapy at Fresh Beginnings awhile longer, she would have likely come to the conclusion—with her therapists' intensive encouragement—that it was not really anger but *shame* that she felt as a result of her mother's abuse. Fresh Beginnings therapists were therefore prepared to encounter, and help clients mine, a thick layer of gendered shame that they presumed to lay beneath their clients' anger.

"Shame on You": Becoming a Woman in Women's Drug Treatment

A number of feminist critics have famously cast discerning and disapproving eyes on the mother-blaming tendencies of the Euro-American therapeutic tradition, devoting the bulk of their attention to Freudian psychoanalysis (e.g., Chodorow 1978; Greenspan 1983; Lerman 1986; Miller 1976). Beginning in the 1970s feminist practitioners also began developing alternative therapies that integrated the convictions and principles of the "second wave," including the foundational idea that "the personal is political" (Evans et al. 2005).[29] Early feminist clinicians asserted that since patriarchy had not only shaped women's experience but their very knowledge of themselves, gender-specific treatments and programs were needed to address the needs of women clients "in their sociopolitical and cultural contexts" (ibid.). In the 1980s, as American society grappled with what many claimed to be an epidemic of childhood sexual abuse, feminist clinicians increasingly focused their attention on the yet unrecognized signs of trauma in their women patients.[30]

In many ways the field of women's addiction treatment followed a similar trajectory. Calls for the gender-specific, if not "feminist," treatment of women drug users began in the early 1980s. In 1982, Beth Glover Reed laid out both the practical reasons why women drug users should be considered a "special population" and the need to theoretically differentiate women users from their male counterparts (see also 1985, 1987). Reed argued, for instance, that women's drug use cannot be explained until there is "understanding of the fundamental role gender plays in defining . . . individual identity, coping style and skills; the structure of a person's life cycle and the nature of life experience, including the psychological, social and cultural realities one faces; and the opportunities and resources available" (1982:1). As the field of women's drug treatment began to take off in the late 1980s and 1990s, this rather anthropological framing of gender-specific treatment began to narrow, as advocates of gender-specific addiction treatment increasingly focused on sexual trauma among women clients in line with the larger clinical trend. Several large-scale studies, conducted in the 1990s, drew a high causal correlation between early sexual trauma and later drug use (e.g., Boyd 1993; Hall 1996; Hall and Powell 2000; Harrison et al. 1989; Medrano, Zule, and Desmond 1999; Miller et al. 1987; Jasinski, Williams, and Siegel 2000; Rohsenow et al. 1988; Stein et al. 1988; Wallen and Berman 1992; Wilsnack et al 1997) and suggested that *shame* was the natural by-product (Barret and Tepper 1994; Carter 1997; Cohen and Mannarino 2002; Finkelstein 1994; Harris 1996; Hurley 1991; Mason 1994; Winick et al. 1992).

As self-described feminists and highly educated practitioners, Laura and Susan were well aware of the astonishing statistics produced by these scholars which suggested that anywhere between 33 percent (Wallen 1992) and 90 percent (Rohsenow et al. 1988) of women drug users have been sexually abused as children.[31] Ella and Mark, the recently minted MSWs and part-time family therapists employed by Fresh Beginnings, were also aware of, and particularly sensitive to, the high reported rates of childhood sexual abuse among female drug users. So whereas program administrators, like Marne, understood the treatment program's "gender sensitivity" to be a matter of providing specific services—such as child care and transportation—which other local treatment programs lacked, the therapeutic staff on Cliff Street felt that being sensitive to gender meant recognizing that their clients had probably been sexually abused as children.

For instance, during a coffee shop interview, I asked family therapist Ella, "What are the biggest challenges of working with clients at [Fresh Beginnings]?" In response, she proposed:

1 E: Most of these women have been sexually *abused* and that has to do with . . .
2   that's one of the *roots* . . . one . . . that's one of the things that led them to use in the
3   *first place* . . .
4 I: Uh-hm.
5 E: And, you know . . . and it *comes out*.
6   Because I know, like, when they're doing the, like when they're in treatment and
7   they go through the *steps* and they're taking inventory of their *life*.

Ella's use of etiologic terms—not to mention the fact that she engages in extensive repair to place those terms in proper order (i.e., lines 1–3)—is noteworthy. Indeed, while Ella corrects herself above before identifying childhood sexual abuse as the singular "*root*" of women's use, her emphatic focus on root cause is unmistakable. For Ella, sexual abuse is not only "one of the things" (line 2) leading to later drug use but is also *"what led them to use in the first place"* (lines 2–3). And, as she continues to describe the process of inventory in similarly sequential and causal terms, we learn that Ella's etiologic starting point is not simply a traumatic event in personal history but also a psychic cluster stored away in the memory. Furthermore, Ella tells us that when clients are "taking inventory" of their life, the stored event *"comes out"* (line 5), presumably in words.[32]

However, as Ella continues, it becomes clear that rooted memories of childhood sexual abuse did not "come out" as simply or naturally as she first suggested. She elaborated:

8 E: A lot of them are saying, you know. "Well, those memories are really painful."
9   It's hard to get through that stuff, it's hard to get past . . . you know.
10   It's hard to get *past* that stuff to the next step because there are a lot of things in the
11   their lives that they don't want to . . .
12 I: Mmm . . .
13 E: . . . take *inventory* of, you know.
14 I: I see.
15 E: They aren't ready to take inventory.

Notice Ella's clinographic terms. Using the term "memories" as a gloss for childhood sexual abuse (line 8), Ella identifies the painful psychic "stuff" stored away, both in the client's psyche and in a historical past (lines 9–10). Indeed, when Ella repeats that "it's hard to get *past*" (lines 9, 10) such stuff, she evokes the image of a psychic blockade. In similar terms, Laura once suggested to me that unarticulated memories of childhood sexual abuse "almost become cystic and are encapsulated but never touched, so real healing doesn't seem to happen." For both therapists, it was a thick and formidable layer of shame that prevented clients from taking inventory of childhood sexual experiences, as we will see below.

If Ella begins with the idea that taking inventory of the inner self is "hard" because of the nature of its contents (lines 8–9), she ends by implying that if painful things do not "come out" in the course of a client's inventory, this indicates a failure to fully engage in the process (lines 11, 13, 15). Convinced of the pervasiveness of childhood sexual abuse among women drug users, Fresh Beginnings therapists often assumed that the client who did not disclose a personal history of childhood trauma had simply not undertaken a proper or thorough inventory. In fact, it was with alarming regularity that the self-inventories clients conducted at Fresh Beginnings yielded evidence of childhood sexual abuse—nearly 90 percent according to therapists and around 65–75 percent according to my own interviews and interactions. And whereas therapists understood clients' reports of sexual abuse as transparent or "clean" representations of their personal pasts, clients themselves indicated that they were something more of a joint therapeutic production. Indeed, some clients suggested that in order to meet their therapists' implicit demands, they had to connect their drug use to early sexual abuse, as few other plot lines were considered legitimate. As one former client attested: "You *got* to be abused there, or they start thinkin' there be somethin' wrong with *you*."

Pushing and Pulling

So although clients frequently reported instances of childhood sexual abuse, they did not always suggest that those reports were rooted in their own psyches, as Ella implies above. More often, clients described intense and highly interactive discussions with their therapists, which led them to identify girlhood sexual experiences as explanations for their drug-using behavior as women. Consider this interview with Louise, conducted soon after she left Fresh Beginnings, in which she describes how she began to understand why she started using drugs:

1 L: And . . . because I was at [Fresh Beginnings] and because we did have to bring out
2   things that's in our past that have made us the person that we are *now*,
3   I eventually, in a one-on-one session, I spoke about this with my therapist.
4 I: Uh-hm.
5 L: And I felt really good after that. I cried while I was telling her this, *you know*.
6   And it was a really long, *four hours*, you know, before I actually got to the point.
7   That the whole point of my conversation was to say that my, I was sexually abused
8   as a child and this kind of thing that's in the back of my head . . .
9 I: Uh-hm.
10 L: [It's] been in the back of my mind for twenty, thirty years, you know?

Recounting the session with her therapist along familiar etiologic lines, Louise not only suggests that sexual abuse makes her the person that she is now (lines 2) but also generalizes this causal relation to other clients, alternating between singular and plural pronouns (e.g., lines 1–3).

Furthermore, in accordance with the local clinical epistemology, the past "things" (line 2) Louise is required to recount are located not in personal history but instead in the "back of her head" and "mind" (lines 8, 10) by the time she finishes her inventory work. It is interesting that both Louise's statements to me as her interviewer and the therapeutic interaction she describes share a plotted crescendo, namely, that "the whole point of [the] conversation was to say that [she] was sexually abused as a child" (lines 7–8).[33] Curious in regard to the rather plodding development of the interaction that Louise recounts, I asked about the unusual length of her individual therapy session. In response, she explained,

11 L: Four hours, because I had . . . I *obviously* had a lot of things inside
12 I: Oh.

13 L: And then once I'm talking with the therapist, oh, she was just like,
14   she was *pulling* that stuff out of me without me knowing it
15 I: Hm.
16 L: You know?

At first, Louise replies with a premise consistent with her therapeutic training at Fresh Beginnings, implying that it was the onus of the "things inside" (line 11) that required so much time for her to verbally unload. However, as Louise continues, she indicates the highly interactive indexes of her seemingly intrapsychic discoveries. Now it is not Louise who "brings out" the stored stuff of sexual abuse, but instead it is the therapist who "pull[s]" it out of her (line 14). Louise's report, rather intriguingly, raises the question of awareness, as she represents herself here as an unknowing container of truths within which the knowing therapist fishes (line 14). Whether or not we accept this suggested lack of self-awareness, it seems rather significant that it only becomes "obvious" that Louise has the referents of sexual abuse "inside" of her (line 11) "*once*" she began talking to the therapist (line 13).

The point here is not to affirm or refute whether Louise was actually abused as a child, nor to determine whether that abuse accounted for her later drug use.[34] Regardless of the ontological status and psychological valuation of Louise's girlhood sexual experiences, the figuring of those experiences as psychically located beyond the grasp of still unrecovered clients is significant. For it is precisely this figuring that allowed therapists to reaffirm their authoritative knowledge of and intimate relationship with clients' inner realities, while suggesting that clients were still sick until they saw themselves and their problems as therapists did. And while this figuration of clients' and therapists' respective positioning in relation to inner truth was intended to be therapeutic, and may have indeed helped some clients to heal, it is important to consider the costs—both clinically and politically—of this economy of self-awareness.

The Gendered Roots of Shameful Substance

As clients like Louise got closer to "the things inside of [them]" (line 11), it was expected that they would no longer bubble over with feelings of anger but would instead encounter a thick layer of shame—a residue left by unprocessed memories that they would need to slog through as they began the work of sorting through the memories themselves. Attesting, as addiction specialist Potter-Efron (2002:80) does, that "defensive anger is frequently used to protect against the revelation of shame", Fresh Beginnings therapists accordingly averred that it was especially important "to *listen for shame in a client's anger*" (ibid., emphasis in the original; see also De Mojá and Spielberger 1997).

Indeed, in line with the current clinical literature on women and addiction, Laura and Susan attested that shame was particularly prevalent among their clientele.[35] They regularly echoed this literature in interviews and conversations with me, suggesting that women commonly try to wash away the "shame" of sexual abuse with drugs and alcohol (e.g., Carter 1997; Cohen and Mannarino 2002; Hurley 1991) and that shame constitutes the emotional dividing line between women users and their male counterparts, who may feel guilt but not shame (e.g., Cohen and Mannarino 2002; Finkelstein 1993; Winick et al. 1992). And although I am unsure where she learned this, Laura once told me that shame is one of the "three emotions that [are] most likely to trigger relapse" in women. In an interview with me, she elaborated:

1 L: One of the things that makes *women's* recovery treatment so much more difficult
2   than men's [is] if the reason you originally started abusing substances is to not *feel*
3   and to not *remember*, you take the substance away...
4 I: Umhm.
5 L: And the healing process starts physically, the healing process begins emotionally,
6   and mentally, spiritually...
7   As you get *stronger*, you're able to handle some of the stuff that you couldn't
8   handle before; these are things that you did or things that were done to you
9   and, usually, those are very *shameful* things that you start to remember.
10   And when those shameful memories come back, the first urge is to shut it down
11   with chemicals.

Here, Laura describes a zero-sum game between drugs and memory: drugs are taken so as not to remember (lines 2–3); drugs are taken away and the memory gets stronger only to recognize "things that you did or things that were done to you" (line 8); these things, once remembered, powerfully threaten to "shut down" the memory all over again with the urge to use "chemicals" (lines 10–11). And although Laura at first implies that any kind of memory can get caught up in such an orbit, as she continues she makes clear that women's memory clearly revolves around the qualifier of shame and its implicit sexual designata. Indeed, Laura asserts that it is usually "*shameful* things" that one starts to remember and works to shut down (line 9), the very same "shameful things," she reasons, that spurred women clients to use in the first place.

When I asked for clarification about the kind of shameful things her clients remembered, Laura responded:

1 L: People bring in everything.
2 I: Ok.
3 L: Because I do believe that chemical dependency affects women very differently than
4   it does men. I also believe the *roots* for women are different than they are for men.
5 I: Ok.

6 L: I know that there are genetic components. I know there are environmental
7   components.
8   And at the same time, most of the women that I have *known* and *worked with*,
9   myself *included*, have used alcohol and drugs to anesthetize pain or shame.
10 I: Uh hmm.
11 L: It's not they, they are like, "let's go get drunk and have a good time and,
12   *ooops* I drank too much." (chuckling)
13 I: Right.
14 L: It's like, "I don't want to *feel*."
15   And it's not about *celebration* and it's not about a *rite of passage* like it is for a lot
16   of men . . . and even though use can become *compulsive*, because that by definition
17   is what makes it a *disease*.
18 I: Okaaay.
19 L: I'm using when I don't *wanna* use. It didn't start out as "this is fun!"

Although Laura begins by stating that people "bring in everything" (line 1), this "everything" is substantially narrowed as she begins to differentiate male and female users. For unlike their male counterparts who engage in celebrations and rites of passage (line 15), women use drugs for psychological rather than cultural reasons—or so the therapist suggests.[36]

Furthermore, in bifurcating addiction along the lines of gender, Laura again focuses on the psychic variable of shame. Inherent to this clinical conception of shame is a tenacious presumption of feminine passivity for, as we see in Laura's account, men use drugs to do or feel something, whereas women use *not* to do or feel something (e.g., lines 9, 15). Note that women users' de facto actions work exactly against their feelings, as in, "I'm using when I don't wanna use" (line 19). Indeed, at Fresh Beginnings, the thesis of shame was regularly evoked in relation to women's presumed inability to act according to their own desires.[37] And since shame was understood as a psychic property, rather than a principle of action, it, too, would have to be mined if clients were to recognize themselves both as women and as addicts.

. . .

Mid-twentieth-century American psychologist Silvan Tomkins (1962, 1963) once likened shame to a yawn. Like a yawn, shame is highly contagious, passed from one agent to another in a mysterious sociality. Shame becomes an individual attribute only to the extent that it is culturally understood as such, just as an inherited yawn is so easily interpreted as a sign that the yawner is tired rather than as a reflexive expression of mutuality. In these terms, Tompkins fuels Eve Sedgwick and Adam Frank's (1995) claim that "shame" is the ultimate performative, one that confers and produces the inner state that it claims to describe (see also Reddy 2001). Yet, if shame, as a sign, can both travel and individuate, the question of just how it does so merits careful analysis.[38] Fresh Beginnings gives us the opportunity to witness the laborious, highly interactive processes that helped to assure that sexual shame would be discovered *inside* the client *as* an explanatory variable of their drug use. As we will see in the following chapter, if therapeutic practices, like inventory, were understood to be private processes of searching one's self for the signs of addiction, this is largely due to professional metalinguistics that obscured the highly dialogical methods by which such searches were conducted.

Conclusions: Topographic Models and Clinographic Measures

As documented above, Fresh Beginnings therapists averred that their clients were constituted by layers of denial, anger, and shame, which prevented them from recognizing their innermost states, including the stored memories and experiences associated with drug use. Taking inventory was accordingly cast as the work of excavating the layers that obstructed clients' ability to accurately know themselves. Indeed, therapists attested that it was only once a client could see and speak what she once denied—including the facts of her addiction—that she was adequately prepared to embark upon the road to recovery. For this reason, a perfectly transparent language—one that clearly identified and cleanly articulated inner states—was the goal of Fresh Beginnings treatment.

It was precisely because therapists believed that the language of inner reference was the best sign of recovery that they were so intent on detecting any deviations from it. In an interview with me, Laura explained:

1 L: Now people can *look* really good, and *sound* really good, and say all the *right stuff*.
2 I: Ok.
3 L: But if they don't *do* . . . I mean, the analogy I always use in treatment is:
4   "Clean out your basement."
5 I: Ok.
6 L: You know, all the stuff you don't want to deal with goes down in the basement and
7   the fuller your basement is, the more unconscious garbage you've got to deal with.

Laura notes that although clients can "sound good" and "say all the right stuff" (line 1), if their words do not correspond to the "stuff" in the psychic basements (lines 6–7), they are not really "*do*[ing]" the work of recovery (line 3). Contrasting an empty kind of talking (line 1) and the deep cleaning of one's basement of unconscious "stuff" (line 7), Laura implies that she is not as interested in the actual contents of what clients actually say as she is in the psychic locales where signs find their signifiers. Indeed, it is clear that "garbage" (line 7) is to be found deep in the psyche rather than in social space, if one hopes to recover from addiction.

Operating in accordance with the logocentric principle that truth is independent of its representation, Fresh Beginnings therapists suggested that clients' language—when healthy and normal—functioned as a vertical channel that reached down into the deepest regions of self where the truths of addiction were stored. Because clients could *sound* really good and say all the *right stuff*, therapists needed sensitive instruments to detect any obstructions or deviations from pure and sober referential rendering (i.e., denial, anger, or shame). So, just as physical engineers need to measure any slants in boreholes before they can build, and miners need to keep a careful eye on the dangerous layers they work their way through, therapists at Fresh Beginnings relied on clinographic analyses in constituting and excavating structures of addicted subjectivity. Thus, in the end, taking inventory was not simply the means of recovering from drug addiction; it was also the measure of therapists' expertise.

. . .

In mining and construction, clinographs measure the deviation from the vertical, assuring that boreholes have the most direct route down. In fields as diverse as drafting, kite making (see Hunt 1971) and statistics (see Yule 1904), however, the clinograph is an adjustable tool, a pair of straight edges united by a hinge that allows them to conform to a desired angle. Of course, the idea of conforming language to "a desired angle" is precisely why—according to Derrida (1995 [1992])—the maverick writer is culturally condemned in a social order that insists upon a language that directly channels Truth. In comparing the writer to the addict, Derrida gestures toward the work with which therapists, like Laura and Susan, have been culturally charged. He suggests that they police a logocentric order that holds a grip on how we think about the treatment of the suffering that can accompany excessive drug use. And, indeed, as the next chapter will demonstrate, the ongoing work of daily therapy at Fresh Beginnings involved what I call "metalinguistic labor" (see also Carr 2006). This labor was rooted in the epistemology that we have seen illustrated here—one that privileges that which bores vertically down to retrieve truth to that which might be adjustable to a variety of desired angles.

CHAPTER FOUR

Addicted Indexes and Metalinguistic Fixes

> Uh, one thing that I used to get flustrated about when I was in group:
> We did a *whole lot* of talkin'. And I'm a person that is very hyper.
> And I, [and] my therapist even talked about it.
> I said, "Can't we have *arts* and *crafts* some days, or *do* somethin' different?
> *Go* for a walk?" Somethin', you know *somethin*', you know, I just, I mean . . .
> It was like a *talk talk talk* place.
> You know, we would leave, we would *talk*.
> Yeah, sometimes we would go to [an AA] meeting and we could come back, and there was always *talk*ing."
> —Tealie, former Fresh Beginnings client

Introduction: Talk, Talk, Talk

As Tealie indicates above, therapy at Fresh Beginnings was predicated on talk. Indeed, behavioral exercises and recreational activities played a secondary role in this "talk, talk, talk place," much to some clients' dismay. Over the years the minutes of Client Advisory Committee meetings documented clients' frustration with the monotony of "always talking," as well as their regular requests for fieldtrips, relapse prevention training, and guest speakers. Therapists, in turn, made sporadic if earnest efforts to respond by introducing alternative therapeutic activities. Such changes in routine, however, were commonly hindered by financial constraints, staffing shortages, and complicated logistical matters beyond therapists' direct control. Moreover, therapists' investment in the therapeutic benefits of talk, shared by many of their colleagues in addiction treatment as well as by a few loquacious clients, firmly instituted talk at the center of the program's clinical regimen.

While Tealie correctly casts Fresh Beginnings as a *"talk, talk, talk* place," it was not just any kind of talk that characterized group therapy. As indicated in chapter 3, therapists worked hard to get clients to speak a language that they believed would help heal them—that is, one that perfectly referenced and revealed inner states. Indeed, clients were dissuaded from recounting a troubling social encounter, unless the speaker's point was to "own her feelings" about it. Commentary about the immediate interaction of group therapy was also tightly controlled, when not specifically prohibited. Rendering a piece of advice in response to a peer's voiced predicament, interpreting another's silence or cultivating one's own, or questioning the very utility of *talk, talk, talking* were clearly devalued speech acts at Fresh Beginnings. And, though therapists sometimes set aside group time for role playing—so that clients could practice effective ways of "saying no" to drugs offered by friends, lovers, or family members—they otherwise discouraged linguistic performances devoid of obvious inner referential content.

Thus it is no wonder that Tealie differentiates talking from "doing" things, like taking a walk or doing arts and crafts. In the therapy rooms on Cliff Street, talking was not about exploring fresh territory or creating something new. Instead, it was about reading the already existing contents of the inner self and releasing them into words. This chapter explores the laborious process by which the language of inner reference was produced by examining the everyday metalinguistic work of Fresh Beginnings clients and counselors.

Cultural Distillation as Institutional Practice

Though millions have been psychologically modeled in topographical terms, and exhorted to reveal their innermost states accordingly, readers who have engaged in modern American psychotherapies may find the restriction and direction of client talk on Cliff Street quite unlike their own experience. After all, many interpretations and implementations of core psychoanalytic principles—such as transference and counter-transference—afford the average American consumer of psychotherapy the opportunity to linguistically explore troubling or puzzling psychological questions without the semiotic presumption that answers will be "found" *already* inside her. Indeed, those who either pay out of pocket or are covered by private medical insurance generally experience therapy as a process of supportive "problem solving" with the contractual understanding that both parties affect, and are responsible for, how personal problems are understood as well as how solutions are formulated.

Furthermore, unlike Fresh Beginnings' adherence to a language ideology of inner reference, modern psychotherapies commonly rely on the idea that language objectifies and thereby distances the speaker from her psychic traumas and dilemmas so that she may rework them. For instance, since the late 1980s, narrative therapists and scholars alike have lauded the *instrumental* potential of talk, suggesting that linguistic interaction with skilled and sensitive therapists allows people to experiment with new or possible selves (e.g., Anderson and Jack 1991; Borden 1992; Bruner 1990; Forsberg and Sands 2009; Ferrara 1994; Fish 1993; Laird 1994; Ochs and Capps 1996, 2002; Mancini 2007; Nye 1994; Riessman 1990, 1992, 2003; Sands 1996; White and Epston 1990). Another relatively new and innovative therapeutic approach, Motivational Interviewing (MI) eschews the stark episteme of inner truth and its denial; MI counselors work instead to co-produce "change statements," which are thought to have both illocutionary force (i.e., they do something in saying something) and perlocutionary force (i.e., they instigate other actions) (cf. Austin 1962; Miller and Rollnick 1993, 2002).

Yet, though MI has made substantial theoretical and practical inroads over the last two decades, the linguistic regimen of inner reference is firmly instituted and continues to dominate the field of American addiction treatment. As the previous chapter elaborated, there is a distinct clinical logic to the theorization of addiction as a disease of insight, the topographical modeling of subjectivity, and the implementation of a linguistic program of inner reference. In understanding the language spoken at Fresh Beginnings, there are *institutional* logics to decipher as well. First, there is professional addiction treatment's debt to the highly successful and quintessentially American cultural phenomenon: Alcoholics Anonymous.[1] Though many have recognized professional programs' use local self-help groups as an ancillary (and extremely cost-effective) arm of treatment, as well as the institutionalization of AA's "disease model" via the ever popular Minnesota Model, the way the linguistic rituals of AA have influenced programs like Fresh Beginnings has not been concertedly analyzed to date.[2] Consider the Twelve Steps, as they have been inscribed in the *Big Book* ever since its original publication in 1939. These steps can be broadly understood as prescribing a way for addicts to manage themselves and their lives considering the theorization of addiction as a chronic and incurable disease. The following "steps," in particular, make clear that such management is impossible without the cultivation of insight, which is achieved through a rigorous process of internal inventory and verbal revelation:

Step 4—Made a searching and fearless moral inventory of ourselves.
Step 5—Admitted to God, to ourselves, and to another human being the exact nature of our wrongs.
Step 10—Continued to take personal inventory and when we were wrong promptly admitted it.[3]

Aside from the fact that Fresh Beginnings therapists accepted many of the basic premises of the "disease model" of addiction, which they combined with psychodynamic, feminist, and dialectical behavioral principles, they most definitely gave credence to these three "steps," using shortened and revised versions of them as metalinguistic prompts for clean and sober talk. It follows that many of the therapeutic slogans, rules of group conduct, and didactic materials discussed in this chapter will be familiar to students and consumers of AA.

Considering both its clinical and institutional proximity, we might be tempted to look no further than AA, and its impressively pervasive practices of "self-help," in uncovering the origins of the ideology of inner reference. Yet this would be near-sighted. As linguistic anthropologists have long noted, the ideology of reference—which works to confine the function of language to the reference of preexisting people, ideas, and things—is the dominant language ideology of Euro-Americans (Hill 2000; Irvine 1989; Silverstein 1979, 1985, 1996, 2003a; Woolard 1998). As Kathyrn Woolard notes, "Examples from European language communities, and especially American English, reveal a tendency to see reference or propositionality as the essence of language, to confuse or at least to merge the indexical functions of language with the referential function, and to assume that the divisions and structures of language should—and in the best circumstances do—transparently fit the structures of the "real world." (1998:13). The further presumption that the structures of language should transparently fit the structures of the *real self* has been explored by anthropologists as well. For instance, Webb Keane has shown how "Christian Moderns" forge and sustain the concept of sincerity out of the "model of words as conventional expressions of inner thoughts" (2007:20; also see Keane 2002). And, Vincent Crapanzano (1992, 1996) has masterfully traced the privileging of the semantico-referential function of language from its roots in classical Greek philosophy to its manifestation in Freudian psychoanalysis.

Michel Foucault's much feted genealogies of confession can also be read as a cultural history of inner reference. Indeed, through his ambitious work, we have learned that confessional techniques have served as the modus operandi for our innermost desires, including our history of sexuality (e.g., 1978, 1993, 1999a, 1999b). Following Foucault's lead, some have further charged that confession is the exemplar of modern, clinical commerce, allowing disease to find root in the denial of inner truth and relief in its articulation (Alcoff and Gray 1993; Rapping 1996; Rose 1990; Young 1994). Several clinical ethnographies have confirmed that inner referential language enjoys particular currency in American therapeutic settings and situations. For example, in his ethnography of a Boston homeless shelter, where many residents had been diagnosed with mental illnesses, Robert Desjarlais notes that "the staff advanced a way of thinking about language that came close to an ideology dominant in many contemporary English-speaking societies which gives priority to the referential, semantic, and propositional functions of language" (1997: 180). Allan Young's fascinating study of a psychiatric unit for Vietnam veterans highlights the clinical demand for patients to verbally disclose the "contents" of their trauma-laden memory as well as the punitive measures reserved for those who do not engage in the "work" of authentic linguistic representation (1995:214–216). It follows that the ideology of *inner reference* would enjoy all the more currency in the treatment of addicts who, according to both clinical and cultural judgment, have tenuous ties with even their own reality.

Notably, the ideology of inner reference has a life in law as well. The 1966 Miranda ruling, which granted suspects a "right to remain silent," works to assure that the suspect's words are motivated by internal rather than external force (Brooks 2000; Shuy 1998). And though one can certainly read the genealogy of Christian contrition and confession as a history of inner reference (Asad 1993; Foucault 1993), it is important to recognize its prominent place in American *civil* religion as well. In the contemporary U.S., the idea that language can tap and reveal inner states has been civilized, in Bellah's (1985) sense, as the quintessential expression of a Protestant American personalism "recovered" from the grips of a self-suffocating society. Television talk shows feature cheating wives, plummeted child stars, once closeted cross-dressers, chronic child molesters, and crack-smoking mothers who seem to talk only of and from their more or less remorseful inner states, without apparent regard to the otherwise obvious demands of their television audience or host-confessors (see Lowney 1999). Indeed, across a wide array of domains of practice, speakers—especially those who have strayed from what is considered healthy, normal, or right—are encouraged and expected to use the language of inner reference. Accordingly, this chapter proceeds from the premise that the language laboriously produced in the therapy rooms of Cliff Street is also quintessentially American.[4]

Given that Fresh Beginnings could have inherited, ready-made, the idea that language primarily functions to denote preexisting psychological facts about the speaker, this chapter asks: Why does it take so much work to protect, patrol, and produce such highly naturalized assumptions about language? I call such work *metalinguistic labor*, arguing that while therapeutic interventions seem to elicit inner signs that are always already there, awaiting cathartic escape into language, Fresh Beginnings therapy was instead an intensive exercise in linguistic production—one that required the labor of therapists, the cooperation of clients, and the use of particular tools and techniques for producing a purely referential language.

Indeed, as we watch therapists so hard at work getting clients to speak in culturally expected ways, we must look beyond the clinical theorization and modeling of the addicted subject to investigate the nature of the relationship between treatment programs like Fresh Beginnings and broader American society. I understand this relationship as a matter of *distillation*, suggesting that, at Fresh Beginnings, cultural ideas about language are purified and reproduced in refined form.

This chapter focuses on three critical sites, or *stations*, of the distillation process: the identification and categorization of linguistic impurities; the filtering and condensation of speech; and the quality control of actual linguistic products. Through their work at each of these stations, therapists hoped to bring clients' inner intentions and emotions in line with their outward expressions. Accordingly, the institutional distillation of cultural forms can be understood semiotically as a process of *indexical iconization*: the discursive collapsing of the spatiotemporal features of a speech act so that it appears to be independent of context and purely denotational (Silverstein 2003, 2004, 2005). We will see that, when properly distilled, the language of Fresh Beginnings clients could be read as pure and simple signs of inner states.

There were both therapeutic reasons for and profound political consequences of the metalinguistic labor on Cliff Street. Primarily, by producing a kind of talk that could not reference anything but inner states—including the immediate circumstances of speaking—the distillation process filtered away clients' institutional critiques and other social commentary. So while this chapter focuses on language as a clinical resource, it addresses it as an institutional resource as well. In this sense my argument proceeds from the premise that institutions are not simply neutral contexts for talk but instead are organized to both demonstrate and enforce the legitimacy of institutional authority (Gal 1991:186; see also Cohn 1987; Desjarlais 1997). Indeed, we will see that as long as therapists labored in accordance with the ideological premises of inner reference, the program and its practices were effectively *insulated* from clients' critical commentary (Carr 2006).

In encountering the troubling by-products of therapists' metalinguistic labor, it is critical to remember that they did not labor alone, nor were they entrepreneurs. Instead, Laura and Susan distilled a language of inner reference not simply because they, as particular kinds of clinical professionals, believed this was the best way to cultivate healthy speakers. They also worked to fulfill the demands of a broader culture that exalts the semantico-referential functions of speech and therefore evaluates people according to how they reference themselves in words. And if there was an intensity and dogmatism to their practice, I believe it was largely because Fresh Beginnings therapists were well aware that their clients would continue to be judged by how they spoke long after they broke free from their therapeutic alliances. They were, after all, American.

How to Sabotage Your Treatment

At Fresh Beginnings the vast majority of clinically guided talk took place behind a carefully sealed door, on which frequently hung a simple sign that warned visitors to keep their own voices down and their ears otherwise occupied. For instance, if coming to pick up Yolanda for a 12:30 court appointment, Cassie might climb the stairs to the second-story group room to find the sign GROUP THERAPY IN SESSION, a signal that she would have to retreat to chance upon an unoccupied colleague downstairs or have a cigarette in her car until that session was done. And though I myself spent many hours in the "group room" during Client Advisory Committee meetings and special sessions, such as clients' sobriety anniversaries, and witnessed countless impromptu therapeutic exchanges, the sign was intended for me as well. Indeed, the only people who experienced, firsthand, the sheer volume of therapeutic "talk, talk, talk" at Fresh Beginnings were CD therapists and their clients.

If talk therapy sessions were generally cloistered affairs, cordoned off even from the most familiar and trusted professionals, visitors to Cliff Street could not help recognize that the program also played host to a tremendous amount of talk *about* talk. In the hallways of Cliff Street, around the boardroom table, and in their everyday conversations with clients, other professionals, and a curious ethnographer, therapists deliberately distinguished healthy and sober talk from the unhealthy and addicted varieties. Though they took this work quite seriously, they also used entertaining educational props that identified and warned clients away from the dangerous impurities that might infect their speech.

For example, at the top of the dingy narrow stairwell just outside the group room, arriving clients were greeted with an array of posted documents, one of which featured critical metalinguistic instructions. A tattered, repeatedly photocopied, and impressively layered document— taken from an illustrated manual that accompanied the original release of the Gerald T. Rogers educational film called "How to Sabotage Your Treatment"[5]—could not help but catch one's eye. Hand-edited in line with immediate institutional concerns,[6] the cartoon warned clients that the fastest way to "sabotage their treatment" was not to relapse on drugs, but rather to relapse into a drug addicted way of speaking (Figure 4.1).

"How to Sabotage Your Treatment" portrays cartloads of self-sabotaging clients riding the roller coaster of recovery. Defeatist statements, each emanating from an individual rider, lurk above the ebbs and peaks of the scaffolded tracks, rendering what could be an exhilarating ride a scary and ineffectual one. The cartoon teaches its viewers that addicts' self-sabotage comes in many forms and flavors, from interpersonal dramas ("the staff

128 • Chapter 4

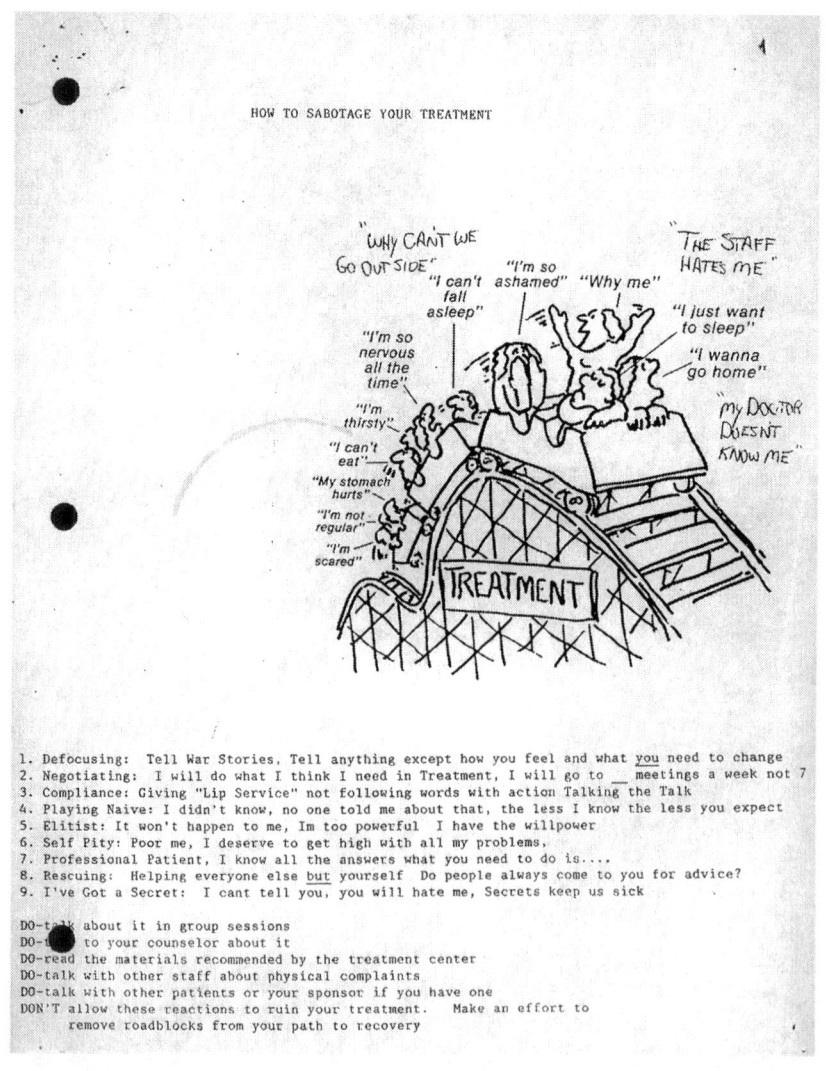

> HOW TO SABOTAGE YOUR TREATMENT
>
> "WHY CANT WE GO OUTSIDE" "I can't fall asleep" "I'm so ashamed" "Why me" THE STAFF HATES ME
> "I'm so nervous all the time" "I just want to sleep" "I wanna go home"
> "I'm thirsty" my DOCTOR DOESNT KNOW ME
> "I can't eat"
> "My stomach hurts"
> "I'm not regular"
> "I'm scared"
>
> TREATMENT
>
> 1. Defocusing: Tell War Stories, Tell anything except how you feel and what you need to change
> 2. Negotiating: I will do what I think I need in Treatment, I will go to __ meetings a week not 7
> 3. Compliance: Giving "Lip Service" not following words with action Talking the Talk
> 4. Playing Naive: I didn't know, no one told me about that, the less I know the less you expect
> 5. Elitist: It won't happen to me, Im too powerful I have the willpower
> 6. Self Pity: Poor me, I deserve to get high with all my problems.
> 7. Professional Patient, I know all the answers what you need to do is....
> 8. Rescuing: Helping everyone else but yourself Do people always come to you for advice?
> 9. I've Got a Secret: I cant tell you, you will hate me, Secrets keep us sick
>
> DO-talk about it in group sessions
> DO-talk to your counselor about it
> DO-read the materials recommended by the treatment center
> DO-talk with other staff about physical complaints
> DO-talk with other patients or your sponsor if you have one
> DON'T allow these reactions to ruin your treatment. Make an effort to remove roadblocks from your path to recovery

Figure 4.1. "How to Sabotage Your Treatment," a cartoon from the illustrated manual published with the 1983 instructional film by the same title (Gerald T. Rogers Productions). The typewritten text below the cartoon, as well as the handwritten text, was added at a later date.

hates me," "my doctor doesn't know me") and physical complaints (e.g., "I'm thirsty," "I'm not regular") to a variety of psychological and spiritual grievances (e.g., "I'm scared," "I'm so ashamed," "Why me?").

Despite this impressive variety, the cartoon is not shy in suggesting a genre. Though all the statements here take the ostensible form of referential self-report, it seems, paradoxically, that a particular kind of semantic barrenness defines the genre of addicted self-sabotage. It is not that the lampooned statements are false, at least not verifiably so. Instead, as referential indexes, they simply miss the point. As indicated in the metalinguistic commentary, probably added below the cartoon at a later date,[7] the number one characteristic of addicts' self-sabotaging semiosis is:

> 1. Defocusing: Tell War Stories. Tell anything except how you feel and what you need to do to change.

We thereby learn that coasting clients' statements are not so much inaccurate as they are misdirected. More specifically, the "defocused" client tells a drug-plotted, war-torn social history rather than rendering aloud her feelings and intention to change. It appears that feelings are such an anathema to the defocused client that she is willing to "tell anything" to avoid articulating them. So, for instance, the second to last client-rider's bowels may *really* be irregular, but, according to the discerning cartoon, the utterance of her feelings is clearly valued as more *focused* than the statement of this physical fact.

Accordingly, under the nine examples of "how to sabotage treatment," there are five positive directives of how to properly "DO" it.[8] Here the reader discovers that one must limit the indexical reach of one's words to preexisting emotional (rather than physical) inner states if one hopes to recover from drug addiction. For instance, although it is conceded that the treatment rollercoaster rider should "talk to other staff about physical complaints" (legal liabilities notwithstanding!), the *real* referent— the "it" that one is supposed to talk to the group and the therapist about—is clearly of a more emotional or spiritual nature. Thus, if properly engaged rather than sabotaging treatment, the "it" is a referential index that points *inside* rather than outside the psyche of the addicted speaker.

Notably, some of the self-sabotaging clients indeed engage in inwardly directed self-talk. For instance, whereas the "Elitist" tells herself, "It won't happen to me" (5), the "Self-Pity[ing]" addict reflects, "I deserve to get high with all my problems" (6). However, this self-talk is clearly characterized as being different from inner reference, and not because of its denotative content per se. Rather, it is the shallow psychic depths from which these statements are presumed to have come that are rendered problematic. More specifically, the cartoon commentary indicates that the speaker has yet to erode the internal, layered residue of denial, shame, and anger to retrieve deeper, realer, and truer inner states. Indeed, in the booklet accompanying the VHS release of Rogers's film, we are given this more personal introduction to "Betty," the self-pitying alcoholic and Valium abuser: "As long as her 'poor me' attitude persisted, she didn't have to look honestly at her drinking and Valium abuse" (Rogers 1983:8).

Reading through the cartoon's attendant list of addicts' self-sabotaging tendencies, another troubling theme emerges. It seems that coasting clients enter into *negotiations* with their therapists rather than following their expert advice (2). "I will do what I think I need in Treatment" is a statement, however adamant, which is apparently not aligned with the "negotiating" client speaker's inner state but instead is directed outward at a more or less embodied therapeutic authority. The negotiating client seemingly shares proclivities with the "professional patient" who "not only knows all the answers" but also apparently counsels her client peers accordingly (7). Similarly, those clients engaged in "rescuing" use language to *advise* rather than self-refer (8). In each of these cases, the self-sabotaging client seems to speak and therefore *act* much more like a therapist than like a recovering addict. As we will see in the following chapter, Fresh Beginnings professional practitioners themselves employed a highly performative language, which—through advising, negotiating, and asserting answers—generated rather than reflected realities. Regardless of the many things professionals did with words, the cartoon clearly encourages its client readers to stick to the linguistic task of inner reference and avoid speaking and acting like the therapists who treated them (cf. Desjarlais 1996, 1997).

In continuing to examine the cartoon commentary, the reader soon finds that drug users' tendencies to "negotiate," "rescue," "act professional," and "play naïve" are themselves symptomatic of a more troubling semiotic malady.

3. Compliance. Giving "Lip Service" not following words with action; Talking the Talk.

Here we have a clear privileging of the referential function of language at the expense of the pragmatic: healthy words should be followed with action rather than being actions in themselves. Of specific concern is the pathological mismatch between the illocutionary force and the semantic content of the coasting clients' statements. In other words, compliant speakers are not properly invested in the propositional content of the words they speak, leaving open the question of just why they speak them. Thus, as a clinical phenomenon, compliance raises the disturbing possibility that the nail-biting addict in the back of the first coaster car might pragmatically mobilize the message, "I'm so ashamed," without proper referential investment—that is, she is not ashamed at all.

Compliance—a clinical term popularized by psychiatrist Harry Tiebout, who was Bill W's psychiatrist and an avid early supporter of AA—describes a linguistic proclivity considered to be both specific to and rampant among addicts, namely, the tendency to produce utterances that are devoid of the referential content that they effectively proclaim.[9] Addiction specialist John Lovern elaborates:

> A major stumbling block to the therapist is chemically dependent people's ability to appear to have relinquished their defenses and accepted their addictions, while they actually continue to inwardly believe themselves innocent of 'all charges' relating to addiction. This ability, called compliance . . . often fools everyone, including themselves, and relieves them of the pressure they find themselves under in treatment to perform the awesome tasks of stopping all drug and alcohol use forever and changing their entire way of life. Some patients who are very good at compliance manage to graduate from treatment dripping with optimism and enthusiasm, having impressed everyone concerned and received sincere congratulations all around, but then go out and get loaded again, much to the surprise of their families, friends, and helpers—and even themselves. (1991:13)

As is discussed in chapter 6, some veteran clients at Fresh Beginnings developed their very own theories about "compliance," or what clinicians more commonly call "lip service" or "talking the talk."[10] Rather than casting it as a practice of "not following words with action"—as the cartoon commentary does above—clients understood that compliance is efficacious precisely because words can be reflexively deployed *as action*. This is precisely why Fresh Beginnings therapists, along with the cartoon they so prominently displayed, worried a good deal about compliance. For instance, therapists were embarrassed and distraught, if not entirely surprised, by the case of Nikki, a client whose elegant autobiographical rendering of recovery wisdom had fueled her swiftly through the phases of treatment. After a maternity nurse called Fresh Beginnings to report that Nikki's newborn baby had tested positive for crack cocaine, a not-so-shocked Laura commented: "These women are real good at telling people what they want to hear . . . that's how they supported their habits."

Knowing clients may have already read what "they wanted to hear," Fresh Beginnings therapists were faced with a dilemma: the possibility that clients may not be speaking inner truths precisely when they seemed to be. Indeed, compliance drove an analytical wedge between clients' self-descriptive reports and therapists' expectations of inner content. By extension, the phenomenon of compliance also directly challenged the hermeneutic nature of therapists' expertise, charged as they were with determining the truth value of their clients' speech. Therefore, Laura and Susan needed a way to separate pure statements of inner reference from the forged ones. Notably, they found their solution in the concept of denial.

132 • Chapter 4

If compliance opened the possibility that their clients were intentionally serving therapeutic goals only with their lips, therapists' mobilization of the concept of denial swiftly shut it down. More specifically, by suggesting that clients could not be trusted to report on inner states simply because they had no access to them, as Lovern does above, therapists effectively converted *lying* into *denying*. Consider, for instance, therapist Susan's explanation:

1 S: Denial is an unconscious defense mechanism.
2 I: Ok.
3 S: If I am in *denial* about my addiction,
4 I: Mmm.
5 S: I'm not *lying* to you.
6 I: Mhhm.
7 S: I'm telling you the truth as I see it.
8 I: Right.
9 S: Ya know, and so, so I could pass a polygraph test based on,
10   ya know, whatever kind of questions I was asked.

Susan evokes the troubling image of the addict as profligate prevaricator, who exercises uncanny linguistic control, able to pass a polygraph with ease (line 9–10). However, armed with a theory of denial, Susan is careful to clarify that the denier passes not because she exercises linguistic agency but precisely because she lacks it entirely, keeping her unnamed secrets from herself (line 7) as well as the truth-seeking technology of the polygraph.

Brilliantly, Susan's commentary not only transforms the highly volatile compliance into a more manageable clinical property; in doing so, she also exalts the expertise of therapists over a technology that is unable to discern the difference between lying and denying. Indeed, by posting the rollercoaster cartoon, therapists advertised to their clients that they could both identify impure speech acts *and* clinically manage them. In the end, denial was transformed from just another way for clients to "sabotage their treatment" to a semiotic antidote for addicts' tendencies to "1: defocus, 2: negotiate, 3: comply, 4: play naïve, 5: be elitist, 6: self-pity, 7: enact the professional patient, and 8: rescue." So although at the bottom of the list of the rollercoaster riders' linguistic failings, readers are warned of the dangers of denial—

9. I've Got a Secret: I cant tell you, you will hate me; Secrets keep us sick—

they are also given a rather dubious reassurance. That is, by positing a secret inner *it*, available to the analyst if not the client, the concept of denial effectively fills the semantic gap left open by the phenomenon of compliance. And if the cartooned client who proclaims "I'm so ashamed" may remain convinced that her spoken signs match her shameful inner signifieds, her therapeutic audience could be assured that although her words may be false, they do not have to remain empty. For once impurities were identified, categorized, and cleansed away, the speech acts of Fresh Beginnings clients could be infused with (inner) truth.

HOW TO RECOVER: *HONESTY, OPENNESS,* AND *WILLINGNESS*

Because therapists were not always able to verify the purity of the denotative *contents* of clients' speech, they simultaneously worked to promote certain *methods* of speaking. They did this by proposing an explicit set of tenets for clean and healthy talk, like a recipe for inner reference. Most prominently, the acronym HOW linked the therapeutic ideals of *honesty, openness,* and *willingness* to specific ways of expressing inner states. Indeed, as a set of metalinguistic principles, HOW was the sieve through which the talk of group therapy passed, filtering out yet undetected linguistic impurities from the sober speech that therapists valued.

In the hallways, offices, and therapy rooms at Cliff Street, therapists repeated HOW like a therapeutic mantra. Sometimes the acronym adorned the group room's central dry-erase board, where it served as a constant reminder to client speakers. At other times, HOW was evoked to mark a particular linguistic achievement. During group therapy Laura and Susan frequently rewarded successful clients with "Certificates of Achievement" that read, for example, "For [Rhonda Smith] who is making a stronger commitment to her recovery, by demonstrating greater HOW (*honesty, openness,* and *willingness*), and for working to raise her awareness." After the brief award ceremony, when I asked Rhonda why she had received this particular recognition, she responded: "I tell it like it *is*, baby. I let it *all* hang out."

However, the practice of HOW was neither as straightforward nor as easy as Rhonda suggested and, in fact, required substantial labor both on the part of therapists and the clients who dutifully spoke in HOW's name. First, those who abided by the acronym had to find a way to graft together *honesty* and *openness*. They did so by theorizing *honesty* as a set of inner signs and *openness* as a process of reading those signs aloud to a therapeutic audience. For example, describing how she "opened up" in regard to her childhood, Yolanda explained:

1 Y: Had I not been at [Fresh Beginnings], I would not have been . . .
2   I would not have even spoken about it, like I said.
3 I: Uh-hm.
4 Y: Because had . . . it not been for them I would not have spoken up *at all.*
5   I would have *internalized* that.

6   Um, they helped me out a lot with opening up, because I was never one to
7   *verbalize* a lot of things. I'm more of the volcano type, you know:
8   Let it mound up, build up until I *explode*!!! Whether it's the anger or hurt,
9   or whatever the feeling *is*. And I never been one to talk about things a lot.
10 And, and, ah, they helped me out a lot with that.
11 And I did learn that it does feel better to talk about it, to *vocalize*, you know.

In strikingly clinical terms, Yolanda portrays herself as constituted by internal "mounds" of unarticulated feeling—singling out anger much like her therapists did (line 8; see also chapter 3). She goes on to credit her therapists at Fresh Beginnings for helping her to verbalize and therefore cathartically release (lines 7, 11) the things she once "internalized" and held silent (lines 2, 5, 9) until she "explode[d]" (line 8).

Significantly, in the above description, the problem is not that Yolanda, before entering treatment, does not recognize or is unable to clearly express her "anger, or hurt, or whatever the feeling *is*" (lines 8–9). According to Yolanda, she suffered from neither denial nor from an inability to self-refer. Instead, in funneling her previous speech acts through the filter of HOW, Yolanda casts the *way* she once communicated the "things" inside her as dysfunctional and destructive. In becoming one who "open[s] up" and "verbalizes" things (lines 6–7) rather than a volcano who lets them build up until she "explode[s]" (line 8), the recovering Yolanda trades a highly dramatic and potentially threatening verbal performance for a cool, calm, and collected act of honest inner reference. (This is not to mention, of course, that in "opening up" the once explosive Yolanda also undoubtedly became more manageable for the therapists, who wanted safe and ready access to her innermost states.)

Because, at Fresh Beginnings, *openness* was the only evidence of *honesty*, therapists made sure that their clients understood that the "O" of HOW was not simply a therapeutic ideal but a requirement of recovery. Although her tenure at Fresh Beginnings lasted less than six weeks, Tealie got this message loud and clear. Indeed, soon after complaining about "talk, talk, talk[ing]," she conceded:

1 T: I got a *lot* of problems that I need to talk about.
2   And I need to share 'em, I need to *share* my problems
3   and I really need to *open up*.
4   [Laura] was always tellin' me, I *got to* open up.

Seemingly equating "talking," "sharing," and "opening up," Tealie suggests—in striking alignment with the ideology of inner reference—that *openness* is a matter of giving reference to the problems *already* inside her. She further asserts, along with her former therapist (line 4), that if she does not willingly "*share*" problems by putting them into speech (line 2), she cannot realize the *honesty* necessary for recovery.

Regardless of her seeming adherence to an epistemological premise in which her problems preexist their linguistic formulation, Tealie also indicates an awareness that her *personal* "need" to open up about her problems (lines 1, 2, and 3) was very relevant to a *professional* need to know about them (line 4). After all, *openness* not only helped clients feel better, as Yolanda indicates above, but also helped therapists do their job of tracking clients' therapeutic progress. Yet, though there may have been good reason to engage in open talk, some clients remained quiet and closed for some time, rejecting what seemed like a strange and unnecessary intrusion.

Louise's Philosophy and Shelly's Chip

As the acronym HOW pithily indicates, in order to be "open" and "honest" one had to be *willing* as well, and some clients, especially as they first began to attend group therapy, were decidedly disinclined. One such client, Louise, explained:

1 L: The thing was . . . is you was supposed to say whatever's on your mind,
2   And I was like, why are they tellin' these people all their *business*, you know?
3   Which is why it was . . . it was such a *long* day for me.
4   Every day was a *very* long day because I was not willing to be . . .
5   Honest, Open, and Willing.
6 I: Hmm.
7 L: Honestly, I was not willing to be open, and that was my . . .
8   my *philosophy*, you know.

In Louise's statement that unwillingness was her "philosophy" (line 8), she identifies HOW as an ideological construct against which she *philosophically* stakes herself. Indeed, she resists precisely what she is "supposed to" do—that is, to say "whatever's on [her] mind" (line 1). Rather than share her "business," Louise attends to the interactional and spatiotemporal indexes of her peers' linguistic performance, asking "why are they tellin' these people all their *business*?" In this regard, what at first appears a convoluted statement that she was not "willing to be . . . honest, open, and willing" (lines 4–5) ends up making a good deal of sense.

Although Louise spent some "very long day[s]" (line 4) on Cliff Street when she first arrived, apparently the principles of HOW eventually affected her speech, if not her philosophy of speaking. She continued:

9 L: . . . eventually I relaxed and got into it, you know.
10   And I became a *major* contributor in group [laughs].
11   They couldn't shut me up! [still laughing].

Notably, as Louise describes her shift from being an unwilling speaker to a "*major*" one (line 10), her characterization of group therapy—as a kind of speech situation—also transforms from an alienating and exhausting place to avoid doing personal "*business*" (line 2) to a relaxing venue that invites intimate contributions (lines 9–10). And although Louise explains her newfound willingness in terms of her own ability to relax and "get into it" (line 9), we might wonder how it is that the linguistic principle of *willingness* "got into" her.

Unlike many of her peers in the program, whose housing and shelter contracts hinged on their participation in treatment, Louise came to Fresh Beginnings relatively voluntarily, believing herself to have psychological issues, if not primarily with drugs and alcohol, which she thought therapists might help assuage. To the extent that Louise's peers felt coerced into treatment by HFC agencies, parole officers, or child welfare workers, they were all the more likely to resist the injunction that they be *willing*, which according to therapists and the acronym they wielded, meant they could neither be *honest* nor *open*. Yet even some of these clients described a trajectory much like Louise's. For example, consider the following comment by Shelly, who believed the custody of her oldest child—not to mention her bed at the Carroll Street Shelter—likely hung in the balance of her participation in drug treatment:

1 S: When I first got there I had a *chip* on my shoulder.
2   I used to sit in the group like this (slouched, arms crossed, head down).
3   "How are you today [Shelley]?" (in falsetto).
4   "I'm fine" (clipped, stern).
5 I: Yeah, I remember when you first came (laughing).
6   What were your first impressions of the program?
7 S: The *worst*, but then, I don't know, something in *me* (pause),
8   started *op-en-ing* up (long pause).

Giving me a command performance of her begrudging participation in the practice of "taking inventory" (see chapter 3), Shelly seems to resist both her therapists' question (line 3) and the program she thought was "the worst" (line 7). However, trading body language (line 2), which once effectively communicated her disinterest and displeasure, for verbal *openness* (line 8), Shelly recasts her initial reactions to the program and its interrogatory practices as a "chip" on *her* shoulder (line 1). By the end of our interchange, Shelly is no longer negatively impressed by the program or its practices but instead is positively focused on her own "*op-en-ing*" (line 8). Interested in this change, I inquired:

9 I: What do you think happened?
10 S: You know I think that, cause you know,
11   I was *addicted* and I talked about it.
12   I wanted the help, but I didn't know how to *ask* for it.
13   And I was just, you know, *acting out*.

We might read Shelly's slouched shoulders and clipped responses as an institutional critique of a program she thought was "the worst" or as signs that she resented the fact that she had not chosen to enter the program voluntarily. However, using HOW as a filter, Shelly herself explains her early communications at Fresh Beginnings as behavioral symptoms of her addiction. According to her, until she started "*op-en-ing*" (line 8), Shelly "didn't know how to ask" for the help she really wanted (line 12),[11] and until she was *willing*, she simply engaged in meaningless "*acting out*" (line 13). By way of this revision, Shelly confirms that she is recovering from addiction in the eyes of her therapists, when she says simply: "I was *addicted* and I talked about it" (line 11).

After many months of treatment at Fresh Beginnings, both Shelly and Louise come to characterize themselves as those who talk in line with the tenets of HOW. Moreover, they also examine their pretreatment talk through its filtering lens as so many signs of addiction. Thus it was not just therapists who worked to distill talk, filtering linguistic impurities from clean, sober, and healthy talk. Yet even if dutifully working alongside their therapists to produce the language of inner reference, some clients ultimately found that the discerning demands of HOW were difficult, if not impossible, to satisfy.

The Lexicon of Lila's Love Life

If clients like Shelly and Louise readily collaborated with their therapists to produce *honest* and *open* talk, the tenet of *willingness* remained a slippery one—at least from Laura's and Susan's perspective. Ideally, HOW worked to arouse the client's will so that she could openly and honestly self-refer. But the very activation of the yet recovered will involved the inherent risk that it would devote itself to complying, negotiating, defocusing, or otherwise "sabotaging" treatment. So while therapists employed HOW in the positive as a metalinguistic prompt for distilling healthy and sober talk, they also used it as a way to catch the linguistic residue of addicted dysfunction. In fact, HOW was such a discriminating filter that it sometimes detected even the slightest deviations from what therapists considered sober talk. The case of Lila, a client who voluntarily left the program after a series of problematic interactions with her therapist,[12] is particularly telling in this regard.

I pieced together the story of how Lila left the program from a number of sources, including interviews with and documents written by Lila, Laura, and Lila's case manager.[13] According to this jointly constructed account, Lila returned to Cliff Street after a week-long holiday break. During the first group therapy meeting she told of a difficult and lonely Christmas, noting—as something of an aside—that she found some comfort in romantic time with a "friend." As she spoke, Lila referred to her "friend" using the third person plural pronoun "they," a grammatical detail that was of much significance in the ensuing conflict.

In the group session, therapists greeted Lila's narrative with the usual array of gentle prompts, but eventually homed in on the gender identity of the plural-pronouned "friend." In response, Lila persisted that the gender of her companion was irrelevant, as she was more concerned with sorting through the causes of her loneliness than with detailing the incidental relief offered by her comforting friend. Days later, during their regularly scheduled individual session, Laura proposed an analytical link between Lila's use of the third-person plural pronoun and stalled progress in recovery, grounding both in Lila's "unwillingness to be honest." In a later report to her supervisor, Laura wrote:

1 This client had been attempting to hide the gender of her romantic partner by
2 using the plural pronoun at times, and using male pronouns at other times.
3 I reminded her that secrets keep us sick.

Laura's report readily highlights the analytical challenge posed by Lila's pronominal usage. As a gender-neutral pronoun, "they" is, grammatically, an absent referent; more precisely, it is an indexical sign that points away from the context in which it is spoken and toward a person, elsewhere, of unknown gender. This was rendered clinically significant for, as reviewed in chapter 3, Fresh Beginnings therapists reasoned that it was not just denial but also *shame* that prevented active addicts from recognizing inner states such as memories, experiences, and desires, especially if related to sexual experiences.[14] Indeed, Laura and Susan claimed that *honesty*—and particularly honesty about sex and sexuality—was essential to recovery from addiction. In this case, Laura was convinced that Lila's hard work in recovery could be derailed if she did not recognize the "truth" of her sexuality—that is, a *real she* that is sickly misrepresented by an empty and false "they."

If Laura's report lays out her dilemma, it also gives some sense of her troubling solution. Namely, the therapist resolves the grammatical ambiguity of the third-person plural pronoun by reading Lila's uttered "they" as a willful attempt to hide a real referent (line 1), a "sick secret" (line 3), and, more specifically, a referent of Lila's presumed gay shame.[15] Indeed, with the ensuing support of her supervisor, Laura made clear that although Lila had not relapsed, her unwillingness to be *open* and *honest* about her sexuality—which the plural-pronouned friend had now effectively come to represent—rendered her vulnerable to do so. Although Lila had tested negative for drug use for more than a year and was moving successfully through phases of treatment, during her individual therapy session with Lila and in a later letter Laura underscored, "As your chemical dependency counselor, I feel it is very important to remind you that 'secrets keep you sick.'"

In response to her therapist's tenacious assertions, Lila maintained that her love life was her "private business"[16] and irrelevant to her progress in recovery. According to both Lila and Laura, the individual therapy session that was normally characterized by "open" sharing had become a formidable standoff. Later in their individual session, still working to elicit a "*she*" from her client's lips, a frustrated Laura suggested to Lila that her case manager as well as the therapeutic staff at Fresh Beginnings "suspected the truth" about Lila's sexuality because of her use of the third-person plural pronoun. On the recorded voicemail of Lila's case manager, whom Laura called immediately after the meeting, Laura recounted:

1 I told her, I said: "It's important for you to know that in all of your efforts to conceal
2 who you are involved with, you've created a great deal of attention about this
3 relationship. And I said, "And by using the plural pronoun, you've led us all to
4 assume that you were with a woman."
5 And that really freaked her out.

While expressing her shock (characterized in line 5 as a "freak-out") at such collective speculation in relation to her pronomial usage, Lila reportedly "slipped" and used the feminine pronoun, thereby confirming Laura's suspicions.

Soon after this harrowing discussion, Lila learned that Laura divulged to her case manager the contents of their therapy session, a move she interpreted as both a violation of her privacy and explicitly counter to the program's confidentiality policies as she understood them. Lila also began to suspect, rightly, that Laura had manipulated her into identifying the gender identity of her friend. One week later Lila made an appointment to tell Laura of her anger and disillusionment, which had culminated in a decision to leave the Fresh Beginnings program. At the meeting, Laura unsuccessfully attempted to dissuade Lila from transferring to a new program but purportedly secured an agreement that Lila come to group one last time to tell members of her impending departure. When Lila did not show up at the next group session, Laura sent a letter that included the following statements:

1 I'm very concerned that you chose not to come to group today as planned and say
2 good-bye to your group members. I hope that you will find the courage to be more
3 *honest* with your new therapist about what you need, more *open* about how you are
4 really feeling, and be genuine about what you are *willing* to do.
5 The only way we recover is through "Honesty, Openness and Willingness" (HOW).
6 It is now clear that this is very difficult for you. (emphasis in original)

Notably, at this point Lila can neither be accused of dishonesty regarding her drug use nor reprimanded for her failure to disclose the gender of her friend. Nevertheless, Laura continues to wield the metalanguage of HOW (line 5). Although Lila had arguably been both *honest* and *open* in expressing anger in relation to her therapist's actions, by qualifying Lila's feelings with the word "really" (line 4), Laura implies that there is something spurious in her client's angry explanations. Recall that therapists theorized anger as a false emotion and poised themselves to listen for "shame in a client's anger," as addiction specialist Potter-Efron has advised (2002:80; see chapter 3). Laboring in line with the ideology of inner reference, Laura contends that there is a still-hidden and more real feeling—one that is *inside* Lila and must be brought out in *honest*, *open*, and *willing* words if she hopes to recover.

Laura's letter also mobilizes a discourse of need (line 3), suggesting to Lila that if she is only "more honest" (lines 3–4) with her (new) therapist about her needs, the path to recovery would be far less "difficult" (line 6). Significantly the metalanguage of HOW effectively streamlines the identification of "feeling[s]" (line 4) and the articulation of "needs" directly to a therapist (line 3), as if there were no intervening variables between the two. Laura is thereby able to signify Lila's expressed lack of trust as a trait that belongs to a still unhealthy client, rather than as a predictable product of their disturbing interaction. So when Laura writes, "The only way we recover is through 'Honesty, Openness and Willingness (HOW).' It is now clear that this is very difficult for you" (lines 5–6), she discursively funnels a host of past and future interactional dynamics into a failed, unrecovered "you" (lines 1, 2, 3, 4, 6).

Laura's metalinguistic labor not only erases critical interactional dynamics but also obscures the institutional surroundings in which Lila's plural pronoun is uttered.[17] For example, conspicuously missing from Laura's various analyses is acknowledgment of Lila's expressed concern that disclosing the gender of her partner would invite the disapproval of her peers, therapists, and case managers, threaten her employment as a client-intern,[18] and damage her hard-won reputation as a senior client. We might gather, then, that Lila retrospectively frames her uttered *"they"* as an index of an institution that may not welcome the gender of her partner. And while Lila evidently shifts pronouns—perhaps strategically—in accordance with her spatiotemporal surroundings, Laura engages in a semiotic process that extracts Lila's "they" from these shifting surrounds and refixes them on the inside of Lila, so they appear purely denotational. In this way Laura labors to prevent what she identified as a *real she* from becoming a felicitous "they."

Although the therapist consistently glossed these tense negotiations in clinical terms, it is nevertheless clear that Laura and Lila became entangled in a very technical grammatical battle. Specifically, they wrestled over a class of indexical signs known as "deictics". According to Emile Benveniste, deictics are "the demonstratives, adverbs, adjectives, which organize the spatial and temporal relationships around the 'subject' taken as referent" (1971:226; see also Hanks 1993; Irvine 1996; Urban 1989). For instance, "I" and "you," as well as "here" and "now," are deictic terms as their meaning depends on the event of an utterance (as opposed to third-person pronouns, for instance). In other words, as a semiotic class, deictics have in common the feature of being defined only in relation to the instances of discourse in which they occur and therefore also rely upon the "I" who speaks. Furthermore, Benveniste (1971) distinguished third-person pronouns, which are independent of the "I" who utters them, and first- and second-person pronouns, which always depend on and "shift" according to situation in which they are uttered (also see Silverstein 1976; Urban 1989). He explained: "The third person must not [therefore] be imagined as a person suited to depersonalization . . . it is exactly the non-person, which possesses as its sign the absence of that which specifically qualifies the "I" and the "you" (1971:200) (see Table 4.1). Why is it, then, that at Fresh Beginnings the third person was imagined and evoked *precisely* as a person—and a distinctly gendered one at that?

As a structural linguist, Benveniste did not methodically consider what is very relevant to Lila and Laura's standoff, something linguistic anthropologist Michael Silverstein (1976) calls "rules of use." Rules of use are site-specific constraints imposed on an entire class of deictics, which determine what they can mean and do in a particular speech context. Along these lines, we can see that the metalinguistic principles of HOW functioned as "rules of use," which rendered what structural linguists would normally call non-indexical terms (e.g., "they") as instances of deixis (e.g., "I"). More specifically, using the metalanguage of HOW as a filter, Laura claimed that the sign "they"—a classic example of a non-deictic term—referred to, and in fact identified, the client speaker. Indeed, Lila's uttered "they" fell victim to what Silverstein (2004) calls *indexical iconic semiosis*—a process that collapses the spatiotemporal properties of signs so that they appear independent of their context and purely denotational. And, by way of this filtering process, the professional need to "bring out" information regarding clients' sexuality is effectively collapsed into Lila's apparent clinical need to "come out" as a lesbian.[19]

It is important to note that Laura did not simply abide by pre-inscribed rules of use, but also went to great lengths to explicitly outline and uphold them. More specifically, the therapist worked hard to justify, both to her client and her colleagues, why it is appropriate to read Lila's "they" as an inner referent of lesbianism and attendant shame. This suggests that

142 • Chapter 4

TABLE 4.1
Interpreting and Anchoring Deictics

	Speech Act	Reception/Analysis	Possible Lx Production
Laura	"they"	she	"I am a shameful lesbian"
Lila	"they"	friend	"My romantic life is my private business" (?)
			"You are/this place is homophobic" (?)
			"I am a lesbian"(?)
			"I am a shameful lesbian" (?)
			Request for diplomatic non-indexicality (Silverstein, 1976) for any or all of the reasons listed above

the process of indexical iconization requires the concerted metalinguistic labor of participants in a given speech event. Nevertheless, the sociological implications of these semiotic processes are especially important to underscore. For, with considerable expertise, Laura effectively deflected Lila's multiple insinuations that the program is homophobic and the program therapists are off-base, leaving the therapist and the institution insulated from her client's criticisms.

Arguably, this institutional insulation would have been difficult, if not impossible, to achieve without Laura making implicit use of the ever looming principle of denial (see chapter 3). For, by way of this principle, Laura is authorized as the one who can see the inner truths that her clients deny. And, indeed, as events unfolded and Lila became more eloquent and loquacious, Laura ensured that her disgruntled client's words would not be taken up as institutional critique, bolstering her metalinguistic labor with a damning, quasi-clinical diagnosis. In her response to the grievance filed against her, Laura wrote: "The client in question has a paranoid personality which has challenged all of her treatment team."

Lila did transfer to another program, and she continued to express regret, hurt, and surprise at the circumstances of her departure while maintaining friendships with several clients still attending the program. Several years after this incident, while working as a travel agent for a small, local company, Lila died of a heart attack. Fresh Beginnings and HFC staff suspected a drug overdose. Talk of shame quietly persisted.

Total Quality Control

Rules for Group Conduct

1. Prompt attendance to all groups and individual sessions is required.
2. There will be periodic drug screens. If the client relapses, it is her responsibility to inform the therapist and group members.
3. Confidentiality must be maintained. Any violation of confidentiality is grounds for termination. Any thing that is shared in the group room must remain in the group room and cannot be discussed during breaks or anywhere with anyone outside the group room.
4. Avoid giving advice to anyone UNLESS the person requests your suggestions.
5. Show respect to others in your group by listening without interrupting, taking responsibility for your feelings without blaming others, and making eye contact when others are speaking.

On first reading, the "Rules for Group Conduct" at Fresh Beginnings seem straightforward enough. One can immediately think of the practical rationales behind the first three, even if further reflection raises some doubts as to their utility. Rule 1 plainly states that clients should come to group on time (despite the fact that they relied upon the chronically tardy program van and overwhelmed van driver to get them there). Rule 2 asserts that clients should admit when they have relapsed (even though they would be drug-tested in any case). And Rule 3 broaches just what kind of conduct will result in client "termination"; at the same time it suggests that confessants can feel confident that their admissions will be contained by the walls of the group room as well as by the clients who speak and listen therein.

Although not as legible to laypeople, Rules 4 and 5 would be readily digestible for clients who had already been taught to talk in line with the acronym HOW. Indeed, when taken together, Rules 4 and 5 are virtual (para)linguistic recipes for acts of inner reference, dividing the copious flow of clinical communication into discrete turns of speaking and listening. More specifically, the rules propound that whereas the *speaking* client has a "responsibility" to articulate her feelings as her own, *listening* clients are to show "respect" for those feelings by refraining from advising, blaming, or otherwise interrupting,[20] and by confining their communication to eye contact.

Indicating that *linguistic* conduct was the kind of group conduct that was of the utmost concern at Fresh Beginnings, all the above rules—aside from Rule 1—are explicitly metalinguistic. Rule 2 warns clients who have relapsed to "inform the therapist and group members" in words before their body does it for them. And just after Rule 2 asks clients to "inform," Rule 3 requests the linguistic confinement of such information.

And, as noted above, Rules 4 and 5 are virtually packed with guidelines for "respectful" and "responsible" communication. Yet, although one might therefore reasonably gather that the five rules were written so as to control the actual linguistic *conduct* of group therapy, just as the heading of the list indicates, consider that Rules 3, 4, and 5 are primarily concerned with the reception rather than the production of speech.

Consider also the actual locale where the rules were posted. Typed in 14-point font on a neatly folded sheet of white office paper, the list was taped to an inside wall of the group room, between the room's single light switch and the wooden doorframe. Thus, when one entered the group room for a talk therapy session, one would naturally pass right by the posted rules without noticing them, though they could certainly be easily spotted on the way out. Why might rules for maintaining eye conduct, abstaining from interruption or advice giving, and not blaming others be advertised in a place where clients would encounter them only *after* a therapy session was over and it was too late to control their actual "group conduct"?

The reason is that the "Rules for Group Conduct" effectively functioned as a "quality control" station in the distillation process, and were therefore attuned to the *inspection, evaluation,* and *interpretation* of talk rather than the actual conduct of it. Indeed, here is where clients and therapists alike evaluated linguistic products—that is, what had *already* been said during group therapy—in line with the principles laid out in the five provisos. On their way out the door, then, the rules effectively encouraged participants to contemplate specific questions: Was eye contact maintained? Was the speaker interrupted? Was advice or blame rendered? They were then expected to evaluate what had been said accordingly. For, if such distracting social indexes could be accounted for, a client's speech act could be packaged as an *honest, open,* and *willing* act of inner reference. A closer look at one of the rules illustrates this point.

Confidence and Confidants

Rules of confidentiality are common in clinical practice, and it is not difficult to appreciate their practical merits. And, unlike the other four rules, it appears to make perfect sense that Rule 3, which is explicitly concerned with confidentiality, was posted so that clients could see it on their way *out* of rather than into the group room. After all, it seems obvious that the point is not to direct who actually says what to whom while group is in progress but instead to control and confine what has already been said to the immediate context of speaking. Indeed, by insisting that things "shared in the group room must remain in the group room" (lines 2–3, below), which is backed by a clear warning (lines 1–2, below), Rule 3 seems intent on constraining how far and by which routes clients' words could travel.

1   Confidentiality must be maintained. Any violation of confidentiality is
2   grounds for termination. Any thing that is shared in the group room must
3   remain in the group room and cannot be discussed during breaks or
4   anywhere with anyone outside the group room.

However, as I came to learn alongside clients, Rule 3 had less to do with directing what clients *actually* said to whom after group was over. Instead, it helped control the *interpretation* of what had been said *during group* as unaffected by the speaker's musings about where her words would travel and who exactly might hear them in the future. After all, if a speaker could be retrospectively cast as unconcerned with who may eventually be party to her words—whether friends and family members or parole officers and child welfare workers—what she said during group could be evaluated as so many signs of inner states rather than as indexes of current or future quagmires, and strategic attempts to negotiate, persuade, or cajole accordingly.

Consider another framing of confidentiality in the document "Rights and Responsibilities," which was distributed to all incoming clients. Here it becomes clear that drawing a stark boundary between the "safe" inside of group therapy (line 3, below) and its implicitly dangerous outskirts (line 1) was intended not only to hinder the flow of talk but to produce quality linguistic products that would be read as such by others. The document reads:

1   It is not permissible to discuss with anyone OUTSIDE of the group room,
2   including your significant other and the person who originally shared the
3   information that is shared by others in group. You need to feel safe that you can
4   control when and how you share sensitive feelings and issues, and know that
5   others will respect that outside of the group room.

First, the responsible reader of "Rights and Responsibilities" might be struck by the insinuation that confidentiality at Fresh Beginnings was not simply a matter of insulating clients' words from uncontrollable forces OUTSIDE the group therapy room walls. More specifically, the reader may wonder why it is that group members who are actually there with the "person who originally shared the information" are not permitted to continue their conversation outside the group room (see lines 2–3).[21]

Reading on, it becomes clear that rules of confidentiality function not only, nor even primarily, to control the flow of confidential information between people but instead to analytically wrap the client speaker in a nest-like security. Indeed, addressing the reader with an intimate deictic term, the document relays that "you need to feel safe that you can control when and how you share your sensitive feelings and issues" (lines 3–4). Such statements, especially when codified, imply that it was perfectly *safe* to speak about inner states. And if a particular speech act did not follow suit, listeners could assume that there was nothing wrong with the conditions of production and presume instead that the linguistic product was itself of inferior or defective quality.

Consumer Reports

When clients first read Fresh Beginnings' rules of confidentiality, they appreciated them as institutional efforts to protect their privacy. For as Yolanda and Lila both clearly indicated, they were not eager to share their "business" unless they could be certain of the terms of trade. All clients were well aware of how fast their business could travel in the urban area, where many of them had lived their whole lives. Some Fresh Beginnings clients had close if delicate relationships with family members, and feared those relationships would suffer if mothers, brothers, husbands, sisters, or cousins caught wind of how they were represented on Cliff Street. Many clients sustained close ties with drug-using circles of friends and family while in treatment, and felt similarly threatened by the idea that their attempts to get sober might be overheard. So if not for the initial assurance rendered by the "Rights and Responsibilities" document, and the regular reassurance given by the rules posted near the group room doorway, they may not have spoken in group therapy at all.

But, over time, many veteran clients came to believe that rules of confidentiality did not actually control how the talk of group therapy sessions traveled but worked, instead, to convince them that their words were "safe" when they really were not. Consider how former Fresh Beginnings clients Mabel and Yvette talked about confidentiality on Cliff Street.

1 M: People come up in there and when you say somethin',
2   it can go outta there, because *it* happen.
3   People done *came* in there and went *back* and *told* things that was *said* about
4   *other* people.
5   Because I have said somethin' there, and *one* person in the group went back
6   and *told* somebody and they came and told *me*.
7 Y: Um, I had I never had that experience. But that is *always* a thought in the
8   back of mind, [and] that kept me from sharin', you know.
9 M: And I knew there wadn't no way they could have *knew* cause they was not
10   *not there.* You know, if I could change anything, I would change that!

Mabel describes the busy coming (lines 1, 3) and going (lines 2, 3, 5) of people who carry "things that was *said*" (line 3) to and from the Fresh Beginnings group room, disregarding the posted rules near the doorway. Whereas Mabel recounts the circular path in which words actually traveled, Yvette suggests that this knowledge alone was enough to preempt her from *sharing* at all (line 8), thereby confirming the fears of her therapists, who wrote the "Rights and Responsibilities" document to persuade clients otherwise. So eventually, loquacious clients, like Mabel, began to reevaluate the relative wisdom of their peers, like Yvette, who rarely spoke at all.

Although Mabel and Yvette seem to target undersocialized clients as the less than cautious carriers of their words, it was, in fact, their seasoned therapists who most frequently extracted words from the group room and injected them into the broader world of talk. In fact, therapists were not only exempt from rules of confidentiality, but they were also expected and indeed bound to share some of what clients said because of their "duty-to-report"—the legal mandate requiring social workers and certain other professionals to report any suspicion of perpetrated child abuse or neglect to the state. Therefore clients frequently had to reckon with the fact that their *honest, open*, and *willing* disclosures could depart quite radically from the presumably "safe" confines of group and land in decidedly punitive places.

Many former Fresh Beginnings clients remember one particular incident with much consternation, often citing it in their critical assessments of the program. The incident centrally involved a widely respected client named Monique who, during a Tuesday morning parenting group, recounted in some detail her recent frustrations with her ill-behaving ten-year-old son. Following the therapeutic injunction that she speak with *honesty, openness*, and *willingness*, and apparently feeling "safe" that her words would be held in confidence given the written documentation to this effect, Monique described various attempts to control the ten year old using prescribed parenting skills and her mounting frustration at their seeming ineffectiveness. Monique, rather nonchalantly, added that she eventually doled out a "good, old-fashioned, whuppin'" when all else had failed. According to clients' reports, the parenting group continued, as therapists offered alternative endings to the family struggle in cognitive-behavioral terms and clients offered words of sympathy and support.

When clients met again the next day for their regularly scheduled group, they were flabbergasted as Laura, flanked by the program's family therapists, announced their decision to report Monique to Child Protective Services presumably based on the narrative she told the day before.[22] In interviews conducted months after the event, clients' astonishment had hardly abated. At issue was not only that therapists had construed the reported "whuppin'" as "child abuse" but, moreover, that they had reported it accordingly. For example, Keisha recalled,

1 K: It was like, *why* did it go out—and she actually *wrote*, wrote her up and
2   reported it, I think, to Protective Services.
3 I: Yeah.

4   K: Yeah, and it had really, we were like *wow*, you know, it kind of made it
5   kind of made it feel like, *dang*, you know, we can't *share* (laughter)
6   some things because we don't want to go to *jail* just for sharing things that we
7   thought we were just honestly speaking on.
8   I: Hmm.
9   K: We were kind of like, "*Dang!* We can't even *trust* her now."
10   But she felt she was doin' her *job*.

Notice Keisha's appeal to the metalinguistic principles that she, like Monique, had been socialized so intensively to speak in accordance with. As she critically traces how what "was honestly [spoken] on" (line 7) "go[es] out" of the group in the form of a damning written report (lines 1–2), Keisha does not question the quality of Monique's narrative nor the language ideology that underscored it. Instead she focuses on how Monique's "honest words" are reinscribed and reported by the once trusted therapist, with the most frightening consequences at stake (line 6). And though what seems an ironic therapeutic violation (notice Keisha's laughter on line 5) is finally acknowledged to be an institutional requirement of the therapist's *job* (line 10), this consumer report blames not the linguistic product itself, which she clearly evaluates as "honest." Keisha instead highlights the unsafe institutional conditions of its production and the dangerous by-products of therapists' metalinguistic labor.

Conclusions: Distilling the Distillers

Fresh Beginnings professionals were well aware of clients' negative reactions to the reports therapists made to state authorities. They collectively mulled both whether they should make a report, and how to relay that they did so to the client involved. Therapists also knew that they would have to brace themselves for the predictable fallout: exhausting weeks of clients' concerted silence, an anathema to their daily exercises in inventory and inner reference.

Significantly, when Laura discussed the hazards of what Keisha called "just doin her *job*," she appealed to the very same therapeutic rationale that her client's critique calls into question. She even dared to directly reference the metalinguistic principle of *honesty* at the very same time she cited the loaded politics of treatment and power imbalances between her and her clients. Laura said:

1   L: There's a lot of class oppression with homeless women and a *real* sense of
2   powerlessness and hopelessness in relation to people in positions of authority.
3   I: Umhm.
4   L: And anybody who's in the role of *therapist* when folks *have* to come to therapy
5   I: Right.

```
 6  L:  is an authority. And so there's a lot of fear and concern about: "Where does
 7      this information go and what are you gonna do with this information?
 8      Am I gonna get in trouble if I tell the truth?" and all of that kind of stuff.
 9  I:  Ok.
10  L:  And so we often times had to talk about what role honesty plays.
11      And that if you want to get better and you want to grow and you want to
12      recover, you have to be honest. To be dishonest in group is not helpful to you.
13      It is not therapeutic and its not gonna serve you.
```

While at first Laura, like Keisha, acknowledges the dangerous by-products of *honest*, *open*, and *willing* talk (lines 6–9), which render verbal disclosure a point of "fear and concern" (line 6) for her clients, by the end of her account these contingencies have all but disappeared. Despite "class oppression, homelessness, and a *real* sense of powerlessness and hopelessness in the face of authority" (lines 1–2), the practical concerns of Laura's orchestrated chorus of wary clients are subsumed into a familiar clinical discourse of honesty and recovery. Directly in line with the ideology of inner reference, the only context of talk that is recognized by the end of Laura's account is a more or less honest client "*you*" (lines 11, 12, 13).

Given that Laura recognizes the serious stakes of her metalinguistic labor, how do we account for her adamant, and some might say *extreme*, dedication to producing *honest* talk? Part of the answer was revealed in chapter 1, where we learned that Fresh Beginnings therapists had signed on to serve an institutional mission that was "commit[ed] to achieving lasting sobriety and self-sufficiency." And in chapter 3 we saw that Fresh Beginnings therapists believed—in line with decades of clinical literature—that the best way to "achieve lasting sobriety" was to elicit sober speech. Given that sober speech was taken as evidence of sober speakers, it also served as evidence of therapists' efficacy and expertise. And, finally, in the previous chapter, we learned of therapists' conviction that their clients would eventually die from their addictions, an idea also supported by clinical literature. It was their care for clients, as well as their hope that they could rescue them, that fueled what can otherwise be read as cold and simple dogmatism.

In this chapter, by focusing on therapists' metalinguistic labor, still other ways of understanding therapists' perspective emerge, in part by showing that if Laura and Susan are addiction specialists, they are hardly entrepreneurs. Indeed, the therapeutic staff at Fresh Beginnings did not dream up the rules of group conduct on their own. Similar rules surely adorn the walls of drug treatment programs all over the United States, and I suspect they function quite similarly. Nor did the therapists on Cliff Street draw that cartoon rollercoaster, even if they had hand-edited the commentary in line with their immediate institutional and clinical concerns. In fact, approximately eighteen hundred copies of *How to Sabo-*

tage Your Treatment, the film with which the cartoon booklet was first released, have been sold since its original release in 1983 (Gerald T Rogers, personal communication, July 31, 2009). And, as students or consumers of addiction treatment know well, the letters HOW have been scrawled across many dry-erase boards and repeated as warnings, prompts, or reminders to countless clients of addiction treatment. So, although we might be tempted to see the incidents detailed in this chapter as an indication that Laura, Susan, and Ella were badly trained or behaved therapists, we must remember that there are thousands of American therapists who have engaged in this kind of metalinguistic work. They do so in an effort to distill clean, healthy, and sober talk—which can, in turn, be taken as evidence of clean, healthy, and sober speakers—and to fulfill their professional charge.

However, this chapter also suggests that we need to look much further than the field of addiction treatment if we want to understand why Fresh Beginnings therapists worked the way they did. For the language laboriously produced in the Fresh Beginnings therapy room is also quintessentially American. Indeed, those who labored on Cliff Street shared ideological assumptions about language long before they walked through a door, which was adorned on one side with a caricatured rendering of how not to speak and, on the other, a set of provisos for evaluating pure and sober speech. This chapter has argued that Laura and Susan were not only charged with upholding and transmitting ideals and standards of healthy language, which were shared and lauded broadly in the society in which they worked and lived. Therapists' work also involved distilling the purest form of what is widely considered an already natural product: referential signs of inner states. And therefore therapists worked to fulfill a cultural as well as a specific clinical and institutional charge as they labored at each station of the distillation process.

If this chapter elucidates why therapists worked the way they did, it leaves open the question of what to make of clients' collaboration. For as we have seen, clients labored alongside their therapists, demonstrating dedication to *honest*, *open*, and *willing* talk. However, clients were also sometimes openly critical of both the process and product of therapeutic talk in a way that therapists certainly were not. The next two chapters address how we can account for the variation of people's awareness about the language they speak, and their specific ability to manipulate social expectations about the structure and function of linguistic forms. And, in traveling from the Cliff Street therapy room to the Fresh Beginnings boardroom—as we do in the following chapter—we will learn that this variation has less to do with the nature of the signs and speech in question and more to do with the way speakers are institutionally positioned and expected to speak accordingly.

CHAPTER FIVE

Therapeutic Scenes on an Administrative Stage

Introduction: Representational Practices and
   Institutional Politics

According to Bruno Latour, contemporary politics has been strangled by a pernicious entanglement of two meanings of the term "representation": representation as the gathering of legitimate political actors and representation as the accurate portrayal of an object of interest.[1] He writes, "For too long, objects have been wrongly portrayed as matters-of-fact. This is unfair to them, unfair to science, unfair to objectivity, unfair to experience" (Latour and Weibel 2005:19). The alternative, he posits, is a form of democratic gathering in which interested assertions, rather than putatively transparent facts, are the currency of political exchange.

In advocating a revision of *Realpolitik* as *Dingpolitik* (or, a politics devoted to things),[2] Latour challenges the dominant notion that politics is primarily a matter of the people who represent—both as those who gather and those who portray—and proposes a politics that is, instead, centered on "matters of concern," along with all their "complicated entanglements" (Latour and Weibel 2005:41). Rather than gathering under passionless "domes of rationality" and "properly speaking parliaments" in which seemingly petty, self-interested rhetoric eventually finds its rational way to the representation of Truth (ibid.), Latour suggests that representation-as-gathering should take place along fault lines that expose difference and cultivate its expression.

The study of Fresh Beginnings highlights the difficulties of realizing a politics premised on generative places rather than preformed people and predictable interests. Focusing on the Fresh Beginnings boardroom as a political forum as well as a central institutional site, I suggest that ways of speaking—particularly modes of representation—tenaciously adhere to "types" of speakers rather than defining specific institutional events or venues. For, as we will see, the ideal of inner reference informed how Fresh Beginnings clients were viewed as actors, as speakers, and, most specifically, as *representatives* well outside the therapy room. Specifically, I unpack program administrators' rationales for resisting the idea of client representation on the advisory board despite their $3 million promise to involve clients in "program design and development" (per their grant application to HUD in 1995). I also trace how explicit efforts to exclude clients from the board gave way to practices that delimited what client representatives could legitimately say and do there. Indeed, this chapter tells the story of how the dynamic arts of rhetoric are practiced and refined at one institutional site largely by managing ideas about who can faithfully represent what.

In this sense, my analysis follows the lead of scholars who note the way that women, and especially women of color, are commonly regarded as "truth tellers" and thereby figuratively stripped of political complexity (i.e., Alcoff 1991; Gal 1991; Haaken 1998; Mohanty 1992; Scott 1991; Spivak 1988). More specifically, these scholars have effectively critiqued popular and scholarly exaltations of women's "voices" as revelation rather than mediation of embodied experience, a warning that resonates well with the central lessons of linguistic anthropology (see, esp., Gal 1991; Inoue 2006; McElhinny 1995). The interesting twist at Fresh Beginnings is that clients—most of whom were women of color—were considered to be *failed* truth tellers by virtue of their addiction; their treatment was thereby devoted to repairing their ability to reference (or represent) inner truths. And although the tethering of people's words to the reference of the inner can always be politically problematic (see chapter 4; Carr 2006), here, I emphasize the costs and gains of holding some people to a language that must accurately refer in order to effectively represent and allowing others to forge new realities with their representations.[3]

As we will see, the boardroom was governed by very different norms of speaking than those characterizing the therapy room. Though board members' linguistic exchanges were certainly directed and policed, requiring their own metalinguistic labors, the rules of speaking posted on the therapy room wall (see chapter 4) clearly did not apply. Interruptions were frequent, eye contact was sporadic, words were spoken primarily to persuade rather than to refer, and seldom was a board member asked to "own" her feelings when her tone sounded angry or inappropriately dispassionate.

In fact, a highly performative way of speaking—replete with euphemism, metaphor, and other context-creating talk—characterized administrative practice at Fresh Beginnings (cf. Silverstein 1996: 93). For instance, board members negotiated internal and external demands for "consumer participation" by creatively employing the highly resonant political and therapeutic discourses of "empowerment" and "enablement." In forging meaningful ties between these potentially conflicting discourses, board members were less concerned with referring to how clients and staff actually interacted than they were with generating ethical and efficacious ideas about those interactions with their words—a practice I call "wordsmithing."

Board members' wordsmithing clearly reveals the peculiar exigencies of providing addiction treatment during a period of rapid welfare-state retrenchment, which arguably requires that professionals learn to speak in a new politico-therapeutic register. In considering the relationship of professional norms of speaking to those inscribed on the therapy room wall, this chapter highlights an important if understudied administrative dynamic in American social services. More generally, in focusing on wordsmithing, I highlight thorny questions about the politics of representation in contemporary American institutions.

Notably, understanding the differences between therapeutic and administrative norms of speaking is not as simple as comparing relevant institutional sites—in this instance, the therapy room and the boardroom. For when clients entered the boardroom as client representatives, they continued to be held to the ideals of inner reference. With this in mind, this chapter attends to the careers of two client representatives who approached their charge very differently, and to the institutional effects of their respective modes of representation. Rhonda strikingly adhered to the rules of speaking posted in the therapy room when she visited the boardroom; the equally eloquent Louise attempted to borrow professional ways of speaking and employ an overtly political language to advocate for the clients she set out to represent. As we will see, Louise received a sore lesson in the institutional efficacy of her representational efforts: she found that the same ideology of language that framed her words in the therapy room followed her straight into the boardroom.

In following Rhonda and Louise from the therapy room to the boardroom, I seek to contribute answers to an ethnographic question of interest to cultural and linguistic anthropologists alike, that is, how do ways of speaking travel from one institutional context to another? Building on relevant linguistic anthropological work (i.e., Briggs and Bauman 1992; Collins 1996; Gal 2005; Mehan 1996; Silverstein 2005; Silverstein and Urban 1996; Spitulnik 1996; Urban 1992, 1996),[4] I bring to bear Louis Althusser's (1971) and Judith Butler's (1993, 1997) discussions of interpellation: the processes of call and response by which speaking subjects are hailed, recognized, and constituted. Specifically, I point to a process that I call *anticipatory interpellation* in which some client representatives, such as Rhonda, not only responded "like addicts" across institutional settings, but also called on powerful others to address them as such. In light of the material and symbolic rewards of this interdiscursive process, the story of the Fresh Beginnings boardroom can be read as a parable about the unexpected political gains, as well as the strategic quagmires, of speaking "like an addict."

Familiar clinical themes run through the story of the Fresh Beginnings boardroom, but its central lessons are broader ones, as readers who have participated in organizational meetings of most any sort (including faculty meetings!) will soon detect. I show, in particular, that the work of wielding institutional power and authority involves the continual forging and stratifying of institutional *identities* or kinds of actors. This is especially evident in institutions predicated on the differentiation of social actors—social workers as opposed to clients, faculty as opposed to students, corporate management as opposed to corporate employees (see Wasson 2004).[5] Rather than simply silencing or excluding actors, such institutions assign ways of speaking to the identities they forge and therefore pre-establish ways of hearing the people who come to inhabit them. And although institutional power is thereby regenerated when these "subalterns speak" (Spivak 1988), people can also inhabit such identities, and speak effectively from these designated locales, in politically efficacious ways.

Before proceeding, a brief note on the locale(s) from which *I* speak in telling the story of the Fresh Beginnings boardroom. In answering Latour's question of "[h]ow to represent . . . the sites where people meet to discuss their matters of concern?" (2005:16), this chapter suggests my own representational quandaries in relation to the "identities" I inhabited at Fresh Beginnings. Of course, I represent as an anthropologist who carefully observed and analyzed institutional dynamics over several years. However, as this chapter makes especially evident, my analytical voice stands in tension with two other voices: anthropologist-as-narrator of a dramatic administrative scene and anthropologist-as-character in this scene, and a particularly interested one at that.[6] As a former student intern, board member, and meeting minute taker, as a more or less tireless client advocate, and as attuned anthropologist now accounting for the complex ways I was implicated in the scenes represented here, I textually enact the sometimes uneasy relationships between these ways of being (and speaking). In so doing, I demonstrate my affinity with both social service professionals and clients in that we all work to anticipate how our words will be read and try to speak efficaciously from our respective institutional positions.

Just a Minute!

Over the years that I attended Fresh Beginnings advisory board meetings, the group gathered in three different settings within a ten-mile radius. Until 1998, board meetings were held at the outpatient services building of Hope Health, a mazelike office park made up of seven two-story buildings that were set off a busy suburban road, just across from the County

Circuit Courthouse. Here, five to ten board members would gather around an oblong faux wood table, settling into tan-cushioned, metal-frame chairs that offered a view of either the car-filled parking lot or a dry-erase board that frequently featured vestiges of a group therapy session held in the same room earlier in the day.

When relations between HFC and Hope Health began to sour, advisory board members convened at the WISH shelter, which was tucked in a small wooded grove just west of the courthouse building. Like all visitors to the massive shelter, arriving board members were carefully monitored—by camera and available staff—as we approached tinted glass doors to be buzzed through. WISH line staff, equipped with large key rings, led us through a series of locked doors in the interior of the building until we reached our meeting room, just off a corridor bleakly adorned with local newspaper articles about county women who had been killed by their boyfriends and husbands.

When board members from the largest HFC agency, HELPNET, complained of the thirty-minute, traffic-laden drive these meeting venues demanded, conciliatory meetings were rotated onto their main site: a grim basement room in the county services building, where refrigerators full of brown-bag lunches hummed and homemade posters from the latest "diversity training" clung to walls on strips of masking tape. Interestingly, the Fresh Beginnings advisory board meeting was never held at the treatment program facility itself, with relative lack of parking on Cliff Street being the most frequently cited rationale.[7]

In theory, advisory board meetings were to be led by Marne, director of HFC, and were to involve the director of each HFC agency, the clinical supervisors from Hope Health, and all therapeutic staff at Fresh Beginnings. In practice, board meetings were attended by an ever rotating collection of agency case and shelter managers who served as emissaries for their frequently overwhelmed bosses. Although one could always count on Marne and Laura, the lead therapist at Fresh Beginnings, to attend the meeting, the board mutated as the demands of members' jobs changed or as they "burned out" or "moved on," leaving HFC altogether. Regardless of these exigencies, Fresh Beginnings advisory board meetings commonly brought together social service professionals of varying institutional rank, from a variety of affiliated agencies, and with disparate, and sometimes conflicting, orientations toward social service provision. Program administrators and clinical supervisors sat beside case managers and therapists. Those involved in the daily operations of the program discussed program policy with those who rarely, if ever, directly interacted with Fresh Beginnings clients. And on the rare occasion when the ponytail-sporting director of the grassroots Carroll Street Shelter had enough time to attend the advisory board meeting, he found himself confronted with a clinician who insisted that the residents in his shelter who smoked marijuana were prime candidates for a *DSM-IV* assessment.

I joined the board in January 1996 as a student intern working to fulfill the nine hundred hours of field experience required to earn a master's degree in social work. I was directly supervised by Marne. At that point, the Fresh Beginnings program had been in operation for a few months, and the board had met only a couple of times, with hiring and other fundamental program development tasks still at hand. (Laura, for instance, was not hired until late March 1996). One of my first charges as intern was to type up schedules for advisory board meetings, based on Marne's verbal directions, and to take "minutes" at board meetings, recording meeting procedures. This work was considered to be administrative assistance—and indeed was taken over by Marne's ever rotating program assistant beginning in May 2006. Nonetheless, Marne offered me the job of minute taker as an educational opportunity to learn about the new program, its incoming people, and its developing practices. Though I did not realize it at the time, by taking minutes I was also taking a crash course on institutional discourse dynamics, replete with intensive lessons on felicity conditions, framing, and the powers of euphemism.

As was often the case in my early months at the program, I had little idea of what I was doing in taking minutes. As a "career student," with little professional experience outside the academy, the textual genre of minutes was not at all familiar. I took my primary cue from the term itself, which dauntingly suggested that my written recording was to somehow reflect the minutest fraction of actual meeting time.[8] As minute taker, I was triply burdened by native theories of representation, as Latour describes them: I was to document (representation/transcription) when and where board members met (representation/gathering) to discuss matters of concern (representation/portrayal). And though I understood that my job was to watch, listen, and record what happened in the board meetings, I soon felt watched and recorded myself, as each subsequent board meeting began with the distribution of the minutes I had spent the week worrying over, editing, and finally printing for all board members to see.

An analysis of my earliest minutes suggests that while I took my task to be an exercise in representing speakers and their speech, I was less consciously involved in the reproduction of institutional authority. I regularly used the items listed in pre-circulated meeting agendas as topical section headers, regardless of how much discursive attention these items actually enjoyed.[9] I proceeded to summarize each board member's contributions to particular agenda items in narrative form, with "action items," decisions, and conclusions highlighted in bold font. Perhaps not surprisingly, these bolded strips of text often bore close resemblance to administrators' (rather than line staff's) contributions. Yet, as my work continued, my minutes became far more parsimonious: bullet points replaced narrative vignettes; highlighted utterances were not always associated with the people who actually uttered them; and I entirely ignored agenda items that I felt unworthy of note.

Indeed, as both a minute taker and then a careful observer of the minute takers who succeeded me, I exercised tremendous influence not just in framing past events but also in shaping the course of future ones. As board members read my renderings of previous meetings, they did not just read about the content of their previous exchanges but also learned what at least one responsible witness evaluated as more or less noteworthy. For instance, they could compare what they remembered of previous meeting exchanges against what had been officially recorded. And, notably, once recorded in the minutes, board members had little chance of editing their contributions to the collective text. Unlike the minute-processing practices of many American professionals, previous meeting minutes were not subject to formal processes of approval by those attending the board meeting, though each meeting began with a silent reading of minutes. In my more than four years of attending these board meetings, I can recall only a handful of occasions when objections to the minute takers' renderings of previous meetings were verbally registered and two in which minutes themselves were rewritten and redistributed.

Considering the rotating nature of membership, meeting minutes were also a pedagogical tool for both newcomers and sporadically attending members alike, which demonstrated not only the matters that had been discussed, but also what really mattered in what was said. And, to the extent that they could determine the minute takers' ascriptions of highlighted statements to particular individuals,[10] newcomers learned not just or even primarily who was powerful around the table; they were also afforded the opportunity to discern the more powerful ways to say things, at least when participating on the Fresh Beginnings advisory board. In this sense, meeting minutes—as textual artifacts—shared a similar function to the rules of speaking posted in the group therapy room; that is, they served as guides for speakers to anticipate how words would be heard, and as an opportunity to strategically adjust in advance.[11]

Although we should not lose sight of the power minute takers have in both rendering program history and shaping its future, we should not fall into the trap of believing that minutes—as texts—transparently reflect what minute makers are "really thinking" any more than we should take a client's soliloquy in group therapy session (or a boardroom meeting for that matter) as transparent. Instead, minutes are always somewhat self-interested renderings of interactive scenes of practice, in which the minute taker is trying to negotiate on paper what has been previously negotiated by others in real time. That is, she is always necessarily representing scenes and strategies of representation, as Latour might put it.

Indeed, one of the first lessons learned by those participating in Fresh Beginnings advisory board meetings is that whereas HFC professionals, in their daily practice, worked hard to get their clients to name their problems—in the sense of properly and accurately denoting preexisting material conditions and/or mental states—the linguistic labor of board meetings consisted of collectively deciding the language that would evoke desired behaviors, practices, and sentiments in clients, staff, and funders alike. In short, board members were skilled wordsmiths who worked primarily to improve the form and function, rather than the denotative content, of a given professional text. So if clinical assessments and group therapy sessions were linguistic lessons in inner reference, advisory board meetings were primers in *metapragmatics,* that branch of linguistic practice devoted to reflexively determining what one can do and make with words in addition to what one can say with them.

Thus, when affiliated program administrators, case managers, and therapists debated whether they should use the term "client" or "consumer," they were not working to refer most accurately to the people they treated or to how they treated them (what I call a "realist crisis"; see Table 5.1, row 1). Nor were they primarily engaged in negotiating and collectively determining who "consumers" really are and how they differ from "clients" (what I call a "nominalist crisis"; see Table 5.1, row 2). Rather, board meetings were devoted to resolving "metapragmatic crises" as participants worked to answer the open question, how do we most effectively and evocatively—rather than most accurately—frame what we do? (see Table 5.1, row 3).

Framing Frames

Thanks in part to a long legacy of philosophers of language—from Plato to Ludwig Wittgenstein and Roman Jakobson, from J. L. Austin to Emile Benveniste and Judith Butler—many scholars consider language performative, meaning they recognize that, in saying something, speakers are *doing* something as well. Austin's examples of "how to do things with words"—such as get married ("I now pronounce you man and wife") or name ships before they set sail ("I name you *Queen Elizabeth*")—have been significantly augmented as anthropologists have documented empirical cases of people reproducing or subverting social hierarchies (e.g., Hill 2007; Irvine and Gal 2000; Kulick 2003a; Rosaldo 1982), displaying features of identity (e.g., Agha 2007; Hall 1995; Silverstein 2004), and managing risk or ritualizing the everyday (e.g., Bauman 1975; Hastings 2008; Keane 1997) with their words. Importantly, Austin laid out a series

TABLE 5.1
Taxonomy of Collective (Meta)Linguistic Crises

1. REFERENT ⟶ WHAT TO NAME? (agreed upon)		= REALIST CRISES
2. NAME ⟶ WHAT IS REFERENT? (agreed upon)		= NOMINALIST CRISES
3. HOW TO FRAME WHAT WE DO?		= METAPRAGMATIC CRISES

of "felicity conditions," which, when not met, render a performance inert: one cannot be married by a monkey, for instance, and a drunkard's swinging bottle cannot christen a ship; however, Austin tended to assume that authorized speakers—across time and space—had equal opportunity to make, take, and break things with words. Linguistic anthropologists, by contrast, have been careful to point out that what one can do with words in a particular time and place is largely determined by local ideologies of language, which establish the possibilities of verbal performance from the start. The ethnographic record, therefore, can be seen as elaborating the conditions in which a particular person in a particular time and place can do something by saying something.[12]

Although philosophical and ethnographic accounts of language-as-performance differ in significant ways, many adhere to the premise that language is not simply or primarily a reflection of the world or of speakers' realities; it is also often a mode of social action that constructs and creates realities. One such creative potential is language's ability to point to (or index) certain features of the complex circumstances in which it unfolds. For instance, through citation, one can index the authoritative language of powerful others and, in so doing, potentially enact the authority of those cited (Bahktin 1984; Urban 1996). However, speakers not only act but also *act on* their (speech) acts by working to establish how their verbal performances are to be interpreted. Through metacommunicative processes, such as keying (Goffman 1974), speakers help establish interpretative frames that cue listeners as to how to understand their words (cf. Bateson 1972; Bauman 1975).

Alongside scholars of language, students of policy process have long noted that framing is an essential part of how social problems are formulated and how policy solutions are attached to them (e.g., Best 1995, 2004, 2008; Coborn 2006; Gornick and Meyer 1998; Linders 1998; Spector and Kitsuse 1987). In their verbal performances the professionals affiliated with the Fresh Beginnings program clearly devoted much attention to explicit framing activities, particularly as they worked to collectively cast clients, their problems, and the practices professionals employed to redress them. Although there was sometimes discord in regard to naming referents so as to best reflect them (i.e., realist crises; see Table 5.1, row 1) as well as some disagreement over what, in fact, constituted the referents of widely traded terms, such as "client noncompliance" or "self-sufficiency" (i.e., nominalist crises; see Table 5.1, row 2), most often board members debated how to establish authoritative interpretative frames about the nature of their work (see Table 5.1, row 3).[13] Indeed, board members knew that if they could productively and evocatively, rather than most accurately, frame what program professionals were doing by sanctioning a client, running a group, or obtaining a urine sample, they could also generate effective ideas about their program and practices.

To be sure, Fresh Beginnings board members were constantly at work anticipating how their words might be picked up by others and what their words could do, both immediately and in an imagined professional future. A conflict-ridden series of advisory board meetings, held in September of 1996, serves as a particularly illustrative case-in-point.

Leading up to the September meetings, conflicts between HFC case managers and Fresh Beginnings therapists had come to a head. The conflict revolved around a group of clients who were not showing up for therapy sessions on Cliff Street, were dodging mandatory AA meetings, and were failing drug tests to boot. Therapists framed these troubling events in the clinical terms of "enabling"—that is, the clinical idea that by ignoring or overlooking a drug user's behavior, not confined to the ingestion of drugs, family, friends and associates unwittingly encourage and implicitly support that behavior.[14] Specifically, Laura and Susan charged that case managers "enabled" clients' continued drug use by either failing to recognize the signs of active drug use or failing to impose proper "consequences" for it—such as terminating housing and other services.

Case managers brusquely responded that Fresh Beginnings therapists were overstepping their professional bounds by trying to dictate how they should do their jobs. They added that Laura and Susan—who were at the helm of a treatment program that was supposed to be "flexible" and "nontraditional" —should be willing to tolerate clients' missed sessions and even relapses. By doing so, case managers further argued that Fresh Beginnings would "empower" clients to make their own decisions about how they wanted to "work" the program. And although many case managers suggested—with significant support from HFC program administrators —that "consumers" should "choose" services within the organization so that they could eventually self-determine their fate outside of it, therapists countered that "addicts," whose very ability to make self-conscious determinations was compromised by their disease, were simply not able to make such rational choices.

By September, the basic terms of the battle were set: in sum, case managers and administrative staff charged that the Fresh Beginnings staff "disempowered" HFC clients by adhering to a myopic clinical orientation; therapists and clinical supervisors worried aloud that HFC staff naïvely "enabled" clients, fueling their life-threatening addictions. These antithetical framings were documented in the meeting minutes by HFC director Marne's administrative assistant:[15]

1 Discussion regarding empowerment vs. enablement. [Marne] questioned whether or
2 not our approach is new and innovative or traditional. It was agreed that are [sic]
3 approach is new but that we need a way of portraying that difference to the Case
4 Managers and clients.

Minute readers are first presented with a "discussion" of empowerment and enablement (line 1), concepts that are positioned on either side of a "vs."—that is, as clearly opposed terms in a discursive standoff. Although it is not initially clear how these positions are peopled, Marne (in minutes) recalibrates "empowerment" as an index of the "new and innovative" and implicitly casts "enablement" as a vestige of the "traditional" (line 2). This framing appears effective, as it swiftly wins agreement: apparently, all involved believe that "[our] approach is new" (lines 2–3).

Notably, board members' discussion, as portrayed by the minute taker, does not focus on the referent of clients and whether they are, in fact, "enabled" or "empowered." Instead, at issue here is the *framing* of the program's "approach" as more or less enabling or empowering (line 2). The interest in framing is quite explicit: board members agree that it is not that the program's "approach is not new" but that this "newness" has yet to be effectively "*portray[ed]* to Case Managers and clients" (lines 3–4, emphasis added). However, if the minute taker—along with the concurring parties she represents—suggests that recent conflicts are matters of framing rather than indexes of more fundamental differences in professional ideology, Laura proposes that Fresh Beginnings clients will not fit into this freshly reinforced "new" and "empowering" frame (lines 5–6, below). The minutes continue:

5 [Laura] stated that there is a need for the CD professional to intervene when the client
6 is unable, due to their addiction, to make viable choices and decisions.
7 [Cecelia] pointed out a need for us to develop a way to incorporate the collective views
8 and opinions of each philosophy represented by the Board, as opposed to delineation of
9 opinions. She also said that we need to work on how to talk to each other.

In the company of her fellow therapist and two clinical supervisors, Laura suggests that case managers' liberal discourse is an inappropriate frame for a program that treats people who, "due to their addiction," are unable to choose their own ends (line 6). Though this move may be read as an attempt to refocus professional debate on the referent of the (addicted)

162 • Chapter 5

client, Laura simultaneously recasts her own professional actions as the CD professional (line 5). Indeed, according to Laura, it is clients' addiction, and more particularly their diseased ability "to make viable choices and decisions" (line 6), that creates a "need" for her professional "interven[tion]" (line 5). Laura's new frame effectively envelops the previous one.

In line with my own observations, the minutes indicate that the battle of the frames continued unabated. Now, rather than reasserting the empowerment frame, Cecelia, the administrative representative from WISH, frames Laura's frame. More specifically, she characterizes Laura's comment as an instance of unproductive "delineation of opinions" (lines 8–9), suggesting that the board's linguistic task was to "work on how to talk to each other" (line 9). The minutes continue in this metacommunicative vein, until one of Laura's clinical supervisors, Angie, intervenes, quadrupling the frame (lines 14–15, below):

10 It was agreed that there is a need to open dialog between Case Managers and Therapists.
11 The October Case mgr. luncheon will focus on [Fresh Beginnings] with an
12 emphasis on where have we been, what have we learned, what can we do better,
13 how is the [Fresh Beginnings] program different, and how is Case Mgr. approach
14 different. [Angie] to look for a survey to give the Case Mgrs. to indicate their attitudes
15 regarding chemical use, poverty and homelessness.

Here, we appear to have indirect reference to the ongoing conflict between case managers and therapists, conflict that Laura is accused of perpetuating in the boardroom. An upcoming, monthly "luncheon" is accordingly portrayed as a pedagogical exercise in "open dialog," directed along the lines of a "different" institutional future (lines 11–14).

Yet though these notes begin with a reference to the institutional "need to open dialog" (line 10), they end with a clinical promise to "survey" case managers' "attitudes" (line 14–15), thanks to Angie's contribution. In other words, the clinical team reasserts the original framing of professional actions as instances of enablement—not despite, but indeed precisely in light of board members' efforts to cast their clinical framings as ideological and narrow. Sighting an opportunity, Laura exploits her clinical supervisor's framing, making a suggestion that most board members (even, perhaps, the minute taker) considered highly offensive:

16 Discussion regarding drug screens for employees. [Laura] stressed that they
17 shouldn't be viewed as disciplinary only, but as helpful and health conscious.

Though clearly an index of case managers' putatively suspicious "attitudes" (line 14), Laura glosses her suggestion that HFC employees be drug-tested not in specifically clinical terms, but rather in a more general professional language of health and healing (line 17). And skillfully, at least as the minutes represent her, Laura desists from the role-specific terms that have characterized the conversation to that point, using the umbrella term "employees" as she suggests that all should be screened not only for their attitudes about drugs but also their actual use of them.

Although frustrated HFC case managers took Laura's suggestion that her colleagues be drug-tested as yet another sign of her clinical dogmatism, here let us consider it as a predictable consequence of a furious battle of frames. As the portrayed board meeting discussion indicates, these battles are fought not to destroy but instead to *colonize* frames that came before them. Indeed, consider the visual representation of the meeting minutes in Figure 5.1.

Remember that this battle of the frames begins with common recognition of the same phenomena: clients were not showing up for group therapy, were refusing to attend AA meetings, and were seemingly failing drug tests more than usual. If therapists cast these happenings as signs that clients were "enabled," case managers insisted, instead, that they

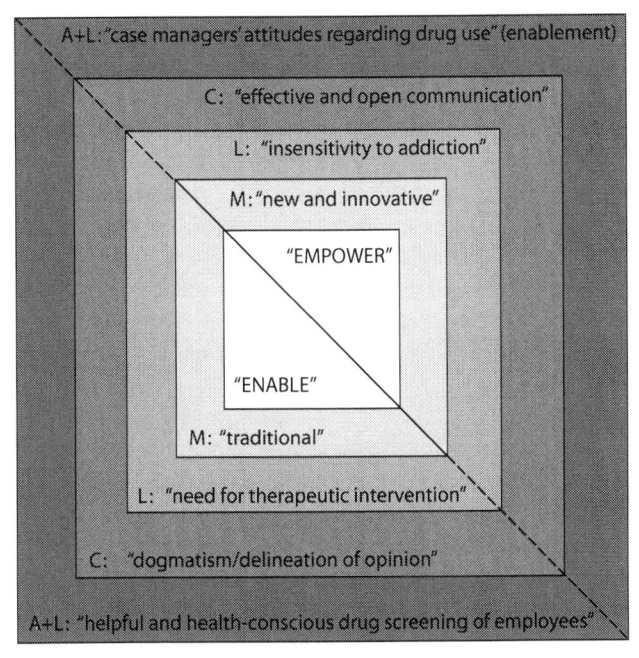

A+L: "case managers' attitudes regarding drug use" (enablement)
C: "effective and open communication"
L: "insensitivity to addiction"
M: "new and innovative"
"EMPOWER"
"ENABLE"
M: "traditional"
L: "need for therapeutic intervention"
C: "dogmatism/delineation of opinion"
A+L: "helpful and health-conscious drug screening of employees"

L: "Laura," the CD therapist   M: "Marne," HFC administrator
C: "Cecilia," WISH administrator   A: "Angie," clinical supervisor

What is bracketed by quotations is not what speakers "actually believed" or "felt," but is instead representation, or objectification, of the minute-taker as interpreted by me.

Figure 5.1. Framing frames: The work of HFC wordsmiths

were signs of being "empowered" (innermost square in Figure 5.1). Meeting minutes indicate that the board meeting began with Marne reframing the fundamental debate in administrative terms, subsuming Laura's "enable" as "traditional" and the case managers' "empower" as "new and innovative" (M in Figure 5.1). In doing so, she recalibrates framings of direct practice as indications of more or less desirable forms of organizational practice while maintaining the bifurcated terms of the debate. Interestingly, Laura responds by *subsuming* Marne's administrative reframing with newly reinforced therapeutic terms: it is precisely such administrative remove that accounts for clinical insensitivity and necessitates Laura's need to govern the day to day practice of the program (L in Figure 5.1). Laura's response is itself colonized again, this time by Cecelia's suggestion that Laura's (re)frame is an instance of poor communication skills and dogmatism, the grist of the very conflict that plagues the program and, potentially, the advisory board meeting itself (C in Figure 5.1). Finally, Angie and Laura collaborate to wrap their original frame around the entire discussion: they return to the case managers' "enablement" and go on to imply that their insensitivity to addiction is fed by "out-of-touch" service administration rather than philosophical differences among line staff (A+L in Figure 5.1).

Of course, drug screens for employees were never instituted, and certainly would not have been at Laura's request. Nor do I believe that this was the goal of her contributions; indeed, she was far more interested in reviving her frame of enablement, now that her colleagues had given her "evidence" of its propriety, thanks to their "insensitive" administration-oriented framings. And although this recorded interaction, and the many board meetings like it, may be correctly understood as a battle of frames, it is important to note the respect the opponents afford to the frames that came before, which they work to control and rework, rather than eliminate.

Indeed, board members knew that for HFC to be successful, they would have to collaborate in building frames since larger discursive battles would need to be collectively waged. To be sure, Fresh Beginnings board members were constantly at work thinking about how their verbal representations would be understood and processed by others—what their words would do within an imagined set of future constraints in addition to the immediate ones. After all, these social service professionals rightly felt themselves on the horizon of a rapidly dwindling welfare state, which would leave them with increasingly fewer resources with which to fulfill their professional charge. In light of these dynamics, they were especially beholden to their primary funder, HUD—a federal agency that itself had done much to cast devolution and retrenchment in the euphemistic terms of "empowerment," "consumerism," and "self-help." It was by way of such critical relationships that board members, as a collective, were endowed with a potentially powerful, if constraining, vocabulary.

THE WORK OF WORDSMITHS

In the early years of Fresh Beginnings, talk of "empowerment" was rampant in U.S. social work. The term served as a particularly potent keyword to describe a wide array of professional practices and ideas that, although often hazily defined, nonetheless held great appeal for scholars and practitioners alike. Rereadings of Paulo Freire's classic text *The Pedagogy of the Oppressed* (1970) and attention to the feminist tradition of consciousness raising inspired a generation of social work scholars, who then held tenure-track positions, to produce scores of publications proposing theories of empowerment (e.g., Breton 1989, 1994; Evans 1992; Gutierrez 1994; Gutierrez et al. 1998; Kieffer 1984; Rappaport 1984; Solomon 1976; Staples 1990) and delineated attendant practice prescriptions (e.g., Burstow 1991; Cohen 1994; Gutierrez 1990; Gutierrez, Delois, and GlenMaye 1995; Mullender and Ward 1991; Parsons 1991; Sohng 1998).[16] Some of this new work was revisionist in spirit, recommending empowerment as an antidote to what had been identified as the "paternalism" of social work. For example, some claimed that empowerment could temper the myopic psychologism of prevention and intervention (e.g., Rappaport 1981; Wallerstein and Bernstein 1988; Yeo 1993), democratize social work education and group work (e.g., Breton 1994; Burstow 1991; Lewis 1991), and relieve professionals of their advocacy tasks by allowing clients to "speak for themselves" (e.g., Rappaport 1995; S. Rose 1990; Rose and Black 1985). Other social work scholars asserted that empowerment defined the "social work tradition" (e.g., Simon 1994), as if the historical practices and ideologies contained therein had finally found their proper moniker.[17]

Of course, talk of empowerment was hardly limited to social work circles. In the national political arena "empowerment" enjoyed broad circulation in the 1990s. Through his urban development initiatives, President Clinton set up "empowerment zones" which offered tax and regulatory breaks for "empowered" entrepreneurs to open businesses in blighted urban zones. He even vowed in 1993 to "change the whole focus of our poverty programs from entitlement to empowerment" (Zippay 1995:263) directly before dealing a crushing blow to the federal welfare state. Empowerment talk was by no means limited to the Clinton administration: the neoconservatives of the 1980s and 1990s were among the most vocal proponents of "personal empowerment" (Zippay 1995:263), an appealing dressing for their agenda of radical government downsizing.

As Barbara Cruikshank has observed, since the late 1980s U.S. politicians "have equated 'empowerment' with the privatization of public services and with market solutions to the problems of urban poverty and racism" (1999:68).

Notably, empowerment talk was especially prevalent at HUD—Fresh Beginnings' funding agency—thanks to the legacy of Housing Secretary Jack Kemp, who led the federal agency between 1989 and 1993. Arguably the lead architect of the empowerment zones later implemented by Clinton, Kemp established Homeownership and Opportunity for People Everywhere (HOPE), a downsizing project that sold public housing units to tenants in the name of citizen "empowerment." The HFC administrators who wrote the grant proposals to HUD artfully responded not just by using the language of "empowerment" and "self-sufficiency" but by promising to establish mechanisms by which the homeless drug users they served would participate in the development and governance of the treatment program itself.[18]

Cruikshank notes that empowerment projects are characterized by an ironic mandate: people should govern themselves through voluntary participation in community-level associations and programs—a striking realization of governmentality that has gained Michel Foucault the status of particularly prescient seer. In fact, recent decades have witnessed the transformation of the very terms of citizenship as applicable to those who are not only able but are also willing to govern themselves. Take, for instance, the widely cited 1984 piece "Citizen Empowerment: A Development Perspective," by social work scholar and practitioner Charles Kieffer, who employs a developmental psychological schema to describe the process of "citizen empowerment" (see also Bernstein et al. 1994; Kaminski et al. 2000).[19] Empowerment, claims Kieffer, is the product of a linear development from an apolitical "infancy" to civic "adulthood" (1984:18).[20] Focusing on the "participatory competencies" of citizen-adults, the author further suggests that the fundamental empowering transformation is the transition from a sense of self as a helpless victim to an acceptance of one's self as an assertive and efficacious citizen.

Given that empowerment is a discourse that seems to perfectly bridge neoliberal ideas about economic and psychological health (Cruikshank 1999; Rose 1990, 1996), there is arguably nothing surprising about its allure among contemporary clinicians and politicians alike. However, a closer look at how people use the language of empowerment in their everyday practice, in precisely the kind of program that Nikolas Rose and Cruikshank critically target, reveals that the individual psyche empowered by institutional noninterference may not be the ideological goal of social workers operating in a rapidly shrinking welfare state. Rather, with an acute awareness of the high stakes of their labor—not the least of which is helping those they perceive to be in dire need—social service professionals use the highly resonant terms of empowerment discourse to appeal to powerful parties, such as private and public funders, who can help them to help others.

Fresh Beginnings affiliates did not simply parrot a neoliberal lexicon to appeal to powerful policy audiences. "Empowerment" was also a frame that helped them manage the everyday ethical and practical challenges of program administration. For instance, for Fresh Beginnings professionals, "empowerment" was not so much an inherited way to denote their own practices and principles as it was a creative way to frame their multifarious interactions with and relationships to clients, without whom their collective expertise could hardly be imagined. A May 1997 board meeting serves as a particularly illustrative example.

"Empower," "Coerce," or "Externally Motivate"

It all began when Fresh Beginnings' lead therapist Laura took charge of revising the program's treatment contract, a document handed to every incoming client and requiring the client's signature. The contract delineated a long list of behavioral expectations that each client-signatory was to heed, including abstaining from drug use, attending daily therapy groups, and providing urine samples on demand. The terms of the contract were substantially undergirded by the requirement that all Fresh Beginnings clients attend daily treatment and follow program rules if they were to keep their housing or shelter, child care vouchers, legal counsel, and other services that affiliated programs provided. Still, feeling the existing treatment contract was "vague" and "uninformative," therapist Laura took on the work of revising the document, securing fellow board members' agreement to review her proposed revisions prior to the May meeting in question. At the meeting itself board members placed copies of Laura's draft—many of which were freshly adorned with prolifically applied red ink—on the boardroom table. Soon it became clear that a particular passage in the draft document was a focus of concern. It read:

1 Experience has demonstrated that clients coerced into treatment tend to be more
2 successful than those who volunteer, and it is [Fresh Beginnings'] experience that
3 most clients were coerced into treatment. With treatment providers working closely
4 with case managers from referring agencies, [Fresh Beginnings] can successfully
5 optimize the value of coercion when a client is still in denial and suffering from
6 impaired judgment and other symptoms of chemical dependency.

In the draft treatment contract, Laura sets up an explicit opposition between "coerced" clients and those who "volunteer" (lines 1–2), placing

Fresh Beginnings clients squarely in the former category. In so doing, she sketches out a clinically informed economy of agency in which her clients' ability to reasonably act is "impaired [by denial] and other symptoms of chemical dependency" (lines 5–6). At the same time, Laura offers a decidedly potent portrait of social work expertise: Treatment providers and case managers, if "working closely" (line 3), can "optimize the value of coercion" (line 5) and thereby compensate for the putative agentive weaknesses of their clients. Indeed, according to this account, whereas clients passively "den[y]" and "suffer" (line 5), professionals collectively and actively "work" (line 3) and "successfully optimize" (lines 4–5).

Although Laura presents professional coercion as a "value" that, when optimized, would help guarantee the success of clients and professionals alike (line 5), at the May meeting in question, not all were in agreement with her drafted passage. At the board meeting, a barely detectable squirm seemed to travel around the crowded boardroom table as Marne listed off "review treatment contracts" while she read aloud the meeting's agenda. Before the word "contracts" had fully escaped Marne's lips, Cecelia, an outspoken representative from WISH, quickly and dramatically interjected, "We do not *coerce* our clients, we *empower* them." She proceeded to distribute photocopies of the dictionary definition of "coerce," transcribed by her hand:

1 Coerce—surround, to restrain and to confine by force esp. by *legal* authority.
2 Curb, to force or compel, as by threats to do something, to bring about by force—
3 enforce. Coercion—the act or *power* of coercing, *government* by force.

Aided by her dictionary definition, and the logic articulated therein, Cecelia effectively re-keyed Laura's use of the term "coerce" from a transparent reference to what Fresh Beginnings professionals may actually do in practice into a term with an array of semantic equivalents that are dangerously evocative. Specifically, Cecelia suggested that if the program can be characterized as "coercing" clients, then it may also be found guilty of "restrain[ing]," "confin[ing] by force," "curb[ing]," "forc[ing]," and "compel[ling] as by threats to doing something" (lines 1–2). Reading her definitions aloud, with clear tonal emphasis on the words *"legal"* (line 1), *"power"* (line 3), and *"government"* (line 3), prosodic gestures made all the more dramatic by her pauses and penetrating gazes directed at those gathered round the table, Cecelia essentially called for a metapragmatic audit: Do we really want to frame what we actually do at Fresh Beginnings in the language of coercion?

As witness to what initially seemed the start of an ideological battle between the service provision philosophies represented on the Fresh Beginnings advisory board, I was surprised when Cecelia's seemingly feminist orientations, born of her domestic violence work, and the discourse of denial and addiction, wielded by clinical staff, found speedy rhetorical resolution. Namely, Cecelia augmented her lexical lesson by reiterating the program's inscribed ideals of "flexibility," "individualization of services," and "consumer empowerment"; Laura and other clinical staff present enthusiastically indicated their dedication to these goals while maintaining that addicted clients—particularly in the early stages of treatment—need strict rules, threatened sanctions, and authoritative guidance. No one objected. With heads soon bobbing in unison around the table, Marne, who always worked hard to generate accord in advisory board meetings, plainly noted, "[The] problem [here] is bald terms, not concepts"—a comment captured and transcribed by the minute taker.

Minute readers thereby learned that it is not necessarily the *idea* of coercion to which Cecelia, with her feminist-inflected professionalism, objects. Nor were there competing ideologies of the client, who all agree needs "external motivation," whether that is cast as a technology of "empowerment" or as one of "coercion." Indeed, board members, representing a number of agencies with explicitly different approaches to service provision, readily agreed that their mutual client is one that can benefit from their external "motivations."

Furthermore, Marne's casting of the boardroom crisis as revolving around the "baldness" of specific terms rather than the legitimacy of collective "concepts" suggests the importance of *wordsmithing*—the practice of textual stylization in which skilled practitioners (wordsmiths) work to improve the form, rather than the content, of a given text.[21] Significantly, the solution was neither to reform the practices and policies that Laura referred to as "coercive"—such as linking clients' shelter and housing services to their participation in treatment—nor to distract the attention of those signing the treatment contract. Instead, the wordsmithing board members found a way to verbally finesse their (coercive-empowering) practices in an efficacious way. Tellingly, the minutes from the May meeting read, "[Cecelia] had a problem with the word 'coerced' in the document. It was agreed that the word would be replaced by 'externally motivated.'"

"External motivation," less hampered by the troubling associations of the "bald" term of "coercion," serves as a poetic alternative to what board members had provisionally agreed was a treatment necessity (i.e., coercion). One might hazard that "external motivation" also served as a euphemism for professional power,[22] which allowed Fresh Beginnings board members to see power as inspired in, rather than exercised over, clients. However, professional practitioners do not just frame their work so as to answer the question, "How do we best think about what we do?" but also must anticipate how their frames will be picked up by others. As wordsmiths, board members expected their words, especially when inscribed, to have social lives over which they had limited control. They therefore used a powerful vocabulary of empowerment and motivation, which was not of their own making, to direct the trajectories of their words within institutional networks of current and future funders, clients, bosses, and other potential readers.[23]

Remember that advisory board members' highly instrumental approach to language was quite different from the metalinguistics that characterized the practice of therapy at Fresh Beginnings. Whereas professionals were at liberty to employ a language that selectively pointed to and framed institutional practices, clients were trained in a therapeutic regimen of inner reference. Quite unlike the wordsmithing practices described above, this regimen allowed clients' words only two possibilities in relation to a singular property: denying or referring to the truth. That is to say, linguistic agency—or what was possible to do with words—was differentially constrained by the organizational identities that people were assigned and inhabited (cf. Kockelman 2007; Silverstein 2004). This held true across the institutional spaces in which clients and professionals spoke, as I demonstrate below.

From Client to Consumer: Discourses and Practices of Participation

```
1  [Cecelia] was also concerned about inviting clients to join the board.
2  Some of her concerns were that during the first couple of years of treatment the
3  client is self-focused. Clients would expect immediate change and would not be
4  able to get that at this meeting. And [clients would expect] that anyone who had
5  completed phase 4 would be invited. A question was asked why would a consumer
6  want to be on the board? The answer was that part of the recovery program is
7  giving back to the community. It enables them to gain personal growth by allowing
8  them to help others who are coming from where they came from. The decision was
9  made that women who had completed phase 4 and had 1 1/2 years of recovery would
10 be considered for the board.
```
Fresh Beginnings Advisory Board Meeting Minutes, May 12, 1997

Cecelia not only "had a problem with the word 'coerced'" in that May 1997 meeting but she also seemed to harbor serious concerns about sitting beside "externally motivated" clients at board meetings. If it seems surprising that the dictionary-toting champion of "empowerment" was also a staunch opponent of clients' efforts to establish a representative position on the advisory board, consider the fact that she was not alone.

Indeed, the minute-by-minute transformation of "the [self-focused] client" (line 3) into "a consumer" (line 5) who "giv[es] back to the community" (line 7) indexes an ongoing struggle over just how Fresh Beginnings clients could and would participate in program development and governance. As we will see, it was in a therapeutic vocabulary of addiction and recovery (lines 2–3, 6), self-focus and personal growth (lines 3, 7), and instant gratification versus self-help (lines 3, 7–8) that the battle lines were drawn. And, it was only by way of these terms that clients eventually found their way into the Fresh Beginnings boardroom.

The saga began when Marne asked me to read the two successful funding applications to HUD soon after I arrived as an eager program intern in January 1996. Aside from orienting me to the brand new Fresh Beginnings program, Marne explained, the grants could serve as a checklist—a way to compare what was promised by grant writers with what the program had actually implemented. Recall that Marne, herself a recently hired employee, had the unforgiving job of coordinating the newly forged Homeless Family Consortium; she was also charged with assuring that HFC's three jointly administered programs, including Fresh Beginnings, were running smoothly, which they almost never were. In my curiosity about organizational practice and program development, Marne found some of the help she desperately needed to identify what the original "vision" of the Fresh Beginnings program was, orient a diverse staff in relation to it, and begin to develop programming accordingly.

As I worked to decipher the unfamiliar lexicon of federal grant applications, I was struck by two themes, which I later came to understand as interrelated. First, scattered throughout the more than one hundred pages of grant narrative, which included letters from over a dozen local programs and agencies promising matching funds, HFC clients were referred to as "consumers." Though the consortium's client base was diverse in many regards, I knew that all clients were homeless and that the receipt of housing and support services required them to follow various staff directives, including, in some cases, mandatory drug treatment. Though I had frequently heard the term "consumer" uttered, both in my MSW classrooms and among HFC staff,[24] it was only upon seeing the word in print that I understood what would long be, for me, a riddle: Why were the clearly non-voluntary terms of receiving Fresh Beginnings services framed in the free market language of "consumerism?"

Though one might expect that "consumers" were portrayed in the grant as those who exercised "choice" among the resources and services provided by HFC agencies, the HFC "consumer" was instead figured as engaged in another kind of action: "consumer *participation*."[25] Indeed, I repeatedly encountered passages that contained clear promises that the Fresh Beginnings program would, in fact, be uniquely characterized by "the active participation of consumers in helping to design the specifics of the model," backed by historical evidence that "all of the programs in the [Consortium] have operated historically with a strong commitment to consumer participation and shared responsibility for program success. All have some mechanism to promote this." And though over the next few months, the advisory board hired therapists, established policies, launched an on-site child care program, designed a highly complex transportation system, and ushered a set of clients into their "second phase" of a newly designed treatment model, I was witness to no discussion of how "to bring consumers and their perspectives directly into the design process," as the grant expressed it. Intrigued, and yet unaware of my powers as minute taker, I felt I had found my first substantive task as a neophyte social worker.

In April 1996, with Marne's hesitant blessings, I took up "consumer participation" as both my charge and, later, as something of a cause, lobbying for the institutional changes I believed would facilitate clients' involvement in program governance. My goal was to include clients, alongside professionals, on the advisory board where I myself had been involved in program development activities for several months. Although armed with grant language, my first soft-pedaled proposal for client representation on the advisory board was swiftly and unanimously ruled out by fellow board members; in fact, it does not even show up in the minutes, a task that had by then been taken over by Marne's newly hired administrative assistant. However, outside the boardroom, Marne indicated her concern to me (and perhaps to others) that HUD, to whom she had to make annual reports, would hold her accountable for "consumer participation" as a principle of practice. Within weeks of my proposal to the board, Marne hatched the idea for a Client Advisory Committee and charged me with the task of serving as its facilitator and liaison. My new job, she explained, would consist of meeting with the clients once a month, eliciting "feedback" on programmatic issues (as narrowly defined by the board), and then translating this back to the board while maintaining clients' confidentiality.

Convening the first Client Advisory Committee in June 1996 was the first time I had laid eyes on a Fresh Beginnings client since arriving at the program in January of that year—an indication of just how much clients "participated" in administrative practice (and, for that matter, how much administrators "participated" in the daily life of the treatment program). Though I have documented my work as the group's facilitator and liaison elsewhere (see Carr 2004), including my involvement in the committee's successful efforts to open and operate a secondhand clothes shop in the program's basement, suffice it to say that I never considered the committee an adequate answer to the grant's demand for "consumer participation." At the time, I believed that my work in carrying information back and forth between committees simply cemented the institutional divide between clients and professionals, along with their respective ability to influence the course of the young program's future. In the meantime, after months of negotiating with the board from a distance as they worked on the Clothes Closet project, several clients indicated a developing interest in who, exactly, was making the programmatic decisions and how they could gain access to them. And while the majority of clients had no interest in joining the board themselves, after months of sending messages back and forth through an increasingly harrowed intern, clients began to talk more and more about the merits of instituting a client representative.

Feeling bolstered by signs of client interest, I broached the idea of a client representative again at the first November board meeting. Thinking I could poach some of the language for my "cause," I strategically timed my request in line with a planned discussion of "phase 4"—the final stage of treatment measured by consecutive months of sobriety and compliance with program directives, and characterized by a "shift to having client take responsibility for treatment" (meeting minutes, November 14, 1996). Attempting to link "responsibility for treatment" to "participation in programming," the minutes document my direct question: "Should a client be allowed to sit on the board?" According to the minute taker, Cecelia swiftly dismissed the idea of clients joining the board as regular members, advocating instead a system of "special meetings" with clients. And although the child care coordinator, Jill, surprisingly suggested that a "committee of clients" come to these special meetings, therapist Laura interjected, reporting that all active clients are "stressed to the limit" and that program alumni are a healthier answer to the question of client representation on the board. Through a canny combination of therapeutic and administrative logic, the idea of client participation on the board was again summarily dismissed.

Rationing Participation and Rationales of Nonparticipation

In 1971 political scientist Michael Lipsky introduced the moniker "street-level bureaucrats" for the social workers, teachers, police, and other workers who shape policy mandates by implementing them. He argued that, by definition, street-level bureaucrats ration services and resources—including institutional information, empathy, and time—and thereby decide *how* policy mandates will affect *which* people (see also Brodkin 1997, 2000; Fording, Schram, and Soss 2005; Meyers, Glaser, and Donald 1998; Pavetti, Derr, and Hesketh 2003; Smith and Donovan 2003; cf. Sosin 2009). HFC board members not only rationed services, but they also rationed *participation*, determining just which consumers could participate in program governance and how. While grant writers cannily appealed to a federal office, which for a decade had promoted federal retrenchment in the name of "consumer participation" and "citizen empowerment," it was HFC's street-level bureaucrats, not HUD bureaucrats, who would ultimately determine precisely what the promised "consumer participation" would look like at Fresh Beginnings.

Over the three and a half years I studied the program, board members articulated rationales for why Fresh Beginnings clients should not participate as client representatives on the advisory board.[26] Most commonly, board members—whether clinically or administratively oriented—cited the nature of addiction and the corresponding requirements of recovery when justifying their stance. Specifically, board members claimed that recovering addicts are unequipped to arbitrate extra-personal matters as would be demanded by participation on the board. Cecelia's comment above about the "self-focused" nature of clients in their "first couple years of treatment" is indicative of this shared rationale (lines 2–3, above).[27] Cecelia was not alone in her further suggestion that drug users' demand for instant gratification carries over into the early stages of recovery, leading them to unreasonably insist on "immediate change" from the institution (lines 3–4). Finally, therapists and clinical supervisors regularly broached the precariousness of recovery and propensity for addicts to relapse; Laura's comment that Fresh Beginnings clients, in all phases of treatment, were already "stressed to the limit" is pertinent in this regard.

In a rare instance of seamless agreement, Laura's clinically oriented claims about clients' "stress" were bolstered by case management staff who also served on the board. Indeed, another rationale for nonparticipation was built around the notion that Fresh Beginnings clients have complicated, chaotic lives and many of them are already *overwhelmed* by their various responsibilities: "Program politics are pretty low on the list of concerns when you are wondering where you and your kids are going to sleep," one program director explained. Curiously absent from this explanation is the fact that HFC programs, by their very mission, served to link clients with housing, giving clients all the more practical reason to want to participate in program governance.

Another commonly wielded rationale for client nonparticipation involved the very *necessity* of a client representative on the advisory board. Early on, board members alleged that clients already had ample opportunity to represent their interests through their case managers and therapists. Board members overlooked the fact that these putative intermediaries were also clients' primary links to much needed resources and services, and that clients may be hesitant to lodge grievances with them. Furthermore, once the Client Advisory Committee was established, board members asserted that if clients were not making the best use of this indirect channel of communication, this indicated that they *lacked interest* in participating in program development at all.

However, as time went on, it became increasingly difficult to sustain the "lack of interest" rationale, as clients sent me back to the board month after month with clear signs of their interest. In Client Advisory Committee meetings, we also experimented with ways to reframe and rework the other rationales that had kept clients from participating, which I subsequently shared with the board with varying degrees of success. However, after months of tireless claims from clients and client advocate, there was evidence of headway as board members began to discuss the imagined problem of *influx*. As one board member plainly put it, "If one comes, then they will all want to come" and "things will get out of control." While previous rationales served to insulate the board from clients' presence altogether, the influx argument was used to control for that presence once it began to appear inevitable.[28] Consider these minutes from a November 1997 meeting, two months before the first client representative would make her rule-bound arrival at an advisory board meeting:

1 It was decided that if a consumer comes to the board meetings they would only be
2 there for a short time at the beginning or ending of the meeting once a month.
3 Summerson will be responsible for setting ground rules.
4 Summerson will come with the first consumer and after that the consumer who has
5 been attending meetings will come with the consumer who will take her place.
6 Only threes and fours [i.e., people in the 3rd or 4th phase of treatment] will be eligible to
7 attend meetings and graduates. People who take the job will need to attend meetings at
8 [Cliff] Street. This would be the 12th step in which they are giving back to the
9 community.

In addition to the bevy of qualifications of *when* clients should participate in board meetings as representational events—articulated above in specific synchronic terms (i.e., line 2)—board members also preemptively evoke developmental temporality to delimit who can participate and how. In honor of the aforementioned rationales, board members pronounce that only clients who are in the third or fourth phase of treatment "will be eligible to attend meetings" (lines 6–7)—a verdict that effectively narrowed the pool to two clients active in the program at that time. Board members delineate certain responsibilities and protocols for client representatives, such as attending meetings on Cliff Street, coming with me to board meetings, and following a set of "ground rules" (lines 3–4), which I am charged with setting. Finally, and perhaps most importantly, the advisory board makes record of a formal frame for client representation: not as a way to make programming more effective or responsive, decision making more democratic, or consumers more empowered by increased participation in program governance. Instead, client representation was inscribed into the program's history as "the 12th step [of A.A.] in which [client representatives] are giving back to the community" (lines 8–9).[29]

If Board members' rationales for nonparticipation were ultimately unable to keep the clients from serving as representatives on the advisory board, client representatives found that their contributions to board meetings were framed using the very same clinical rationales that professionals once used to control their access. For example, when the first client representative registered complaints about the significant administrative disarray of the program's affiliated child care center—a problem of which board members were very much aware—therapist Laura noted:

1 L: [A] lot of the clients that we work with have some ... ego defenses that are hard
2   for a lot of people to deal with, like projection, *blaaaame* and just walls of anger.
3   And when that stuff got directed at child care staff, who were *not* supervised,
4   *not* properly trained, were *not* properly supported.
5 I: Mm-mm.
6 L: And were not *paid* well. And there *were* lots of problems. There were.
7   But I use it therapeutically to talk about, "how do you *feel* when they don't
8   take care of your kids?" Ya know, "how do ya *feel* when they're late?"
9   I try always to bring it back to personal responsibility.

Although Laura acknowledges "there *were* lots of problems" (line 6) about which clients might legitimately complain, she begins and ends by attending to the psychological attributes of the people complaining. Specifically, Laura suggests that the *"blaaaame"* (line 2) that clients placed on unsupervised, untrained, unsupported, and poorly paid child care staff (lines 3–6) was a "projection" (line 2) of their own issues—an "ego defense" (line 1) and sign of an internal state rather than a legitimate, critical sign of an external one. According to Laura, clients are not really denoting child care staff when they complain about them; instead they are indexing their own less-than-responsible states of mind (line 9).

Laura is also quite explicit about how she handled clients' complaints about the administration of the child care center— that is, she "use[d them] therapeutically" (line 7) as the fodder for further investigation into clients' feelings (lines 7, 8). As Laura "bring[s] ... back" (line 9) clients' criticisms about the program toward the familiar referential terrain of how they *"feel"* (lines 7, 8) and their "personal responsibility" (line 9), she provides poignant evidence of the formidable challenges clients would face when working to represent, whether in the boardroom or in the therapy room. Although not as clearly articulated as other rationales for nonparticipation, the idea that addicts were constitutionally disinclined to speak in meaningful ways affected each and every client representative, whose complaints, critiques, and contributions were always at risk of being heard and handled as not quite representative of existing internal or external realities.

TALKING IN AND OUT OF TURN: TWO CLIENTS IN THE BOARDROOM

We are tightly packed in the Fresh Beginnings group therapy room, three to a loveseat, for a 2:00 meeting of the Client Advisory Committee. Zoe is placing frustrated phone calls to the Family Independence Agency regarding her recently curtailed food stamp allotments. Yolanda and Nikki are engaged in enthusiastic whispers, and Shelly slouches, pale and half-asleep, after a harrowing night with her ex, who has just been released from prison. Mabel tells me of the latest debacle with her teenage "daughter," who is, technically, her granddaughter. Others dig in worn-out purses or fill out various forms with borrowed pens.[30]

We are tacitly waiting for the arrival of Mattie, the senior client representative who, for six months, has run the Client Advisory Committee meetings. More recently she had also begun to make bimonthly, twenty-minute trips with Shelly, the junior representative, and me to advisory board meetings in her beat-up Ford. Here, often with evident trepidation, she has worked to translate the copious notes on her peers' concerns and complaints to a table of nodding professionals, mentally recording their responses to take back to "the ladies." As a program veteran, with one year clean and a gentle but firm demeanor, the twenty-six-year old Mattie seems much more comfortable with her command of the Client Advisory Committee, where she has artfully garnered her peers' attention and interest in programmatic matters, than she does at the Board meetings, where she says little and squirms a lot.

As the first (and only) successful graduate of the program, Mattie is seen on Cliff Street much less often these days. During our chats on the telephone, she has assured me that she is still interested in serving as senior representative. But Mattie has only attended one of the weekly Client Advisory Committee meetings in the six weeks since her graduation party, and, when I call, a recorded voice tells me that her phone has been disconnected. In her absence, clients exchange information on the porch in clouds of cigarette smoke and February fog: Mattie has lost her new job at Pick 'n' Pay; Mattie is doing "just fine;" Mattie isn't getting phone calls because the "asshole" moved back in. And, of course, there is the seminal accusation attached to anyone who has not been seen in over a week: Mattie has "gone back out"—that is, resumed regular drug use.

Yet now—while we silently hope for Mattie to come through the door of the group room, gently insist that we "hush up," and coax conversation toward constructive criticism of program administration—there is no such speculative talk. And as the minutes tick by, counting off Mattie's continued absence, inquisitive and exasperated eyes settle on me, as if to say, "What do we do *now*?" I am at a loss. Our committee notebook, in which Mattie has scrupulously recorded meeting minutes, has been languishing in the corner bureau drawer beneath a stack of pamphlets on crack cocaine, codependency, and HIV testing. Shelly, the junior representative, is ill equipped to take notes: she can barely read, let alone write. Furthermore, Shelly has never shown the senior representative's inclination or talent for the group facilitation demanded by the task at hand. Deflecting eye contact, I refuse to retrieve the notebook or run the meeting myself, still desperately clinging to the principle of self-representation that, as a social work intern, I have come to know as "empowerment." We wait some more.

Breaking away from her whispering confidant, Yolanda relieves the growing silence: "You all waitin' for Mattie? Well, she ain't gonna come." Delivered with the definitiveness we have all been awaiting, even if with some trepidation, Yolanda's comment inspires discussion as we wonder what to do next. Zoe, normally a stringent nonparticipant in our committee meetings, announces with characteristic sarcasm, "looks like its time to find someone *else*." Indeed, although Mattie had been elected as the program's first client representative by a unanimous "vote" of her admiring peers, there was, quite frankly, no competition. Although the Client Advisory Committee had fought long and hard to establish client representatives on the advisory board, few were eager, interested, or willing to serve in this role once the board had conceded to it. And when, with foresight, clients had decided to establish a rotating "train-the trainer" model with "senior representatives" passing skills and knowledge to "junior representatives," Shelly beat out only one other volunteer.

As I mentally compose an impromptu pep talk, premised on our short but inspiring history of "client action" in the program—including our recent success in convincing a hesitant advisory board to establish a client representative position in the first place—an enthusiastic voice chimes in: "I'll do it." It is Rhonda. Some wary glances are exchanged of which the broadly smiling Rhonda seems wholly unaware. Rhonda has never been particularly active in the Client Advisory Committee, nor does she seem to have the skills necessary for the job she has just nabbed. Noticeably, outside the circle of friendships that other clients have developed, Rhonda has also recently been quietly implicated in the petty thefts of purses from the client-operated Clothes Closet in the basement of Cliff Street. Perhaps we have misjudged her, I think, as I watch the enthusiastic Rhonda pull out her black date book and ask for the next advisory board meeting date as well as my phone number. Then, without explanation, Rhonda gathers her things and exits the room, leaving the client advisory group, for which she is now responsible, in a not-so-stunned silence.

Less than one week later, the afternoon of the advisory board meeting arrives. Rhonda, whom I have plied with information about board members, dynamics between participating agencies, and general meeting procedures, follows me through traffic-jammed streets in her brand new, forest green SUV. As we enter the building and then the meeting room, I am surprised at Rhonda's placid demeanor, which stands in striking contrast to that of Shelly and Mattie, who both refused to take off their winter coats during their first board meetings. As board members arrive, they notice Rhonda's presence immediately, welcome her, and take seats around a makeshift conglomerate of institutional folding tables. Freshly copied meeting agendas soon arrive with fresh-faced Marne, who warns of a busy two hours, scans the room to tally absentees, and exchanges a hearty hello for Rhonda's inquisitive gaze.

In acknowledgment of the new "board member," Marne calls for a round of self-introductions before taking a seat on the less populated side of the tables. Straightening up a bit in their chairs, board members haltingly comply, fiddling with pens and paperclips as Marne sets the stage with her own introduction. In classic institutional fashion, the others around the table take turns identifying themselves in terms of their organizational role and function, with friendly smiles but little personal embellishment: "Hi, I'm Polly Barth and I am the shelter manager at HELPNET"; "Charles Rankin, clinical supervisor. I make sure all clients' needs are being met from a clinical point of view"; "I'm Letitia, I'm the HFC administrative assistant. I help Marne out." Although others look on, likely with varying degrees of critical assessment, each board member explicitly directs his or her introduction to Rhonda, the only new face at the table. She nods and returns smiles until the circling discourse makes its way to her seat. Now, it is Rhonda's turn to identify herself.

Without hesitation and with seemingly unimpeachable confidence, the newest board member announces, "Hi, my name is Rhonda, and I am a recovering crack addict." As in an Alcoholics Anonymous pair structure, her professional audience responds with a semi-synchronized but vigorous, "Hi Rhonda" and continue their introductory round.

Confession and Critique

Rhonda's boardroom debut clearly indicates that, at Fresh Beginnings, therapeutic talk was not limited to the confines of the group room or to the interactions between therapist and client. Much to my initial surprise, Rhonda carries a prototypical Alcoholics Anonymous prologue from the group therapy room to the boardroom, announcing herself as a recovering addict as readily as those in her audience of professionals introduce themselves in terms of their institutional roles and functions.

How might one explain Rhonda's boardroom confession—that is, her acts of inner reference on the highly performative boardroom stage? One possibility is that Rhonda has adopted the very same addict identity that she puts into words. Like psychic baggage, her identity as a "recovering crack addict" is carried from the therapy room to the boardroom and simply released into words. Certainly, this explanation would be favored by Rhonda's therapists, who not only worked to help clients forge cross-contextual identities as recovering addicts but also taught a way of using language that indexes inner states regardless of the contextual features of speech events. Rhonda's confession, they might therefore assume, is not just a sign of her success in recovery but also an indication that their metalinguistic labor has not gone to waste.

If it is true that Rhonda's introduction is a transparent reflection of an inner state, radically insulated from the contingencies of context, one would expect her to introduce herself as an addict across other speech events, or at least those events in which introductions are elicited or expected. However, in the course of my fieldwork, I observed Rhonda introduce herself simply as "Rhonda" to incoming clients, clients' kin, and new staff members. I even have a record of Rhonda introducing herself—as part of a formal introductory "round" quite like the one in the boardroom—during a client focus group run by a cadre of program evaluators and making no mention of crack, addiction, or recovery. So, if Rhonda has adopted something like an "addict identity," she is highly sensitive to context—including intra-institutional contexts—when indentifying herself accordingly.

In trying to understand Rhonda's boardroom confession, we might also consider Foucault's (1978, 1988, 1993, 1999a, 1999b) famous inquiry into confession as a "ritual of discourse" key to the making of the modern subject. His work has been indispensable in understanding how confession wields power in the desire to know and speak innermost truths. Along Foucaultian lines, one might suggest that, through her boardroom confession, Rhonda is expressing not inner truth per se but instead a form of institutional power that has manifested as self-knowledge. So, whereas board members might readily respond to Rhonda's representation of herself as a recovering addict (i.e., "Hi Rhonda"), they have no need to explicitly elicit it: Rhonda confesses in the boardroom because she has been "disciplined" to do so in the therapy room. Like his teacher, Louis Althusser, Foucault explains confession by way of a theory of subjectivity, in which "the subject acts insofar as he is acted by the [. . .] system" (Althusser 1971:170).

Althusser's discussion of interpellation, that process of hailing by which individuals are transformed into subjects, also offers a seductive way to analyze Rhonda's boardroom confession. Most apparently, Rhonda both recognizes and responds to the genre of "the introduction"—continuing a round initiated by Marne and perpetuated by each party gathered around the table. And although Rhonda's self-introduction may seem strikingly at odds with those of her fellow board members, she actually follows in perfect suit; after all, it is precisely Rhonda's institutional role to function as and speak from the position of a "recovering crack addict." Recall, too, that Fresh Beginnings professionals have devoted much work to assuring that clients' role on the board is to inhabit this very position. This may partially explain how readily those gathered around the boardroom table respond "Hi Rhonda" to her words, almost as if on cue. Although Rhonda seems to volunteer herself as an addict in introducing herself as one, she is simply responding to a subject position and a possibility for recognition that is already well established.

However, there is a formal precision to Rhonda's performance as client representative that necessitates a finer-grained account than, arguably, is offered by the lines of analysis reviewed above. Significantly, as Rhonda made several successful requests from her professional audience at the two board meetings she attended, she entirely eschewed the pronoun *we* in favor of a clinically elaborated *I*. More specifically, Rhonda faithfully abided by her therapists' political pedagogy, articulated by Laura above: She carefully couched her requests in "feeling statements" and enacted "personal responsibility" by refusing to *"blaaaame"* others for the substantial problems in the program. Notably Rhonda also adhered to the rules for speaking posted in the therapy room while visiting the boardroom—never interrupting or interjecting (Rule 5) and providing opinions only when asked (Rule 4), for instance—although her fellow board members almost never followed suit.

As an observer of what I had yet to recognize as a form of political representation, I was particularly impressed when, on her way with me to her second board meeting, Rhonda declared, with marked bravado, that she would be leaving the meeting having secured promises of respite child care.[22] As a mother of several small children, Rhonda had a clear individual interest in doing so. However, the understaffing of the child care center and, more generally, the decaying quality of services for children was also the subject of her fellow clients' most pressing complaint. At the Client Advisory Committee meetings, they plied Rhonda with troubling anecdotes and trenchant critiques of the center as well as with their concerns that new state welfare provisions would require them to seek work after hours, necessitating respite care for their children. Some agitatedly coached a seemingly placid Rhonda on just what to say when she reached the boardroom. There were suggestions for speaking that indexed the terms of institutional contract (i.e., "you tell 'em, this here is not what they *promised* when they signed us up for this shit"). Others advocated for a more descriptive approach, a detailing of the day-to-day problems at the center keyed either as a "report from the trenches" respectfully delivered to commanders-in-chief or as an implicit critique of administrators' remove from and ignorance of their own program's failings.

Rhonda's representation of the problems at the child care center nonetheless took quite another form at the boardroom table, one that adhered to a strikingly familiar institutional logic: "I just feel like respite child care would really *help me* not to feel so overwhelmed, you know, 'cause *as an addict*, you know, that is dangerous, you know, to feel so *overwhelmed*." Board members were thereby treated to their own rationales for resisting client representation, now articulated by the client representative and as an implicit threat. If Rhonda was slated to speak like an addict, she did so as a properly recovering one, reminding her professional audience that she was ready to translate their institutional failures into personal ones. And, notably, Rhonda's boardroom performances of inner reference were well received. At the time, no one knew the results of her most recent drug test, which would swiftly end her career both as client and client representative.

Admittedly, I squirmed through Rhonda's self-presentation, assuming I was witnessing confirmation rather than mobilization of board members' rationales for client nonparticipation. Yet, ultimately, I could not ignore the nodding heads and displays of empathy that greeted Rhonda, along with assurances that she would receive temporary respite child care, despite the program's struggle to replace regular line staff. In eliciting professional action and garnering program resources, Rhonda was far more successful than her predecessors or successors precisely because she faithfully represented the very terms in which she could represent. She studiously spoke in the ways that had been laid out for her and gained tangible, not to mention intangible, rewards by doing so. Rhonda's boardroom confession was an acutely anticipated response to an institutional demand, which might best be cast as *anticipatory interpellation*: she called on board members to recognize her as an addict—and therefore recognize their own categories of recognition—by introducing and presenting herself as one. In other words, she effectively hailed those who hailed her.

Clients called this practice "flipping the script," which will be explored in more detail in the following chapter. Script flippers learned to inhabit the identity of a recovering addict and strategically replicated clinically and culturally prescribed ways of speaking from that position. Although Rhonda engaged in a reproductive rather than an explicitly resistant linguistic practice when representing in the boardroom, we must not overlook the efficacy of her practice. In speaking precisely as she was expected to, she successfully worked her way through the Fresh Beginnings program, garnering an impressive cache of resources and services for herself, her family, and her peers. Clients who chose other modes of representation enjoyed little of script flippers' gains.

Representing Louise

After Rhonda "retired,"[31] program veteran Louise was elected client representative, and board members were greeted with a new style of representation—one that combined Rhonda's apparent ease in acting as a representative with her predecessors' dedication to representation in the sense of accurate depiction. From the beginning of her tenure, Louise vowed that she would employ *honest*, *open*, and *willing* talk in the boardroom as she did in the group room—thoroughly and transparently representing her peers' concerns and complaints. And, indeed, at the same time that Louise worked to faithfully transmit the content of Client Advisory Committee exchanges—which she had carefully documented in notes if not committed to memory—rather than her own "inner feelings," she was concertedly unconcerned with the context in which she spoke. A good representative, Louise explained, was faithful to the people and the ideas she represented and undeterred by the indexes of actual performances (i.e., audience, script, etc.). So, whereas Rhonda was committed to felicitous performances of inner feelings, Louise was interested in transparent representations of clients' collective opinion.

Over the months of her work as representative, I observed Louise carry clients' words to the advisory board like precious cargo, hesitant to edit clients' trenchant critiques (in either their form or content) as her predecessor dramatically had. In an interview conducted after she left the program, Louise described her approach in response to my question, "What was it like being the client representative?"

```
1  L: Now that was something I enjoyed. I enjoyed . . . getting points of view from the
2     women, taking it back to our leaders, you know, um . . . and bringing the information
3     back. You know what I'm saying? Relaying the information and, and
4     um, letting people know what the people who were using the program . . .
5  I: Okay.
6  L: I figure if we're the ones that's using the program, then we should definitely have an
7     input into how it should be run.
8  I: Right, right.
9  L: And, um, I think that the ladies enjoyed having me doing that type of thing for them
10    because I, hm! excuse me, because I made sure what they said was brought to the
```

11 table, you know. You know, and then I made sure that everybody knew what was
12 being, you know, what the *boss lady* and the boss man said, was brought back to
13 them, you know.

Louise describes an enjoyable process of playing linguistic liaison, eliciting "points of view from the women," "taking it . . . to . . . leaders," and "bringing the information back" (lines 1–3) to the therapy room. As she figuratively circles around the institution, she articulates a classically liberal philosophy of representation, which values the transparent revelation of linguistic content and distrusts elaboration (cf. Bauman and Briggs 2003). Indeed, although clients' "points of view" (line 1) are transformed into programmatic "input" (line 7) and "what the *boss lady* and the boss man said" (line 12) is rendered and returned as "information" (line 2) by virtue of her representational labor, Louise was consistently faithful to linguistic content regardless of these transformations. Note that she emphatically *"made sure"* (line 10) that the clients she represented were privy to what board members said, just as she had relayed clients' "points of view" to professionals.[32]

As Louise continued with her representational work, she seemed to enjoy the job less and less while continuing to show dedication to it. Specifically, Louise began to suspect that board members were working hard to circumvent her representational efforts.

1 L: They . . . the thing that . . . it's as if they were attempting to talk *around* me.
2 I: I see.
3 L: You know what I'm saying? It could have been just my own feeling but . . .
4   I don't think so.
5 I: Like they'd use certain *terms* or something?
6 L: Yeah, and then . . . then, you know, to think that I didn't know what the hell
7   they were talking about, you know. And then I was . . . you know, it got on my
8   nerves so much that instead of sitting quiet, I'd have to jump up like,
9   "Yeah, and . . ." you know, so that way they was like, "Oh, she *understood*."
10 Like, I'm not *sitting* here, you know what I'm saying?
11 I'm just a sweater in a chair, you know. It was not good. *Really*, not good.
12 I: Okay.
13 L: You know, so in no uncertain terms, I, well, actually in *certain* terms,
14 I had to, you know, "Hey, I know what you're saying, *okay?*" And I had to
15 do that by the raising of the hand, or "*helloooo!* I've got something to say,
16 recognize me" (waving). In other words, almost to the point of being *rude*.
17 I: Okay. Like very assertive.
18 L: Right. Exactly, because other than that it was like "she's not here."

Suspecting that board members were "attempting to talk *around*" her (line 1), Louise implies that professionals did not share her goal of transparent verbal representation. She also indicates that board members treated her as something less than a speaking subject—a "sweater in a chair" (line 11), to which she takes clear offense.[33] Proving her mettle, Louise therefore engages in a game of linguistic chase, tracking and pinning down board members' circuitous talk and establishing, "in *certain* terms" (line 13), that she "know[s] what [they]'re saying" (line 14) but will not participate in talk that performs at the expense of accurate reference. Indeed, Louise's frustrated call to board members (i.e., "*hellooooo!*") suggests a metalinguistic formulation quite consistent with her therapeutic training, one in which recognizing that "[she has] something to say" is also, fundamentally, "recogniz[ing her]" (lines 15–16). However, at the same time, Louise is seemingly forced to play along in quite a different language game: in board meetings, she infuses her representational efforts with dramatic signs of her comprehension (lines 8–9) and supplements steady words with paralinguistic markers, such as raising her hand and waving (lines 15–16).

Although Louise, in my estimation, was never "rude" to board members (line 16), as she suggests above, her words became more and more difficult for her new colleagues to ignore. More vociferous, more assertive, and less susceptible to her listeners' linguistic machinations than other client representatives, Louise attended board meetings determined to get through a long list of clients' concerns and document, in detail, board members' responses. And when the program found itself grappling with institutional crises, Louise's tenacious representations of clients' concerns and critiques clearly began to ruffle some professional feathers.

Perhaps most troubling to program administrators was Louise's insistence on garnering information about the transition between recently fired therapist, Laura, and the yet-to-be-announced appointment of a new therapist, Lizzy. After many weeks of tolerating substitute therapists on Cliff Street, Louise began to demand satisfying answers about the program's hiring plans to "bring back" to her consternated peers.

1 L: We still hadn't met the new therapist, although they kept telling us that there was
2   somebody, that "You're *going* to get a new therapist," blah-blah-blah-blah-blah-
3   blah-blah-*blah!* That's all I kept hearing. I, no, I took my job as a representative,
4   *client* representative, very seriously.
5 I: Uh-hm.
6 L: And I had been on the phone prior to [Laura] leaving to, um . . . the advisory rights
7   people and all that, trying to find out, um, *who, what and where and how,*
8   and when we were going to get our new therapist and so forth and so on.

Framing administrators' explicit, definitive promises as just more "blah-blah-blah-blah" (lines 2–3), Louise indicates that she has caught on to the logic of board members' wordsmithing. She also implies that it is board members, rather than recovering addicts, who use language in empty ways. And, in another striking role reversal, Louise initiates a familiar interrogation by quizzing the advisory rights people,[34] whom she had called for procedural advice, much as Fresh Beginnings assessors quizzed their incoming clients (lines 7–8).

In retrospect, Louise surmises that both the direction of her questions, and the role reversal they implied, got her into trouble at Fresh Beginnings. She explained:

1 L: You know, as a client yourself, you can . . . you have a better overall *picture* of
2   what it is that the clients want or need. You know what I'm saying?
3   The client representative, the client is there *every day* so, you know.
4   They, like I say, they have a better overall view of what *actually* is going on, you know.
5   Which I . . . hm-m, never mind.
6 I: What?
7 L: (laughs). I was going to say, which I think was their . . . I feel that was their whole
8   purpose is *not* to have a client representative.
9   Oh, boy, okay. I speak on *personal* terms.
10   With . . . with me, once I get comfortable in anything, I'm a talker.
11   And, um, any representative that's doing their job, I feel is going to bring to
12   those who need to know what . . . the thing they need to know.
13   And I feel that I was saying more than what they wanted to hear.

Note that Louise breaks frame in line 5, shifting gears from a "report" elicited in an interview to an implicit comment on that report, and this continues through line 9. She seems to acknowledge by way of her extensive qualifications (lines 7–9) and expressions of hesitance (line 5) that the way she figured the people she represented—as well as herself as a representative—was taken up by some as an institutional threat. After all, she suggests that it is clients, rather than therapists or administrators, who best know what clients "want [and] need" (line 2). In doing so, Louise turns an institutional logic on its head in implying the superiority of an "*every day*," experientially based knowledge that reflects "what *actually* is going on" (lines 3–4) and the "overall *picture*" (line 1).

In suggesting that she was "saying more than . . . they wanted to hear" (line 13), Louise also acknowledges that clients were expected—by board members and therapists alike—to speak only of, as well as from, their inner selves. Indeed, as both "a talker" (line 10) and one who evidently hesitates to speak on "*personal* terms" when not in the therapy room (line 9), Louise was not talking as a recovering addict should, irrespective of her explicit dedication to representation-as-accurate reference. Recall that addicts are commonly thought to suffer from a disease of insight. As a result, they inappropriately and unhealthily index the contextual features of social life, including speech events themselves, when talking about why they suffer. This logic was clearly at play in the Fresh Beginnings therapy room. The question here is why this very same logic served in the *boardroom* as a representational filter through which the words of clients were heard and understood. And although one might suggest that client representatives—whether healthily indoctrinated, powerfully disciplined, or simply duped—carried ways of speaking from the therapeutic to the administrative stage, it is notable that in defending the board against client representation in the first place, one administrative member of the board once stated, "Women [in recovery from drug addiction] tend to be externally focused and need to [be] encourage[d] to be internally focused." Thanks to the minute taker, board members could read and potentially reuse this statement in their future wordsmithing work.

So, whereas Rhonda was seen by board members as demonstrating that she was a recovering addict—and therefore that the institution was successful in its therapeutic efforts—Louise was ultimately read as failing to recover precisely because she so often explicitly relayed her "overall view of what actually [was] going on" (line 4) around her. (After all, a critical view was not the inner state to which an addict should give reference.) I differentiate Rhonda and Louise as representatives along different lines. Rhonda, as a relatively more experienced and therefore skilled client in social service agencies, anticipated how she would and could be heard and adjusted accordingly in advance.

In the end, it is hard to measure exactly how much less effective Louise's referential talk was than Rhonda's script flipping in terms of spawning institutional change or garnering specific resources. One thing is certain, however: Rhonda's strategy was much less risky. Soon after her therapist's controversial departure, Louise, who had relapsed and completed her inpatient time, returned to Cliff Street to sign the probationary contract that awaited her. While reading the contract—with the new therapist Lizzy, Lizzy's supervisor, Angie, and her case manager from WISH looking on—she was surprised to find a personalized provision that read: "#8: [client will] participate appropriately in all groups at [Fresh Beginnings]." Louise found this strange and, indeed, according to my observations and the reports of her case manager and former therapist, Louise not only acted "appropriately" in group but was considered a particularly dedicated adherent to the principles of group conduct posted on the group room wall. Saying nothing, Louise put pen to paper but was stopped by Angie, who pointedly asked if she was "sure she understood and was willing to comply with provision #8." In frustrated response, Louise held up her hand, as if to stop the interchange, rolled her eyes, and again began to affix her signature. Angie abruptly swiped the contract from underneath Louise's pen, saying something to the effect that "those gestures are exactly what we mean by 'inappropriate'—it appears you are not ready to participate again in group." Without further ado, Louise was informed that she was terminated from Fresh Beginnings and escorted out of the building and into the rain, with her stunned case manager in tow.[35]

On the phone later that night, a crying Louise poignantly asked me, "You know they didn't discharge me for rolling my eyes, right?" As a former program intern who had once encouraged Louise's political approach, and as an interested anthropologist who had witnessed it, I did not know what to say. This chapter is an attempt to answer her.

Conclusions: Language, Latour, and Louise's Losses

Although Latour's emphatic calls to jettison a politics improperly focused on people and to initiate an "object oriented" democracy is quite compelling, the study of Fresh Beginnings suggests the complexities of simply getting "back to things." All client representatives eventually found that their representations of clients' concerns about institutional matters, no matter how artfully or persuasively formulated, were taken up by board members as clinical issues. Whether "things," such as problems at the affiliated child care center, were greeted as therapeutic opportunities to cultivate the insight clients are thought to lack (e.g., "How do you *feel* when they don't take care of your kids?") or as chances to cultivate psychologically developed citizens, clients were preconfigured as types of speakers before they uttered a word in advisory board meetings. Indeed, the diverging career trajectories of Rhonda and Louise suggest the difficulties of circumventing ideologies of language—which construct people as kinds of speakers and as more or less equipped to represent—well before they engage in acts of representation.

Consider a final example. After Louise's departure, the energetic clinical consultant Diane worked to institute a new client representation system, this time without any noticeable client enthusiasm. Board meeting minutes read:

1 [Diane] wants to legitimize working within systems, and not wait until people
2 are mad. It's an empowerment issue, a way to be a responsible citizen.
3 In fact, we think the best time to teach this is when there are no 'issues,' and
4 therefore the learner is less likely to be so judgmental.

Strikingly in line with the definitions of empowerment in the scholarly literature reviewed above, Diane, and her colleagues, link empowerment with "responsible citizen[ship]" (line 2), on the one hand, and psychological development, on the other. Diane's client is not just a "citizen" (line 2) but also a "learner" who is taught to "work . . . within systems" (line 1). In this sense, Diane's political pedagogy is strikingly at odds with Laura's: Diane wants to teach clients to work within systems in a decidedly non-emotive way. Empowerment, here, is a matter of trading a person's anger for a citizen's "responsib[ility]" (line 2).

All the more striking is the consistent promotion of a kind of "empowerment" that is explicitly divorced from systematic critique or judgment (line 4). In terms directly antithetical to the kind of "object oriented" politics that Latour promotes, the advisory board (using the rare moniker *we*) envisions a form and forum of client politics that is issueless as well as passionless. More specifically, under Diane's pedagogy, clients will learn to work within systems when "there are no 'issues'" (line 3) in relation to which clients might develop angry "judgment[s]" (line 4). Instead, her lessons in empowerment aim at the (developing) psychology of the empowered "learner" (line 4) rather than at judgment-provoking "issues."

Although their wordsmithing suggests that they had much more legitimate(d) room to linguistically maneuver than clients did, professionals were also constricted and enabled by the institutional identities assigned to them, along with attendant ways of speaking. The transition from liberal to neoliberal modes of governance imposed new rhetorical as well as material demands on social service professionals, who were told that the best way to help people was to allow them to help themselves. "Self-help" entails new practices of participation and representation that are often quite at odds with practitioners' professional, institutional, and clinical goals—a conundrum they worked to resolve by their wordsmithing. If treating addiction means teaching clients to use a language that denotes inner states, and program administration is an exercise in wordsmithing, "client participation" in administrative venues, such as board meetings, put Fresh Beginnings professionals in an understandable bind. And whereas some clients got caught in this metalinguistic bind, others found ways to productively untangle it.

Louise's losses and Rhonda's gains suggest that speakers, as well as forms and forums of speech, are always already products of semiotic ideologies and that an effective politics must take this into account. As many of her peers seemed to realize in coaching and warning her, Louise's representational strategies were bound to be ineffective as long as she tried to circumvent rather than mobilize the expectation that she would speak like an addict. Although there were also risks and losses associated with the practice of flipping the script, as a representative, Rhonda demonstrates how carefully rehearsed scripts and perfectly enacted representational roles can alter scenes of political performance. After all, and as we will see in the following chapter, there are many things that skillful speakers can do with words.

CHAPTER SIX

Flipping the Script

> For the acting consciousness itself, its act needs no hero (that is a determinate person); it needs only goals and values that regulate it and determine its sense. My act-performing consciousness as such poses questions only of the following type: what for? how? is it correct or not? is it necessary or not? is it required or not? is it good or not? it never asks such questions as the following: who am I? what am I? what kind am I?
>
> M. M. Bakhtin, *Art and Answerability*

Introduction: Flipping the Script as the "Science" of Clienthood

I first heard the term "flipping the script" one summer afternoon, ten months into my formal fieldwork.[1] Nikki and Shauna were engaged in an intensive, hushed, but clearly entertaining exchange, as the rest of us quietly lounged against the cool stone steps of the porch on Cliff Street, watching people pass by. I gathered little about the conversation at the time, except that it seemed to involve an encounter one of the two women had had with a social worker (perhaps within the Homeless Family Consortium, but this was also unclear). A couple of months later I had the opportunity to interview Shauna, who was no longer a client at Fresh Beginnings. I asked her:

```
 1 I:  One time you said something and I, I wondered, I thought it meant, or had to do
 2     with . . . like, "talking the talk." You said, "flipping the script" in the treatment,
 3     like, 'cuz you haad, like, if you were
 4 S:  Oh, I did that good. Oh yeah, I had that down to a science.
 5 I:  So whadaya mean you had it down to a science? Like, how'd you do it?
 6 S:  When you've been to more than three treatment centers you learn how to say
 7     exactly what they want ta hear, ya know.
 8     And that, that's what kept me fucked up, being able to do that, ya know,
 9     bein' able to know what a person wanna hear and tell 'em exactly that.
10 I:  Mmmm.
11 S:  You forget, I'm a prostitute, that's what I do.
12 I:  Um hm
13 S:  I tell people what they wanna hear.
```

14 I: And you had to be pretty convincing about it how you said it, right?
15 S: Well, yeah. You have to um . . . kinda, it's really hard to explain you have ta . . .
16   You have to almost be a fly on the wall to understand.

Trying to give her bumbling interviewer (lines 1–3) a quick lesson on script flipping, Shauna lays out some of the basic premises of the practice. Most emphatically, she describes an anticipatory practice of telling people "what they want to hear" (lines 7, 9, 13)—much like Rhonda did at the boardroom table—and implies that this requires both analytical and rhetorical skill. Indeed, Shauna suggests that script flipping is a mimetic practice of discerning "*exactly*" (line 7) what is wanted by listeners and satisfying those desires "exactly" (line 9) in speech.

Highlighting the precision involved in script flipping, Shauna declares that she was not just "*good*" at flipping the script but "had it down to a *science*" (line 4). Interestingly, what she describes resembles an ethnographic science. Shauna explains that she "learned"—over time and across particular institutional contexts (line 6)—how to "know what a person wanna hear" (line 9) as well as how to calibrate her verbal performance accordingly. Indeed, Shauna portrays script flipping as a kind of procedural knowledge (or know-how) derived from careful and continuous attunement to one's immediate environment.

Furthermore, as Shauna implies and my research confirmed, flipping the script at Fresh Beginnings involved analyzing and responding to a set of institutional and clinical practices *as* linguistic and metalinguistic practices. More specifically, flipping the script was a matter of perfectly reproducing therapeutic scripts, in both their generic form and textual content, with one big exception—script flippers did not match their spoken words to their inner signifieds (i.e., their thoughts, feelings, and intentions) as "healthy" speakers should. Just like the prostitute who gives her body without her heart (line 11),[2] script flippers produced the language of inner reference devoid of its requisite inner referents. In this sense, script flipping is an instance of what M. M. Bakhtin (1984) has called "varidirectional double-voiced discourse," in which one's speech has a semantic intent contrary to that which one mimics (also see Lee 1997:300). As a "double-voiced" practice, script flipping both theoretically challenged and practically reproduced the semiotic ideology at play at Fresh Beginnings. After all, script flippers fluently and eloquently spoke the language of inner reference without abiding by its principles (i.e., *honesty, openness, willingness*). In short, at Fresh Beginnings, flipping the script was the *performance* of inner reference, and this chapter explores the theoretical, institutional, and clinical implications of this sort of performance.

. . .

Derived from the Latin *scribere* (to write), the word "script" can refer to various constituent features of a text such as its lexical content, the writing system employed (i.e., alphabetical, logographic), or the style of hand in which it was written (i.e., cursive as opposed to print). Yet, at Fresh Beginnings, the term "flipping the script" also indexed a general orientation toward language. Accordingly, in their elicited explanations of script flipping, clients appealed to the definition of script as a particular kind of text: one that is produced so as to be performed. In this sense, "scripts" are text artifacts that store the rules and roles of performances, so that each instance of their enactment is never original in any pure sense (cf. Bauman 1996; Jackson 2005; Silverstein and Urban 1996). And, indeed, Shauna describes a dramatic practice that is much more like learning lines appropriate to a stage (i.e., "a treatment center") and expected by an audience (i.e., clinicians) than improvising to sway, move, or surprise—as many actors do. At Fresh Beginnings, script flippers like Shauna knew that although performers can and do take various liberties with scripts, audiences commonly scrutinize such deviations carefully.

In Erving Goffman's useful terms (1981), we might say that a script is a kind of text whose *author* (the one who selects the ideas and sentiments expressed) is not the same person as its *animator* (the one who actually utters those ideas and sentiments).[3] It follows that one's verbal rendering of a script is never true or false, but rather more or less successful, faithful, or believable. Accordingly, J. L. Austin (1962) chose the term "performatives" for that class of speech acts that cannot be said to be true or false but only more or less successful (or, in Austinian terms, "felicitous"). It is perhaps for this very reason that, in the contemporary United States, the term "script" has a pejorative meaning as well. For to say that a particular strip of speech is "scripted"—take a public apology, for instance—is to indicate that it is out of line with the speaker's true thoughts or feelings or has been authored by another. In a culture in which the ideology of inner reference has been so scrupulously institutionalized, an apparently scripted speech act is commonly deemed not simply insincere but also fundamentally false. This is precisely why "performance" and "reference" are so often considered antithetical terms.

However, semiotically speaking, performative speech acts are also always referential ones and often have multiple points of reference, including their adherence to a guiding script. For instance, as Shauna explains, script flippers engage in *exact* reference and, more specifically, reference what a particular audience, whether social workers or Johns, "want to hear" (line 7, 9, 13).[4] Yet, to be sure, in flipping a script one circumvented a highly valued point of reference, and with it the therapeutic and cultural goal of matching one's words to one's inner states. At Fresh Beginnings a flipped script was not a verbal demonstration of self-knowledge—

as therapists would have it—but rather an acute, highly attuned know-how (line 9) of how one's words aligned with the desires, intentions, and motivations of those who listened. Significantly, this knowledge was accrued as clients participated in the highly recursive verbal practices of group therapy, where they learned the formal features and content of the script as well as how to perform it successfully.

Indeed, script flippers managed to perform the role of the recovering client so well that it seemed they were not performing at all, but simply referencing inner states. In other words, having determined that abstract questions such as "who am I? what am I? what kind am I?" (Bakhtin 1990:139) were grist for the verbal mill of group therapy, script flippers figured out how to answer them aloud to their therapists' satisfaction. In order to do this, clients like Shauna also had to ask themselves what they took to be more fundamental and critical questions about their own verbal performances: "what for? how? is it correct or not? is it necessary or not? is it required or not? is it good or not?" (ibid). In short, script flipping was an enactment of the act-performing consciousness—that is, a consciousness of "a life lived by performing actions at every moment of it" (ibid.:138), a consciousness freed from the charade that our acts are simple expressions of ourselves, and a consciousness that understands the act rather than the actor as the essential determinate entity (ibid.:140).

In order to answer the pragmatic questions posed by the act-performing consciousness, script flippers schooled themselves in what Gumperz (1982) calls "contextualization cues"—the communicative indexes that let people know what is going on in any given situation and how they are expected to proceed. We will see that clients like Shauna were ethnographers of language in their own right, reading and analyzing the language of their immediate cultural surroundings. Indeed, if Shauna's first lesson on script flipping is that it requires knowing how to use language to respond to social expectations rather than divulge personal inclinations, her second point is that script flipping requires a heightened—even scientific— awareness of what kind of talk is expected in particular circumstances and by specific interlocutors. In this light, Shauna gives us reason to reconsider and build on the current thinking on "metalinguistic awareness"—that is, the knowledge people have about the language they speak (e.g., Briggs 1986; Jakobson 1980; Lucy 1993; Silverstein 1985; 1993, 2001; Kroskrity 2000).

In an influential paper, Michael Silverstein notes that metalinguistic awareness is tied to certain properties of the linguistic sign. These properties include the sign's presuppositional qualities—the extent to which it presupposes the existence of what it refers to—and the relative pragmatic creativity of the sign—the extent to which it helps establish or can manipulate aspects of its context, such as the relative positioning of participants. Silverstein claims that "we can best guarantee native speaker awareness for referential, segmental, and presupposing functional forms in his or her language" (2001:400; see also Duranti 1997:201), and that the more "context-creating" a linguistic sign is, the more difficult it is for native speakers to be conscious of just what it can do. This leaves open the question of how people manage to manipulate and mobilize the pragmatic possibilities of ostensibly presupposing, referential forms—that is, "flip the script." Through an examination of script flipping, this chapter seeks to answer this question by suggesting that metalinguistic awareness has more to do with situated practice—and, more specifically, the skills one develops in one's history as a speaker in situ—than with the nature of the linguistic signs in question.

If metalinguistic awareness is not necessarily correlated with the nature of the linguistic sign, it is also not easily attributed to the personal qualities of the script flipper. I have no reason to believe that those who flipped scripts at Fresh Beginnings used drugs more heavily or frequently than their fellow clients; nor does my research suggest that they were less fond of their therapists, nor even less interested in achieving sobriety. Toward the end of the chapter, I also address to what extent—if at all—flipping the script at Fresh Beginnings can be considered a specifically African American practice. Shauna herself launches this line of analysis by indicating that anyone—presumably regardless of race—who has been to "three treatment centers" can "learn ta say exactly what they want ta hear" (lines 6–7).

Accordingly, rather than pointing to particular qualities of signs or speakers, the pages that follow attest that metalinguistic awareness is the *practiced ability to read the range of authorized, acceptable discursive possibilities within an institutionalized set of recursive linguistic practices*—in this case, the discourses of mainstream American addiction treatment. So while this chapter might highlight the impressive abilities of a few skillful script flippers, the focus remains on the contextual dynamics of the linguistic practice at Fresh Beginnings rather than the innate verbal talents of particular people.

Shauna's Science and Ethnographic Evidence

If successfully performed, it was difficult if not impossible for Fresh Beginnings therapists to tell the difference between a flipped script and a followed one. For, as Bakhtin proposes, in order to succeed, mimetic practices must re-create the mimed language as an authentic whole (1981:364); and, indeed, the clinical scripts that were flipped at Fresh Beginnings were identical, in both form and content, to those that were not. This is not to say that the therapists were unaware that scripts could be flipped—quite to the contrary. By suggesting that clients might "talk the talk" (see chapter 4), Laura and Susan indicated that they were on guard for insincere performances of inner reference.

However, the primary effect of script flipping was not to fool naïve therapists but rather to create evidentiary crises for them. After all, to flip the script was to exploit a clinical regime based on the ideology of inner reference: an ideology that evaluated clients' words as either truly or falsely revealing inner states. Whenever a language ideology is characterized by such a sincerity condition, insincerity is also possible (Searle 1969; also see Hill 2000; Irvine 1982), and considering the particular challenges of verifying inner states, the language of inner reference was particularly vulnerable to being flipped. As the discussion of urine screens below demonstrates, clients not only posed evidentiary puzzles by flipping scripts, but they also discursively managed and sometimes disabled their therapists' means of detection.

Significantly, script flipping creates evidentiary crises for anthropologists as well as therapists, who cannot ultimately verify whether a script is flipped or followed. As Nikki once demonstrated in an interview with me (see the introduction), one can flip a social science script just like one can flip a clinical one. For this reason, I cannot simply fill this chapter with clear instances of "flipped scripts" and differentiate them from "followed" ones. However, what seems a built-in methodological limitation of ethnographic interviewing may be better seen as an opportunity.[5] Indeed, when Shauna notes that flipping the script is "really hard to explain" (line 15), she lends a few more lessons on script flipping, this time of a methodological order.

First, Shauna implies that an analyst can only understand a linguistic practice if she is intimately acquainted with the context in which it unfolds—like "a fly on the wall" (line 16). In other words, she suggests that just like script flippers, I should practice reading contextualization cues and develop an awareness of the various pragmatic values of ostensibly presuppositional signs. Accordingly, as I focus below on cases identified by clients as script flipping, I do so not in confidence that I can detect which words I hear are true or false in relation to speakers' inner states. Like Shauna, I instead take comfort in the knowledge that I have learned to rigorously consider what people say in relation to a specific set of institutional and linguistic practices.

Shauna also sheds light on a second methodological issue, one that has long concerned anthropologists: the limits of informants' awareness about native cultural forms and how that awareness can be accessed. Linguistic anthropologists are particularly interested in the relationship between metalinguistic description—the use of language to describe language in the course of an interview, for instance—and metalinguistic awareness. Along these lines, note that Shauna claims, on the one hand, that she has developed an acute, even "fly-like" awareness of her linguistic surrounds and, on the other hand, that it is "really hard to explain" what she does in the abstract. In doing so, she implicitly warns against analytically conflating speakers' knowledge about their language (i.e., metalinguistic awareness) and what they can describe in the abstract during an ethnographic interview (i.e., metalinguistic description). I would go further to argue that when ethnographers do not separate out what informants *say* about their language from what those informants are *aware of*, we confine ourselves, methodologically, within the boundaries of a language ideology that takes words as signs of what speakers "really" know and think. Thus this chapter is written with an understanding that what are sometimes taken to be the limits of speakers' awareness are in fact the limits of ethnographic methodology—limits that nonetheless provide other analytic opportunities (cf. Mertz 1993).

What Shauna says less about during her lesson on script flipping is *why*, exactly, a Fresh Beginnings client would flip a therapeutic script. Perhaps she thought this was already obvious to me, even if I had not yet quite managed to manifest as a "fly on the wall" at that stage of my fieldwork. As highlighted in previous chapters, there were various practical reasons for engaging an act-performing consciousness as a client at Fresh Beginnings, all of which can be summarized as follows: to successfully flip a script was to control the evaluative dimensions of their therapists' labor so as to control the distributive ones. After all, contemporary American social work—as a multifaceted field of expertise—combines evaluation of people and problems with the distribution of goods and services, with the latter task generally hinging on the former. Whether in shelter intakes and clinical assessments (see chapter 2), in group or individual therapy (see chapters 3 and 4), or even in the boardroom (chapter 5), case managers and CD therapists alike relied both on what clients said about themselves and how they said it when undertaking their evaluative and distributive work.

This being the case, clients' linguistic interactions with therapists—even in the most seemingly intimate and personal exchanges—were commonly characterized by carefully constructed, institutionally astute, and strategic performances rather than simple acts of self-reference. Indeed, a prerequisite of script flipping was a clear recognition of how words spoken in the physical confines of the therapy room on Cliff Street were subject to a distant range of institutional interlocutors and bore a number of material consequences. Accordingly, this chapter proposes that flipping the script is a *political act* not only because practitioners engage in the value-laden work of redistributing basic goods and services, but also because they develop an acute awareness of referential speech as an efficacious mode of social action.

Practice Makes Perfect

Though clearly socialized to think and talk about their problems in accord with the ideal of inner reference (see chapters 3 and 4), clients' descriptions of therapy at Fresh Beginnings were strikingly *metapragmatic*—that subcategory of metalinguistics that pertains to what language *does* in contexts of speaking (cf. Briggs 1993; Lucy 1993; Silverstein 1991, 1993).[6] Indeed, in interviews with me about their treatment, clients commonly focused on the many things they did with words when it appeared that they were simply denoting inner states. For example, in an interview conducted several months after she was terminated from Fresh Beginnings (see chapter 5), Louise described her "one-on-one" therapy sessions with therapist Laura in the intriguing terms of "hidden agendas:"

1 I: You said something about hidden agendas? I didn't get that?
2 L: Um, you know, things in my head that I want to do that are no good for me.
3   Things that there's no way I'm gonna tell [the therapist].
4 I: Yeah.
5 L: Ah, you know, as a *user*, you think about all kinds of stuff.
6   But you don't think about the reasons *why*.
7   All you think about is "this is what I *want* to do," you know.
8   And *those*, that's hidden agendas, you know what I'm sayin'?

One might readily read Louise's comments as an indication that Laura's and Susan's metalinguistic labor has not gone to waste. First, notice where and when Louise locates referents, whether they are to be eventually spoken or continuously hidden: "things" are "in her head" (line 2), already formulated and organized in an "agenda" (line 8), and clearly prior to speech events such as encounters with interested therapists. Second, Louise suggests that, were she willing, her agendas could simply unfold into words; that is, she could relay her agenda—at least theoretically—in an unfettered, transparent, and exhaustive way. Third, Louise evokes the familiar clinical terms of denial, implying that whereas her therapists cannot readily recognize her agenda because she intentionally hides it from them, she more fundamentally lacks the ability—or insight—to read her agenda on her own. More precisely, Louise explains that, as a "*user*" (line 5), she thinks about "all kinds of stuff" (line 5) but routinely fails to "think about the reasons *why*" (line 6).

Although Louise's description of "hidden agendas" may well please her therapists, who would take it as indication that their recovering client

198 • Chapter 6

now relays in *honest*, *open*, and *willing* talk what she used to hide, Louise employs strikingly metapragmatic terms in recounting the practice of inner reference. For instance, in the reported self-talk on line 7, Louise suggests that she uses language—and specifically the phrase, "this is what I want to do"—to identify a plan of action (i.e., "an agenda") based on a want or desire. In doing so, she seems to conjure "the back of her head" as a context, a place where she uses language in an entailing—or creative—way (cf. Silverstein 1993; Voloshinov 1973). Furthermore, when engaged in individual therapy, Louise reportedly uses language strategically to keep her formulated "agenda" hidden—either through talking around it or simply not talking at all. And, unlike the way she is taught to use language to cleanly and clearly denote inner states, without reference to the contingencies of context, Louise demonstrates that she is acutely attuned to the institutional context in which she speaks, and most specifically to her therapist's authority. Indeed, in saying "there's no way I'm gonna tell" (line 3), she both theorizes her own linguistic agency (i.e., she can form, articulate, and cache agendas) and indicates the practical reasons to keep the "things in her head" well hidden, even if they are "no good" for her (line 2).

Based on my knowledge of Louise, I have reason to believe that she agreed with her therapists about what agendas were "no good" for her well before she set foot on Cliff Street. Yet, as she explains below, Fresh Beginnings' primary aim was neither to change the content of clients' agendas nor even to extract transparent representations of those agendas in language; therapists instead worked to change her and her fellow clients' ideas about how language properly functions. Louise continued:

9 L: With me going to [Fresh Beginnings], they make you realize that this is why you
10   want to do this. You know, if you know the reason *why*, then you don't have to. . .
11   you know what I'm saying? You can change your method of *thoughts*, you know?
12 I: Ok.
13 L: Yeah.
14 I: So you can't really have a hidden agenda there?
15 L: Right, you know. Because you know *why* you're doing things. You know?
16 I: Right.
17 L: And not just an *excuse*, like, "Yeah, I just *want* to," you know.
18 I: Ok.
19 L: You know *why* do you want to, you know what I'm saying?
20 I: Right. Okay. I gotcha.
21 L: Yeah.

Note that the new "method of thoughts" (line 11) Louise learns at Fresh Beginnings is a new method of thoughts *about language*. Indeed, Louise describes an analytic shift from language as a way to make and hide agendas; metalinguistically reformed, she now casts such self-talk as "an excuse" (line 17). As a dedicated student of a rigorous program whose central aim is to answer the question "Why?" (lines 9, 10, 15, 19), Louise now anchors strings of signs like "Yeah, I just *want* to" (line 17) to a set of yet undiscovered inner referents rather than to aspects of her institutional circumstances, for instance. And more than simply replacing the (meta)pragmatic use of language to make and pursue plans, the method of inner reference enervates those plans, assuring that they are never pursued in practice; Louise suggests: "If you know the reasons why, then you don't have to" (line 10).

Territories of Talk

Louise demonstrates above that although Fresh Beginnings clients commonly studied themselves through the language of inner reference, they also studied the metalinguistic terms they were trained in. And though all clients eventually learned of the socioeconomic consequences of the words they spoke in the name of health and healing, the difference between those who flipped scripts and those who followed them often came down to experience and practice. Shauna—who claimed she had been in several treatment programs from the tender age of fourteen—had considerable experience analyzing the institutional and ideological circumstances in which she spoke. By contrast, as a "first-timer" in treatment, Louise arguably struggled *within* the ideological terms of inner reference: her strategy was limited to "hiding" the "agendas" that she was clinically urged to reveal.

However, script flipping did not just require practice. More specifically it demanded *situated practice*, which allowed practitioners to both learn the script—in its generic features and textual context—and also witness more or less successful performances of it (cf. Lave and Wenger 1991). Each institutional setting, after all, afforded a new set of contextualization cues that clients had to understand if they hoped to successfully flip a script. So even highly skilled script flippers could not do their work when unfamiliar with their linguistic surrounds. This became evident to me when I interviewed Nikki, the client I regarded as the consummate script flipper, who insisted that she was actively using drugs fourteen out of the eighteen months that she attended Fresh Beginnings.[7] During the interview Nikki explained how her rhetorical skills—on which she had long relied to obscure her continued drug use—finally failed her:

1 N: They [Laura and Susan] had, didn't have a *clue*.
2   And then I, I slacked off for awhile and um . . .
3   That Protective Services thing came up, cause I went to the doctor and I was

4   pregnant with [LaShaun] at the time...
5 I: Ok.
6 N: And um, then when he was born positive, I ended up with [Child] Protective
7   Services [PS] and ... so *that's* why I stayed.
8 I: Ohhh ...
9 N: That's why I continued with [Fresh Beginnings] ...
10 'cause I had to continue with them for another six *months* in order to get
11 PS off of me, for [LaShaun] bein' positive for cocaine.
12 So I *had* to just, ya know, it's kinda like, really, more or less ...
13 I: Ok.
14 N: Uh, uh, I had to just *play it off*. I just had to play it until I couldn't do it no more.
15 And once I got um, got off, PS, I really didn't give a fuck no more.

Significantly, Nikki notes that it was hospital nurses, rather than program therapists, who finally procured evidence of her continued drug use, and not by way of her own person. LaShaun is readily read as "positive" by her doctors and nurses (line 6)—a determination that precipitated a child protective services report and another six-month stint at Fresh Beginnings (lines 9–10).[8] Nevertheless, Nikki emphasizes that although "she slacked off for awhile" (line 2), she never betrayed her thriving drug habit in her own words. Indeed, before she "went to the doctor" (line 3), Nikki claims that Fresh Beginnings therapists, who relied so heavily on clients' words, "didn't have a clue" (line 1) about her continued use of cocaine.

Of course, like hospital nurses, Fresh Beginnings therapists also regularly administered drug tests. However, as we saw in chapter 2, clients had various ways to explain away positive results. Recall the case of the assessed client who, when confronted by her case manager with a dirty urine screen, claimed that she had used her young daughter's urine, thereby buying herself time to procure "clean" evidence. Recall, too, that case managers and therapists alike acknowledged that there were many ways in which clients could manage both the process and the results of urinalysis or, in Nikki's terms, "play it off" (line 14). Yet because clients' procedural knowledge could not simply be transferred from one context to another, script flippers, like Nikki, had to retune their strategies to the particular demands of new environments and interactions, initiating an entirely new round of study.

Although Nikki still speaks with the bravado of a rhetorical expert, she makes her foible clear: relatively unfamiliar with the hospital where she gave birth, the medical professionals with whom she interacted, and their drug-testing procedures, she was unable to manage LaShaun's testing while in the hospital. Indeed, as an uninitiated patient—not to mention as a woman in labor—Nikki simply did not have the time, nor the information needed to acclimate her verbal performances to her new context.

And if there is one thing script flipping required, it was the "orientation to an immediate and urgent environment" (Silverstein 1991:399).[9] In the end Nikki describes, with what appeared to me to be some wounded pride (line 10–11), what she finally *had* to do (line 12): admit that "it's kinda like, really more or less" (line 12) that she had been using drugs, a fact that required her to attend six more months of treatment at Fresh Beginnings.

Note, however, that whereas Nikki is forced into a confessional corner at the hospital, she is quickly back on her game at Fresh Beginnings. Released into the familiar discursive territory of Fresh Beginnings, Nikki spends the next six months *"play[ing] it off"* (line 14)—creating puzzles for program therapists with her words. Now subject to increased monitoring, Nikki had to be even more convincing in her verbal performances of inner reference, a challenge she seemed to savor. And while the urine screen is a technology that uses the body as ground to check the voice, Nikki instead proposes that she used her voice to check her body:

16 I: How did you do it? Whaddya mean "play it off?"
17 N: Ya know, explain it away—talk 'em *through* it. I shifted things around
18   until they left me alone.
19 I: Oh.

To the extent that Nikki can "explain [a dirty screen] away" and "talk 'em *through* it" (line 17), she disables her therapists' systems of detection—whether the language of inner reference or the testing of urine—all the while seeming to abide by their terms. Considering that there are few discourses that enjoy a more "durable locus" (cf. de Certeau 1984) than modern scientific ones, Nikki's ability to strategically "shift" (line 17) the urine screen from its bifurcated grounds of positive/negative and true/false seems particularly noteworthy. And while urine screening seemed an "extra-discursive" element of that regimen—a bodily screen for the client voice—script flippers assured that what came from their body was always subject to their words.

As Judith Butler proposes, "bodies that matter" (1993) are not the asocial grounds upon which culture works or from which language derives. Indeed, feminist scholarship on corporeality suggests that bodies can never be separated from the discursive processes and regulatory norms that give them their meaning (e.g., Bordo 1989; Butler 1990; 1993; Grosz 1995; Hall 1995; Haraway 1991; Marcus 2002; Martin 1987; Robertson 1992, 1998). While proposing that sexed bodies, as ideals, are forcibly materialized over time, Butler argues that materialization is never complete nor does it ever gain the full compliance of its subjects (1993:2). Nikki and her colleagues show just why this is: whether throwing salt into urine or rhetorically responding to a given script (in this case, urinalysis results), people manage their bodies so that they are always in creative process and therefore never subject to acts of perfect reference.

Below, we learn more about how Nikki artfully evaded fourteen months of urine screening on Cliff Street, as well as increased monitoring after her stay at the hospital —that is, not just by manipulating chemical compositions, but also by linguistically composing her own body as an ambiguous text. Put differently, Nikki is able to "shift things around" (line 17) with her words so that her body cannot be read as "negative" or "positive" for drugs. So, on the one hand, Nikki's linguistic strategies disable therapists' discursive technologies from reading her body as "either (positive for drugs)/or (negative for drugs)" and her attendant words as "true or false." On the other hand, Nikki's script flipping also reproduces such epistemic dichotomies, continuing to use the language of inner reference and filling cups on demand.[10]

Flipping Feminism; or, Why "It's Obvious that AA Is Not Safe for Women"

Nikki and Shauna imply above that script flipping is a solo performance. And, if we hearken back to the previous chapter, it appears that Rhonda's boardroom confession was the work of a virtuoso, as she seemed intent on keeping fellow clients clueless as to how she would act on an administrative stage. However, through the course of my research at Fresh Beginnings, I learned that script flipping was sometimes more concerted.[11] And, when it came to required AA meetings, it seems that clients worked to flip the script in concert.

Since Fresh Beginnings' inception in 1995, Alcoholics Anonymous had been formally incorporated into the treatment regimen. After each Thursday afternoon therapy session on Cliff Street, the program van was supposed to transport clients to an open community meeting that was held at a large church less than three miles off site. And, although all Fresh Beginnings therapists acknowledged that the women of Fresh Beginnings had little in common with the majority of local AA attendees—predominantly white, middle-class, professional men and a smattering of their female counterparts—all clients were nonetheless encouraged to find a "sponsor," that is, a mentor within AA whose role it is to encourage sobriety and help less experienced attendees abide by program principles.[12] Significantly, therapists Susan and Laura, and Laura's successor, Lizzy, also commonly used AA as a sanction. Clients who were determined to have relapsed were signed to stringent treatment contracts requiring them to attend ninety AA or NA meetings in ninety days (known as a "90/90," as pointed out earlier) in addition to their four days-a-week at Fresh Beginnings. The stated consequences for not complying with the contract were hefty: termination from the Fresh Beginnings program and loss of ancillary services, including shelter and transitional housing.

Whether or not they were subject to these special contractual terms, many clients came to consider AA less like therapy and more like probation or punishment. Indeed, clients claimed that the Thursday afternoon AA meeting felt tedious, even intolerable, after a long week of meeting-filled days on Cliff Street. After all, there was work and housing to find, family obligations to meet, and legal and bureaucratic matters to handle—all of which was especially difficult when relying on public transportation, as most clients did. With few exceptions, clients consistently complained of having too little time and far too much to do. Thus, from the early days of the program, it was not unusual for an individual client, complaining of illness or citing a domestic emergency, to cajole an AA-bound van driver into taking her straight to her home or shelter, thereby circumventing yet another round of therapeutic talk.

When Laura and Susan first learned of these tactics, they tried to control them by requesting "rider logs" from van drivers. However, with little faith in and cooperation from the drivers—not to mention the attendant blow to therapists' expertise in having to enlist the assistance of paraprofessionals—therapists soon loosened their monitoring of clients' participation in Thursday meetings. And while both therapists continued to give "90/90s" to clients who had relapsed or who, by not showing up for therapy sessions on Cliff Street, were suspected of doing so, and though Susan still strongly encouraged clients to attend community meetings on a weekly basis, Laura subtly made it known that she was not wholly unsympathetic to her clients' attempts to avoid AA.

Laura was a longtime moderator of "Women for Sobriety" (WFS), a nonprofit, women-only corollary of AA launched in 1976. WFS's founding and development were spurred by charges that AA does not welcome female participants and is insensitive to the specific "issues" of women alcoholics (see Berenson 1993; Kaskutas 1989, 1992, 1996), ideas that Laura largely shared.[13] Laura responded to her clients' distaste for AA by initiating on-site WFS meetings for her AA-dodging clients and urged, but did not require, them to attend. In an interview with me, Laura explained the philosophy of Women for Sobriety and her rationale for instituting the on-site meetings:

```
1 L:  It's sort of like a self-help support group corollary for people who did not find
2     12-step programs that helpful. A lot of 12-step programs are not welcoming for
3     women, because it is a program that was started by middle-class, white males and,
4     there's more men in attendance than there are women, and it's not a place where a
5     lot of women feel safe talkin' about their feelings or their sexual abuse issues.
```

6 I: Uh, hmm.
7 L: And in a lot of areas, it's a place that's kinda like a meat market where
8   women are preyed upon as sex objects . . . that make it feel unsafe to open up.

Laura explains that because AA is both *for* men, with more of them in attendance (line 4), and *by* men, founded by "middle-class, white males" (line 3), it is not welcoming of women (lines 2–3), "their feelings" or "their issues" (line 5). Appealing to the tenet of linguistic safety (lines 5, 8), Laura cites two interrelated, androcentric dangers of AA. First, women are the "meat" of the AA marketplace, preyed upon as "sex objects" (lines 7–8). Second, and perhaps partially as a result, AA-attending women feel linguistically inhibited from "open[ing] up" (line 8), particularly regarding their "issues"—which here again are assumed to involve sexual abuse (line 5; see also chapter 3).

Held in the Fresh Beginnings building on Cliff Street, conducted by Laura, and involving the same clients as other therapy groups, WFS groups were much more convenient, if not more comfortable or "safer" for clients. Indeed, when I inquired in the weeks after Laura launched them, clients suggested that the weekly WFS meetings were almost indistinguishable from their other activities at Fresh Beginnings—just another round of talk. This rather agnostic acceptance of Women for Sobriety shifted dramatically, however, when Susan resigned, talk of Laura's departure loomed, and a decidedly pro-AA therapist, Lizzy, took the helm. Clients who survived the transition between therapists—with a few notable exceptions[14]—swiftly took up Laura's feminist critique of AA, adopting it with striking similitude. No longer was AA inconvenient, troublesome, or just plain "stupid, *embarrassing,* people cryin' all over themselves and telling all their *business*"—as a particularly recalcitrant client once put it. Instead, well-schooled clients began to insist that AA was started and run by men, not welcoming of women, and therefore an "unsafe" place for women to "open up," especially about sex. For instance, during an interview conducted soon after Laura left Fresh Beginnings, one client told me:

1 R: AA is for men. And it's *obvious* that you don't speak about some things
2   that you would when you're just females, you know.
3 I: Like what?
4 R: Okay. Like, when I went to, um . . . to AA one week, that one time I went,
5   it was an *all-male* group and it made me extremely nervous. And there's just some
6   things that you *won't* talk about, you know. Like your sex life, for instance.

Of course, what this client casts as "*obvious,*" that is, "AA is for men" (line 1) and there are "just some things that you *won't* talk about" (lines 5–6) around men, was also obvious to her departed therapist, as we saw above (i.e., line 5). However, notice that the client does not simply parrot

Laura's criticism of AA, but also weaves the fundamental therapeutic lessons that she learned on Cliff Street through a clearly gendered analysis of AA. Drawing implicitly on the metalinguistic tenets of HOW (*honesty, openness, willingness*) and citing her nerves (line 5), the client echoes Laura's portrayal of AA as an unsafe venue for verbal disclosure, particularly when that disclosure relates to one's sex life (line 6). Although we might suggest that this client came to this conclusion independently of her therapist, notice that she refers to "that one time" she attended an AA meeting— a scant experiential base from which to launch such a critique (line 4).

Clients also seemed to scaffold feminist critiques of AA (cf. Cain 1991). In talking with each other, they effectively pieced together the critical content of Laura's feminist script in what appeared to be their very own words. For example, in a group interview conducted as part of an independent program evaluation, two clients responded to the question of whether Fresh Beginnings was "a good program for women?" as follows:

1 A: Um (clears throat), like she said, I, I, I, I *tried*, you know, and I *still* don't feel
2   comfortable going to um, I , *most* NAs[15] anyway.
3   But I don't, don't feel comfortable talkin' around men about the personal things, I
4   just, I don't know, I like to think that it's just women there.
5 B: Right! That's the way.
6 A: Just women to talk to.
7 B: That's the way I am. When I went to AA, I could *not* sit in the *mixed*
8   group with men and, um, women, where the men sit and speak.
9   I had to be with *women*, you know.
10   'Cause I felt more un*comfor*table. *So* I know what she's sayin'.

While clients' reasoning sounds eerily familiar, we cannot find ready resolution to the question of whether they flipped or followed their therapist's feminist scripts. This was, in fact, the whole point of the practice. If allowing for the instrumental or context-creating potential of talk, we might suspect that clients poached Laura's anti-AA'isms in a wily attempt to outmaneuver their new therapist. Or, in line with the ideology of inner reference, we might suggest that clients' reports transparently reflect their actual experiences and heartfelt criticism of a "truly" misogynist AA. Of course, there are a number of other complex possibilities. For example, from a historical perspective, we might posit that clients' anti-AA consensus indexes a feminist consciousness raised during the Women for Sobriety meetings on Cliff Street. Some might aver instead that clients' anti-AA statements reflected a natural, or at least pre-institutional, yearning for an insulated, feminine therapeutic milieu.

In any case, clients' vociferous critiques of AA constituted a formidable puzzle for Laura's replacement, Lizzy, as she took the helm as the primary (and, for awhile, the sole) therapist at Fresh Beginnings. As an AA-advocate (for reasons she explains below), Lizzy promptly wrote the Thursday AA meeting back into the weekly treatment schedule and also advised clients to attend additional meetings on their own time. Like Laura and Susan, she began to dole out 90/90s to those who relapsed or broke the other conditions of their treatment contracts. (On more than one occasion, Lizzy qualified that 90/90 required clients to attend *any* drug and alcohol focused self-help group, not just AA. However, she also acknowledged that, after Laura left town, there were no local Women for Sobriety meetings for clients to attend, rendering this point moot.)

Clients collectively and loquaciously resisted all their new therapist's AA-related policies. True to feminist script, filled with compelling clinical content, and delivered with adamancy, clients' objections to AA posed a formidable conundrum: although Lizzy doubted that her clients really believed that they could not "open up" in AA meetings, especially for the gender-based reasons they cited, she nevertheless had no proof to the contrary. In an interview with me, several months into her tenure at Fresh Beginnings and seemingly exhausted by clients' protests, Lizzy retrospectively staked out the terms of her response:

1 L: And the way that I feel about AA is that AA has been more successful than
2   *any other treatment ever* for alcoholics, *including women* (sarcastic tone).
3   And for me to not recommend AA is un*ethical*.
4   Because it is the best treatment ever.
5   The best treatment is AA combined with treatment. (pause)
6   Research has proven this over and over.
7   And it is oriented towards *men*, but that's what we have and I think sucks too,
8   you know, um, but [it has] the highest rate of success.
9   And the reason you'll hate it is 'cause people are telling, you know,
10   pouring out their *guts* and that's *weird*.
11 I: Uh-huh.
12 L: We don't do that, I mean, in this society people just don't go up and say:
13   "My name is [Lizzy] and I am an alcoholic and I beat up my wife and I . . .
14   It's very peculiar.
15   Now what happens is that lot of women grab onto the idea that "it's not good for
16   me because I'm a woman and men created it" and "doctors, white male *doctors*!"
17   And those are all *true* things and I'm not going to *disagree* with that,
18   but I'm saying: it *works*, including with women, better than treatment.
19   I cannot treat you alone and be very effective.

In defense of AA and its inclusion in the weekly treatment schedule, Lizzy pulls science on her side (lines 1–5), and particularly that brand of science known as "evidence-based practice" (EBP).[16] Evidence-based practice is a methodological program of determining which clinical practice or combination of practices works "best" for the most people in a given population (e.g., "for women," as Lizzy notes above), and selecting and implementing interventions accordingly. Heavily reliant on evidence gleaned from randomized controlled trials and other quantitative research designs, some advocates of EBP conflate the *effectiveness* of a treatment modality—as determined by what they call the "hierarchy of evidence"—and its ethical implications, as Lizzy does above (line 3; see also Myers and Thyer 1997; Thyer and Myers 1999). For instance, Lizzy highlights AA's therapeutic functionality (lines 1–2, 4, 5, 6; 17–18) in a way that works to enervate the societal indexes of clients' objections (lines 9–14), constructing her narrative so those objections are literally enveloped by her scientific claims. And though conceding that there is some sociological "truth" in clients' criticisms (line 16), the new therapist questions the psychological validity of their protests, suggesting that they had "grab[bed] onto" an exogenous, feminist "idea" (line 15).

Embellishing her recitation of clients' critiques with doses of sarcasm (lines 2, 15–16), Lizzy points to her epistemological bind: the truth of science and society can be confirmed by research, whereas the truth of the client remains tenaciously evasive. Perhaps most frustrating was the fact that clients had successfully pulled her into a guessing game with their words. Indeed, when I proposed later in our interview that perhaps clients "really *didn't* like AA" precisely for the reasons they stated—a referential premise of my own—Lizzy responded with a strikingly elaborate *metapragmatic* analysis:

1 L: *But* but they would be talking and I would *see* their interactions and the way that
2   they were. And I would *hear* things that they said. But when they started talking
3   about AA, they were using someone *else's* words. It *felt* very different to me.
4   Um, because they were saying things like, *like* "doctors developed AA, and that's
5.   not good for women, and and and" (sarcastic).
6   And they would use all kinds of things that were not their ordinary way of *talking*
7   or relating to the world.

Rather than relying upon the ideology of inner reference, which allows one to connect the "things that they said" (line 2) with "the way that they were" (line 1–2), Lizzy is forced to consider a number of other points of reference. For instance, Lizzy accounts for observed "interactions" between clients (line 1), including the generic features of their "ordinary way of talking or relating to the world" (lines 6–7) in relation to the feminist critiques of AA that they voiced directly to her.

Furthermore, in recognizing and comparing two different ways of speaking, which we might call "the everyday" and "the critical," Lizzy is also compelled to reflect on the register of clients' critiques—that is, the way their talk is associated with social practices and personae (cf. Agha 2001, 2007). This puts her in yet another analytical bind. On the one hand, if she accepts clients' words as clinical critique emanating from a legitimately staked-out gender base (lines 4–5; also lines 15–16 above), she is directly implicated by the content of those critiques. After all, new at the helm of a self-proclaimed "gender-sensitive program," Lizzy was surely aware that this particular script required delicate handling, though—when talking to me—she again laces sarcasm through her voicings of clients.

Yet this sarcasm may, in fact, index the flip side of the new therapist's bind, namely, that clients are not the authors of the critiques they voice, another claim she has to carefully manage. After all, Lizzy had just taken a position in which *honest*, *open*, and *willing* talk was precisely the measure of her expertise. Furthermore, the new therapist had recently become acquainted with her colleagues at HFC, many of whom were dedicated to running an "empowerment-oriented" program, and in fact had just agreed to client representation on the advisory board in the name of these principles (see chapter 5). Lizzy therefore knew that any suggestion that clients were less-than-authorized speakers could well be met with suspicion, even hostility, by the professionals—not to mention the clients—with whom she worked.

Nevertheless, Lizzy clearly pursues the second of these two analytical options in her conversation with me, positing that clients strategically parroted others' critical words. In doing so, she recognizes yet another metapragmatic feature of clients' AA-protests—their historicity. Indeed, when Lizzy notes that "when they started talking about AA, they were using someone *else's* words" (lines 2–3), she acknowledges the existence of a group of possible, non-immediate interlocutors, including the clients' former therapist. Unable to "*see*" (line 1) or monitor clients' interactions with these parties, a defeated Lizzy suggests that these unknown interlocutors will continue to exert force on clients' words: in closing her quotation with an exasperated "and and and," Lizzy indicates that she was prepared for the criticism of AA to keep coming in a number of skillfully deployed versions (line 5).

Such metapragmatic analyses rendered decidedly unsatisfying answers compared to the ideologies on which Lizzy and her predecessors generally relied. For whether calling upon the ideology of science or the ideology of inner reference, Fresh Beginnings therapists generally drew clear distinctions between truth and falsity. Now faced with a linguistic puzzle exceeding those sincerity conditions, and with the "evidence" of therapeutic practices thrown into question, Lizzy must rest upon her intuitions, conceding that "it *felt* very different to me" (line 3). So whether clients' AA protests were "really" their own or whether they were wily attempts to evade burdensome institutional requirements, they radically shook the epistemological basis of Fresh Beginnings' therapeutic program which worked so hard to align speakers' words with inner truths. As such, they constituted a powerful strategy that trumped even the highly intelligent Lizzy's attempts to understand them.[17]

The efficacy of the AA protests became all the clearer as I continued to talk with Lizzy, asking her to elaborate on her earlier statement that some Fresh Beginnings clients had never gone to AA meetings (line 7 below), even before Laura instituted the WFS "alternative."

1 I: But they said that they hadn't been going to AA when [Laura] was there?
2 L: I don't even *know* if they told her that, but it became very clear from the van
3   drivers, and that kind of thing, that they weren't going there in *the van*.
4   And I would say, "what other meetings are you going to?"
5   And they would say, "we're *not*."
6   And *finally* people started telling the truth: "I haven't been to an AA meeting in
7   five months, nine months," or something like that, or "I've *never* gone to one."
8   And again, who *knows* what the truth is.
9   Is the truth that they never went?
10 Is the truth that they went and hated it?
11 I don't know, and it would be hard to speculate at this point.

Now, with the ideology of inner reference—and along with it "the truth"—in radical suspension (lines 8, 9, 10), Lizzy is forced to treat clients' talk as dynamic performance, verifying words by connecting them to the travel logs and reports of paraprofessional van drivers (lines 2–3). And though Lizzy seems to arrive at an intertextually derived conclusion by comparing van drivers' accounts with the *"finally"* truthful admissions of clients (lines 6–7), in the end, she concedes that the truth was still in active conjecture—even six months after the height of the protest. Posing the question with apparent consternation, "And again, who knows what the truth is?" (line 8), Lizzy indicates the destabilizing work of script flipping. The new therapist is now left to "speculate" on the truth rather than procure it, as she has been hired to do.

Considering the aims of Fresh Beginnings treatment, which had as much to do with procuring clean words as producing clean bodies, such speculation on the part of truth-seeking therapists had serious implications, both clinically and institutionally. Clinically the program was dedicated to producing *honest*, *open*, and *willing* selves whose language reflected and relayed the inner truths that therapists sought to know and treat. Script flipping forced therapists to look for the "truth" in social space rather than "in" their clients, and thereby engage an epistemology quite out of line with inner reference. And since therapists' charge to distribute goods and sanctions radically depended on their evaluations of what their clients said to them, script flipping was also an institutional intervention that influenced the distributional aspects of social work labor by troubling the evaluative ones. After all, while therapists tried to keep up with script flippers' discursive maneuvers, clients were freed from a requirement to attend AA, which they claimed was an onerous and unimportant element of their treatment.

210 • Chapter 6

Believing that script flipping posed a threat to the clinical and institutional health of the program, therapists worked hard to convince the advisory board that preventative measures were necessary. More specifically, as script flippers found ways to manipulate the rigors of *honest, open, and willing* talk, therapists came to believe that they needed more rigorous technologies to detect these troubling deviations.

SCREENING THE VOICE

> "Treatment is structured as three phases of treatment based upon each woman's progress, and includes regular random urinalysis, required recovery support meeting attendance (e.g., 12-Step and Women for Sobriety), and aftercare services."
> Fresh Beginnings Program Description

> "[Laura] suggested the use of chemical tests to judge the validity of the clients [sic] voice. Empowerment is the key part of the efficacy of a treatment program."
> Fresh Beginnings Advisory Board Meeting Minutes

Despite their striking differences, there is an important similarity in these two framings of urinalysis at Fresh Beginnings—the first, issued to each and every incoming client in a small packet of orientation materials, the second, recorded in the minutes of an advisory board meeting and distributed to professionals affiliated with the treatment program. Whereas the program description straightforwardly informs clients to expect "regular random urinalysis" and the meeting minutes more mysteriously cast "chemical tests" as a matter of "empowerment," both documents are clear that urinalysis is an integral part of Fresh Beginnings' therapeutic regimen.

Laura, the primary author of both these texts, also indicates to readers that urinalysis is, fundamentally, about the procurement of signs. The meeting minutes frame urinalysis as a way to procure nonverbal signs to "validate" the verbal ones collected in group and individual therapy. And although the program description seems simply to notify incoming clients that they could expect—randomly and regularly—to provide liquid evidence on demand, they would soon find that urinalysis was carefully integrated into daily rounds of talk therapy. Indeed, in everyday conversation as well as in writing, Laura delicately framed urinalysis so as to stave off the criticism of clients and colleagues who objected to the practice. However, through their very exposure to these framings, all readers learned that urinalysis was a script that could be flipped or reframed.

Notably, their ability to do one or the other depended on their relative institutional position.

Reframing Revisited

In comparison to the straightforward way that Laura informed her clients that "random" drug screens were a "regular" part of the program, her proposal to fellow board members about the very same practice seems quite byzantine. Certainly, HFC professionals would be no less shocked than incoming clients to find that urinalysis was as much a part of Fresh Beginnings "structure" as aftercare services and AA meetings. After all, urine screening was also a standard part of the intake and assessment process at most HFC agencies.

HFC professionals generally justified drug testing at their agencies—both to me and to incoming clients—in explicitly pragmatic and functional terms. They asserted that since all HFC agencies prohibited clients from possessing and using drugs while staying in their shelters, urine screening worked to assure that shelters, as well as the clients within them, would remain drug-free (cf. Sosin and Yamaguchi 1995). Nevertheless, drug screening was controversial within the Homeless Family Consortium. As discussed in chapter 2, WISH refused to conduct on-site drug screening on the grounds that it was potentially "traumatizing" and "disempowering" for clients who had been victims of violence, particularly of a sexual nature. At other HFC agencies, individual workers expressed quiet discomfort with urine screening in less theoretically elaborated terms.

Although Laura had been employed at Fresh Beginnings for less than six months when she crafted the correlation between "chemical tests" and "empowerment" at the advisory board table, she had apparently already learned the local keywords with which to address, if not quell, her new colleagues' concerns about drug testing (see chapter 5). Yet, even more telling than Laura's casting of urinalysis in the powerful term of "empowerment" is the distinctly metalinguistic commentary that characterizes the meeting minutes. Specifically Laura—as she was recorded—does not represent "chemical tests" as a measure for *identifying* bodily signs (i.e., the presence or absence of certain "chemicals") but instead as a clinical means of *validating* linguistic ones. Indeed, while she employs strikingly scientific terms (i.e., "chemical tests" and "validity"), it is the implication that both she and Susan had the ability to detect truth or falsity in "clients['] voices" that does most to relay their relative expertise to their new colleagues.

If Laura's boardroom framing of urinalysis was a site-specific enactment of expertise (cf. Carr, 2010a), she would soon have to redouble her efforts as circumstances at Fresh Beginnings began to challenge her ability to procure evidence of inner truth, which she understood to be her primary therapeutic charge. Indeed, faced with scores of negative drug-test results, and therefore potentially a threatening legion of script flippers, Laura and Susan had begun advocating for stricter urinalysis policies, which would face opposition from HFC professionals and clients alike. Namely, therapists proposed that HFC case managers conduct "random drops" with Fresh Beginnings clients during home visits, in addition to the tests they conducted at the shelter, in order to snag those they felt sure were trumping the tests. Reaction was swift and almost uniformly negative. While some case managers muttered about therapists' attempts to "pass off" the clinical responsibility to monitor clients' drug use, others shifted from the institutionally established and highly functional framing of urinalysis to a set of clearly ethical arguments about the nature of the practice (cf. Brodwin 2008).[18] More specifically, case managers became increasingly adamant that off-site drug testing of clients would violate the professional bond and trust between case manager and client, and therefore implicitly undermine the very essence of their own expertise.

Case managers' irritation with therapists' insistent proposals mounted to the point where a special meeting was called to discuss the matter. Moderated by Diane, a trusted program consultant, HELPNET case managers and supervisors, as well as the two Fresh Beginnings therapists and their supervisors from Hope Health, attended. Notes from the meeting read:

1 [Kelly] noted that she sees the primary role of the CM [case manager] as
2 supportive. For example, asking a consumer for a urine drop feels uncomfortable
3 to [Kelly] and other CMs, because it feels too intrusive, and feels like she is
4 policing the consumer.

Kelly provocatively frames the work of case management as a matter of being "supportive" of "a consumer" rather than "policing" or "intrud[ing]" upon her (lines 1–3). Though she repeatedly refers to her "feelings" (lines 2, 3), and therefore seems to speak in a therapeutic rather than an administrative register, Kelly's comments—as they are represented by the minute-taker—are distinctly moral in character. Indeed, although urinalysis was both expensive and time-consuming, the meeting minutes make no mention of this. As other case managers in attendance followed Kelly in casting their objections to urinalysis in explicitly ethical terms, they were able to secure an agreement that "random drops" would and *should* not be procured during home visits.

Moreover, as a result of Kelly's reframing, "policing" would be left to the therapeutic staff at Fresh Beginnings, and clients were thereby granted more room to evade attempts to detect and validate a clinically and institutionally valued set of truths. Of course, seasoned clients knew that it was not chemically derived truths that their therapists sought, and this knowledge was critical in their attempts to flip the script of urinalysis.

From Framing to Flipping

Laura wisely dressed down empowerment-inducing "chemical tests" as "random, regular drug tests" in the program description she distributed to incoming clients. After all, the very idea of "tests" that could determine "the validity of the clients' voice" was a ready sign to the discerning client-reader that therapists needed technological assistance in their work of evaluating the *honesty, openness, and willingness* of clients' self-reports. Indeed, for those who labored within the disciplined terms of inner reference, the very use of urinalysis threatened to expose the limits of what therapists could know about their clients through talk alone. Accordingly, when addressing her clients, Laura framed urinalysis as just another part of the program's structure rather than an inner truth-detecting device per se.

For these very same reasons, in their daily exchanges with clients, therapists framed urinalysis not as a "test" to validate whether a client's voice was truthful but instead as a kind of linguistic *prompt*—a reminder to clients that therapists already knew the truth, whether or not it had yet to be properly put into words. In this framing, "random drops" provided an opportunity for clients to "get *honest*" (line 3, below). Shelly, a veteran client, explained:

1 S: When we would do our random drops, or somebody, if they weren't clean,
2   we would be in group and [Laura] would say:
3   "Does anyone need, does anybody here, uh, need to get *honest* about anything?"
4 I: And then what would happen?
5 S: And then, you know, the people *knew* who they were.
6   They knew what they had *used* or not. And then they would *talk* about it.
7   You know whoever it was who, you know, *relapsed*.
8 I: And so they, what would they explain, why or how [they relapsed]?
9 S: Oh, *everything*, you know.

After untying her tongue (line 1), Shelly casts the client who relapsed as the keeper of knowledge, saying the "people *knew* who they were. They knew what they had *used* or not" (lines 5–6). At the same time Shelly clearly grants her therapist the ultimate authority in deciphering the truth. According to the above account, the less than "clean" results of "random drops" (line 1) are quickly subsumed by Laura's rhetorical query: "Does anybody here . . . need to . . . get *honest* about anything?" (line 3). In this sense, the therapist seemingly plays the moral provocateur (who also just so happens to be on the chemically validated side of the truth). Significantly, in the end, Laura's question precipitates a response from her relapsed client that can be read clinographically rather than chemically (see chapter 3).

While Shelly, like her therapists, represents the use of chemical tests as a way to promote "honesty," the exercise she describes opened the door to script flippers to "play it off," as Nikki once put it. As soon as Laura opens up the possibility that clients could comment on their urinalysis results—even if it was simply to confess a set of believable actions that produced those results—she renders urinalysis a script vulnerable to flipping. The most obvious way to "play it off," then, was to readily confess in perfectly *honest*, *open*, and *willing* terms. Indeed, since Fresh Beginnings therapists measured clients' recovery primarily by how transparently they referenced inner states, the apparent cleanliness of a client's words was at least as important as the cleanliness of the corresponding vial sent off for chemical analysis.

Of course, there were risks involved in flipping scripts: an *honest*, *open*, and *willing* confession of drug use sometimes landed the confessant in an inpatient program or instigated a call to a Child Protective Services worker, even if it was simultaneously lauded as a sign of therapeutic progress. In considering such risks, the question arises: Why did Fresh Beginnings clients flip the script of urinalysis rather than reframe it, as HFC professionals did? Simply put, clients were not afforded the luxury of obviously creative linguistic performance. Indeed, whereas professionals were endowed with the linguistic rights to make things with their words, including reframing urinalysis as "policing," clients were expected to speak within the terms of inner reference. After all, to speak outside the disciplined tenets of *honesty*, *openness*, and *willingness* was to indicate to therapists that one still floundered in addiction, and this held true in the boardroom as well as the therapy room, as chapter 5 demonstrated. Thus, if a client like Lila, Louise, or Nikki charged that therapists were trying to "police" them by conducting urinalyses, they would quickly be met with suspicion that they had something to hide.

Therefore, script flippers had to work *within* the terms of given clinical scripts. And, in challenging their therapists' urinalysis practices and policies, they found the clinical discourse of "shame" particularly effective. Moreover, in mobilizing the discourse of shame, script flippers recruited professional framers to work with them in reformulating program policy.

Script Flipping as Policy Making

Even though script flippers were limited to performing acts of inner reference, they found ways to collaborate with those endowed with other kinds of performative powers. Indeed, with some effort, script flippers could learn critical tidbits from framers, namely, their HFC case managers. Clients could become "flies on the wall," for instance, while they waited in program offices as case managers unwittingly complained about Laura's latest antics. Or during the rare but eventful case conferences that convened her case manager, CD therapist, and family therapist, a script flipper might be a spectator as much as a participant, watching carefully for signs of professional conflict. As skillful speakers as well as analysts, script flippers could feed case managers' critiques of Fresh Beginnings right back to them, potentially doubling their force. And although I found it impossible to trace the lines of influence, as neither clients nor case managers acknowledged (and/or recognized) that they worked in unison, there is no doubt that when it came to monitored drug testing, framers and flippers collaboratively worked to shape program policy.

It all began when Laura and Susan—continually dogged by clean drug screen results from bodies they suspected were decidedly drugged, and unable to secure agreement from case managers to conduct drug tests off-site—quietly instituted a policy of monitored urinalysis. In practice, this meant that one of the two therapists stood in the cramped Cliff Street bathroom, watching to make sure each initialed vial was filled by the appropriate body and preventing water, salt, or sweetener from being added by those determined to alter the chemical composition of their product. Fresh Beginnings therapists could not help but be aware that professional affiliates of the program would object to monitored urinalysis in principle. And, indeed, hearing rumors that Laura and Susan were monitoring clients, advisory board members registered their concerns in swift and definitive terms, enervating the practice. Meeting minutes read:

1 The group discussed the use of urine screens.
2 It was agreed that monitored screening brings shame and is demoralizing.

Considering therapists' theories of women's addiction, which draw casual links between sexual abuse, ensuing shame, and numbing drug use, administrators' reference to the shame-inducing quality of one of Laura and Susan's practices (line 2) is particularly striking. And though we might readily take this as another instance of creative reframing, it appears that the journey of the sentence "monitored screening brings shame and is demoralizing" was more circuitous.

Although I never determined for certain whether Fresh Beginnings clients originally complained to their case managers about the "shame" induced by monitored screenings, or if they later learned this particular moral plot line from HFC professionals, I believe the former was the case. After all, through their lessons on Cliff Street, Fresh Beginnings clients had learned that female addicts are constituted by layers of denial, anger, and shame; case managers may or may not have been privy to this particular clinical discourse. Clients also knew, through their daily therapeutic interactions, that Laura and Susan—as well as their family therapists—claimed that shame was a deeper and more fundamental emotion than anger, and the inevitable result of sexual victimization (see chapter 3). Evocations of shame, therefore, were especially likely to elicit concern and sympathy from their therapists.

Wherever it began, the content of clients' critiques of monitored screening closely resembled those documented in the advisory board minutes above: they both appealed directly to "shame." Indeed, according to the clients I spoke with directly, and the case managers who reported what they had been told, monitored screening was "embarrassing," "traumatizing," and even "violating," especially—as one WISH/Fresh Beginnings client put it—"considering all I've been through." Furthermore, not long after Nikki returned from the hospital, some clients began to weave a more elaborate theory of shame, which would be most familiar to their therapists. Specifically, they claimed that being monitored, especially by those who were supposed to care for them, induced shameful memories of childhood sexual abuse, which in turn triggered intense urges to get high (and sometimes, by extension, dirty drug screen results).

Perhaps in citing the "shame" evoked by monitored screenings, Fresh Beginnings clients were flipping scripts. Or, perhaps they were simply referencing what they actually felt and believed. The very point of script flipping was to raise the definite possibility that either could be the case, and the latter was too serious to be ignored by professionals, considering the threatened consequences. In either case, by successfully performing inner reference, clients contributed to and sustained HFC professionals' objections to monitored screening. They also effectively suspended the practice of monitored screenings as professionals debated its ethics.

. . .

Notably, when it came to the Fresh Beginnings program, few policies endured, suggesting that organizational-level policy might best be understood as temporarily coalesced and officially authorized discourse about a collectively constructed object of concern (cf. Latour and Weibel 2004). Thus to say that clients effectively participated in policy making when they flipped professional scripts does not mean that they had a direct hand in establishing the content of enduring policy mandates. Rather, by contributing to and influencing the flow of discourse about urinalysis, AA, and other collective concerns, script flippers engaged in the ongoing policy work of debating and legitimating, stabilizing and destabilizing, and naturalizing and denaturalizing program practices. Indeed, script flippers' work sometimes congealed in temporary decisions, or non-decisions, that benefited many clients such as the suspension of required AA meetings and regular drug testing in the shelters. And, interestingly, in the case of monitored urinalysis, script flippers' contributions to program policy were eventually officially recognized, even if they were also eventually devalued.

Many months after the advisory board curtly appraised and effectively halted the practice of monitored screenings, well-substantiated rumors surfaced that Fresh Beginnings clients who were staying at the WISH shelter were using drugs rampantly on-site. Considered a crisis by WISH and Fresh Beginnings professionals alike, Laura and Susan convinced the shelter to institute on-site testing, which they had adamantly resisted up to that date. In the powerful terms of "crisis management," Fresh Beginnings therapists took the opportunity to persuade the advisory board that monitored screening should be reinstituted. At a particularly momentous board meeting, therapists directly referenced the skillful work of "creative clients" (lines 4 and 7, below) in defending the need for the monitored screenings. The minutes read:

1 Drug Screens: [WISH] will not do drug screens on site. However the [Fresh
2 Beginnings] staff can do the screenings. [Fresh Beginnings] has gone to observed
3 urine screenings for everyone due to the fact that some clients have found a way
4 to creatively get around the drug testing. A question was raised about the concern
5 that some women may have about sexual abuse? Most consumers understand and are
6 not having a problem with the observed testing. The ones that are having a problem
7 with the testing are the ones who are being creative.

Note the collective assent therapists are able to secure in relation to what board members, HFC staff, and clients had all once agreed was a decidedly "shameful" practice. While that critique is referenced and raised in interrogative form (lines 4–5), the long-standing objection is quickly resolved by pitting it against the wily workings of "creative" clients (lines 4, 7).

Carefully distinguishing between the majority of clients who "understand and are not having a problem with observed testing" (lines 5–6) and the problematic clients who are "being creative" (line 7), the meeting minutes trace a troubling connection between the "creativity" involved in "get[ting] around the drug testing" (line 4) and the voiced concerns about sexual abuse (line 5). Indeed, the question raised in lines 4–5 is definitively answered by pointing to the ways in which clients had "flipped" their professional scripts, with the disastrous consequences left silently hanging in the air for board members to ponder. Clients had analyzed their discourse, adopted it, and fed it back, resulting in months of undetected drug use, and—arguably—the failure of the program to meet its mission to "achieve sobriety and self sufficiency" (see chapter 1).

As the program, with the approval of the advisory board, began to implement more rigorous means of detection to crack down on those who continued to evade them, script-flipping clients were faced with the negative consequences of their political practice. These consequences were not just the losses of specific opportunities once gained through their honed ability to read and mobilize the scripts of their therapists and case managers. They also temporarily lost their status as legitimate speakers and actors in the eyes of Fresh Beginnings therapists and HFC professionals alike, who—in line with the cultural and clinical ideology of language—judge the value of a person to the degree that she transparently reveals her innermost thoughts, feelings, and intentions in words.

Against these grave losses, script flippers arguably gained something much greater than temporary relief from arduous meetings and therapists' intrusions. Script flippers, like Shauna, Nikki, and Rhonda, developed their skills in institutional and linguistic analysis, which allowed them to intervene in how institutionally powerful people, like their case managers and therapists, engaged in evaluations of relatively less powerful ones, such as themselves. They also influenced the consequences of those evaluations, and helped direct the distribution of both material and symbolic goods. And although clients did not always get to keep what they earned in flipping the script—whether the suspension of an onerous treatment requirement or ancillary services such as respite day care—they were able to participate in policy debates that would have otherwise been off-limits to them.

Conclusions: The Politics and Ethics of Script Flipping

Politics is the interplay between acts that make what is contingent seem natural and just, thereby excluding other possibilities for how things could be, and acts that demonstrate the contingency of what has been accepted as natural and just, thereby introducing alternative possibilities for how things could be (cf. Mouffe 2005).[19] In showing that one could perform inner reference in more than one way, script flippers demonstrated that the relationship between spoken words and inner states is not a natural or given one. They also troubled a cultural regime of personhood—which was potently distilled at Fresh Beginnings—which insists that fully formed selves exist prior to their speech acts, that a person's words should be valued primarily as signs of selfhood, and that language is a window to the psyche if not the soul. As we saw above, the practice of script flipping demanded that the analyst, whether anthropologist or therapist, approach clients' narratives not as transparent reports of the contents of individual psyches, but instead as the joint products of many speakers, and as effective social actions in the world with histories and futures of their own.

Many might argue that script flipping is a specific kind of *racial* politics. And, indeed, the very term "flipping the script" has origins in cultural sites where race and rhetoric are enduring concerns. It appears that the term was first used in American hip-hop and, more specifically, in an improvisational form of rap known as "freestyle."[20] Among freestyle artists and audiences, the term "flip the script" has been used to connote the highly valued ability to seamlessly introduce a new theme (or script) or to skillfully respond to such introductions all the while staying on beat (ibid.; Keyes 2004).[21] By the mid-1990s the writings of black scholars, activists, and bloggers about race—and particularly race and education—used the term to denote the critical examination of dominant roles, and especially of white privilege (i.e., Gilyard 1996; Duncan and Jackson 2004).[22] Most recently, "flip the script" has been used to interpellate young black people who are thought to use the term themselves. In these uses, to "flip the script" means to volitionally change one's social trajectory, from "gangbangin'" and a "culture of no accountability" to "credible choices and opportunities." Such is the stated mission of the "Flip the Script Program", run by the Goodwill Industries of Greater Detroit, described on the program's Web site as a "16 week life changing male minority empowerment program [that] emphasizes a holistic curriculum that transforms the self to realize the power within"(Goodwill Industries of Greater Detroit). Indeed, in line with the empowerment rhetoric described in the previous chapter, such programs suggest that "flipping the script" is not about challenging white authority, but instead about engendering a sense of personal power.

Along similar lines, Reverend Kathi Martin calls on young parishioners of a black Atlanta congregate to "flip the script on our lives and walk into a new reality of love, justice, and hope" (Atlanta Church of Christ). Likewise, East London rapper Dizzee Rascal's lyrics sound less like his hip-hop predecessors and more like an Oprah Winfrey Show confessional refrain (save the expletive, of course):

> I'm from the street, you're from the street
> We've all done dirt
> Now it's time to flip the script
> Fuck the suffering and the hurt
> Because I've seen the bigger picture, it's all good
> There really is a world outside the hood.
>
> (Dizzee Rascal 2008)

Considering this recent chapter in the now twenty-six-year life of the term, the College of Office Technology advertisement, published in the

Figure 6.1. "Flip the Script in 2008." Advertisement for the College of Office Technology, *Chicago Sun Times*, January 28, 2008, Chicago Sun Times

January 28, 2008, issue of the *Chicago Sun Times*, might well be read as an exemplar (Figure 6.1).[23]

At Fresh Beginnings clients' script flipping certainly entailed the trumping of a rhetorical opponent (as in freestyle), the critical examination of power relations (as in critical race scholarship), and perhaps even, to some degree, the volitional reframing of identity (as in more recent interpellative uses of the term). And though I have no doubt that many Fresh Beginnings clients were familiar with these uses of the phrase, and paid homage to the cultural domains where its meanings have been developed and defined by adopting it, it does not necessarily follow that flipping the script of Cliff Street was a form of racial politics.

I also have no doubt that the disproportionate number of African American women in the Fresh Beginnings program was a reflection of both social and institutional racism, and in the course of my research I found evidence that white clients were systematically, if not intentionally, favored (Carr 2010b). However, clients and therapists did not enter the Fresh Beginnings program with already formulated alignments with language and ideology, which can be simply mapped, analytically, onto their race and class backgrounds. For, like all Americans, Nikki, Shauna, and Rhonda were socialized into the ideas about language and personhood that were distilled at Fresh Beginnings well before they arrived on Cliff Street, through their interactions in educational, religious, medical, and legal institutions, and their consumption of mass media (see chapter 4). And, like their white fellow script flippers, not to mention their white (Laura, Lizzy) and black (Susan, Ella) therapists, script flippers invested in these cultural ideologies and generally conducted themselves accordingly.

So, although some might argue that African American clients like Shauna and Nikki had unique ways of theorizing as well as using language, and therefore a critical distance on the Euro-American ideology of inner reference, that is not the argument I make here—and not just in acknowledgment of Fresh Beginnings' multicultural crew of script flippers.[24] For if flipping the script was a manifestation of a specifically African American language ideology, how could we explain the fundamental difference in the boardroom performance of Rhonda and Louise, two black women of approximately the same age, class, and religious background? Indeed, while practices like pointed indirectness (Morgan 1996) and other kinds of signifying (Gates 1988; Labov 1972a; Mitchell-Kernan 1999; Morgan 2002) have long been cultivated and valued among African Americans, the story of Fresh Beginnings is not a story of a linguistic "culture clash" between therapists and clients. Instead, it is a story of how institutions recruit people into roles and expect them to speak accordingly. It follows that people's differential awareness of the function of language, and ability to manipulate social expectations about ideological linguistic forms, has less to do with the nature of the signs and speech in question and more to do with institutional practice. Because of a long legacy of American racism, and the specific discrimination against black women, they have had a disproportionate amount of practice in settings like Fresh Beginnings and many have become especially skilled and highly aware speakers as a result.

The anthropologist Robert Desjarlais (1996, 1997) also makes the point that people speak from institutionally assigned positions. Desjarlais draws on Michel de Certeau's famous distinction between "strategies" (as the province of the powerful) and "tactics" (as the weapons of the weak).[25] Desjarlais argues that shelter staff's language relied upon an extra-contextual logic of reason, promoting ideas of causality, regularity, reliability, and responsibility. For example, Desjarlais notes that shelter staff used the pronoun "we" in their self-descriptions while referring to their clients in the singular (e.g., "we think it's time for you to get some rest, Buddy")—a strategy that leant professionals' "we-ed" advice the semantic markers of authority. Desjarlais differentiates this "strategic" language of staff from the "tactical" language used by shelter residents—language characterized by questions, pleas, complaints, and entreaties. From this difference, Desjarlais draws a clear conclusion: clients' verbal tactics did not stand a chance in relation to the linguistic strategies of staff, grounded as the latter were in a durable locus of reason (cf. de Certeau 1984). More specifically, Desjarlais explains that residents' tactics were enfeebled by their tendency to locate agency in the staff listener, thereby providing an opportunity for a rationalized, strategic response. In the end Desjarlais found that residents' linguistic maneuvering came at the great cost of losing the coherent or stable identity that staff encouraged (see also Wilce 1998, 2003).

Desjarlais did not observe or account for mimetic practices like flipping the script. Such a practice essentially borrows the "strategic" language of powerful parties—to use de Certeau's and Desjarlais' lexicon—and skillfully redirects its illocutionary and political force. While successful script flippers certainly located agency in the staff listener, as the Boston shelter residents reportedly did, they also troubled the staff's capacity to respond definitively, effectively, or in any kind of immediate way. Thus, Fresh Beginnings clients were neither destined to use the weak weapon of a "tactical" language nor were there such grave costs for their linguistic practices; as long as they perfectly performed and reproduced the language of inner reference, their intent in doing so remained undetected. As a varidirectional practice (Bahktin 1990), flipping the script was, arguably, both strategic and tactical.[26]

Nevertheless, Desjarlais's ethnography raises an important consideration about the potential risks, if not the certain costs, of deviating from culturally valued ways of speaking that has its precursor in Erving Goffman's famous study of asylums: the risk of losing the social recognition necessary in sustaining a culturally authorized "self." Goffman's work has received much attention for its brilliant description of how the preserve of the self is "mortified" in what he called "total institutions." Much like Desjarlais, Goffman writes, "To prescribe activity is to prescribe a world; to dodge a prescription can be to dodge an identity" (1961:187). However, like Bahktin, Goffman addresses mimetic practices and therefore acknowledges inmates' decidedly strategic capacities. He writes, "Inmates' use of the official staff language and staff philosophy in discussing or publishing gripes is a mixed blessing for staff. Inmates can manipulate the staff's own rationalization of the institution and through this threaten the social distance between the two groupings" (ibid:97).

Goffman goes on to suggest that while an inmate might engage in prescribed activities, including authorized ways of speaking, his "capacities" may have migrated—that is, he does not believe or invest in what he dutifully does. Not only can an inmate be "an absentee" of his own activities, Goffman further explains, he can also conceal his own leave taking. In doing so, the inmate does not shirk authorized ways of acting and speaking but instead plays with prescribed ways of being (ibid:188). Goffman wisely ends this section of *Asylums* with a methodological warning, which I have worked to heed throughout this book. Specifically, while acknowledging that "absenteeism" could be analyzed as a psychological phenomena, I follow Goffman in holding at bay the question of just what an individual "gets out of" a practice. Indeed, Goffman warns that, from a sociological point of view, the initial question should be not what a particular practice means to and for the practitioner. Instead, we should inquire into the nature of the social and institutional relations that require the acquisition and maintenance of practices like flipping the script (1961:200–201).

Although this book does not offer a psychological portrait of script flippers, I end this chapter where I began: that is, with the suggestion that script flipping entails an alternative ethic of personhood, one that Bahktin once called an "act-performing consciousness." This is a way of being that does not rely on the idea of a self that preexists and stands before its acts, deliberating in the abstract about the "right thing to do." It is a way of being that does not see the self as a collection of signs, gathered over a personal history, so that when one speaks, one simply releases what is believed, desired, or intended. Rather, it is a way of being that is intensively historical, making note of what has been said and done, and intensively ethnographic, keenly attuned to what others say and do. Script flipping entails a kind of reflection that does not ask "Who am I?" and then seeks others' confirmation and authorization of a seemingly self-derived conclusion; instead, it involves reflecting on one's actions as they relate to others by asking "what for? how? is it correct or not? is it necessary or not? is it required or not? is it good or not?" (Bahktin 1990; see also Jackson 2005).[27] In short, without dismissing the risks and the costs of script flipping, or stopping at the delineation of its gains as a mode of politics, my encounters with script flippers ultimately taught me about an ethic of personhood I had never really appreciated: the cultivation of a consciousness of "a life lived by performing actions at every moment of it" (ibid. 138) with an audience and fellow performers always in mind.

So although there was something profoundly sad about the evening I met Nikki in that Bob's Big Boy restaurant—in part because I correctly predicted it would be the last time I saw or spoke to her—I never thought to be hurt or offended when, after I cited the contents of our previous oral history interview, she laughingly relayed: "*Girl*, don't you know, I flipped a *script* on you?!" In fact, what I took to be her revelation that evening I also understood as confirmation of the many years I had devoted to the study of culture. And though anthropologists differ in how they go about this charge, Nikki pointed me in what I think was the right direction: the self is an actor who is radically dependent on where, when, with whom, why, and under what circumstances she acts; culture is the sum total of such interactions. So rather than being offended, I was, and continue to be, impressed by the bravery, skill, and ingenuity with which she performed inner reference by enacting a beautiful—if culturally devalued and institutionally illegitimate—way of speaking and being.

Conclusion

Scripting Addiction highlights what mainstream American addiction treatment reveals about American ideologies of language and personhood. Taking Fresh Beginnings to be a distillery where cultural ideals are processed and reproduced in purified form, the book elaborates six theoretical points, briefly reviewed below.

First, we have witnessed the sheer amount of work it takes to put dominant cultural ideologies of language into practice and thereby reinforce their authority. For instance, by identifying, categorizing, and filtering linguistic impurities, therapists rigorously refine what is commonly taken to be a natural and normal way of speaking—or, what I call "the ideology of inner reference". This *metalinguistic labor* distills the language of inner reference by delineating specific rules and methods of representing oneself, clearly and cleanly, in words. Indeed, *Scripting Addiction* shows that in the contemporary United States, sobriety is a way of speaking as well as a way of being. The preceding pages also demonstrate the myriad ways that the ideology of inner reference affects institutional and political, as well as therapeutic, practices, thanks to the labors of people who speak in its name.

Second, this book illustrates the co-constitution of ideologies of language and personhood. For, as we have seen, the idea that addicts are the kind of people who cannot read and render their inner states generates a rehabilitative program of reproducing, protecting, and patrolling highly valued but rarely questioned linguistic norms. Conversely, the cultural privileging of the presupposing, denotational function of language not only lays the foundation for the clinical construction of the addict; it also and by extension establishes what it means to speak like—and therefore be—a healthy, clean, and sober person. It follows that chemical dependency therapists strive to fulfill a cultural as well as professional charge when they work to produce sober people by distilling sober ways of speaking.

Third, *Scripting Addiction* suggests that institutions are organized by representational economies (Keane 2007), which naturalize roles such as "client" and "professional" by designating *who* can talk about *what* (as well as *when* and *how* they can talk about it). The preceding chapters have mainly focused on how people are socialized to speak like, and therefore inhabit the role of, the recovering addict. Chapter 5, however, details the linguistic routines and resources that constitute the role of social service professional. It shows that whether employing a given lexicon of resonant terms to appeal to powerful funding bodies, or exploiting coworkers' framings to establish their own expertise, the speech of professional practitioners is both constrained and empowered—and so too, therefore, is their ability to act. As Murray Edelman once sagely argued, examining the "special language of the helping professions . . . can help us understand more profoundly than legislative histories or administrative or judicial proceedings how we decide upon status, rewards, and controls for the wealthy, the poor, women, conformists, and nonconformists" (1974:297).[1]

Fourth, we have learned that people can anticipate how they are expected to speak and make use of given scripts, however they invest in the content of what they say. As documented in chapters 5 and 6, some clients carefully analyzed local speech conditions, very much like linguistic anthropologists, in order to play the role of "recovered client" and perform effective acts of speech. Accordingly, *Scripting Addiction* proposes that precisely because it involves determining how one can speak and represent authoritatively, metalinguistic awareness is a powerful institutional and political resource. With this point in mind, the reader should recall that—from boardroom to therapy room—Fresh Beginnings therapists also evinced metalinguistic awareness. Like their fellow professional wordsmiths, they were keenly attuned to what they could *do* and *make* with their words, as well as what they could state with them. This book allows us to consider this metapragmatic sensibility and better understand the multiple reasons why therapists—as fluent speakers of a highly pragmatic tongue—nevertheless insisted that their clients confine their speech acts to the reference of already existing inner states.

Fifth, this book demonstrates that people do not simply pursue professional projects and interests by using language in specific ways (as in the deployment of jargon). Realizing one's self as an expert commonly entails figuring others as less aware, knowing, or knowledgeable, and therefore establishing differential relationships between people, words, and valued objects, such as inner states (see also Carr 2010a).[2] As argued in chapter 3, the efforts of Fresh Beginnings therapists to help and heal their clients, run an effective and stable program, and establish themselves as clinical experts hinged on their claim that they intimately knew the inner states that their clients, as addicts, denied. Yet, significantly, these expert claims served as the fodder of script flipping. After all, script flippers mobilized expert discourses to their own ends, not simply or even primarily by using the jargon of addiction science and treatment, but rather by adroitly managing situated exchanges with their therapists and case managers. Therefore, HFC professionals and script flippers alike demonstrate that although mastery of a professional register is an important aspect of cultivating expertise, emerging as an expert may have as much to do with learning how to control an interactional text as deploying a denotational one (cf. Carr 2010a; Matoesian 2009; Silverstein 2004, 2006).

Sixth, by documenting the various ways that clients act as efficacious, if not legitimated, institutional actors, *Scripting Addiction* makes an intervention in the study of power in institutions, particularly in the realm of social services. Specifically, in elaborating the practice of flipping the script, I offer a viable alternative to theories of power that suggest a simple equation between ideology and resistance—whether cast in the terms of zero-sum or in Foucault's popular formulation (i.e., where there is power, there is resistance).[3] After all, script flipping, as a mimetic practice, simultaneously reproduces and undermines therapeutic practices, as well as the semiotic ideologies that underlie them. For, on the one hand, clients can influence professional evaluations, and therefore direct the flow of resources and influence program policies by flipping the script. In creating evidentiary crises for professionals, who can not readily decipher a flipped from a followed script, script flipping also attacks inner reference at its ideological core. On the other hand, because "flipping" means perfectly reproducing therapeutic scripts in form, if not in prescribed "content," the language of inner reference continues to be articulated in actual practice. And, to the extent it is suspected, if not detected, script flipping also impels therapists to continuously refine their efforts to produce clean and sober acts of inner reference.

In sum, *Scripting Addiction* is a story about what it means to be "addicted" and "sober" in contemporary American society, what it means to reflect upon and use language given a set of cultural and professional norms of speaking, and therefore what it means to engage in institutional practice and politics. Though the primary purpose of this book has been descriptive and analytic rather than prescriptive, I conclude by highlighting select implications of this study for social work education and American addiction treatment.

Professional Social Work as Practical Ethnography

> The one thing to be dreaded in the Settlement is that it lose its flexibility, its power of quick adaptation, its readiness to change its methods as its environment may demand. It must be open to conviction and have a deep and abiding sense of tolerance. It should demand from its residents a scientific patience in the accumulation of facts and a steady holding of their sympathies as one of the best instruments for that accumulation. It must

> be grounded in a philosophy whose foundation is on the solidarity of the human race, a philosophy which will not waver when the race happens to be represented by a drunken woman or an idiot boy.
>
> Jane Addams, *Forty Years at Hull-House*

While completing this book, I have been teaching in one of the oldest and most distinguished schools of social work in the United States. Here, I have encountered scores of students who have the intelligence, patience, and flexibility that it takes to be a good social worker. "Patient" and "flexible" are not adjectives commonly used to describe social workers, who are more often cast as idealistic, caring, and frequently controlling—"the friendly arm of the state." Social work is powerful work, a point both widely recognized and poorly understood. In this book, and in my scholarship more generally, I have sought to think through and illuminate the complex circumstances, material and ideological, that my students face as they engage their professional charge.

When we consider, for instance, how welfare state retrenchment affects the labor of social service professionals, we recognize that they work not only with a dwindling cache of resources but also with a new vocabulary of "personal responsibility" and "work opportunity" (Finn and Jacobson 2000). In classrooms all over the country, social work educators accordingly devote themselves to mapping out the rapidly shifting material and symbolic terrain of social service provision. Yet considering both the breadth and dynamism of the social work profession, it is all the more important to teach students the methods and skills of *quick adaptation* and *a scientific patience in the accumulation of facts* required to generate such maps on their own (Addams and Wald, 1910). In light of the observations accrued in the course of researching *Scripting Addiction*, as well as my experience teaching young social workers how to best navigate the complexity of their professional environments, I conclude that social work students can especially benefit from learning to practice the methods and skills of ethnography.

Teaching social work as ethnography means, first and foremost, instilling in novice practitioners an *inductive* approach to practice, engaging in what Jane Addams called "scientific patience in the accumulation of facts" (ibid.:126) before concluding what kind of people clients are, the problems they are facing, and how to best ameliorate them. As in participant observation, inductive social work builds theories based on evidence accumulated from grounded interactions with clients and colleagues, along with evidence and theoretical perspectives accrued in training and research. Contrary to the idea that social work is practical rather than theoretical work, the professional practitioners I witnessed were continually drawing on a wide range of formal psychological, sociological, and political explanations about why their clients were suffering and what would most likely alleviate that suffering; they also relied heavily on folk theories of language and personhood in the course of their everyday work. This, in and of itself, is unproblematic. Yet problems did arise when these practitioners jumped to conclusions, hatched theories too quickly or systematically—e.g., whether they expected their assessees to suffer from denial well before they assessed them (see chapter 3) or presumed that a client's word choice indexed gay shame despite her claims to the contrary (see chapter 4)—or clung to their convictions despite the accumulated experience of interacting with clients. As Jane Addams so eloquently notes, "a steady holding of one's sympathies"—that is, the conclusions toward which one might be generally or naturally inclined—is one of the best instruments for the patient "accumulation of facts" as well as for the sustenance of a humanistic profession (ibid.).

Arguably, the conditions of professional social work practice do not often afford practitioners the luxury of practicing induction, making it all too easy to indiscriminately apply prepackaged explanations and rely upon comfortable "sympathies."[4] Indeed, social service professionals engage in their work under tremendous, immediate structural pressures, not the least of which is the fact that their clients' lives can be radically transformed by their evaluations and decisions. Therefore, social work educators should not only work to familiarize students with the psychological, sociological, and organizational theories they can employ in future work; we must also instill a spirit of theoretical "flexibility" (ibid.; see also Borden, 2009). This will allow them to decipher—from what they actually observe in, and gather from, the everyday interactions that comprise their practice—the very real, if often elusive, problems they are facing. After all, these problems are always subject to reframing and revision, which is central to any effort to solve them. As Addams noted, the thing "most dreaded" (ibid.) in the practice of social work is conceptual inflexibility, and an unwillingness to adapt to an ever-changing environment.

Like students of ethnography, who are taught to recognize how culture and politics manifest in even the most intimate interactions and conversations, social work students should be provided with multiple ways to think about matters of *scale*. As a professional field uniquely dedicated to the idea of Person-In-Environment (see chapter 2), theorizing the relationship between sites of human activity is clearly of central importance. To this end, social work educators have relied heavily on particular ecological models, such as Urie Bronfenbrenner's, which figure the person as encapsulated in concentric circles of context or environment (see chapter 2, Figure 2.1). Printed in countless social work textbooks, these models typically portray the individual surrounded by a small circle of family, friends, and peers, otherwise known as the "microsystem," which is itself surrounded by the larger "exosystem," which includes institutions such as schools, social welfare services, and legal organizations.[5] An even larger circle, known as the "macrosystem," figuratively engulfs the exo- and microsystem and includes within it such diverse phenomena as politics, economy, and the "attitudes and ideologies of the culture" (Dockrell and Messer 1999:39). According to this visual rendering of social life, culture and politics are not only "bigger" than the individual, but are also at the furthest remove. Though the ecological model is taught to show the complexity of the "Person-In-Environment," given its nested figuration, students may reasonably leave the classroom and enter the field thinking that therapeutic activities are insulated, if not isolated, from politics, economy, and culture, at least when it comes to selecting a site of intervention.

If another way to think about relations of scale has yet to concertedly challenge the ecological model's dominance in social work classrooms, the categorical division between micro- and macro-level practice has most definitely been vigorously discussed and debated since the Progressive era, and has involved some of the profession's most prominent commentators.[6] Many agree that the micro/macro distinction—so frequently modeled in textbooks as gradated circles of context—loses significance when considering what social workers actually do in the course of their professional practice. Clearly, large-scale social transformations—like the growth of contracting in the human services (see Smith 2009)—affect how clinical professionals care for their clients. And, as *Scripting Addiction* demonstrates, the so-called micro practices of group therapy sessions or clinical assessments are inherently political, precisely because they are sites of evaluation where processes of resource distribution are symbolically motivated.

With these critical points in mind, teaching social work as practical ethnography would entail showing how sites of social service practice, no matter how clinically oriented, are also always cultural and political. Accordingly, novice social workers can be prepared to approach their professional domain as interconnected sites on a map rather than differentially scaled circles (cf. Ferguson 2008; Floersch 2002).[7] For instance, sharing maps like the one in chapter 2 (see Figure 2.5) can help students understand how a psychotherapeutically driven interaction with a single client in one agency can affect a myriad of other social service, juridical, and penal transactions. The therapeutic encounter is therefore best conceived not as "smaller" than a social welfare policy, nor as isolated from it. Indeed, in the preceding pages, we learned that a drug test conducted in a shelter or a clinical assessment undertaken in a therapist's office can travel many miles to influence a decision about whether a family can keep their subsidized housing. Thus, if we teach social work students to think about the context of their work as interconnected and similarly scaled sites of professional activity, they will not only be better prepared to understand the wide-reaching stakes of therapeutic practices and appreciate the inevitably political nature of clinical work. Novice social workers will also learn how to better anticipate and potentially control how the information generated from their own professional interactions is likely to travel and the myriad effects it can have.

As the assessment map in chapter 2 clearly portrays, linking the sites of social work practice together are acts of speech such as program intake interviews, consultations with colleagues, and phone calls to parole officers or child welfare workers, as well as the texts generated by these interactions such as case notes, professional memos, urinalysis results, meeting minutes, and completed assessment forms. Indeed, no matter what field of practice novice social workers enter, they will be charged with producing information about the people and problems they encounter, which means that they will be responsible for generating texts. And, as suggested in chapters 1 and 5, novice social workers will also be expected to collaborate with colleagues to effectively frame problems, people, and the nature of their own work. After all, as HFC administrators once implied, framing a particular set of professional practices as "empowering" rather than "enabling" may be just the ticket to scoring a three million dollar grant from HUD.

Accordingly, this book suggests the benefits of providing formal opportunities for social work students to develop and refine their skills in written and spoken communication. For, just like ethnographers, social work practitioners are regularly called upon to effectively and sensitively represent the complex worlds where they find themselves at work. In curricula devoted to social service communications, students can learn to write organizational memos, case notes, and grant applications, and practice the art of verbally advocating a course of action or representing a client to a recalcitrant audience. In such courses, students can also be prepared to better anticipate the potential consequences of their representations. For, as the practice of script flipping keenly demonstrates, to be reflexive about how one can most effectively speak in particular circumstances is also to be reflexive about power and institutional practice.

Social work educators commonly emphasize the importance of a reflexive approach to practice (e.g., Heron 2005; Kondrat 1999; Taylor and White 2001). *Scripting Addiction* suggests the benefits of extending the practice of reflexivity to include consideration of how cultural ideologies or "folk theories" of language shape professional practices. Furthermore, following a bevy of social work and welfare scholars who call upon practitioners to reflect upon how they "construct" clients (e.g., Hasenfeld 1972; Hall et al. 2003; Lipsky 1980; Margolin 1997; Tice 1998), this book proposes that practitioners be especially critical of the way they construct clients' ability to know and speak authoritatively. For, as illustrated by the story of the Fresh Beginnings boardroom, therapeutic ideas about how recovering clients should speak severely circumscribe how they can contribute to program development and administration. And whether or not novice social work practitioners are inclined to provide such opportunities, they must be reminded that how they construe clients' ability to know and speak will profoundly affect how they will end up working with them.

Teaching social work as practical ethnography suggests, in line with Marilyn Strathern's (1988) elegant description, a practice of reflexivity grounded in the idea of "parallel worlds." This means that the practitioner must always account for his or her own way of interpreting specific circumstances in relation to how his or her clients interpret them. As I regularly tell my own students: only when they are able to account for the difference between their own situated interpretations and those of the people with whom they work will they be prepared to formulate sensitive and effective interventions. I underscore that this does not mean that they abandon their interpretations, but rather that they work to patiently formulate them in tandem, or parallel, with their clients. Just as good ethnography is not simple reportage of the "native point of view," good social work is not a matter of simply adopting or valorizing a client's perspective over one's own.

As *Scripting Addiction* has shown, many clients have learned to become astute and critical ethnographers in their own right. Indeed, over the course of interacting with professionals in social service settings and institutions, clients gain skills in reading, analyzing, and strategically responding to the social service transactions that involve them. They do this analytical work because their fates often hang at least partially in the balance of social service professionals' evaluations and actions. So when they gauge that their own valued ways of thinking about and being in the world diverge from those of their social workers, they sometimes use the ethnographic knowledge they have accrued, and especially what they have learned about the language of social workers, and "flip" it to their advantage.

Of course, this can be disheartening and frustrating for social work practitioners, as we have seen above. Nonetheless, practitioners should be taught to read the whole range of clients' reactions and responses as significant, including the act of adopting—in form—their very own interpretations and analyses, which clients sometimes perform as scripts. After all, clients tell us much about professional scripts when they flip them. Imagine what might have happened had Fresh Beginnings board members read Rhonda's boardroom confession ethnographically rather than as a simple sign of who she "really" believed herself to be (i.e., a "crack addict"). At the very least, they would certainly have had to recognize that their own professional practices made it difficult, if not impossible, for Rhonda to represent herself in other ways, thereby delimiting her contributions to program administration and development.

The most important lesson of this book is that clients' statements are always more than simple signs of mental states (whether glossed as "attitudes," "feelings," or "readiness to change"). They can and should also be read as cultural diagnostics, which indicate local dynamics of clinical and social service provision. After all, careful attention to the many things clients say and do with words can be the novice social worker's greatest resource in the process of learning the science and art of social work.

On Drugs and Treatment

> Because of [the] diversity of experience, the visitor is continually surprised to find that the safest platitude may be challenged. She refers quite naturally to "the horrors of the saloon," and discovers that the head of her visited family does not consider them "horrors" at all. He remembers all the kindness he has received there, the free lunch and treating that goes on, even when a man is out of work and not able to pay up; the loan of five dollars he got there when the visitor was miles away and he was threatened with eviction. He may listen politely to her reference to "horrors," but considers it only "temperance talk."
> Jane Addams, *Democracy and Social Ethics*

Anthropologists have long documented and analyzed drug use and exchange, including that which is culturally coded as problematic (e.g., Agar 1973; Bergmann 2009; Bletzer 2004; Bourgois 1996, 2003; Bourgois & Schoberg 2009; Cassinelli 1986; Douglas 1986; Heath 2000; MacAndrew and Edgerton 1969; Pine 2007; Rogers 2005; Taussig 1986, 2004; Tomlison 2004; Westermeyer 1979; Van Wetering and Van Gelder 2000). *Scripting Addiction* joins forces with a relatively new ethnographic literature on addiction and drug treatment, including the examination of how culturally and historically specific ideas about addiction translate into particular forms of therapy (e.g., Garrity 2000; Meyers 2009; Raikhel 2006;

Saris 2008), and studies of the relationship between addiction therapeutics and the figuring of the addict as "a criminal type" (Garriott 2008; see also Moore 2008; Skoll 1992). Other ethnographers have presented portraits of addiction treatment as mismanaging, even violating, the phenomenological experience of addiction and the subjectivity of addicts (e.g., Garcia 2008) or have theorized addiction treatment as a site of governmentality (e.g., Bourgois 2000; Fairbanks 2009; Friedman and Alicea 2001). *Scripting Addiction* contributes uniquely to this literature by approaching addiction treatment as a site where ideologies of language are refined and reproduced, processing people along the way.

Ethnographic studies play an important role in the much broader, interdisciplinary literature on addiction treatment. For although there is excellent work focusing on political and financial influences, program characteristics, and organizational dynamics (e.g., D'Aunno, Sutton, and Pryce 1991; Durkin 2002; Friedmann, Alexander, and D'Aunno 1999; Sosin 2002, 2005), less attention has been given to the ways that addiction treatment—a field acknowledged to be highly value-laden—integrates and reproduces cultural values and norms (D'Aunno 2006: 222; D'Aunno, Vaughn and McElroy 1999). There is also little literature that has focused specifically on substance abuse counselors and administrators (D'Aunno 2006; but, for a recent notable exception, see Pollack and D'Aunno 2008), and none to my knowledge that shows how counselors draw on and integrate both clinical theory and folk theory in their interactions with clients. This book suggests that to know more about addiction treatment as it is actually practiced, we must look more closely at how counselors are trained, how they make sense of and conduct their everyday work in light of this training, and how they revise and refine their approaches as they accrue on-the-ground experience in organizations and with clients.

Although my purpose in writing this book has never been to propose or prescribe new interventions, therapeutic approaches, or modes of service delivery, I have, of course, developed perspectives about how the institutional and therapeutic practices I describe here could be productively reworked. For instance, since completing the research for this book, I have become an advocate of "housing first" and harm reduction housing strategies, which consider housing a right or a basic need and do not require clients to attend treatment in order to access or retain it (Padgett, Gulcar, and Tsemberis 2006; Tsemberis, Gulcur, and Nakae 2004; Milby et al. 2005; Schumacher et al. 2000).[8] In other words, such programs reverse the sequence of services of "continuum of care" and "treatment-first" programs, such as HFC's, which require clients to attend drug treatment in order to gain or retain access to transitional and subsidized housing services.

We still have much to learn about the dynamics of housing programs that do not have abstinence-based contingencies.[9] Aside from my opinion that housing is a human entitlement, this book highlights clear reasons to move away from treatment-first approaches. First, and most obvious, drug users who are already stably housed will undoubtedly be better prepared to benefit from drug treatment. Second, by eliminating the coercive linkage of treatment to housing and other ancillary services, addiction treatment practitioners will likely encounter a more invested group of clients, which will both strengthen therapeutic alliances and positively affect interactions between clients.[10] *Scripting Addiction* suggests that clients in contingency-based housing programs, such as HFC, may attend addiction treatment simply to access other services, especially when living in an environment of increasingly scarce and hard-to-obtain resources. Indeed, one can read the practice of flipping the script as diagnostic of political economic conditions and a social service delivery system that make it difficult to focus on much more than accessing and retaining shelter, food, and other basic services.

Since completing my research at Fresh Beginnings, I have also refined my understanding of and position on gender-specific addiction treatment.[11] In general, I continue to support offering ancillary services such as child care and transportation, which is consistent with reports of client satisfaction in current service research (Smith and Marsh 2002).[12] However, for the reasons articulated above, I do not believe that it benefits programs, professionals, or clients to use ancillary services to persuade or coerce clients into treatment. Considering that some Fresh Beginnings clients prolonged their treatment so as to retain free child care, a resource that allowed them to work part-time jobs or take GED classes, programs need to think carefully about *how* and *under what terms* ancillary services will be provided. And to the extent that scholars and practitioners of addiction treatment are driven by goals of gender equality, we would be wise to advocate offering ancillary services, such as child care and transportation, to middle- and low-income men as well.[13] This would obviously make it easier for them to share the responsibilities and benefits of raising children.

While I have strengthened my support of the provision of ancillary services under the conditions delineated above, I have become more skeptical of "gender-sensitive" therapeutic approaches since completing my research at Fresh Beginnings. Indeed, *Scripting Addiction* suggests that such approaches can potentially *prescribe* gender difference rather than respond to already existing, gender-specific states or qualities. For instance, recall how Fresh Beginnings therapists theorized and approached "shame"—a quality that they, in line with literature on gender-sensitive addiction treatment, believed to be an attribute specific to women drug users. Shame, they further proposed, had a specifically sexual etiology, which connected childhood sexual abuse to women's later abuse of drugs. Although the literature contains evidence of this connection, estimates vary dramatically. A Fresh Beginnings client provided one way to explain this variation when she said: "You got to be abused [at Fresh Beginnings], or they start thinkin' there be somethin' wrong with *you*."

Surely, some women at Fresh Beginnings had been sexually victimized as children, which may have indeed been relevant to why they used drugs later in life. Yet to the extent that clinical scholars and practitioners conceptualize women as a social grouping that share certain socio-psychological characteristics—regardless of class, race, or country of origin—we risk funneling clients' complex histories and circumstances, along with their clinical and political significance, into predictable narratives about why women use drugs and what best helps them to stop (narratives, by the way, that clients are well poised to flip— as we saw in chapter 6). This tendency arguably becomes all the more problematic when explanations about why women use drugs are so keenly focused on early childhood sexual victimization and routinely downplay the traumas entailed in adult poverty, homelessness, and racial discrimination.

My research at Fresh Beginnings suggests that the one aspect of treatment that might make the most immediate and enduring positive impact on American addiction treatment is a reworking of the concept of denial. As detailed in chapter 3, this concept has long stood at the ideological center of the field and enjoys a wide range of professional adherents across otherwise distinctive theoretical orientations. Throughout the book we saw how the casting of clients as unable to read and know themselves, and therefore unable to speak authoritatively, profoundly affected the way therapists clinically engaged their clients. Furthermore, as a metalinguistic as well as clinical heuristic, denial also influenced how clients could engage in program governance, as was dramatically illustrated by Rhonda's and Louise's respective experiences in the boardroom (see chapter 5). Given these double binds, we might also hazard that the analytical sensibility that many clients cultivated, which sometimes manifested in acts of script flipping, owes much to therapists' conceptual reliance on denial. Considering these wide-ranging effects of the idea of addicted denial, we must wonder how, in its absence, the clinical encounter and the institutional environs might positively transform, allowing therapists and clients to re-channel their analytical energies in more creative and collaborative ways.

This appears to be precisely the goal of an innovative counseling method known as Motivational Interviewing (MI), formulated in the mid-1980s for the treatment of drug users and now enjoying popularity across a number of professional fields. Staked explicitly against "traditional" and "confrontational" approaches to addiction treatment, MI casts itself not simply as a novel set of clinical techniques, but also as a special "style," "spirit," or "way of being with people" that "can be likened to that of a dance, where the practitioner leads in a delicately balanced collaborative effort" (Miller and Rollnick 2002:280).

Thanks to its dedication to intensive and ongoing clinical training programs, MI has developed a number of ways to enhance practitioners' reflexive awareness as they lead clients in the delicate "dance" of the therapeutic encounter. Most important, MI proponents understand both denial and motivation as possible discursive products of the clinical encounter rather than the latent qualities of the drug-addicted person. In a foundational text, lead proponents William Miller and Stephen Rollnick put it this way:

> Some people believe that resistance occurs because of a client's character armor . . . Primitive defense mechanisms such as denial were once believed to be an inherent part of, even diagnostic of, alcoholism. In this way of thinking, resistance walks through the door with the client. We question this view, which attributes resistance primarily to the client. Instead, we emphasize that, to a significant extent, resistance arises from the interpersonal interaction between counselor and client. (2002:98)

Motivational Interviewing may be an ideal example of how much can change with the reworking of a single if central clinical heuristic. Indeed, MI's recasting of denial is accompanied by what appears to be the elaboration of a new semiotic ideology, as well as a set of attendant linguistic rituals, which reconfigure the therapeutic relationship between language and personhood. Namely, whereas Fresh Beginnings therapists understood talk therapy to be a matter of eliciting inner states that are always already there, awaiting escape into words, MI practitioners are trained to co-produce "change statements" with clients, which are endowed with a social, psychological, perhaps even mystical, force of their own. More specifically, "change statements" are considered efficacious not because they refer to an already formulated inner state (i.e., a preexisting desire to change) that one comes to see and then puts into words but instead because they prompt and produce the change that they index. Accordingly, MI practitioners understand their practice as a matter of orchestrating productive conversations rather than eliciting acts of inner reference.[14]

Rather than getting clients to see what they once denied, the practice of MI appears to involve exploring the parallel interpretations of counselors and clients, and closing the potentially conflictual gap between those symbolic worlds (cf. Strathern 1988). This fascinating therapeutic modality deserves the same careful ethnographic analysis as the mainstream addiction treatment practices investigated here, work I am currently undertaking. Considering the cultural roots and resonances of the language ideology distilled in programs like Fresh Beginnings, there is every reason to suspect that ideas about denial and language-as-inner reference will persist and coexist alongside the novel approaches offered by proponents of Motivational Interviewing. But one way or another, we can expect—as always—that change is on its way.

. . .

In the end, *Scripting Addiction* tells a story about contemporary Americans, with a special interest in who we think we are and how those reflections relate to what we think we can reveal about ourselves when we speak. Indeed, if this story has sounded eerily familiar to readers previously unfamiliar with addiction treatment, it is because Fresh Beginnings distills distinctly American ideas about what it means to speak as and therefore *to be* a healthy, clean, and sober person, the kind of person who is valued and legitimated by others. Because institutions always distill culture, they can show us what we believe in disturbingly clear and potent form. How might we productively revise the forms and formulae of being and speaking documented here, given the impossibility of wholly fresh beginnings?

Notes

INTRODUCTION

1. I use the terms "professionals," "professional practitioners," and "social service professionals" somewhat interchangeably in this book to designate the broad category of workers—including case managers, chemical dependency counselors, clinical consultants, domestic violence advocates, family therapists, program directors and administrators, and shelter managers—whom I studied during my fieldwork. Most of these practitioners had master's degrees in social work (MSWs); a couple had received master's degrees in counseling or related professional disciplines, among them one of the two therapists at Fresh Beginnings. A few of the case managers and domestic violence advocates had only a bachelor's degree in social work (BSW) or were enrolled part-time in local MSW programs during the period of this study.

2. Although this book focuses on three central domains of American social work—addiction treatment, housing and homelessness services, and domestic and family violence services—the profession is vast, including fields such as child welfare; community development and organizing; community-based mental health; hospital social work; hospice care; inpatient mental health; juvenile and adult corrections; occupational social work and income support; private clinical practice with individuals, couples, and families; school social work; probation and parole services; long-term and respite care for the elderly; social insurance; and public welfare.

3. Jane Hill (2000) notes that every regime of personhood selects exemplary speech acts, evaluating the integrity or efficacy of speakers accordingly. For instance, as the late Michelle Rosaldo's work on Illongot *tuk*, or commands, brilliantly demonstrates, gender- and age-stratified commands are not expressions of what Illongot speakers want or need but instead are highly valued ways to organize labor and channel energy (Rosaldo 1980, 1982). Valued for the communal things they do rather than the personal things they express, *tuk* throw acts of inner reference into particularly stark cultural relief, though both can be considered exemplars.

4. Alessandro Duranti's excellent ethnographic critique of "personalist" ideologies (e.g., 1988, 1993)—which espouses that "the meaning of an utterance is fully defined in the speaker's mind before the act of speaking" (1988:13–14)—is relevant here. In an effective critique of Speech Act Theorists such as Grice (1957, 1989) and Searle (1969, 1983), who suggest that speech acts can be judged by discerning the intention of speakers, Duranti uses evidence from Samoa to suggest the limits of personalist ideologies in understanding the interactional dynamics of meaning making (see also Rosaldo 1982). However, the ideology of inner

reference differs from the personalist ideologies that Duranti critiques in that speaker intention is a far less valued point of reference than other "inner states," such as feelings and memories. Indeed, as illustrated in chapter 3, the intention of client speakers at Fresh Beginnings was seen as a potential barrier to "healthy" speech rather than a measure of it.

5. Sobriety, or being sober, has become conventionally associated with abstaining from the excesses of alcohol and drugs (e.g., "clean and sober"). Historically, the term carried broader connotations of avoiding that which alters. Sobriety, then, is not just avoiding intoxication but also entails maintaining a pure and natural internal state, unfettered and unburdened by external agents. It is in this vein that sobriety is associated with the will and, more specifically, cast as an *ethical* means for the ends of selected, recognizable goals (cf. Weber 1958). More generally, Americans have come to understand that to be sober is to be dispassionate, solemn, serious, and, above all, demonstrably sensible in one's disposition and orientation. The idea that being sober is best marked by a sober language can be traced back to the nation's beginning. As Jay Fliegelman has shown, the Declaration of Independence was itself a document developed to be expressed through a natural rhetoric cleansed of the excesses of oratory and an ungrounded sophistry. "The language of natural sound and gesture sought to satisfy [the] needs for precision and control, and in addition, to counteract and undermine the dangers of eloquence, the dangers, that is, *of calculating language empty of real feeling*" (1993:47, emphasis added; see also Bauman and Briggs 2003).

6. The "disease model" of addiction—which posits that addiction is an incurable if treatable disease, caused by biological and environmental factors beyond an individual's control and negatively affecting the self-knowledge or insight of the drug user—was adopted by the American Medical Association in 1956 (Quinn, Davis, and Koch 2004). The disease model serves as the philosophical basis of both Alcoholics Anonymous (AA), and the Minnesota Model, which most professional programs relied upon through the early 1990s (Spicer 1993). And although the therapists at Fresh Beginnings program drew from a number of clinical traditions in both their everyday practice and in their elicited explanations of that practice, their commitment to the disease model was clear. Considering the pervasiveness of the Minnesota Model, especially during the time I conducted my research for this book, I use the term "mainstream addiction treatment" to indicate those programs and practitioners that follow the basic premises of the "disease model," which is elaborated throughout the text.

7. This is not to say that "reference" and "performance" are mutually exclusive types of semiotic phenomena. Indeed, as Silverstein (2004) has argued, pragmatic and performative acts are dependent on relationships of reference (see also Reddy 2001:97–98), and the following chapters explore the semiotic relationship of reference and performance in depth. Ethnographically, my goal is to decipher speakers' ideas about what a speech act indexes, the extent to which that act presupposes its point of reference, and what the act *does* via what it putatively denotes.

8. There are four levels of addiction treatment set by the American Society of Addiction Medicine Patient Placement Criteria for the Treatment of Substance-Related Disorders, 2nd ed. (ASAM-PPC-2)—a clinical guide for placing people in

the appropriate intensity of services in relation to the assessed level of need. Intensive Outpatient Programs (IOPs), along with partial hospitalization, are considered Level II services and require clients to attend treatment minimally nine hours a week on at least three different occasions. As a result of increasing decentralization and privatization of health and social services in the United States, the addiction treatment systems that emerged in the 1960s and 1970s have shifted from inpatient to outpatient services (see Weisner and Schmidt 1993; National Institutes of Health [NIH] 1997 [97–4107]), restricting the number of outpatient service sessions (Durkin 2002) and circumscribing the length of stay in remaining inpatient programs.

9. Fresh Beginnings was located in a county characterized by wide disparities in household income. While the 1990 median household income was approximately $36,000 and about 6.5 percent of households earned $100,000 per year or more, more than 12 percent of the population lived below the poverty line. Median rent in the county was almost $500 per month, and more than 40 percent of households spent 30 percent or more of their income on rent. A mother with one child living at the 1990 poverty level of $8,420 would need to spend almost 70 percent of her monthly income to afford an apartment at $500 a month (U.S. Census Bureau 1990).

10. According to the U.S. Code Collection (TITLE 42 CHAPTER 119 SUBCHAPTER I §11302) the category "homeless" includes individuals who lack a fixed, regular, and adequate nighttime residence; it also includes individuals who have a primary nighttime residence that is a supervised publicly or privately operated shelter designed to provide temporary living accommodations (including welfare hotels, congregate shelters, and transitional housing for the mentally ill); an institution that provides a temporary residence for individuals intended to be institutionalized; or a public or private place not designed for, or ordinarily used as, a regular sleeping accommodation for human beings (Cornell Legal Institute 2007). The definition of "homelessness," according to the National Office of Housing and Urban Development (HUD), has been interpreted to include persons and family being evicted within a week from a private dwelling, or being discharged within a week from an institution in which they have been a resident for more than thirty consecutive days, or fleeing a domestic violence situation. If children are involved in the "homeless event," the definition can also be interpreted to include those "doubled up" in friends' or relatives' dwellings due to loss of housing, economic hardship, or foster care placements.

11. In 1995, best countywide estimates indicated that approximately 1,000 families, in a county of approximately 120,000 households, met the federal criteria of homelessness. This number did not include homeless individuals, who, by virtue of local homeless service agencies' "family-centered" approach, were not included in its count. Over 90 percent of the families these agencies served were female-headed, in line with national trends. Of these female-headed families in the county, almost 25 percent lived under the 1989 federal poverty line, which was set at $9,990 for a family of three (i.e., two children, one parent).

12. In the then still shocking wake of late-twentieth-century American homelessness, many social work and welfare scholars worked to understand (and address) the similarly paired terms of "social drift" and "social causation" (e.g.,

Benda and Dattalo 1990; Dohrenwend et al. 1992; Dooley, Catalano, and Hough 1992). Generally, those who espouse the social drift hypothesis argue that people with mental illness, including addictions, plummet into poverty and mental illness because they lack the ability to "cope" socioeconomically (e.g., Weyerer 1994; Levav el al. 1987). Those who emphasize social causation argue that the stresses of poverty and homelessness cause once mentally healthy people to slip into mental illness (e.g., Rogler 1996; Link and Phelan 1996; McLeod and Kessler 1990). Several anthropologists have undertaken compelling genealogies of American discourses of homelessness (e.g., Gounis 1993; Hopper 1987, 1990, 2003; Susser 1996), and have productively questioned the practical and political consequences of these theses, as well as the more general scholarly tendency to frame homelessness as "crisis" (see Hopper and Baumohl 1994, in response to Lipsky and Smith 1989).

13. The idea that women drug users have distinctly different treatment needs than their male counterparts—because of unique social and psychological factors—was formulated in the early 1980s and developed through the 1990s (see Reed 1982, 1985, 1987; Brown and Gillespie 1992; Finkelstein 1993, 1994). Single-sex treatment programs, such as Fresh Beginnings, as well as women-only self-help groups, like Women for Sobriety, are manifestations of this early scholarship, which is characterized by both cultural feminist rationales, which suggest, for example, that women are "relational" and therefore should be treated with relational therapeutic techniques (i.e., Cook 1995), and liberal feminist arguments about equal access to therapeutic and material resources. The practice of "gender sensitivity" in addiction treatment is explored in some length in chapter 3 and is also addressed in the conclusion.

14. "Cultural sensitivity," both at Fresh Beginnings and in HFC more generally, was a common and official gloss for the acknowledgment of the race and class differences between professional staff and their clients, rather than among the clientele itself. This finding is consistent with Yoosun Park's (2005) argument that the "culture" in the social work project of "cultural sensitivity" is commonly read by professional practitioners as difference, though she goes on to argue that culture is approached as "deficit" as well. Along similar lines, Vilma Santiago-Irizarry's ethnographic study of "bicultural" psychiatric programs in New York City (e.g., 1996, 2001) documents the ethical and clinical dilemmas involved in the project of cultural sensitivity. Arguably, such dilemmas are particularly pronounced in mainstream American addiction treatment, where professionals are especially reluctant to consider cultural mediation of the relationship between (individual) mind and (narcotic) matter, thanks in part to the dominance of the disease model (see Miller and Carroll 2006 on the challenges of considering the social dimensions of drug-using behavior).

15. According to Asif Agha, a *register* is a linguistic repertoire that members of a cultural group associate with both particular social practices and the people who are imagined to engage in those practices (Agha 2001:212). He points out that such repertoires are not static and, indeed, must be instantiated or *registered* through a consensual social process that involves metalinguistic evaluation (see also Agha 1998, 2007). Chapter 1 is an ethnographic illustration of the process Agha calls "enregisterment."

16. In 1995, the year before the Personal Responsibility and Work Opportunity Reconciliation Act (PRWORA) was passed, families receiving benefits from the program Aid to Families with Dependent Children (AFDC) had cash incomes roughly equivalent to 40 percent of the federal poverty line which was set at an annual income of $7,740 for the head of household plus $2,560 for each additional household member.

17. Aside from its use in welfare reform debates, the discourse of dependency was recently put to work characterizing those struggling to survive in the devastating wake of Hurricane Katrina. Claiming that federal economic development efforts would harm poor and displaced New Orleans residents left homeless by the storm, Senate Republicans proposed four amendments to the labor and health and human services spending bill in October 2005. Senate Republican Conference Chairman Rick Santorum (PA) stated that, "The whole idea is to change the cycle of dependency. . . . If spending money is the answer we would have solved poverty a long time ago" (*Washington Times*, October 26, 2005). Santorum's proposed amendments focused on promoting marriage and responsibility among New Orleans fathers, which South Carolina Republican Jim DeMint agreed would do much to address the "root causes" of poverty. The lexicon of dependency has also been mobilized across international lines in the debates about whether to sustain or withdraw American forces in Iraq. Responding to President Bush's January 10, 2007, televised call to deploy additional troops, Dick Durbin sounded as much the concerned parent of a spoiled teenager as the Democratic Whip debating the most important political event of our time. Stating "we've given the Iraqis so much," Durbin implicated the Iraqis as underdeveloped democratic citizens as much as he criticized the president's botched war planning. Indeed, Durbin ended the Democrats' official response that evening by saying, "The Iraqis must understand that they alone can lead their nation to freedom. They alone must meet the challenges that lie ahead. And they must know that every time they call 911, we are not going to send 20,000 more American soldiers."

18. I explore the genealogy of the term "consumer" in American social services at some length in chapter 5.

19. Mariana Valverde (1998) argues that North American alcoholism—and, by extension, other chemical addictions—have been culturally cast as diseases of the will (see also Levine 1978). Based on readings of the clinical literature on addiction going back to the 1930s, I propose instead that addiction is approached and treated as a disease of *insight* and, more specifically, as a failure to translate inner desires into linguistic signs rather than consumptive behavior. And as I demonstrate in chapter 3, therapists contend that any disorder of the will corrects itself once addicts learn to *see* their true inner selves, presumably including what they will.

20. According to the 2007 National Survey of Substance Abuse Treatment Services (N-SSATS), 13,648 substance abuse treatment facilities reported that 1,135,425 people were being treated on March 30, 2007, with about 95 percent of facilities reporting. Of these, 11,078 (or 81.2%) are outpatient facilities, like Fresh Beginnings, and 4,337 (or 31%) have women-only programs, which is down substantially from 2002 when there were 5,150 such programs. Almost 1.9 million people were admitted to substance abuse treatment facilities in 2005. The

National Institute for Drug Abuse reports even more striking figures. In 2004 the Institute estimated that 22.5 million persons over age 12 were classified with substance dependence or abuse (9.4% of the population). An estimated 3.8 million people aged 12 or older (1.6% of the population) received some kind of treatment, and 1.6 million of these people received treatment in outpatient facilities like Fresh Beginnings.

21. The dual role of language in therapeutic settings, as both the instrument of diagnosis and the talking cure, has been noted both by clinical ethnographers (e.g., Young 1995; Lakoff 2005) and linguists interested in therapeutic language (e.g., Labov and Fanshel 1977; Ferrara 1994). *Scripting Addiction* builds on these studies by delving into the ideological assumptions about language, as well as the practical mobilization of those assumptions, that allow it to function both as the mode of diagnosis and the means of a cure.

22. The Minnesota Model relies heavily on group therapy, often using individual sessions on an as-needed or ancillary basis, and employs recovering professionals who connect on an experiential level with clients; it also frequently uses confrontational methods, and requires or strongly encourages participation in AA or NA (Chiauzzi and Liljegren 1993:305; see also Galanater, Glickman, and Singer 2007; Veach, Remley Kippers, and Sorg 2000; Quinn 2004). A comprehensive overview of the Minnesota Model, written by Patricia Owens, can be found on http://www.drugabuse.gov/ADAC/ADAC11.html (accessed August 1, 2009). Although the Minnesota Model is generally taken to be a philosophical offshoot of AA, particularly because of the clear commitment to the disease concept in both cases, see Miller (2003) for the ways that the principles of AA and the Minnesota model diverge.

23. Although Weber's discussion of the Puritanical evaluation of sobriety of spirit—and the development of the "ethical appreciation of the sober, middle-class, self-made Man" (1958:163)—is certainly relevant, St. Augustine's distinctly metalinguistic theory of the sober memory—which stores designata that is cleanly and clearly relayed by the properly penitent confessant—bears uncanny resemblance to the clinical ideas explored in chapter 3.

24. Marsha Linehan developed Dialectical Behavior Therapy (DBT) specifically for the treatment of borderline personality disorder (BPD), but it has been used in the treatment of other personality disorders and mental illnesses classified in the *Diagnostic and Statistical Manual (DSM) of Mental Disorders*, including chemical dependence. Linehan defines her approach as "the application of a broad array of cognitive and behavior strategies to the problems of BPD, including suicidal behaviors" (1993a:19). What makes the approach unique is its focus on a dialectical balance between acceptance and change, which she suggests "flows directly from the integration of a perspective drawn from Eastern (Zen) practice with Western psychological practice" (ibid.:19). Linehan also references Hegel and Kant, suggesting that these philosophers "discussed dialectics as a means of understanding or synthesizing apparent contradictions," which apparently leads to her premise that "from a dialectical worldview, behavior is conceptualized as interrelated, contextually determined, and systemic" (Rosenthal, Lynch, and Linehan 2005:617). Linehan suggests that *Cognitive-Behavioral Treatment of Borderline Personality Disorder* (1993a) and the accompanying *Skills Training*

Manual for Treating Borderline Personality Disorder (1993b) together provide a comprehensive guide to DBT.

25. For discussions of theoretical eclecticism and integrationism in American psychotherapeutic practice, see Applegate 2000; Borden 2009; Lazarus 1989, 1992, 2006; Norcross 2005; and Norcross, Karpiak, and Lister 2005.

26. The practice of script flipping poses a formidable methodological challenge to anthropologists and therapists alike: after all, successfully flipped scripts are identical—in both form and content—to those that are "followed." To the extent that my own interviewing techniques relied on the referential merits of their clients' words (Carr 2010b), I myself was not immune to the linguistic strategies of script flippers.

CHAPTER 1. IDENTIFYING ICONS AND THE POLICIES OF PERSONHOOD

1. One of these women, Lillie Harden, a former welfare recipient and starring character of Clinton's favorite anti-AFDC anecdotes (Carcasson 2004), spoke to the audience gathered in the Rose Garden before the president gave his framing address. According to the *Washington Post* (August 23 1996, A01), Harden, a forty-two-year-old mother of three from Clinton's hometown of Little Rock, Arkansas, received welfare for two years before finding work at a supermarket.

2. In the wake of twelve years of Republican executive rule, Clinton announced his "New Covenant" at a 1991 Democratic Leadership Council meeting in Cleveland, Ohio, as part of his bid for the presidential nomination. Centered on a "contract" that promised "opportunity" in exchange for "personal responsibility," the Covenant laid the rhetorical groundwork for the New Democrats' attack on the federal welfare system and was, in fact, instantiated in the very name of the 1996 Act. For an excellent overview of Clinton's rhetorical framing of welfare reform, see Carcasson 2004, 2006.

3. In his 1992 campaign book, *Putting People First*, Clinton laid out his plan to dismantle the federal welfare program. According to this plan, federal spending for child care, medical care, housing, job training, and so on, would accompany the eventual bill. When Clinton's plan was legalized in 1996, the share of national income going to the top 5 percent of households rose to 21.4 percent, the highest level ever recorded by the Census Bureau. By contrast, the share of income received by the bottom four-fifths of the population was close to an all-time low.

4. Clinton touted himself as particularly tuned into the experiential worlds of welfare recipients, claiming to have spent more time with them than any other elected official. He also insisted that welfare recipients hated being on welfare and he told stories of their demoralization, announcing in a roundtable discussion with Southern Illinois University students that he "almost never met anybody who didn't want to get off" (Clinton 1995, 2: 1340).

5. Lewis's work was first officially picked up by the late senator Daniel Moynihan, who wrote the renowned policy text, "The Negro Family" (1965). In this controversial and influential text, Moynihan charged that the "Negro Family" was a "tangle of pathology," linking this pathology as much with black "matri-

archy" as with poverty. Notably, while Moynihan's text was used to support many anti-welfare platforms over the last four decades, he was staunchly opposed to Clinton's PRWORA.

6. Remarks by the president at the signing of the Personal Responsibility and Work Opportunity Reconciliation Act, Office of the Press Secretary, August 22, 1996.

7. Ibid.

8. Foucault was consistently disdainful of the ideas that history is progressive and that discourse is "authored" by humans. However, Foucault's early career is distinguished by an archeological method that he later rejected, which can be characterized by its interest in the relationship *between* discursive forms and an attention to intratextual relationships. For Foucault, shifting to a genealogical method entailed broad sociological attention to what is *behind* discursive forms—as exemplified in *History of Sexuality, Volumes I and II* (1978, 1985). Arguably it is the ethnohistorical nature of the later work that has so appealed to anthropologists and cultural historians. However, from a linguistic anthropological perspective, there are costs to abandoning archeological attention to "the anticipatory power of meaning" (Foucault 1984a:83), as sometimes such intratextual relations are precisely what account for the generativity of discourses. For an explication of his shift from archeology to genealogy, see Foucault 1984a, 1984b.

9. Strauss et al.'s (1963) work gives some sense of the place of such "retreats" in the life of social welfare institutions and falls nicely in line with anthropological practice theories. Known for their work on the hospital as "a negotiated order," Strauss et al. suggest that although hospital workers shared a common goal (e.g., to produce healthy patients and turn them out into the world), they disagreed on how to achieve it. Rather than operating in accordance with a set of formal rules of conduct, which were not widely known, workers' sense of institutional order was achieved by daily negotiation among themselves. Although negotiations became patterned as staff worked together for long periods of time, they were continually subject to change. When negotiations broke down, institutional crises were solved by a formal, committee-made decision that was practiced as a rule until it was again forgotten and the cycle would begin again (see Wright 1994).

10. Most HFC administrators called clients "consumers." Line staff—like therapists and case managers—often used this term as well, especially during board meetings and in less formal conversations with administrators. Therapists at Fresh Beginnings—and case managers to a lesser extent —generally called clients "women," a term clients themselves often used (clients almost never referred to themselves as "consumers"). When referring to their collective experience in the program, clients frequently used the term "clients," which is why I adopt this appellation. The use of the term "consumer" at Fresh Beginnings and a brief history of its use in American social services more generally are discussed in chapter 5 (see also Carr 2009). Here it is important to remind the reader that almost none of the women who attended Fresh Beginnings did so voluntarily, and all were obliged to "service contracts" both at their home HFC agencies and in the treatment program.

11. In addiction treatment, as well as in American social work more generally, there is much discussion about the importance of maintaining "boundaries." As

was the case at Fresh Beginnings, this boundary talk generally falls into two categories. First, there is a prominent psychosocial discourse about the importance of having good boundaries between self and other that is applied to clients in treatment (and, arguably, especially women in treatment; see Haaken 1993). This psychosocial discourse clearly has philosophical roots in the dominant model of personhood in the United States as bounded, independent, and endowed with an autonomous will. Second, social workers commonly discuss the importance of firm boundaries between professionals and clients. While this kind of boundary talk is implicitly focused on institutional concerns and explicitly cast as an ethical matter, it is clearly intertwined with psychosocial boundary talk, not the least because of its common philosophical grounding (see Scott 2000 on boundaries in addiction counseling; also see Davidson 2005; Strom-Gottfried 1999; Taleff 2006).

12. For ethnographic treatments of case management, see Brodwin 2008; Estroff 1981; Floersch 1999, 2002; and Sullivan, Hartmann, and Wolk 1994.

13. In response to the relatively ineffectual New Construction program, which gave government grants to build public housing, Section Eight is a certificate program that pays 70 percent of the rent to low-income families if their housing is under fair market rent. By 1990, less than 5 percent of government housing funds went to public housing construction, channeling funds to the more conservative, voucher-based Section Eight program. At the time of this study, HFC administrators and clients estimated that there was an average eight-year wait for a Section Eight in the county, though I know of a case in which a client applied for and received a Section Eight within a three-year period.

14. Script flipping is fully explicated in chapter 6. Here, however, is an excellent demonstration of one its practical capabilities, namely, filling in semantic gaps in recognized ways or registers of speaking (i.e., "what you people are failing to *realize*" [line 1]). Arguably, Nikki recognizes an institutional discourse, sees that it is faltering, and then finds a way to rescue it rhetorically. Her appeal to the joint-smoking, beer-guzzling client does not simply serve as an empty warning of institutional failing, but is also an emphatic reminder that staff is "supposed to be" (line 13) focused on "giv[ing] us some kind of support" (line 16).

15. Notably, this practice of removing support services and resources as "reward" is precisely the opposite of the practice of "Contingency Management" (CM), in which clients in addiction treatment are given prizes (often cash) when they reach predetermined recovery goals. For the rationale and practice of CM, see, for example, Petry 2000, 2002.

16. Such statements are consistent with some of the scholarly literature on homelessness that HFC professionals may well have been exposed to during the course of their bachelor's or master's degree training in social work. For example, connecting homelessness with disintegration of family structure, Ziefert and Brown (1991) write, "A home provides women and children with the rootedness from which they can master daily living. Without this stable base, families often begin to disintegrate. Role boundaries begin to loosen within the family, and specific functions are usurped by people outside the family" (212). On the other hand, scholars such as Hopper and Baumohl (1994) argue that rather than focusing on homelessness as a problem of personal or familial structure, we should

248 • Notes to Chapter 2

instead focus on failures of political economic structures, viewing homelessness as a "standing pattern of residential instability" (527).

17. The idea of instilling structure through addiction treatment counseling is not at all idiosyncratic. Indeed, in a popular textbook on substance abuse, David McDowell and Henry Spitz (1999) write, "The group therapist sets the stage for a constructive group experience by supplying a group structure and setting limits for the members. This is particularly important in substance abuse work since so many people with problems of addiction come from families in which appropriate limits were not set and inter-generational boundary lines were not successfully delineated" (165).

18. Laura arrived at our last interview with two brown grocery bags of personal and professional documents, including her own performance reports.

19. See, for example, William White's (1993) *Critical Incidents: Ethical Issues in Substance Abuse Prevention and Treatment*. The general premise of the book, which presents more than two hundred "critical incidents" or ethical quandaries typically faced by substance abuse counselors, is that the field has lost its ethical way and must develop shared styles of ethical reasoning (see also Dove 1995; Chapman 1997; and Williams and Swartz 1998). An entire section of the book is devoted to client-professional relationships, which are often articulated in relation to "boundaries." Boundaries are in danger of being violated when the therapist has more than one kind of relationship with a client. The resulting "dual relationship" threatens to "compromise the quality and integrity of the service process" (White 1993:148; see also Chapman 1997). Along these lines, Laura's actions are cast as "boundary lapses" (line 7) not just because she crosses the boundary from therapeutic space into domestic space, but because her visits and calls suggest to her supervisors that she is acting as a mother, friend, or girlfriend as well as a therapist.

CHAPTER 2. TAKING THEM IN AND TALKING IT OUT

1. Ideas about privacy are embedded in the larger conceptual constellation commonly called "subjectivity" and, more particularly, the culturally and historically variable line drawn between "person" and "public." Jay Fliegelman has brilliantly shown how ideologies of language come to shape notions of privacy and personhood during the Jeffersonian eighteenth century, a period in which "all expression [is reconceived] as a form of self-expression, an opportunity as well as an imperative to externalize the self, to become self-evident" (1993:2). In line with Fliegelman's treatment of Jefferson as "an especially sensitive register of the social costs and benefits of such a view of language" (ibid.:2), I suggest that Shelly, Mabel, and Yolanda—in their careers at Fresh Beginnings—demonstrate the social consequences of particular modes of self-expression that have roots in the "natural language" of the Jeffersonian era and have continued to expand and exploit the region of "the private," as the contemporary recovery movement so aptly illustrates (see also Bauman and Briggs 2003; Hacking 1975; Lowney 1999).

2. Although the majority of clients filtered in and out of the HFC system in a matter of weeks, and sometimes days or even hours, HFC's transitional housing program—which primarily served to place people in low-rent housing—allowed clients to stay connected with HFC and receive housing assistance and ancillary services for up to two years. A couple of HFC programs also had active internship programs, which hired clients into paraprofessional roles after their tenure as clients. However, the 1996 changes in federal and state welfare assistance, and decreasing governmental support for the poor and homeless more generally, meant that HFC clients were increasingly pressured into jobs and out of HFC agencies toward the later stages of my research.

3. Textbook assessment guides commonly suggest that assessors begin with open-ended questions to "establish rapport" with assessees (e.g., Boyle et al. 2005; Hepworth, Rooney, and Larsen 2002; Soriano 1995) or, more rarely, to allow assessees to establish the definitional terms of the interchange (Greenfield and Hennessey 2004:102).

4. Historical sociologist Leslie Margolin and Jerry Floersch—a social work scholar and ethnographer of Assertive Community Treatment (ACT)—have both addressed the power and politics of case files. Margolin claims, simply, that "the control of writing gives investigators power over clients, making it impossible for people at risk of being labeled as child abuser to 'negotiate' on an equal basis." (1997:148). This point fits into his broader claim that social work has historically operated "under the cover of kindness," the title of his 1997 book. In determining the nature and effects of case files, Jerry Floersch (1999, 2000, 2002) argues for the methodological importance of linking written texts (like case records) to spoken texts (such as interviews with workers who compile those records, and with clients who are portrayed in them). I hope this chapter adds another dimension to this debate by suggesting that clients, as well as case workers, find ways to manage written accounts, often through carefully calibrated verbal performances on occasions such as assessment interviews and program intakes. For further critique of Margolin's provocative history of social work, see Wakefield 1998.

5. As has been recognized by a diverse group of social work and welfare scholars (Chambón 1999; de Montigy 1995; Hasenfeld 1987; Margolin 1997; Saleebey 1994; Tice 1998) and anthropologists (Asad 1973; Clifford and Marcus 1986; Marcus and Fischer 1986; Silverstein and Urban 1996; Tedlock and Mannheim 1995), it is not just the task of gathering knowledge that is power-laden but also the re-rendering of it as text that others can read.

6. Although assessors claimed that their work entailed finding out who people are, they were simultaneously involved in what Ian Hacking calls "making people up" (1991, 1999). In his acute matter-of-factness, Hacking notes that "many of our sortings of people are evaluative" (1999:130), including (social) scientific ones. And, indeed, because of the social scientific interest in deviance, our classifications of people tend to evaluate "who is troubling or in trouble" (ibid.:131). This is particularly true in social work, as Hacking seems to acknowledge (see 1991:266; see also Hall et al. 2003, 2006; Margolin 1997; Tice 1998). In fact, as a number of social work and welfare scholars have demonstrated, social service

institutions serve to "process" people as "clients," which Hasenfeld calls "people processing" (1983, 1992)—an idea that I engage throughout this book. Unlike social scientific categorization, social workers are interested not only in creating and refining categories of trouble, but also in intervening in the lives of the people who come to inhabit them.

7. In their study of human service encounters, sociologists William Spenser and Jennifer McKinney argue that intake interviews involve the production of "trouble" and define trouble as "a divergence between the service preferences of clients and social workers as expressed in their discourse during human service encounters" (1997:186). Amir Marvasti builds on this work by examining how social workers and clients in an emergency homeless shelter engage in what he calls "collaborative narrative editing" to "reach a definition [of homelessness] that rationally fits the mission of [the] shelter and facilitates the administration of limited resources" (2002:615). Both these studies suggest that social problems and institutional solutions are the product of joint labor on the part of social workers and clients, and therefore are consistent with the analysis this chapter pursues.

8. In this sense my approach responds to Goffman's idea of "trimming" as articulated in his masterful work, *Asylums* (1961). According to Goffman, the admissions process into the asylum is a process of trimming away what he calls an "identity kit"—one's feelings about one's self, one's thoughts, one's physical body and one's possessions, or all that we culturally recognize to be within the "territory of self." While clearly the language of self-as-kit is commentary on culture outside the institution as well as within it, Goffman's later ideas of the self as an ideological effect of particular performances (as in his famous essay on "footing," for example) suggest that the asylum's collecting of the dossier of information is at once the violation and the construction of "the informational preserve regarding the self" (Goffman 1961:23).

9. Consider Trudy's response in contrast to Spenser and Mckinney's description of intake interviews in a homeless shelter: "[Social workers'] soliciting requests at the beginning of the interview provided the opportunity for clients to rhetorically construct biographical narratives as accounts for those requests. In this way, narratives were not mere descriptions of clients' biographies, they were accountable reasons for their service requests" (1997:191–192).

10. The *Encyclopedia of Social Work* (Edwards 1995:335) notes that the assessment of clients' needs is one of five basic functions of case management: "Case managers typically are assigned responsibility for identifying and engaging clients, assessing their needs, locating appropriate services and planning for their use, linking clients to resources, and monitoring the process for targeted or desired outcomes. . . . Case managers also are supposed to ensure the timely and adequate delivery of appropriate services." Genograms are among a number of key assessment tools listed in the *Encyclopedia of Social Work*.

11. In their widely read text on conducting social work assessments, now in its third edition, family systems theorists Monica McGoldrick and Randy Gerson supply readers with genograms of a number of well-known public figures, including Sigmund Freud, Eleanor Roosevelt, and Henry Fonda, as well as Gregory Bateson and Margaret Mead. Information about the Bateson and Mead family is

gleaned from a number of biographical and autobiographical texts (e.g., Bateson 1984; Brockman 1977; Mead 1972), yet Bateson's influence on systems therapies goes curiously unmentioned. Whereas McGoldrick and Gerson never mention Bateson's influence on systems therapies (all the while genogramming his family!), Stuart Lieberman is cognizant of family therapy's long relationship with Batesonian anthropology (see also Keeney and Sprenkle 1982; Keeney and Ross 1983; Inger 1993; and Beels 2002); accordingly, he views the family therapist as analogous to the anthropologist working "in a strange kinship system" (1998: 200). Lieberman further suggests that the genogram has much in common with the kinship charts of anthropologists, both of which are used as "a tool to explore a kinship's *heritage*, the social and ideational environment, the knowledge, expedients, habits and institutions handed down from one generation to the next" (ibid.:200).

12. McGoldrick and Gerson emphasize that "there is no generally agreed-upon 'right way' to do a genogram . . . just a loose consensus about what specific information to seek, how to record it, and what it all means" (1985:1). Nonetheless, their 1985 book includes several dozen genogram symbols and accompanying text that prompt readers just what to seek and how to render and interpret it. Notably, the number of genogram symbols has grown over the years. By the second edition of their book, McGoldrick, Gerson, and Shellenberger (1999) list thirty-seven "Standard Symbols for Genograms." And though HFC assessors were not privy to them, several genogram software programs have recently emerged that have further expanded the number of symbols that can be used. For instance, GenoPro, a commercially available genogram software package, offers a total of sixty-four symbols. The software includes thirty-one types of line symbols representing different types of relationships, from "fused-hostile" to "in love" to "fan/admirer" and allows the addition of digital photos of family members beside their symbol on the genogram (see Figure 2.4).

13. The material in this chapter, in fact, could be effectively analyzed in the analytic terms of role recruitment—the interactional process by which people are drawn into institutional and sociological taxonomies by being identified and asked to respond as particular "types" of people. Asif Agha (1993, 2007) and Michael Silverstein (1998, 2004, 2005) have elaborated the semiotic processes involved in role recruitment and in so doing have unpacked the process that Louis Althusser (1971) calls "interpellation." Althusser asserts that individuals are already always subjects (of the Ideological State Apparatus, as Althusser would more particularly have it) as they are called upon or "interpellated" by proper names, gendered pronouns, and other forms of direct address. Hailings such as "Hey, you there" (ibid.:175), precisely because they elicit the questioning response (i.e., "who me?"), compel subjects to recognize that they have a "fixed residence" where they can be called (ibid.:178). See chapter 5 for further discussion and illustration of role recruitment and interpellation. Also see Carr 2009.

14. WISH retained a number of expert legal advocates, whose role it was to coach clients through court cases, where their initial responses to social workers were passed along, repeated, modified, or refuted as "evidence." In an otherwise excellent ethnography about social problems work in domestic violence shelters, Donileen Loseke (1992) seems to underplay such legal pressures involved in

social workers' everyday constructions of battered women and domestic violence. For anthropological treatments of the production of legal texts, see Matoesian 1993, 2001, 2009; Mertz 1996, 1998, 2007; and Philips 1998).

15. This includes the assessment tool known as the "Person-In-Environment System" or "PIE" system. In the early 1980s, with the help of a grant from the National Association of Social Workers (NASW) and explicitly "using the organizing construct of 'person-in-environment,'" social work scholars Jim Karls and Karin Wandrei developed PIE as "a new system for identifying, describing, and classifying the common problems brought to the social worker" (1994:1818). The authors suggested that their instrument "provides social work practitioners in all settings with a common language for describing the problems of their clients. This language can facilitate work with the client and clarify aspects of the client's problems that are in the domain of social work" (ibid.). Indeed, the authors are explicit that the PIE system was developed in direct response to diagnostic instruments such as the DSM–IV (discussed in the following chapter), and in an effort to create a standardized, distinguishing, and unifying assessment instrument for social workers.

16. Chenot (1998) writes, "In social work, beginning where the client is, stands out as one of the most commonly held and essential values" (304), and, indeed, the adage "meeting the client where she is" or "beginning where the client is" enjoys the status of an ethical precept in contemporary American social work. According to some clinical social work scholars, the adage has its roots in the work of self-psychologist Heinz Kohut (Eisenhuth 1981; Chenot 1998), yet clearly it has been widely adopted across particular clinical orientations (e.g., Bardill 1996; Burack-Weiss 1988; Coholic 2003; Leon and Armantrout 2007; Marsh 2002; Pomeroy, Walker, and McNeil 1996; Saari 1986).

17. For instance, Fresh Beginnings expected that assessees who had a positive screening for marijuana (the metabolites of which last up to six weeks in the urine of regular users) would be referred along with habitual users of "harder" drugs. Most case managers made fairly sharp distinctions between crack cocaine use, which they unanimously felt warranted a referral to Fresh Beginnings, and marijuana use, which they found relatively unproblematic. For instance, one case manager relayed the common sense that "if, if somebody's using crack, they probably need to get some help, but uhm, with but with certain level of alcohol or marijuana use, some of us might feel like: 'ok, maybe it's recreational.'" However, most HFC case managers would likely concur with the case manager's further statement that *"philosophically my idea* is that if you're *homeless*, you got no business spending money or even any, very much *time* drinking or smoking pot, 'cause you got too much other stuff to deal with and you've got *kids*, and you're living in a *shelter*, and you *really should be* focusing *all* your energies on getting everything together so that you can move on and get into your own."

18. First employed in VA hospitals with Vietnam veterans returning from war, urine screening is now a common aspect of contemporary addiction treatment in the U.S. Since Reagan ordered the drug testing of all federal employees in the early 1980s (an order struck down by the Supreme Court, excepting pilots and conductors), drug testing has made its way into other areas of public life, including the workplace (see Osterlo and Becker 1990). There now appears to be a

movement toward increased reliance on drug testing as an addiction treatment modality; indeed, the National Institute of Justice recently suggested that expensive treatment programs for criminal justice populations be replaced with frequent testing (William Garriott, personal communication).

19. This is not to say that "sugarcoating" did not involve extra-institutional considerations. Clients were well aware of, and indeed invested in, cultural norms about drugs and the complex valuations that render some drugs (alcohol, marijuana) more acceptable than others (opiates, amphetamines). Clients were also acutely aware that the relative valuation of powder versus crack cocaine was (and still is) built into our legal system, even though they are the same substance. Since 1988, those charged with possession of one gram of crack cocaine could expect the same sentence as those charged with possessing one hundred grams of powder cocaine—a policy that substantially accounts for the soaring rates of incarceration of black and Latino men and women in the United States.

20. A few clients, in interviews, demonstrated their knowledge of an array of tactics used to trump urinalysis, though only a few claimed that they had engaged in any themselves. Specifically, clients told me that some of their peers regularly toted vials of their sober children's, family members', or friends' urine in their purses, pockets, or bras, carrying them straight into the Cliff Street bathroom when subjected to random drops. And even during the brief, officially legitimated period of monitored drug screening (which is discussed in chapter 6), clients claimed that an active user—if experienced—could evade his or her therapist's detection. One client described a process of bleaching or salting her fingers before entering the bathroom, and then rubbing them surreptitiously on the inside of vials as they opened them, purportedly lacing their "dropped" urine as a result.

21. The law that governs mandated reporting of child abuse and neglect in the state where this research was conducted does not mention whether a parent's or child's use of controlled substances is considered child abuse or neglect. The law does require, however, the mandated reporting of infants born with alcohol or a controlled substance in their bodies and children exposed to the manufacturing of methamphetamine. Companion materials to the mandated reporting law are similarly vague on the issue of substance abuse. The guide lists specific actions and situations that warrant a report to Child Protective Services. Drug use by parents or children is not included in this section, but a subsequent section of the guide instructs reporters to be prepared to answer questions about parental drug use when making a report of suspected "physical neglect."

22. Cocaine can be detected in the urine approximately two to four days after use. Alcohol has the shortest "shelf life" and can only be detected in the urine for twelve hours after usage. When using urine (rather than hair or blood tests), the detection period for methamphetamines and amphetamines is one to two days; for heroin, morphine, and codeine, two days; for barbiturates, two days to three weeks; for benzodiazepines (if used chronically), six weeks; and for cannabis, up to eight weeks (LabCorp, Inc. 2007).

23. Many HFC staff employed the term "termination" to refer to the cessation of services due to a client's lack of compliance. The term "discharge" was generally reserved for clients who ceased services on their own volition, left a program in good standing, or left willingly in light of more minor infractions.

24. Drug testing is also expensive. In a study of the costs of employee drug testing, Ozminkowski et al. (2001), report that off-site testing for amphetamines, opiates, cocaine, marijuana, and PCP cost an average of $41.67 per test, not including the cost of employee time related to the administration of the test. In recent years a number of testing companies have developed simple-to-use, on-site drug-testing kits that cost as little as $10 per test when purchased in bulk. HFC sent all testing kits off site for lab analysis, and on more than one occasion I heard administrators mention the high cost of doing so.

25. Cassie articulates a fairly standard way of collecting information about a client's substance use, in which the client's age when she first tried each drug is thought to have diagnostic implications. For instance, Robins and Przybeck (1985) and Willis et al. (1996) suggest that people who use a drug before the age of fifteen are "at risk" for abusing it later in life. Greenfield and Hennessy (2004) suggest that assessments should address the following eight areas: (1) age at first substance use; (2) frequency of substance use; (3) amount of the substance used; (4) route of administration for the substance; (5) consequences associated with substance use; (6) treatment history; (7) periods of abstinence; and (8) relapses.

26. Posing an alternative to the Freudian slip and drawing on Goffman's (1981) idea of response cries, Jane Hill (1995) suggests that moments of consciousness can emerge between words rather than manifesting by or in words. In this sense, she suggests that stutters can be indexed to "a responsible self which attends to precise representation" (1995:135; cf. Irvine 1990). Accordingly, we can say that Yolanda and her stutters indicate her efforts to square the three sets of intricately related speech events and their corresponding frames: her first assessment interview in which she initially discussed her drug use (lines 1–2), her later revisions to that discussion with her WISH assessors (line 5), and the enveloping frame of the ethnographic interview (lines 1–15), which essentially asks her to square all three of her reports.

27. These criteria, and Fresh Beginnings therapists' mobilization of them, are discussed at length in the next chapter.

28. Although the drug and alcohol field has long operated on the assumption that there is underreporting on drug and alcohol assessments (whether conducted for research or practice purposes), and, according to Midanik, "over-reporting is almost never seen as a possible behavior" (1989:1421), recent research suggests otherwise. Employing the Paulhus Deception Scales (PDS) (Paulhus 1998) and the Texas Christian University Drug Screen I (Simpson and Knight 1998), Richards and Pai (2003) found that, when screening for a voluntary in-prison substance abuse treatment program, almost 37 percent of participants produced protocols of questionable validity, with 22 percent "faking-good" (that is, downplaying or disguising a drug habit) and 14.7 percent "faking-bad" (or exaggerating or fabricating a drug habit). Midanik found, as early as 1982, over-reporting of new entrants into a treatment program of up to 57 percent and concludes that, "by overreporting their alcohol consumption, they have the impression that they were generally in need of the treatment program itself and its secondary benefits such as food and shelter" (1989:1421). Such findings have led some addiction researchers, such as Davies, to regard self-reports of drug use as "acts of con-

struction rather than merely degraded versions of the truth" (1987:1273, as cited in Midanik 1989:1420).

29. Section 1.01 of the 1996 National Association of Social Workers Code of Ethics, reads: "Commitment to Clients: Social workers' primary responsibility is to promote the well-being of clients. In general, clients' interests are primary. However, social workers' responsibility to the larger society or specific legal obligations may on limited occasions supersede the loyalty owed clients, and clients should be so advised. (Examples include when a social worker is required by law to report that a client has abused a child or has threatened to harm self or others)." In such cases, social workers are cautioned to reveal "the least amount of confidential information necessary to achieve the desired purpose" (ibid.). The Code of Ethics also demands that social workers discuss with their clients these limits of the client's right to confidentiality. Social workers and other mandated reporters in HFC's home state who fail to report suspected child abuse or neglect are guilty of a misdemeanor and can be subject to both fines and imprisonment.

30. This estimate does not include the reports made by the second chemical dependency therapist, Susan, nor those filed by the two child and family counselors on staff—though reports were generally made with team discussion and support and were therefore probably included in Laura's count.

31. As we have already seen, it was not unusual for HFC social workers to reenact previous conversations—especially when those conversations were with clients. They did so not just with me but also with one another, and most often when the represented interchange explicitly or implicitly involved questions of authority (i.e., confronting a client who had broken the rules, recounting a conversation with a client who refused to follow up on a psychiatric referral, etc.). These reenactments allowed opportunities for therapists and case managers alike to edit and repair what they had said and done before, and were therefore highly valued linguistic resources within the HFC system. More generally, these reenactments can be thought of as a way that HFC social workers developed and cultivated social work expertise—reworking what they said and did when alone with their clients for an audience of colleagues who could evaluate, comment upon, and critique based on their own history of interactions.

32. It is well documented that poor, and particularly homeless, parents have far more contact with child welfare systems than middle-class parents do (Hutchison 1989; Jenkins et al. 1983; Katz 1983; Lindsey 1994; Nelson 1984; Wolock 1982). There are various reasons for this, aside from individual worker discrimination. First, the poor and homeless make more use of social service systems that subject them to increased state surveillance. Second, because children can be and most often are removed for "neglect" rather than abuse, parents with fewer economic and social supports are more likely to, for example, leave children under the age of twelve home at night while they work a late shift. This is one of the more concerning consequences of the policy coupling of child abuse and neglect.

33. Although researchers have yet to find a direct causal relationship between substance abuse and child maltreatment and neglect (Tomison 1996), the extent to which substance abuse alone, whether or not in the case of *in vitro* exposure, is reported *as* abuse or neglect varies by state and by report. In the case of Fresh

256 • Notes to Chapter 3

Beginnings, I heard of at least two cases in which relapse was reported as neglect, without evidence of subsequent acts of maltreatment, and the numbers are likely higher.

34. This interview was conducted as part of a program evaluation of HFC, and though I was part of the evaluation team, I did not conduct this particular interview. The interview was conducted off site, at a nearby university, where most of the evaluation staff was employed or attending as a student. In the case cited here, the interviewer, in fact, was working on her doctorate in social work and disclosed early in the interview that she was "in recovery"—features of this text that should be considered in analyzing it. For a further discussion of the dynamics of interviewing as they pertain to this project, see Carr 2010b.

CHAPTER 3. CLINOGRAPHIES OF ADDICTION

The sources of the definitions given in the epigraph to the chapter are the following: definition 1: http://www.healthexpertadvice.org/medical_dictionary/index.php?l=C&page=119 (retrieved August 8, 2009); definitions 2 and 3: *Webster's Unabridged Dictionary*, 2nd ed. (New York: Random House, 2001).

1. Derrida reminds us that it is not consumption per se that renders the addict culturally problematic nor even the consumption of drugs (after all, think of caffeine or the two-martini lunch). Within a constellation of political and cultural ideas that links some consumables (such as caffeine or Adderall) with production and does not recognize the productive potential of others (such as crack cocaine or heroin), it is consumption that is thought to *produce nothing* in return that is condemned. Indeed, following Derrida, drug addiction is a kind of consumption in which nothing is produced except the drive to consume more.

2. Motivational Interviewing (MI), an innovative counseling method first formulated in the mid-1980s for the treatment of drug users, is a significant exception. In short, MI proponents have retheorized denial as the discursive product of the clinical encounter rather than a latent quality of the drug-addicted person. In the foundational text, founders and lead proponents William Miller and Stephen Rollnick (2002:98) put it this way:

> Some people believe that resistance occurs because of a client's character armor . . . Primitive defense mechanisms such as denial were once believed to be an inherent part of, even diagnostic of, alcoholism. In this way of thinking, resistance walks through the door with the client. We question this view, which attributes resistance primarily to the client. Instead, we emphasize that, to a significant extent, resistance arises from the interpersonal interaction between counselor and client.

This chapter works to ethnographically demonstrate this very point.

3. Cynthia Scott goes further, warning that "the tendency to reduce all client resistance to denial often obscures the possibility that the problem may lie in the treatment model, not in the client" (2000:210).

4. For instance, in his classic genealogical paper, "The Discovery of Addiction," Harry Levine identifies Locke's differentiation between desire and will

as the conceptual impetus of the modern formulation of addiction. He writes, "In the 19th and 20th century versions, addiction is seen as a sort of disease of the will, an inability to prevent oneself from drinking" (1978:494). According to Levine, Dr. Benjamin Rush, the earliest American addictionologist and signer of the Declaration of Independence, himself identified addiction as a "disease of the will" (ibid).

5. In Alcoholic Anonymous Bateson found illustration of the following cybernetic principles: the mind is imminent in the system, any ensemble of events has mental characteristics, and no part of an internally interactive system can have unilateral control over any other part. According to Bateson, these principles are rejected by the alcoholic, whose willful maxim, "I will fight the bottle," is always bound to fail, precisely because the system (i.e., liquor–mouth–throat–stomach–blood–brain–liquor) is neither bounded nor controlled by the individual consciousness (whether inebriated or not).

6. This does not mean that denial permanently disappears with treatment. In accordance with the notion that addiction is a lifelong disease, therapists warned clients that they needed to stay vigilant against reoccurrence. For instance, in the aforementioned document, "What Is Denial?" clients could read the following caveat: "Denial does tent [sic] to recur, and, if left unchecked, it can lead to resurgence of defense mechanisms and undermine self-awareness and honesty."

7. In recovery parlance, a "dry drunk" is one who continues to behave like an addict, denying her problems and responsibilities, even when not actively using drugs or alcohol.

8. As we will see in the next chapter, group therapy sessions at Fresh Beginnings were largely devoted to self-talk. However, short lectures, films, and occasional guest speakers—the stuff of psychoeducational training—were sometimes interspersed with talk therapy.

9. Of course, Freud had much to say about the topographical arrangement of subject as a compound of ego, superego, and id (e.g., 1959 [1926]:266; 1955 [1939]:96; 1940:163), as he divided the psyche into subsystems that, while interreliant, have distinct functions and accordingly can be treated, metaphorically, as points in physical as well as psychical space (See Laplanche and Pontalis 1973: 449). As Laplanche and Pontalis note, the term "topography"—or theory of "places"—can be traced back to Greek antiquity and has enjoyed a prominent role in Western philosophy, particularly in the work of Kant and his interest in "the decision as to the place which belongs to every concept" (1965:281, as cited in 1973:449). Laplanche and Pontalis add: "The Freudian hypothesis of a psychical topography has its roots in a whole scientific context embracing neurology, physiology, psychopathology" (ibid.). That said, therapists' ideas about addicted denial, and the structures of subjectivity these ideas imply, may owe as much to Western religion—and particularly St. Augustine's formulation of memory as an internal storehouse and his delineation of the referential capacities of human speech—as they do to Western science and philosophy.

10. Because program therapists relied upon a widely shared, if culturally distinct, set of epistemological presumptions about the self and how to know it, it is no wonder that what they built in practice seemed to already exist in nature.

11. These terms are commonly used in the clinical literature on addiction treatment as well. For example, Spiegel and Fewell write that "to *pierce* through the

denial of active alcoholism and clearly see the turmoil and damage in its wake is a painful awakening" (2004:135). Similarly Rinn et al. write: "For some, denial is fragile and is easily *penetrated* when they are supportively confronted with the facts (e.g., liver disease, drunk driving arrests, repeated detoxifications). For others, the denial is fixed and is unaffected by confrontation with the evidence" (2002:52, emphasis added).

12. In 1971, with the passing of the Comprehensive Alcohol Abuse and Alcoholism Prevention, Treatment, and Rehabilitation Act of 1970 (Public Law 91–616), which involved the public testimony of a number of alcoholics, the NIAAA was established. The NIAAA is a branch of the National Institutes of Health (NIH) within the U.S. Department of Health and Human Services. Its mission is to "develop and conduct comprehensive health, education, research, and planning programs for the prevention and treatment of alcohol abuse and alcoholism and for the rehabilitation of alcohol abusers and alcoholics" (P.L. 91–616, 1). Only six years after its establishment, Melvyn Kalb and Propper (1976) declared in the *American Journal of Psychiatry*: "A new type of manpower, the professional alcohologist, has emerged on the alcoholism treatment scene as an outgrowth of the recent rich infusion of federal attention and funding through the establishment of the . . . NIAAA" (641). They added that prior to 1971 professionals comprised a "scant fraction of the manpower in the field" (ibid.). In 1974 NIDA was established as part of the Alcohol, Drug Abuse, and Mental Health Administration, and in 1992, it was incorporated into the NIH.

13. According to the Addiction Research Institute at the University of Texas, Austin, there are more than 160 assessment instruments for clinical practitioners and researchers available on the NIAAA Web site.

14. Myrick et al. (2002) found that assessees' self-reports were higher when paraprofessionals—that is, practicing clinicians who are not licensed or degreed—were conducting the assessment interview.

15. Butler et al. (1998) note that the long dominant ASI has a lengthy interview format, taking nearly an hour to administer, in addition to the time required for scoring and interpreting results (see also Carroll 2002:332). Since the development of the ASI twenty years ago, developers of alternative assessment instruments increasingly attend to the brevity with which their tests can be administered, scored, and interpreted.

16. The stages-of-change model has spawned the development of a wide range of clinical instruments to measure motivation, and related constructs (Carroll and Rounsaville 2002). It has also been influential in the development of a number of clinical practice models, including Motivational Interviewing (see Miller and Rollnick 1991; Miller and Tonigan 1996), which will be addressed in the book's concluding chapter.

17. Relevant here is the clinical distinction between signs—that which a clinician sees—and symptoms—that which a patient experiences. Whereas the biopsychosocial portion of the assessment records *symptoms* by eliciting historical information from clients in narrative form, the psychiatric portion of the evaluation clearly works to circumvent the subjective experience of the client in an attempt to record *signs*.

18. The definition of addiction was originally derived from the study of opiate use and, more specifically, the observation that repeated use of opiates results in the development of what is known as "tolerance"—the need for increased doses

of the drug in order to achieve the desired high (See Paolino 1991:218). Although alcohol is thought to be similar to opiates in this regard, some argued that tolerance is not observed with cocaine, which, interestingly, did not lead to the conclusion that cocaine is not addicting but led instead to the development of a new conception of "psychological" addiction characterized by three basic criteria: loss of control in using the drug, craving and compulsion, and continued use regardless of negative effects on the user or others or both (see Smith 1984; Paolino 1991). These criteria are clearly represented in the *DSM-IV*.

19. According to Fulkerson et al. (1999) there was much debate about the relationship between the two diagnostic categories of "substance abuse" and "substance dependence" between the writing of the *DSM-III* in 1980 and the 1994 publication of the *DSM-IV*, which Laura and Susan used. In the former, substance dependence was defined by the presence of functional impairments in social or occupational life in conjunction with physical manifestations of tolerance or withdrawal. Despite pressures on the Substance Use Disorders Work Group to do away altogether with "substance abuse" as a diagnostic category, it was retained as a residual category as the definition of substance dependence broadened substantially, and this has remained the case through the most current revisions of the manual. In 1988, the Substance Use Disorders Work Group was again charged with revising the diagnostic schema and spent most of its time considering—often contentiously—whether abuse and dependence could be merged into a single category. As it stands, "substance dependence" remains the category of clinical interest, with some consensus that people pass through substance abuse before developing substance dependence (ibid.) so that the former can be considered predictive, to some degree, of the latter. For especially informative accounts of the development and uses of the *DSM*, graced with particularly stimulating examples of how ideas about evidence, specification, and generalizability have changed over time, see Young 1995, 1999, 2001.

20. In his study of the globalization of diagnostic routines and measures of mental illness, Andrew Lakoff demonstrates that, much like our Laura, some Argentinian clinicians oppose a theoretical reliance on *DSM* categories, believing them to generalize across cases and thereby erase the uniqueness of clinical encounters. The clinicians Lakoff studied also associate the *DSM-IV* with neoliberalism, privatization, and the dismantling of the welfare state—an association that I never heard articulated at Fresh Beginnings, where therapists nevertheless used it as a foil in establishing their expertise.

21. A common exercise in group therapy confirms this point. On several occasions therapists distributed a "recovery quiz" with empty boxes awaiting clients' check marks in two columns titled, respectively, "recovery bound" and "relapse bound." Those making progress proudly noted, "I'm honest and realistic about myself and my problems" whereas "relapsers" failed, admitting, "I deny and distort reality."

22. By the mid-1990s the confrontational techniques associated with the Hazelden group and Vernon Johnson had lost support among many addiction specialists (Morgan 2006). Proponents of Motivational Interviewing have been particularly trenchant and rigorous critics of confrontational tactics, and have developed principles of intervention accordingly (Miller and Rollnick 1991, 2002). Nevertheless, Johnson's family confrontation model—widely known as

"the intervention"—is still commonly practiced in programs like Fresh Beginnings and other community-based settings across North America.

23. Bobbi vanished from Cliff Street within weeks of receiving this award, suggesting that—in practice—self-recognition and admission did not always line up the way that therapists wanted.

24. If we hearken back to the assessments described in chapter 2, which figured client assessees as products of problem-laden environments and complex pathohistorical trajectories, we may well be struck by the contrast in the terms to describe the very same people here. HFC clients are now "diagnosed" (line 2) with a "*primary* disease" (line 4), with "environmental factors" clearly playing a secondary role (line 5). Addicts' cognitive impairments are also described in some detail (lines 7–9), indicating that Fresh Beginnings therapists did not trust clients to be reliable historians of themselves as HFC assessors commonly did.

25. While Bahktin (1984) describes double voicing as both part and parcel of discourse, since an utterance never belongs to a single author, he also indicates that double voicing is a specific literary strategy in which a speaker brackets part of his or her speech with quotations so as to demarcate the voice of another. Double voicing was a particularly common practice among direct service providers across HFC, a phenomenon I plan to explore in depth at a later date.

26. More recently, neuropsychologists have become interested in identifying executive control impairments in the prefrontal cortex that would provide new scientific support for addiction specialists' long-standing belief that addicts have impaired capacity to experience affect (e.g., Aguilar de Arcos 2005; Carvajal et al. 2006; Panksepp et al. 2004; Verdejo-Garcia 2006).

27. In fact, in a widely cited 1974 article, Leon Wursmer proposed that addicts suffer "a curtailed ability or inability to symbolize [that] pertains particularly to the patient's inner life, his emotions, his self-references" (1974:837). And while Wurmser is clear that "affects remain preverbal" (ibid.), he goes on to suggest that drugs function to replace "the not perceived and not articulated affect"—presuming that the lack of articulation naturally follows from a lack of perception.

28. Anthropologists have challenged the idea of emotion as a property or product of individual bodies by ethnographically documenting various political and cultural processes by which emotions are publically produced (e.g., Besnier 1993, 1995; Brenneis 1990; Irvine 1982, 1990; Lutz 1988; Lutz and Abu-Lighod 1990; Ochs and Scheifflein 1989; Rosaldo 1980, 1982). This chapter follows their lead in demonstrating the production of emotions in interpersonal and institutional interactions, even against the powerful backdrop of the well-institutionalized American folk theory that emotions are private property. For an analysis of the history of emotions, including the treatment of emotions in anthropology, see Reddy 2001. Reddy's discussion of emotional expression, which productively connects cultural ideas about emotion to ideologies of language, is particularly pertinent to the issues raised in this chapter.

29. For a comprehensive overview of feminist therapies and their roots in various schools of feminist thought, see Enns 2004.

30. Janice Haaken (1998) traces the clinical and cultural division between those who argue that recovered memories are veridical accounts of sexual trauma and those who claim that therapists are implanting memories of abuse in their

patients. Haaken suggests that in jettisoning the concept of fantasy, both camps of the debate tend to reify memories as (only) "true" or "false"—and thereby sacrifice the complexity of traumatic experience.

31. Though a discussion of the research methodology of the cited studies is beyond the scope of this chapter, we may be wise to note—particularly in light of the discussion of interviewing methods in chapter 2—that studies of clinical populations (i.e., those in addiction treatment) consistently find much higher rates of correlation between childhood sexual abuse and drug abuse than populations not recruited or studied in treatment settings. Consider that whereas Rosenhaw et al. (1988) found that 71– 90 percent of adolescent women in addiction treatment reported, during "routine questioning about sexual abuse," that they were victims of childhood sexual abuse (as cited in Polusny and Follette 1995:150), Harrison et al. (1989) found that a much lower 35 percent of adolescent women made these reports after the completion of their treatment. In other words, it appears that adolescent girls are much more likely to report sexual abuse while they are in treatment than after they complete it.

32. This way of talking about the memory can be traced back to Augustine, who in Book 10 of the *Confessions*, elaborates his portrait of a human memory as a vast storehouse that can contain experience as thing-like ideas. As I have argued elsewhere (Carr, n.d.), Augustine also proffers a theory of semiotic replication: what has been experienced is available to the rememberer if s/he ventures inward to retrieve them from the vast hall of memory. For Augustine, as for Fresh Beginnings therapists, "confession" is a matter of marshaling the messy contents of the penitent memory into a tidy semiotic bundle that can be matched with and released into spoken signs. Here, we can see more specifically the similarity in Louise's description of therapy and Augustine's delineation of a confessional discipline which suggests that, in order to examine one's memory, its contents "have to be brought together (*cogenda*) so as to be capable of being known; that means they have to be gathered (*colligenda*) from their dispersed state" (1991:189).

33. This is a good example of the kind of parallelism described by Elizabeth Mertz in her study of language socialization in law school classrooms. Mertz finds that the structure of narrative practice reinforces the underlying language ideology, thereby transforming mental processes and transmitting a theory of language not through direct semantic description but instead through pragmatic demonstration (1996:233; see also Mertz 2007). Here the suggestion is that the therapeutic dialogue took so long because the "contents" that Louise recounts during the process of inventory are so far from being able to be clearly articulated.

34. During an interview with me, Louise also reported a troubling sexual encounter as a teenager with her older brother. But she suggested that she ranked this incident very low on a long list of traumatic experiences. Interestingly, after leaving the program, Louise also told me that she was surprised and confused when, after describing what she believed to be a consensual relationship with a slightly older female cousin, therapists reframed the relationship as "abuse."

35. Addiction specialist and author of *The Mask of Shame* (1981), Leon Wurmser, also argues that childhood sexual abuse commonly results in shame and is one of the key determinants of adult drug abuse and addiction. Notably, scholars

who focused primarily on the clinical study of childhood sexual abuse (i.e., Polusny and Follette 1995; Rodriguez et al. 1996; Zierler et al. 1991) have also explored the correlation of shame, childhood sexual abuse, and drug abuse.

36. Here we have a clinical instantiation of the "woman is to nature as man is to culture" equation, long of interest to feminist anthropologists (i.e., Ortner 1996, 1998; Ortner and Whitehead 1981). Note that male users celebrate and participate in rites of passage, whereas female users are mired in *disease*.

37. As is illustrated in the "My Ego" cartoon shown in Figure 3.1, Laura aligns insight and will. On the one hand, Laura gives her client a voice that seems in touch with what she wants and does not want to do. But, on the other hand, Laura is also clear that the client uses even when she recognizes that she does not want to because that is the "compulsive" nature of the disease (see line 16). Although it appears that Laura is suggesting here that addiction is, in fact, a disease of the will, note that the self-talk Laura channels through the figured client begins with the seemingly highly willful statement: "I don't want to feel" (line 14) and a drive to "anesthetize pain or shame" (line 9). Thus, while Laura indeed suggests that the will may be taken over by compulsion in active addiction, she is clear that the disease begins with a willful abandonment of self-recognition.

38. For anthropologies of shame, see Kulick and Klein 2003, and Wilce 2008.

Chapter 4. Addicted Indexes and Metalinguistic Fixes

1. There have been a number of excellent anthropological accounts of AA, some of which have traced its cross-cultural proliferation. For instance, Stanley Brandes (2002) explores the rapid spread of AA into Latin America, Amy Borovoy (2001, 2005) studies the rise of Adult Children of Alcoholics (ACOA)/codependency discourse in Japan, and Eugene Raikhel (2009) tells of the Russian articulation of the 12 steps in relation to placebo therapy (see also Fainzang 1994; Swora 2001; Spicer 2001). Several studies have highlighted the linguistics and metalinguistics of AA, including Carole Cain's fascinating study of "scaffolding" (1991), Norman Denzin's interpretive interactionist portrait of AA socialization (1987, 1993), and Paul Antze's anthropological account of AA as symbolic action (1987). For a "native" ethnographic account of AA language ideology and "alcoholic thinking," see Wilcox 1998.

2. The Minnesota Model of treatment is theoretically premised on AA and serves as the basis of many professional programs like Fresh Beginnings. The Minnesota Model has several components: (1) psycho-education to build clients' awareness about addiction; (2) the use of recovering professionals who connect on an experiential level with clients; (3) the acceptance of the "disease model" of addiction; (4) the emphasis on self-help groups like AA; and (5) the reliance on group and individual counseling to confront denial (Chiauzzi and Liljegren 1993:305).

3. The full text of the Twelve Steps reads:
   1. We admitted we were powerless over alcohol, that our lives had become unmanageable;

2. Came to believe that a Power greater than ourselves could restore us to sanity;
3. Made a decision to turn our will and our lives over to the care of God as we understood Him;
4. Made a searching and fearless moral inventory of ourselves;
5. Admitted to God, to ourselves and to another human being the exact nature of our wrongs;
6. Were entirely ready to have God remove all these defects of character;
7. Humbly asked Him to remove our shortcomings;
8. Made a list of all persons we had harmed and became willing to make amends to them all;
9. Made direct amends to such people wherever possible, except when to do so would injure them or others;
10. Continued to take personal inventory and when we were wrong promptly admitted it;
11. Sought through prayer and meditation to improve our conscious contact with God as we understood Him, praying only for knowledge of His will for us and the power to carry that out;
12. Having had a spiritual awakening as the result of these steps, we tried to carry this message to alcoholics and to practice these principles in all our affairs.

4. This is not to say that ideologies of language are uniformly practiced. Indeed, some Americans are held to the demands of inner reference more than others, as I address in chapter 5.

5. "How to Sabotage Your Treatment" is a professionally produced treatment film whose ironic title comes into focus as viewers follow the flashbacks of several clients who have gathered for a reunion at their former treatment center. The now sober clients reminisce about the myriad ways in which they each attempted to sabotage their treatment, demonstrating the nine ways listed in the accompanying booklet.

6. Therapists' hand editing is particularly interesting here, as in each case the added "commentary" is indicative of actual complaints lodged by Fresh Beginnings clients. Indeed, the discerning might recognize Tealie's commentary: "Why can't we go outside?" Such strategies of taking up clients' words and turning them to different uses (here a lesson about what is an unhealthy way of speaking and acting) were quite analogous to the tactics of script flippers and are described at some length in chapter 6.

7. Indeed, it appears that the list of the nine ways to sabotage treatment was added at a later date, as it does not exactly correspond with either the text of the manual or the VHS insert. And though I am certain that Laura added the handwritten commentary that hovers over the riders' heads, I cannot be sure who typed the list immediately below the image.

8. These "Do's" are taken directly—and verbatim—from the treatment manual, unlike the nine ways to sabotage treatment, which appear to be a summary, with a bit of editorializing, of the nine ways to sabotage treatment dramatized in the film and listed in the inset of the film's VHS release.

9. Thus the definition of "compliance" should not be confused with the more commonsensical use of the term to denote the dutiful following of program rules and the recommended regimen of counseling, and so on. However, the fact that the term means both to properly follow rules and regimens *and* to emptily or falsely follow rules and regimens indicates a key problematic of mainstream American addiction treatment.

10. Anthropologist Geoffrey R. Skoll (1992) has underscored the importance of this treatment maxim. Though Skoll conducted his research in the mid-1980s and focused on a Synanon program for male ex-convicts, there are striking similarities in the institutional practices that he and I document. And although he does not elaborate on the linguistic dimensions of clinical rituals and institutional routines of treatment, as I do here, one can find similarities in the rituals of talk in both programs. Sociologist Darin Weinberg's study of two treatment programs, which focuses on the relationship of addiction, mental illness, and social marginality as both "constructed" and "lived reality," can also be considered an interesting companion text (2005), as can Dawn Moore's (2007, 2009) and William Garriott's (2008) studies of addiction programs, which focus on the supposedly casual links between addiction and crime, on the one hand, and therapy and the law, on the other.

11. The idea of "wanting help but not knowing how to ask for it" has a robust life in mainstream addiction treatment and bears an interesting—if somewhat awkward—relationship to the theory of denial.

12. Since clients' treatment at Fresh Beginnings was so often linked with their housing, parole requirements, and/or custody of their children, very few clients could leave Fresh Beginnings voluntarily without serious consequences. To my understanding, there were only a handful of such cases among the dozens of clients who filtered through the program during the course of this study, including Lila's.

13. The delicate data presented here were obtained from both Lila and Laura. In addition to the letters that Laura wrote Lila, I was given written exchanges between Lila's case manager, who objected to Laura's handling of the case and filed a formal grievance, and Laura's ten-page response to her supervisors. Both these documents (which Laura gave to me after she left the program) included verbatim transcriptions of relevant verbal exchanges between the two parties. The case manager's grievance included a two-page transcription of a message that Laura had left on her voicemail.

14. We might also take the story of Lila as perfect articulation of how 'gay' shame can be semiotically conferred, much as Silvan Tompkins suggested (1963).

15. A similar linguistic bind is described by Allan Young (1995) in his study of a specialized psychiatric unit for Vietnam veterans. In group therapy, patients' linguistic and paralinguistic behaviors are analytically funneled into categories of flaunted secret and healthy disclosure, with ideas about trauma, rather than addiction, at stake.

16. Lila's use of the term "business" may be of some significance. In contrast to Laura's categorization of sexuality as a state, Lila (who had been romantically involved with men and women) portrays her sexual life as a matter of practice and desire, both of which were decidedly private. This epistemological difference

inflected the ongoing conflict, as Laura accused Lila of "shame" about "who she was" and Lila responded with surprise at what she saw as Laura's voyeurism into her "private business."

17. Irvine and Gal (2000:38) explain that language ideologies must ignore or transform elements that do not fit into their interpretive structures. According to Irvine and Gal, "erasure" is one of three semiotic processes that sustains a given language ideology, the others being iconization and fractal recursivity. My discussion builds on their work by suggesting that the "erasure" of spatiotemporal indexes of clients' talk is achieved by an a priori process of indexical iconization.

18. Some HFC programs had "consumer intern" programs in which former clients were hired into the organization, usually in low-skilled, low-wage, and high turnover positions. Lila's case was an exception, since she was still attending Fresh Beginnings when she was hired, causing much ado among some staff members regarding the propriety of resulting messy "boundaries."

19. For relevant work on the relationship between language and sexuality, see Besnier 2002; Cameron and Kulick 2003; Hall 1995; and Kulick 2003b.

20. Prohibition of "cross-talk" is typical in the mainstream treatment of addiction but only in formal clinical and self-help settings. For example, AA, specifically and formally, discourages cross-talk as people take turns telling their stories. Women for Sobriety (WFS) is a notable exception to the rule: not only is cross-talk allowed but dialogue is encouraged during meetings. Indeed, Kaskutas (1989:182) suggests that WFS explicitly circumvents confessional techniques altogether; she writes, "Stories about one's drinking history are avoided as unnecessarily focusing on negative thoughts and memories. Women do not announce themselves as alcoholics."

21. At one point, therapists also tried to forbid clients from talking to each other when not in the group, by discouraging phone calls, for example. This effort was wholly unsuccessful, as many clients formed close friendships while at Fresh Beginnings, and some were friends (or family) before they arrived.

22. Fresh Beginnings CD and family therapists were to follow the protocol laid out below when contacting Child Protective Services. This document is generally stored in their files, and they shared it with me. It reads:

> Each step below should be followed in succession until a person feels that the problem has been taken care of: 1) The person finding the alleged abuse or neglect should first report their concerns to their immediate supervisor. 2) The supervisor should then talk to the clients [sic] case manager. 3) The alleged case of abuse or neglect should then be reported to the case managers [sic] supervisor. 4) If it is felt that a P.S. [Protective Services] Report needs to be made the parent of the child involved should then be informed of the concern and the fact that a report will be made to P.S. 5) File a report with P.S. A phoned in report must be followed up with a written report within 48 hours.

It is important to note that Ella and Laura may have had additional information about Monique that precipitated their report, even if it did come immediately after the therapy session recounted above.

Chapter 5. Therapeutic Scenes on an Administrative Stage

1. Dedicated as he is to "Making Things Public" (see Latour and Weibel 2005; also see Bruno Latour's Web site n.d.), Latour is well aware of a third (or meta) meaning of "representation," which certainly pertains to the task at hand—that is, "how to represent, and through which medium, the sites where people meet to discuss their matters of concern" (Latour and Weibel 2005:16). Amahl Bishara's 2008 article on the politics of Palestinian news making and reporting also works, ethnographically, with Latour's three senses of representation. I find that her language of representation-as-gathering and representation-as-depiction is helpful and therefore borrow it to gloss Latour's taxonomy.

2. Latour uses the German word *ding* to refer both to "an issue that brings people together *because* it divides them" (Latour and Weibel 2005:23) and a form of "archaic assembly" such as the Icelandic Althing, in which people gather on fault lines. Indeed, division is at the heart of Latour's efforts to revive political representation—in both senses of the word: "If the Ding designates both those who assemble because they are concerned as well as what causes their concerns and divisions, it should become the center of our attention: Back to Things!" (Latour and Weibel 2005:23).

3. Although these distinctions are often drawn along the lines of race, class, and gender, my broader point is that they are inevitably drawn, and any theory of political representation must take this into account. As Judith Butler notes, "The one who acts (who is not the same as the sovereign subject) acts precisely to the extent that he or she is constituted as an actor and, hence, operating within a linguistic field of enabling constraints from the outset" (1997:16).

4. For instance, Michael Silverstein and Greg Urban suggest that, if politics is a "struggle to entextualize authoritatively" (Silverstein and Urban 1996:11), success is measured by how texts are strategically situated in institutions and interactions by interested actors. Silverstein's (2005) work on "axes of eval" offers a further distinction between "intertextuality," in which a structural feature of a text remains constant and recognizable across speech events, and "interdiscursivity," in which a relationship is forged between spatiotemporally distinct speech events by a "message" sent from one participant involved in those events to another participant. This useful distinction suggests the need to provide evidence and develop theories that account for the various ways that people serve as messengers.

5. This, of course, is not to say that social workers or clients were considered internally homogeneous groups. Indeed, both groups drew clear, and often hierarchical internal distinctions. In the case of staff, rank in the institution, relative proximity to clients, and degree of education were regularly noted as criteria to differentiate administrators, clinical supervisors, clinicians, case managers, other "line staff," and paraprofessionals, with the class coordinates of these distinctions left implicit. In the case of clients, experience within the organization, number of services procured, and quality of relationship with staff were the explicit categories of differentiation, although some clients pointed explicitly to class background and gradations of skin color to differentiate themselves from others.

Nevertheless, firm institutional boundaries were undoubtedly drawn between "staff" and "clients," and the few who strayed across these lines were criticized and punished by both groups.

6. One might argue that there is nothing unusual about the triple-voicing of ethnographic accounts, premised as they are on participant observation. Indeed, as Thomas Lyons (2001:185), drawing on Silverstein (e.g., 1993), eloquently notes: "voicing within a text produces an implied alignment of the pragmatic roles of narrator, characters, and so on with real world social actors, including the author" and that ethnographies "can presuppose, in fact create, multiple 'points of view' or 'authors' that each in different ways 'originate' it." I, too, credit Michael Silverstein for encouraging me to develop the potentially productive tensions of ethnographic "voicing" based on his reading of an early draft of this chapter.

7. This makes the "retreat" described in chapter 1 a unique event in that it was held in the treatment program itself, where some program affiliates spent their working days and others had visited only once or twice, if at all.

8. Oddly, while many organizational researchers have used board minutes as a more or less transparent source of data for their studies (i.e., Adams 2004; Arino and de la Torre 1998; Lamoreaux 1986; Miller 2002; Peck 1995), very few scholars have examined board meeting minutes as organizational artifacts, worthy of analysis in their own right (for noteworthy exceptions, see Schwartzman 1989:130–132, 147; Tracy and Muller 2001).

9. A colleague, who teaches organizational theory and practice to professional students, recently informed me that she advises her students always to make sure that their issue of interest appears both on the meeting agenda and in the meeting minutes (Susan Lambert, personal communication, 2008). As a minute taker, I was not aware of these sorts of external pressures, though I certainly understood that I was becoming increasingly (self-)interested in engaging in the practice.

10. Although the names of minute takers were always included in the list of those "present," it was not standard practice to textually denote who the minute taker actually was; part of newcomers' work, therefore, was discerning who wrote the minutes and the nature of person's relationship to other board members.

11. However, much unlike the group therapy rules, minutes were not located in a permanent or predictable place where readers could find them. There was no central file to which all board members had access. Therefore, board members had to rely on their own, inevitably incomplete files of hard copies of minutes that were distributed at the meetings they attended. Minute sharing was made difficult by the geographically dispersed nature of HFC agencies, as well as by the fact that not all workers had ready access to computers. Though minutes were written and stored on office word processors—often shared by five to ten workers—they were not generally sent by e-mail attachment. Therefore, if a board member did not actually attend a meeting, she had to work hard to get hold of the minutes of the previous meeting.

12. This is not to mention the anthropological critique of speech act theory, launched most notably by the late Michelle Rosaldo (1982). In short, Rosaldo argued that Austin's and Searle's propositions relied on sincere and intentional speakers, which they failed to acknowledge as a culturally specific model of personhood.

268 • Notes to Chapter 5

13. Anthropologist Paul Brodwin's (2008) work on "everyday ethics" in Assertive Community Treatment also addresses the evaluative and distributional elements of "post-institutional" social service provision and has inspired my own thinking on this question.

14. "Enabling," as used in substance abuse treatment literature, refers to a range of behaviors by friends, family members, treatment professionals, and important others that serve to protect a person with an addiction from its negative consequences. William White provides several prototypical examples of enabling: "the spouse who calls in sick for the person who is really hung over, the coworker who covers up for the person's drug-related behavior on the job, the family members who make excuses for the individual whose drunken behavior ruined last Christmas, and the parent who rushes in to bail the teenager out of jail for a drunk and disorderly charge" (1998:10). White (1996) suggests that enabling by treatment professionals is also exemplified by "mistaking compliance for enduring changes in [client] attitudes and behavior, as well as doing things for addicts that they should be doing for themselves" (1996:194), which is particularly pertinent to the framing case at hand. For a classification of six types of enabling behaviors, see Weiss et al 1994.

15. My use of minutes here *as data* has not lost sight of the above discussion of minute taking as a practice; accordingly, minutes are read here as representations of scenes and practices of representation.

16. Indeed, as a student of social work, I myself became invested in the discourse (see Carr 2003). Although my work critiqued what I found to be the troubling implications of empowerment discourses in social work scholarship, I laid out my own prescriptive model of "empowerment practice" based on my readings of feminist scholars such as Linda Alcoff and Theresa de Lauretis.

17. These social work and community psychology scholars were hardly alone in this regard. In the academy many lauded the analytical merits of "empowerment," including scholars in women's studies (Bell 1996; Benmayor 1991; Fine 1992; Young 1994), education (e.g., Benmayor 1991; Weiler 1991; Zacharakis-Jutz 1988), the anthropology of education (Lima and Gazetta 1994; Mitchell 1994; Shethar 1993), political science (e.g., Bookman and Morgan 1988; West 1990), and public health (e.g., Braithwaite et al. 1994; Coombe 1997; Eng and Parker 1994).

18. For a discussion of discourses of "participation" in relation to visions of political process—and, particularly, to visions of democratic process—see Paley 2001. The "paradoxes of participation" Julia Paley describes in post-dictatorship Chile, wherein "participation" simultaneously serves as a mode of social control and a call to action, constitute an interesting comparative case.

19. According to Google scholar (August 3, 2009), Kieffer's piece has been cited 369 times since its publication.

20. Others agree that empowerment is essentially "a developmental construct" (Bernstein et al. 1994:286) but describe a much less linear process than Kieffer proposes. For example, consult Michelle Kaminksi and colleagues' (2000) use of Kieffer's developmental schema in their study of union activists. These authors suggest that people move through stages of empowerment, developing skills, understandings, and resources in a more or less linear and progressive way.

21. In this case, they were not as concerned with denoting elements of their program as indexing the institutional accountability implied by the genre of the American contract. For instance, board members surely understood that in describing their program and its practices to clients, they were also setting the terms of institutional accountability. In other words, clients (or client advocates) might not only rely upon the document as a promise but might hold the program accountable—in a referential sense—to its representation of itself. This was exactly the case when Louise, a client representative, filed a recipient's rights claim with the county for what she felt was a wrongful termination of services. Though state action was never taken against the program, the result of Louise's complaint was yet another time-consuming revision of the "Rights and Responsibilities" document.

22. Social theorists have long suggested that euphemism is a metalinguistic practice central to institutional stability (e.g., Bourdieu 1977, 1991; Goffman 1979; Weiner 1976). Through euphemism, a speaker can connect a term or terms of interest to a limited range of positive other terms, in effect creating or exploiting analogic relations. One might suggest that euphemism is a quintessential performative practice, because it (ideally) affects how speakers feel about what they are talking about (cf. Cohn 1987).

23. As Susan Phillips (1998) has noted, the contemporary linguistic anthropological study of institutions and organizations has been dedicated to showing how language practices within institutions are linked with various state projects and processes. It is in this vein that I remind the reader of social workers' rhetorical and practical ties to the state and, particularly, to the neoliberal project of "empowerment."

24. According to David Austin (personal communication, July 11, 2006), American social work shifted away from the term "client" in the mid-1960s, as the term implied "a dependent status of the service user." Austin adds that there was a more general effort "to avoid language which implied unequal status when the relationship [between service provider and recipient] also crossed ethnic lines" (ibid.). The use of the term "consumer" to refer to American social service recipients can be traced back to the late 1960s and, more specifically, to Edith Back's (1969) scathing critique of the increasing technocratization of social work; she clearly uses the term pejoratively. However, by the early 1970s the term is widely used as a synonym for "client," (cf. Beck 1970; Buttrick 1970; Daniels 1971; Kamerman 1974; Kahn 1976; Patti 1974). Having gained the status of a "keyword," surprisingly few social work scholars have concertedly or explicitly challenged the term in writing, as Kramer did in noting: "Despite its increasing popularity, the term "consumer involvement" is somewhat of a misnomer because of the usual absence of choice and pricing mechanisms in the social service 'market'" (1975:341).

25. This connection of consumerism and participation is well reflected in the early social service uses of the term (i.e., Beck 1970; Daniels 1971; Kramer 1975; Kahn 1976). Somewhat later, social work scholars like Neil Gilbert (1979, see also Gilbert, Specht, and Lindeman 1981), who studied "participation oriented" housing projects sponsored by HUD in the 1970s, charged that "consumerism," and particularly "consumer participation," was empty rhetoric (see also Gulati

1982). By the 1990s, consumer participation was increasingly glossed in terms of "having a voice." With the dismantling of the federal welfare state, and, in particular, the institution of work requirements and time limits, social work scholars have also witnessed mandated "consumer participation." In 1993, O' Looney presciently observed: "The welfare reform movement to link benefits to responsibilities suggests one potential means of promoting collective consumer voice: in essence service recipients could be mandated to participate at some level in [. . .] planning and decision-making" (1993:524).

26. Indeed, even before I had decided to take on Fresh Beginnings as the site of my dissertation research, I submitted a research project proposal to both HFC and my University Human Subjects Committee in the summer of 1996 with the intention to document these rationales, and continued this work for the remainder of my time at Fresh Beginnings.

27. Several years after this series of meetings, Cecelia met with me to copy everything that was in her Fresh Beginnings file. It included a handwritten script, which she evidently wrote out to be read aloud at the board meeting (indeed, it was never distributed to other members). After a brief description of her own qualifications to serve on the advisory board, Cecelia states: "I want to go on record that I am not comfortable with simply inviting consumers to join the Ad Bd [advisory board]." Notably she begins to explain her position with explicitly clinical ratiocination: "Women tend to be externally focused and need to encourage to be internally focused" and follows with a rhetorical question: "Does participation on the Bd conflict with this?" Quite interestingly, Cecelia's script then goes on to ask if board members are "ready to deal with clients? Can we treat them respectfully w/o dismissing demeaning or belittling their viewpoints and experiences?" It is significant that this point was never, according to my records, verbalized in board meetings by Cecelia or any other board member.

28. It is noteworthy that these rationales were alternately used in combination and in rapid succession. At first, board members agreed that clients would not be interested in attending board meetings. A month later, when I told the board that the clients had almost unanimously agreed to the *idea* of client participation, the board director replied that the clients would probably not follow through and that no one client was likely to volunteer. Several weeks later, when two clients *volunteered*, both the addiction and the necessity rationales were cited once again.

29. AA's Twelfth Step reads: "Having had a spiritual awakening as the result of these steps, we tried to carry this message to alcoholics, and to practice these principles in all our affairs." "Giving back" is frequently used as shorthand for the Twelfth Step.

30. During the course of this study, Fresh Beginnings clients experienced substantial cuts in or elimination of various sources of state and federal aid, as well as a bevy of new eligibility requirements, changing rules and regulations, and a "new culture of welfare" (see Finn and Underwood 2000). Aside from the work requirements and time limits that came with the implementation of TANF, the newly renamed state Family Independence Agency no longer counted addiction treatment, whether court-ordered or not, toward mandated work hours. These policies took some time to be implemented, and, when they were, many clients

(with the support of their therapists and case workers) found ways to circumvent work requirements so as to continue in treatment. Forms were almost always involved.

31. Rhonda was discharged from the program after testing positive for cocaine. She was already on a probationary contract for repeatedly failing drug tests over a sixteen-month time span.

32. Although Louise portrayed her institutional work in client representation much as she did her therapeutic work in inner reference, it was clear to me that, like her new colleagues, she was also a skilled wordsmith. For instance, Louise framed her representational work as an entitlement, born of and supported in extension by the moniker "consumer," a term rarely used by clients. Although Louise pays her respects to "the *boss lady* and the boss man" (lines 12–13), she is unequivocal that clients, as users of the program, "should definitely have an input into how [the program] should be run" (lines 6–7). It was "that type of thing"—that is, communicatively connecting clients and "bosses"—that both "the ladies" and Louise "enjoyed" (lines 1, 9).

33. In this sense, Louise reads and responds to the idea that "one can be interpellated, put in place, given a place, through silence, through not being addressed, and this becomes painfully clear when we find ourselves preferring the occasion of being derogated to the one of not being addressed at all" (Butler 1997:27).

34. Louise contacted the county community mental health office devoted to the investigation of "consumer appeals and grievances regarding denial, suspension, reduction or termination of services" in substance abuse programs. Her first call to this office was to investigate if and how Fresh Beginnings clients could lodge complaints regarding Laura's firing. She would be in contact with them a few months later in relation to her own termination from the program, as I subsequently describe in the text. Louise's interaction with these parties is further indication of her sense of the political: she consistently lodged complaints along formal institutional channels and was consistently disappointed when powerful parties seemed to ignore or dissipate her claims.

35. This account is pieced together from several sources, including interviews with Lizzy, Louise, and Louise's case manager as well as the accounts of recipient rights "advocates" who investigated Louise's subsequent complaint. No action against the program or its staff was ever taken and Louise was not reinstated to the program.

Chapter 6. Flipping the Script

1. I can only assume that clients did not mention "flipping the script" in my presence until they determined my positioning within HFC and my relationships with staff. I also found that some Fresh Beginnings clients did not use or seem to know the local meaning of this term, suggesting that script flippers were generally guarded about elaborating the practices the term indexed.

2. Shauna does more than simply suggest that her role as prostitute informed her performances at Fresh Beginnings; she also draws a theoretical parallel between the work of prostitutes and the work of clients in addiction treatment,

suggesting both earn their way by telling people what they want to hear. Kira Hall's (1995) brilliant discussion of the use of extremely gendered language among telephone sex workers is relevant here, in that she implies a high degree of consciousness and intentionality involved in the linguistic reproduction of "sex[y] lines."

3. The degree to which a performer emerges as a particular script's "principal"—that is, the one whose position or beliefs are being represented and is responsible for the content of the expression—varies, depending on how the textual and performative aspects are brought together (see Goffman 1979).

4. As I have worked to demonstrate in previous chapters, it is precisely because American institutions like Fresh Beginnings exalt one particular function of language—that is, the referencing of preexisting inner states of speakers—and, in doing so, instantiate both a semiotic ideology and an ideology of healthy personhood, that "performance" and "reference" are so commonly cast in opposition.

5. Many have critically addressed the idea that one can access speaker awareness through elicitation techniques such as interviewing (Briggs 1986, 2007; Carr 2010; Hanks 1987; Labov 1972b; Mertz 1993). Among linguistic anthropologists, there is also broad agreement that the best way to piece together a picture of speaker awareness is to combine direct elicitation with other methods (i.e., participant observation, including the careful attention to so-called naturally occurring discourse), an approach I obviously follow here.

6. Russian linguist Roman Jakobson (1980) introduced the concept of metalinguistic function, that is, the use of language to describe and analyze language. Metalinguistic function is an essential feature of native speakers' awareness of their own language, including their ability—highly valued by anthropological linguists—to isolate terms (plant names, kinship terms, etc.) and identify their meaning (or "function"). In differentiating speakers' awareness of the ostensive definition and pragmatic value of words, and suggesting that the former is far greater than the latter, Jakobson's student, Michael Silverstein (1976, 1991, 1993), developed the concept of metapragmatic function: the use of language to describe what language can *do*. See Alessandro Duranti (1997) for an excellent overview of these developments in linguistic anthropological scholarship.

7. This assessment was confirmed by other clients including Louise, Nikki's closest friend in the program.

8. In 2000, the U.S. Supreme Court ruled in the case of *Ferguson v. City of Charleston* that drug testing pregnant women without their consent was unconstitutional in that it "violated the Fourth Amendment's prohibition on unreasonable search and seizures" (Schroedel and Fiber 2001:227). The careful wording of this ruling, however, left other routes open through which pregnant women suspected of drug use could be prosecuted. As of 2001, fourteen states required hospitals to report all positive drug tests of pregnant women to proper authorities. Half the states required reporting the results to the state's child welfare department, and the other half required hospitals to treat positive drug tests as they would other suspected cases of abuse or neglect, calling in reports to child protective services (Schroedel and Fiber 2001).

9. More specifically, Silverstein writes, "the native speaker, faced with tasks that require orientation to an immediate and urgent environment, trying to 'think

out' a response, or even to 'think about' the referential properties of his or her native language in specific situations, is hopelessly at the mercy of the so-called 'phenotypic,' or as we now say 'surface' lexicalized forms of language . . . to which, in piecemeal fashion, he or she attributes true referential effect in segmenting the cultural universe" (2001:399).

10. Judith Butler makes a similar point in her discussion of hate speech. She writes: "The political possibility of reworking the force of the speech act against the force of injury consists in misappropriating the force of speech from . . . prior contexts. The language that counters the injuries of speech, however, must repeat those injuries without precisely reenacting them. Such a strategy affirms that hate speech does not destroy the agency required for a critical response" (1997:40–41). Butler's work has inspired my attempt to trace, more closely, the semiotic processes by which this reworking occurs.

11. It seems that collective script flipping was anticipated by therapists as well. In the personal files Laura gave me when she left Fresh Beginnings was a document titled "Behaviors Likely to Destroy Therapy." It listed an array of destructive acts, such as "parasuicidal," "suicide crisis," and "violent" behaviors, and ended by noting the pernicious effects of "united rebellion of clients against the therapist." Perhaps there was no more threatening a rebellion on Cliff Street than that posed by a united front of script flippers.

12. In his masterful on-line glossary of addiction terminology, William White defines sponsorship as "the practice of mentorship between one recovering person and another." He traces the tradition back to the Washingtonians (circa 1840s) but notes that the practice was institutionalized within Alcoholics Anonymous; http://www.bhrm.org/advocacy/add-rec-glossary.pdf (accessed October 5, 2008; see also White 1998).

13. Explicitly eschewing a "radically feminist" approach and discouraging "polemic[s] against men" (Kaskutas 1996:78), WFS might best be considered culturally feminist in orientation in that it posits that deeply held, if not essential, socio-psychological differences exist between males and females (cf. Daly 1978; Gilligan 1982; Rich 1977). Like other therapeutic approaches that are culturally feminist in orientation, WFS is devoted to providing a "women's space" for the treatment of distinctly "women's issues." See Linda Alcoff's excellent discussion of cultural versus post-structural approaches to gender, which she identified as the "identity crisis in feminism" (1988).

14. Lizzy took over at Fresh Beginnings in place of Laura, who was the lead therapist at Fresh Beginnings from March 1996. Laura handed in a letter of resignation in January of 1999, and before she could retract it, she was fired. Lizzy took over the next month. Susan, who played a far lesser role in the program for many reasons, left after a maternity leave in November 1998. Thus, for more than a year, Laura was the only therapist on the payroll at Fresh Beginnings—a situation that purportedly precipitated her resignation.

15. Narcotics Anonymous sprang from AA in the late 1940s, hosting its first meetings in Los Angeles. NA follows the same format and principles as AA but is focused on those who use drugs other than alcohol. Mabel was one of the few clients who attended local NA meetings; there were relatively few in the county but one happened to convene very close to her apartment.

274 • Notes to Chapter 6

16. Evidence-based practice was originally developed by the Evidence-Based Medicine Working Group at McMaster University, Ontario, Canada, a team of doctors and researchers who sought to improve the effectiveness of medical interventions through doctors' conscientious use of formal research as opposed to intuition, tradition, or other factors in making clinical decisions (Sackett et al. 1997). EBP has since been widely adopted by a number of clinical professions, including social work, psychology, and nursing.

17. Lizzy is essentially faced with what Judith Irvine (1982) calls a "sincerity problem"—that is, the inability to decipher whether a particular expression or speech act aligns with some real referent (i.e., a sentiment, opinion, etc.) without a thorough consideration of relevant contexts, including, of course, the context of speaking.

18. In his study of Assertive Community Treatment workers (2008), and drawing on his previous work (2000, 2002, 2005), anthropologist Paul Brodwin examines how front-line workers cope with and resolve everyday moral quagmires by drawing on "high order" ethical notions.

19. Chantal Mouffe inspires my thinking here, writing that "things could always be otherwise and so every order is predicated on the exclusion of other possibilities" (2005a:18).

20. Originating in the South Bronx in the 1970s (Keyes 1996; Newman 2001; Pihel 1996), and popularly portrayed in the 2002 movie *Eight Mile,* freestyle is a live demonstration of rapping skills in which two opponents take turns crafting clever, spontaneous responses to each other—often with minimal musical accompaniment and with far less reliance on predetermined lyrics than other forms of rap (cf. Foytlin et al. 1999; Perry 2004). While it clearly involves intertextual elements—importing lines from previous freestyle encounters or making use of pre-inscribed phrases that demonstrate cultural sophistication—freestyle entails composing and performing raps simultaneously, which accounts for why it is sometimes called "off the head" or "rapping off the top of the dome" (Pihel 1996). Thus, like Fresh Beginnings script flippers, successful freestyle artists are always also analysts intensively interactive with their opponents, keenly attentive to their audience, and highly attuned to contextual features of the event itself.

21. This feature of freestyle is so iconic of the art form that the verb "flip the script" has been used as a synonym for the successful freestyle performance. For example, by the early 1990s two songs about the art of freestyle were released by hip-hop artists Da King and I and Gang Starr—titled "Flip the Script" and "Flip Da Script," respectively—and Big Daddy Kane's 1993 Billboard hit about his freestyle prowess, "Looks like a Job For," boasted, "I flip the script, like a movie director." All three songs emphasized one or more of these features of successful freestyling: taking advantage of flaws or foibles in an opponent's performance—whether in content, rhythmic qualities, or diction; seamlessly introducing a new theme into the dialogue; or trumping or spinning to whatever an opponent may say. In using the term "flip the script," rap artists have also pointed to their rhetorical sway over audiences. For instance, Big Daddy Kane provocatively noted that, in flipping the script, "I'm makin' non-believers believe what I'm dishin' up," a comment that—as we will see—resonates with Fresh Beginnings clients' use of the term.

22. For instance, in 1996, English professor and poet Keith Gilyard wrote, *Let's Flip the Script: An African American Discourse on Language, Literature, and Learning*, a book that addresses the remedialization of Black English in undergraduate classrooms. He focuses on spontaneous creative readings and responses rather than basic, scripted "skill and drill" teaching practices that so often characterize undergraduate composition classes. Other scholars suggest that to "flip the script" is not just to analyze but to use dominant parties' rhetorical tools against them. For instance, in a scholarly piece on urban education, Garrett Albert Duncan and Ryonnel Jackson (2004) lauded the actions of a young man who outsmarted—or "flipped the script"—on a school security guard known for racially profiling students; citing the school's stringent tardiness policies, the script flipper claimed that he ran in the halls only to make it to class on time.

23. The advertisement for the College of Office Technology, shown in Figure 6.1, calls on young black men, such as the one pictured here, to "Flip the Script in 2008!" This imperative is accompanied by two others (i.e., Build it! Take it Home!), as well the promise that "Your NEW Technology Career is just a phone call away." Yet other and only slightly subtler signs give us a better sense of what exactly it would mean to "Flip the Script in 2008." Pictured is a young, broadly smiling black man who holds what appears to be a flat screen computer monitor, presumably procured by way of his "new technology career." While the man sports urban street garb (crooked cap, baggy clothes, and goatee), suggesting that his daily business is conducted far from office cubicles, the screen he holds in front of him changes everything; he is, in essence, *reframed* as a well-tailored businessman—that is, once he heeds the advertisement's call. The message is clear: by "calling the number," "building it," and "taking it home," the man is transformed from one who uses the term "flip the script" to one who is living proof of the bootstrapping mentality that the term has come to connote, even in one of the least stable and financially rewarding sectors of the economy (i.e., "office technology"). It appears that to flip the script in 2008, then, is to accept that one's social positioning is the cumulative effect of one's everyday actions and dispositions, and to change those actions and dispositions accordingly. Cleansed of implications that script flippers are those who challenge existing power arrangements, this marketing strategy makes sense, in part, because it distances itself from any impediments to social advancement by using the putative lingo of the advertisement's target consumers.

24. Linguistic anthropologist Marcilyena Morgan has argued, for instance, that the African American language ideology "incorporates the knowledge that the construction and assessment of social face and character are simultaneously performed and grounded with the notion of multiple audiences" (2002:37).

25. Of course, James Scott famously discussed the weapons of the weak in his 1987 book bearing that title, and then again in his 1992 book, *Domination and the Arts of Resistance*. Linguistic anthropologist Susan Gal's (1995b) review essay of the book keenly analyzes Scott's assumptions about the nature of language and suggests the limits of a vision of politics based on these assumptions.

26. Aside from his suggestion that the tactic is the art of the weak (e.g., consumers, improvisational artists, TV viewers, immigrants) and that strategy is the province of the powerful (e.g., producers, proprietors, scientists, politicians), de

Certeau (1982) further differentiates tactics and strategies as follows: (1) a tactic has no place of its own and is dependent upon context, whereas a strategy is independent of context, isolatable, and autonomous; (2) a tactic makes use of time and is opportunistic, whereas a strategy has its own place; a strategy is the "triumph of space over time" (ibid.:36); (3) a tactic cannot establish a place from which it can see, whereas a strategy is panoptical; (4) a tactic can therefore not establish truth but instead works on deception, whereas a strategy is defined by the presence of power and, as such, has the ability to establish static truth; (5) a tactic is therefore like rhetoric, whereas a strategy is like a grammar.

27. John Jackson's brilliant ethnography, *Real Black*, has discussed this ethic in terms of "racial sincerity." Beginning with the premise that race-based authenticity tests—as epitomized by the question, are you "really" black?—are a constraining and potentially self-destructive feature of identity politics, he draws on his Harlem informants' notion of sincerity: a way of being in the world that demands performance. Jackson writes, "In short we play the role of being ourselves, we sincerely act the part of the sincere person, with the result that a judgment may be passed upon our sincerity that it is not authentic" (2005:14). In the end, Jackson accounts for how "people think and feel their identities into palpable everyday existence, especially as such identities operate within a social context that includes so many causal forces beyond their immediate control" (ibid.:11), a way of being in the world that I associate with script flipping without necessary or direct reference to racial identities and identifications.

Conclusion

1. In this vein, a number of European social welfare scholars have focused on the "special language of the helping professions" with a clear focus on how professionals use language as an instrument to construct clients. (See, especially, Hall, Slembrouck, and Sarangi 2006; Hall et al. 2003; Wahlstrom 2006; and Forsberg and Vagli 2006). In his ethnography, *Social Working*, Gerald de Montigy (1995:chap. 3) offers a provocative account of how social workers discursively construct professional identities and boundaries, as well as their clients, though his analysis is not as fine-grained as the reader might like.

2. Indeed, inspired by Greg Matoesian's work on expertise (1999, 2009), *Scripting Addiction* suggests that to be an expert is not only to be authorized by an institutionalized domain of knowledge or to make determinations about what is true, valid, or valuable within that domain; expertise is also the ability to "finesse reality and animate evidence through mastery of verbal performance" (Matoesian 1999:518). Matoesian's portrait of expert testimony (2008) and Silverstein's discussion of oinoglossia (2004, 2006) are particularly entertaining examples. For a review of anthropological treatments of expertise, see Carr 2010a.

3. More specifically, Foucault writes, "where there is power, there is resistance, and yet, or rather consequently, this resistance is never in a position of exteriority in relation to power" (1978:95).

4. Advocates of evidence-based practice are also concerned with the problem of how to create the conditions for practitioners to carefully evaluate evidence to

ground their analyses and actions (e.g., Gambrill 1999, 2006; Gibbs and Gambrill 2002; McCracken and Rzepnicki 2009; Thyer and Myers 1999). And though our assumptions about the nature and accumulation of evidence may differ, this book underscores the need to cultivate a "scientific patience" in practitioners even in the pressing circumstances of their daily work. I also am convinced that we, as scholars of social work, need to understand more about processes of translation—in the case of EBP, the translation of research findings into clinical practice, and vice versa.

5. Bronfenbrenner also describes a "mesosystem"—a relational domain that, by bringing teachers and parents together, for instance, connects the microsystem with the exosystem.

6. For instance, in the 1980s and early 1990s, as social work scholars digested the implications of targeted federal block grants, the decentralization of social services, continued deinstitutionalization, and the burgeoning of "self-help" practices, many debated the proper mission of social work, with the psychotherapeutic (or "micro") and the (re)distributional (or "macro") dimensions of social workers' labor pitted, theoretically, against each other. For instance, Specht and Courtney (1993) sounded an alarm that an increasing number of social workers—as "unfaithful angels"—had abandoned the poor, community-level work and their traditional "social justice" mission to pursue private practice instead with middle-class clients. Jerome Wakefield (1988a, 1988b), drawing on the liberal philosophy of John Rawls, countered that psychotherapeutic work and social justice were not antithetical aims and that, in fact, psychotherapy is social justice work because "self respect" is, in Rawlsian terms, a "primary social good" (1971). In an important sense, Wakefield's argument echoed a decade of feminist social work scholarship, which, in addition to demonstrating how sexism and racism are built into human service work (e.g., Abramovitz 1988; Gordon 1986, 1988a, 1988b), argued that direct services should incorporate the feminist mantra, "the personal is political" (Collins 1986; Davis 1986; Nes and Iadicola 1989; Van den Bergh and Cooper 1985).

7. British social work scholar Harry Ferguson (2008) has recently argued that social work should be reexamined in terms of mobility rather than in static terms (presumably including a map, with movement indicated by arrows, as I offered in chapter 2). In demonstrating the imbrication of political and clinical practices, or what Ferguson calls "a flow of mobile practices between public and private worlds" (2008:561), I believe his proposal has great merit for getting social work educators to rescale practice and prepare their students for the realities of the field.

8. On July 30, 2008, the White House released HUD figures suggesting that the number of chronically homeless persons in the United States has dropped by approximately one-third between 2005 and 2007. Aside from putatively improved data collection techniques, housing officials attributed the drop to the advent of "housing-first" strategies around the country (Swarns 2008).

9. Although some research has shown that no significant difference in substance use and psychiatric symptoms exists between those in housing-first and treatment-first programs (i.e., Padgett, Gulcar, and Tsemberis 2006; Tsemberis, Gulcur, and Nakae 2004), other researchers have maintained support for

abstinence-contingent programs such as Fresh Beginnings (i.e., Milby et al. 2005). Still other research in this area points to an interesting puzzle, which deserves further investigation. Specifically Marsh, D'Aunno, and Smith (2000:1246) have found that participation in an enhanced drug-treatment program, which provided transportation, child care, and outreach services, was negatively related to drug use; however, those clients who actually made use of ancillary services were less likely to abstain from drugs than a control group who, while in drug treatment, did not have access to these services. To explain this seeming paradox, the authors propose that the women who accessed services and continued to use had the most severe psychiatric, family, and drug problems.

10. Indeed, as suggested by the influential work of Prochaska, DiClemente, and Norcross (1992), clinical advantages also likely exist to treating those who actively seek or feel they need drug treatment separately from those who do not feel in need of treatment or are resistant to it.

11. Fresh Beginnings opened its doors at the heyday of women's treatment; between 1995 and 2005 outpatient (non-methadone) programs offering some group therapy have declined from 64 percent to 37 percent. After a decline in the 1980s, as federal block grants effectively pitted women's treatment against other local interests (Finkelstein 1994), women-specific programs reemerged in the 1990s with the help of federal guidelines (RL 98–509) requiring states to set aside 5 percent of block grant funding to women's drug and alcohol treatment (Sun 2007). In recent years, those interested in improving the quality of addiction treatment have increasingly focused on "tailored care" or "service matching" to the specific needs of client subgroups (Alexander et al. 2008) and have found themselves frustrated by a lack of adequate services and resources.

12. In a meta-analysis of studies of women in drug treatment, Sun (2007) found that not all researchers agree that women-only programs produce better treatment outcomes than mixed-gender programs; however, there is more agreement that programs offering child care have a positive impact on treatment outcomes. Smith and Marsh (2002) found that matched counseling services (like domestic violence and family counseling) were associated with reduced drug use, and ancillary services (such as legal services, job training, and housing) were associated with clients' satisfaction with treatment.

13. See the research by Marsh, Cao, and D'Aunno (2004) on the gender differences in the impact of comprehensives services.

14. Though its moniker may imply that the motivational interview elicits an internal quality, namely, motivation, through dialogic routine, MI is more interested in the production of behavioral change. My research thus far further suggests that practitioners of MI are also interested in cultivating the conditions for the emergence of two complex, less apparent qualities: a kind of clinical expertise premised on collaboration with clients and what the MI's founder, William Miller, calls "quantum change" (2004, 2009; see also Miller and de Baca 2001).

References

Abbott, Andrew D. 1988. *The system of professions: An essay on the division of expert labor.* Chicago: University of Chicago Press.
———. 1995. Boundaries of social work or social work of boundaries. *Social Service Review* 69 (4): 545–562.
Abramovitz, Mimi. 1988. *Regulating the lives of women.* Boston: South End.
Adams, Brian. 2004. Public meetings and the democratic process. *Public Administration Review* 64 (1): 43–54.
Addams, Jane. 1915. *Democracy and social ethics.* New York: Macmillan.
Addams, Jane, and Lillian D. Wald. 1910. *Forty years at Hull-House: Being "twenty years at Hull-House" and "The second twenty years at Hull-House."* New York: Macmillan.
Agar, Michael. 1973. *Ripping and running: A formal ethnography of urban heroin addicts.* New York: Seminar.
Agha, Asif. 1993. Grammatical and indexical convention in honorific discourse. *Journal of Linguistic Anthropology* 3 (2): 131–163.
———. 1998. Stereotypes and registers of honorific language. *Language in Society* 27 (2): 151–193.
———. 2001. Register. In *Key terms in language and culture,* ed. Alessandro Duranti, 212–215. Malden, Mass.: Blackwell.
———. 2007. *Language and social relations.* New York: Cambridge University Press.
Aguilar de Arcos, Francisco, Antonio Verdejo-García, Maria I. Peralta-Ramírez, Maria Sánchez-Barrera, and Miguel Pérez-García. 2005. Experience of emotions in substance abusers exposed to images containing neutral, positive, and negative affective stimuli. *Drug and Alcohol Dependence* 78 (2): 159–167.
Alcoff, Linda. 1988. Cultural feminism versus post-structuralism. *Signs* 13 (3): 405–436.
———. 1991. The problem of speaking for others. *Cultural Critique* 20:5–32.
Alcoff, Linda, and Laura Gray. 1993. Survivor discourse: Transgression or recuperation? *Signs* 18 (2): 260–290.
Alcoholics Anonymous. 1939. *Alcoholics Anonymous Big Book.* Alcoholics Anonymous World Services.
Alexander, Jeffrey A., Tammie A. Nahra, Christy H. Lemak, Harold A. Pollack, and Cynthia I. Campbell. 2008. Tailored treatment in the outpatient substance abuse treatment sector: 1995–2005. *Journal of Substance Abuse Treatment* 34 (3): 282–292.
Althusser, Louis. 1971. *Lenin and philosophy and other essays.* London: New Left Books.
Altschul, Sol. 1968. Denial and ego arrest. *Journal of the American Psychoanalytic Association* 16:301–318.

References

American Psychiatric Association. 1980. *Diagnostic and statistical manual of mental disorders—III.* Washington, D.C.: American Psychiatric Association.

———. 1994. *Diagnostic and statistical manual of mental disorders—IV.* Washington, D.C.: American Psychiatric Association.

Anderson, Kathyrn, and Dana C. Jack. 1991. Learning to listen: Interview techniques and analyses. In *Women's words: The feminist practice of oral history*, ed. Sherna Gluck and Daphne Patai, 11–26. New York: Routledge.

Antze, Paul. 1987. Symbolic action in Alcoholics Anonymous. In *Constructive drinking: Perspectives on drink from anthropology*, ed. Mary Douglas, 149–181. New York: Cambridge University Press.

Applegate, Jeffery S. 2000. Theory as story: A postmodern tale. *Clinical Social Work Journal* 28 (2): 141–153.

Arino, Africa, and Jose de la Torre. 1998. Learning from failure: Towards an evolutionary model of collaborative ventures. *Organizational Science* 9 (3): 306–325.

Asad, Talal. 1973. *Anthropology and the colonial encounter.* Ithaca, N.Y.: Ithaca Press.

———. 1993. *Genealogies of religion: Discipline and reasons of power in Christianity and Islam.* Baltimore: Johns Hopkins University Press.

Augustine. 1991. *Confessions.* Translated by H. Chadwick. New York: Oxford University Press.

Austin, J. L. 1962. *How to do things with words.* Cambridge, Mass.: Harvard University Press.

Back, Edith B. 1969. Technocracy and the ethic of social work. *Social Service Review* 43 (4): 430–438.

Bakhtin, M. M. 1981. *The dialogic imagination: Four essays*, trans. C. Emerson and M. Holquist, ed. M. Holquist. Austin: University of Texas Press.

———. 1984. *Problems of Dostoevsky's poetics*, trans. and ed. C. Emerson. Minneapolis: University of Minnesota Press.

———. 1990. *Art and answerability*, trans. V. Liapunov, ed. M. Holquist and V. Liapunov. Austin: University of Texas Press.

Ball, Samuel, Ken Bachrach, Jacqueline DeCarlo, Chris Farentinos, Melodie Keen, Terence McSherry, Douglas Polcin, Ned Snead, Richard Sockriter, Pauleen Wrigley, and Kathleen Carroll. 2002. Characteristics, beliefs, and practices of community clinicians trained to provide manual-guided therapy for substance abusers. *Journal of Substance Abuse Treatment* 23 (4): 309–318.

Bardill, Donald R. 1996. *The relational systems model for family therapy: Living in the four realities.* New York: Routledge.

Bateson, Gregory. 1971. The cybernetics of "self": A theory of alcoholism. *Psychiatry* 34 (1): 1–18.

———. 1972. *Steps to an ecology of mind: Collected essays in anthropology, psychiatry, evolution, and epistemology.* Chicago: University of Chicago Press.

Bateson, Mary Catherine. 1984. *With a daughter's eye: A memoir of Margaret Mead and Gregory Bateson.* New York: William Morrow.

Batteau, Allen W. 2000. Negations and ambiguities in the cultures of organization. *American Anthropologist* 102 (4): 726–740.

Bauman, Richard. 1975. Verbal art as performance. *American Anthropologist* 77 (2): 290–311.

———. 1996. Transformations of the word in the production of Mexican festival drama. In *Natural histories of discourse*, ed. Michael Silverstein and Greg Urban, 301–327. Chicago: University of Chicago Press.

Bauman, Richard, and Charles L. Briggs. 1990. Poetics and performances as critical perspectives on language and social life. *Annual Reviews in Anthropology* 19 (1): 59–88.

———. 2003. *Voices of modernity: Language ideologies and the politics of inequality*. Cambridge: Cambridge University Press.

Beels, C. Christian. 2002. Notes for a cultural history of family therapy. *Family Process* 41 (1): 67–82.

Bell, Lee Anne. 1996. In danger of winning: Consciousness raising strategies for empowering girls in the United States. *Women's Studies International Forum* 19 (4): 419–427.

Benda, Brent B., and Patrick Dattalo. 1990. Homeless women and men: Their problems and use of services. *Affilia* 5 (3): 50–82.

Benmayor, Rita. 1991. Testimony, action research, and empowerment: Puerto Rican women and popular education. In *Women's words: The feminist practice of oral history*, ed. Daphne Patai and Sherna Berger Gluck, 159–174. New York: Routledge.

Bennett, Larry, and Marie Lawson. 1994. Barriers to cooperation between domestic violence and substance abuse programs. *Families in Society* 75 (5): 277–285.

Benveniste, Emile. 1971. *Problems in general linguistics*, trans. by M. Meek. Coral Gables, Fla.: University of Miami Press.

Berenson, David. 1991. Powerlessness—liberating or enslaving? Responding to the feminist critique of the Twelve Steps. In *Feminism and addiction*, ed. Christine Bepko, 67–84. New York: Haworth.

Bergmann, Luke. 2009. *Getting ghost: Two young lives and the struggle for the soul of an African American city*. New York: New Press.

Bernstein, Edward. 1994. Empowerment forum: A dialogue between guest Editorial Board members. *Health Education Quarterly* 21:281–294.

Besnier, Niko. 1993. Reported speech and affect on Nukulaelae atoll. In *Responsibility and evidence in oral discourse*, ed. Jane Hill and Judith Irvine, 161–181. New York: Cambridge University Press.

———. 1995. *Literacy, emotion, and authority: Reading and writing on a Polynesian atoll*. New York: Cambridge University Press.

Best, Joel. 1995. *Images of issues: Typifying contemporary social problems*. 2nd ed. New York: Aldine De Gruyter.

———. 2004. Theoretical issues in the study of social problems and deviance. In *Social problems: A comparative international perspective*, ed. George Ritzer, 14–29. Thousand Oaks, Calif.: Sage.

———. 2008. Historical development and defining issues of constructionist inquiry. In *Handbook of constructionist research*, ed. James A. Holstein and Jaber F. Gubrium, 41–67. New York: Guilford.

Bezdek, Majorie, and Paul Spicer. 2006. Maintaining abstinence in a Northern Plains tribe. *Medical Anthropology Quarterly* 20 (2): 160–181.

Bishara, Amahl. 2008. Watching U.S. television from the Palestinian street: The media, the state, and representational interventions. *Cultural Anthropology* 23 (3): 488–530.

Bletzer, Keith V. 2004. Open towns and manipulated indebtedness among agricultural workers in the New South. *American Ethnologist* 31:530–551.

Bond, Michael P., and Jean S. Vaillant. 1986. An empirical study of the relationship between diagnosis and defense style. *Archives of General Psychiatry* 43 (3): 285–288.

Bookman, Ann, and Sandra Morgen. 1988. *Women and the politics of empowerment*. Philadelphia: Temple University Press.

Borden, William. 1992. Narrative perspectives in psychosocial intervention following adverse life events. *Social Work* 37 (2): 135–141.

———. 2009. *Reshaping theory in contemporary social work: Toward a critical pluralism*. New York: Columbia University Press.

Bordo, Susan. 1989. The body and the reproduction of femininity: A feminist appropriation of Foucault. In *Gender/body/knowledge: Feminist reconstructions of being and knowing*, ed. Alison Jaggar and Susan Bordo, 13–33. New Brunswick, N.J.: Rutgers University Press.

Borovoy, Amy. 2001. Recovering from codependence in Japan. *American Ethnologist* 28 (1): 94–118.

———. 2005. *The too-good wife: Alcohol, codependency, and the politics of nurturance in postwar Japan*. Berkeley: University of California Press.

Bourdieu, Pierre. 1977. *Outline of a theory of practice*. New York: Cambridge University Press.

———. 1991. *Language and symbolic power*. Cambridge, Mass.: Harvard University Press.

Bourgois, Phillipe. 1996. *In search of respect: Selling crack in El Barrio*. New York: Cambridge University Press.

———. 2000. Disciplining addictions: The bio-politics of methadone and heroin in the United States. *Culture, Medicine, and Psychiatry* 24 (2): 165–195.

———. 2003. Crack and the political economy of social suffering. *Addiction Research and Theory* 11 (1): 31–37.

Bourgois, Phillipe, and Jeffrey Schonberg. 2009. *Righteous dope fiend*. Berkeley: University of California Press.

Boyd, Carol J. 1993. The antecedents of women's crack cocaine abuse: Family substance abuse, sexual abuse, depression, and illicit drug use. *Journal of Substance Abuse Treatment* 10 (5): 433–438.

Boyle, Scott W., Grafton H. Hull, Jannah H. Mather, Larry L. Smith, and O. William Farley. 2005. *Direct practice in social work*. Boston: Allyn & Bacon.

Braithwaite, Ronald L., Cynthia Bianchi, and Sandra E. Taylor. 1994. Ethnographic approach to community organization and health empowerment. *Health Education & Behavior* 21 (3): 407–416.

Brandes, Stanley. 2002. *Staying sober in Mexico City*. Austin: University of Texas Press.

Brenneis, Donald. 1984. Grog and gossip in Bhatgaon: Style and substance in Fiji Indian conversation. *American Ethnologist* 11(3): 487–506.

———. 1990. Shared and solitary sentiments: The discourse of friendship, play and anger in Bhatgaon. In *Language and the politics of emotion,* ed. Catherine Lutz and Lila Abu-Lughod, 113–125. Cambridge: Cambridge University Press.

Breton, Margot. 1989. Liberation theology, group work, and the right of the poor and oppressed to participate in the life of the community. *Social Work with Groups* 12:5–18.

———. 1994. On the meaning of empowerment and empowerment-oriented social work practice. *Social Work with Groups* 17 (3): 23–37.

Breznitz, Shlomo. 1983. The seven kinds of denial. In *The denial of stress,* ed. Shlomo Breznitz, 257–280. New York: International Universities.

Briggs, Charles L. 1986. *Learning how to ask: A sociolinguistic appraisal of the role of the interview in social science research.* Cambridge: Cambridge University Press.

———. 1993. Metadiscursive practices and scholarly authority in folkloristics. *Journal of American Folklore* 106 (422): 387–434.

———. 1998. "You're a liar—you're just like a woman!": Constructing dominant ideologies of language in Warao men's gossip. In *Language ideologies: Practice and theory,* ed. Bambi B. Schieffelin, Kathryn A. Woolard, and Paul V. Kroskrity, 229–255. Oxford: Oxford University Press.

———. 2007. Anthropology, interviewing, and communicability in contemporary society. *Current Anthropology* 48 (4): 551–580.

Brockman, John. 1977. *About Bateson: Essays on Gregory Bateson.* New York: Plume.

Brodkin, Evelyn Z. 1990. Implementation as policy politics. In *Implementation and the policy process: Opening up the black box,* ed. Donald J. Palumbo and Dennis J. Calista, 107–118. New York: Greenwood.

———. 1997. Inside the welfare contract: Discretion and accountability in state welfare. *Social Service Review* 71:1–33.

———. 2000. Investigating policy's "practical" meaning: Street-level research on welfare policy. In Joint Center for Poverty Research Working Paper series, Northwestern University. Chicago.

Brodwin, Paul. 2002. Genetics, identity, and the anthropology of essentialism. *Anthropological Quarterly* 75 (2): 323–330.

———. 2005. "Bioethics in action" and human population genetics research. *Culture, medicine, and psychiatry* 29 (2): 145–178.

———. 2008. The co-production of moral discourse in US community psychiatry. *Medical Anthropology Quarterly* 22 (2): 127–147.

Brooks, Peter. 2000. *Troubling confessions: Speaking guilt in law and literature.* Chicago: University of Chicago Press.

Brown, Karen, and Dair Gillespie. 1992. Recovering relationships: A feminist analysis of recovery models. *American Journal of Occupational Therapy* 46 (11): 1001–1005.

Bruner, Jerome. 1990. *Acts of meaning.* Cambridge, Mass.: Harvard University Press.

Bryant, Mary. 1986. *My ego.* Stroudsbourg, Pa.: Quotidian.
Burack-Weiss, Ann. 1988. Clinical aspects of case management. *Generations* 12 (5): 23–25.
Burstow, Bonnie. 1991. Freirian codifications and social work education. *Journal of Social Work Education* 27:196–207.
Bush, George W. 1999. *A charge to keep.* New York: William Morrow.
Butler, Judith. 1990. *Gender trouble: Feminism and the subversion of identity.* New York: Routledge.
———. 1993. *Bodies that matter.* New York: Routledge.
———. 1997. *Excitable speech: A politics of the performative.* New York: Routledge.
———. 2004. *Undoing gender.* New York: Routledge.
Butler, Stephen F., Frederick L. Newman, John S. Cacciola, Arlene Frank, Simon H. Budman, A. Thomas McLellan, Sabrina Ford, Jack Blaine, David R. Gastfriend, and Karla Moras. 1998. Predicting Addiction Severity Index (ASI) interviewer severity ratings for a computer-administered ASI. *Psychological Assessment* 10 (4): 399–407.
Buttrick, Shirley M. 1970. On choices and services. *Social Service Review* 44 (4): 427–434.
Cain, Carole. 1991. Personal stories: Identity acquisition and self-understanding in Alcoholics Anonymous. *Ethos* 19 (2): 210–253.
Capps, Lisa, and Elinor Ochs. 1995. *Constructing panic: The discourse of agoraphobia.* Cambridge, Mass.: Harvard University Press.
Carcasson, Martin. 2004. Negotiating the paradoxes of poverty: Presidential rhetoric on welfare from Johnson to Clinton. Ph.D. diss., Texas A&M University, College Station.
———. 2006. Ending welfare as we know it: President Clinton and the rhetorical transformation of the anti-welfare culture. *Rhetoric and Public Affairs* 9 (4): 655–692.
Carr, E. Summerson. 2003. Rethinking empowerment theory using a feminist lens: The importance of process. *Affilia* 18 (1): 8–20.
———. 2004. Accessing resources, transforming systems: Group work with poor and homeless people. In *Handbook of social work with groups*, ed. Charles D. Garvin, Lorraine M Gutiérrez, and Maeda J. Galinsky, 655–687. New York: Guilford.
———. 2006. "Secrets keep you sick": Metalinguistic labor in a drug treatment program for homeless women. *Language in Society* 35 (5): 631–653.
———. 2009. Anticipating and inhabiting institutional identities. *American Ethnologist* 36 (2): 317–336.
———. 2010a. Enactments of expertise. *Annual Review of Anthropology* 39:1–21.
———. 2010b. Qualifying the qualitative social work interview: A linguistic anthropological approach. *Qualitative Social Work*.
Carroll, Jerome F. X. 1980. Similarities and differences of personality and psychopathology between alcoholics and addicts. *American Journal of Drug and Alcohol Abuse* 7 (2): 219–236.

Carroll, Kathleen M., and Lisa S. Onken. 2007. Behavioral therapies for drug abuse. *Focus* 5 (2): 240–248.

Carroll, Kathleen M., and B. J. Rounsaville. 2002. On beyond urine: Clinically useful assessment instruments in the treatment of drug dependence. *Behaviour Research and Therapy* 40 (11): 1329–1344.

Carter, Carolyn S. 1997. Ladies don't: A historical perspective on attitudes toward alcoholic women. *Affilia* 12 (4): 471–479.

Carvajal, Cesar, Yvan Dumont, and Remi Quirion. 2006. Neuropeptide Y: Role in emotion and alcohol dependence. *CNS* 5 (2): 181–95.

Cassinelli, Lee V. 1986. Qat: Changes in production and consumption of a quasilegal commodity in Northeast Africa. In *The social life of things: Commodities in cultural perspective*, ed. Arjun Appadurai, 236–257. Cambridge: Cambridge University Press.

Chafetz, Morris E. 1997 [1959]. Practical and theoretical considerations in the psychotherapy of alcoholism. In *Essential papers on addiction*, ed. Daniel Yalisove, 315–324. New York: New York University Press.

Chambón, Adrienne. 1999. Foucault's approach: Making the familiar visible. In *Reading Foucault for social work*, ed. Adrienne Chambón, Alan Irving, and Laura Epstein, 51–82. New York: Columbia University Press.

Chapman, Charlotte. 1997. Dual relationships in substance abuse treatment: Ethical implications. *Alcoholism Treatment Quarterly* 15 (2): 73–79.

Chenot, David K. 1998. Mutual values: Self psychology, intersubjectivity, and social work. *Clinical Social Work Journal* 26 (3): 297–311.

Chiauzzi, Emil J., and Steven Liljegren. 1993. Taboo topics in addiction treatment. *Journal of Substance Abuse Treatment* 10: 303–316.

Chodorow, Nancy. 1978. *The reproduction of mothering*. Berkeley: University of California Press.

Clark, Hewitt B., Barbara Lee, Mark E. Prange, and Beth A. McDonald. 1996. Children lost within the foster care system: Can wraparound service strategies improve placement outcomes? *Journal of Child and Family Studies* 5 (1): 39–54.

Clifford, James, and George E. Marcus. 1986. *Writing culture: The poetics and politics of ethnography*. Berkeley: University of California Press.

Clinton, William Jefferson. 1992. *Putting people first: How we can all change America*. New York: Three Rivers.

———. 1995. Public Papers of the President.

———. 1996. Remarks by the President at the Signing of the Personal Responsibility and Work Opportunity Reconciliation Act, ed. Office of the President Secretary.

Coburn, Cynthia E. 2006. Framing the problem of reading instruction: Using frame analysis to uncover the microprocesses of policy implementation. *American Educational Research Journal* 43 (3): 343–349.

Cohen, Alex, and Paul Koegel. 1996. The influence of alcohol and drug use on the subsistence adaptation of homeless mentally ill persons. *Journal of Drug Issues* 26(1):219–243.

Cohen, Judith A., and Anthony P. Mannarino. 2002. Addressing attributions in treating abused children. *Child Maltreatment* 7 (1): 82–86.

Cohen, Marcia B. 1994. Overcoming obstacles to forming empowerment groups: A consumer advisory board for homeless clients. *Social Work* 39 (6):742–749.

Cohn, Carol. 1987. Sex and death in the rational world of defense intellectuals. *Signs: Journal of Women in Culture and Society* 12 (4): 687–718.

Coholic, Diana. 2003. Incorporating spirituality in feminist social work perspectives. *Affilia* 18 (1): 49–67.

Collins, Barbara G. 1986. Defining feminist social work. *Social Work* 31 (3): 214–219.

Collins, James. 1996. Socialization to text: Structure and context in schooled literacy. In *Natural histories of discourse*, ed. Michael Silverstein and Greg Urban, 203–228. Chicago: University of Chicago Press.

Cook, Christopher C. 2006. The Minnesota Model in the management of drug and alcohol dependency: Miracle, method or myth? Part I. The philosophy and the programme. *Addiction* 83(6): 625–634.

Cook, Mary Ann. 1995. Substance-abusing, homeless mothers in treatment programs: A question of knowing. *Contemporary Drug Problems* 22 (2): 291–316.

Coombe, Chris M. 1997. Using empowerment evaluation in community organizing and community-based health initiatives. In *Community organizing and community building for health*, ed. Meredith Minkler, 291–307. New Brunswick, N.J.: Rutgers University Press.

Cornell Legal Institute, 2007. *TITLE 42 CHAPTER 119 SUBCHAPTER I § 11302.* Edited by U. C. Collection: Cornell Legal Institute.

Crapanzano, Vincent. 1992. *Hermes' dilemma and Hamlet's desire: On the epistemology of interpretation.* Cambridge, Mass.: Harvard University Press.

———. 1996. "Self"-centering narratives. In *Natural histories of discourse*, ed. Michael Silverstein and Greg Urban, 106–130. Chicago: University of Chicago Press.

Cruikshank, Barbara. 1999. *The will to empower: Democratic citizens and other subjects.* Ithaca, N.Y.: Cornell University Press.

D'Aunno, Thomas A. 2006. The role of organization and management in substance abuse treatment: Review and roadmap. *Journal of Substance Abuse Treatment* 31 (3): 221–233.

D'Aunno, Thomas, Thomas E. Vaughn, and Peter McElroy. 1999. An institutional analysis of HIV prevention efforts by the nation's outpatient drug abuse treatment units. *Journal of Health and Social Behavior* 40 (2): 175–192.

D'Aunno, Thomas A., Robert I. Sutton, and Richard H. Price. 1991. Isomorphism and external support in conflicting institutional environments: A study of drug abuse treatment units. *Academy of Management Journal* 34 (3): 636–661.

Daniels, Robert S. 1971. The future of medical care delivery systems. *Social Service Review* 45 (3): 259–273.

Davidson, Jennifer C. 2005. Professional relationship boundaries: A social work teaching module. *Social Work Education* 24 (5): 511–533.

Davidson, Virginia. 1977a. Psychiatry's problem with no name: Therapist-patient sex. *American Journal of Psychoanalysis (Historical Archive)* 37 (1): 43–50.

———. 1977b. Love and hate in methadone maintenance. *American Journal of Psychoanalysis* 37 (2): 163–166.

Davis, Liane V. 1986. A feminist approach to social work research. *Affilia* 1 (1): 32–47.
de Certeau, Michel. 1984. *The practice of everyday life*. Berkeley: University of California Press.
De Mojá, Carmelo A., and Charles D. Spielberger. 1997. Anger and drug addiction. *Psychological Reports* 81 (1): 152–154.
De Montigny, Gerald A. J. 1995. *Social working: An ethnography of front-line practice*. Toronto: University of Toronto Press.
Denzin, Norman K. 1987. Under the influence of time: Reading the interactional text. *Sociological Quarterly* 28 (3): 327–341.
———. 1993. *The alcoholic society: Addiction and recovery of the self*. New Brunswick, N.J.: Transaction.
Derby, Karen. 1992. Some difficulties in the treatment of character-disordered addicts. In *The chemically dependent: Phases of treatment and recovery*, ed. Barbara C. Wallace, 115–126. New York: Psychology Press.
Derrida, Jacques. 1995 [1992]. The rhetoric of drugs. In *Points de suspension . . . interviews, 1974–1994*. Stanford: Stanford University Press.
Desjarlais, Robert. 1996. The office of reason: On the politics of language and agency in a shelter for "the homeless mentally ill." *American Ethnologist* 23 (4): 880–900.
———. 1997. *Shelter blues: Sanity and selfhood among the homeless*. Philadelphia: University of Pennsylvania Press.
Dick, Hilary. 2006. What do to with "I don't know": Elicitation in ethnographic and survey interviews. *Qualitative Sociology* 29(1): 87–102.
DiClemente, Carlo C., and James O. Prochaska. 1982. Self-change and therapy change of smoking behavior: A comparison of processes of change in cessation and maintenance. *Addiction Behaviors* 7 (2): 133–142.
Dockrell, Julie, and David Messer. 1999. *Children's language and communication difficulties: Understanding, identification, and intervention*. London: Cassell.
Dohrenwend, Bruce P., Itzhak Levav, Patrick E. Shrout, Sharon Schwartz, Guedalia Naveh, Bruce G Link, Andrew Skodol, and Ann Stueve. 1992. Socioeconomic status and psychiatric disorders: The causation-selection issue. *Science* 255:946–952.
Dooley, David, Ralph Catalano, and Richard Hough. 1992. Unemployment and alcohol disorder in 1910 and 1990: drift versus social causation. *Journal of Occupational and Organizational Psychology* 65 (4): 277–290.
Dorpat, Theo L. 1983. The cognitive arrest hypothesis of denial. *International Journal of Psycho-Analysis* 64:47–58.
———. 1987. A new look at denial and defense. *Annual of Psychoanalysis* 15: 23–47.
Douglas, Mary. 1986. *How institutions think*. Syracuse, N.Y.: Syracuse University Press.
———. 1987. *Constructive drinking: Perspectives on drink from anthropology*. New York: Cambridge University Press.
Douglas, Mary, and Steven Ney. 1998. *Missing persons: A critique of the social sciences*. Berkeley: University of California Press.

Dove, William R. 1995. Ethics training for alcohol/drug abuse. *Alcoholism Treatment Quarterly* 12 (4): 19–30.
Doweiko, Harold. 1996. *Concepts of chemical dependency*. Pacific Grove, Calif.: Brooks/Cole.
Dumit, Joseph. 2004. *Picturing personhood: Brain scans and biomedical identity*. Princeton, N.J.: Princeton University Press.
Duncan, Garrett Albert, and Ryonnel Jackson. 2004. The language we cry in: Black language practice at a post-desegregated urban high school. *GSE Perspectives on Urban Education* 3 (1): 1–22.
Duranti, Alessandro. 1988. Intentions, language, and social action in a Samoan context. *Journal of Pragmatics* 12 (1): 13–33.
———. 1993. Truth and intentionality: An ethnographic critique. *Cultural Anthropology* 8 (2): 214–245.
———. 1997. *Linguistic anthropology*. New York: Cambridge University Press.
Durkin, Elizabeth M. 2002. An organizational analysis of psychosocial and medical services in outpatient drug abuse treatment programs. *Social Service Review* 76 (3): 406–429.
Edelman, Murray. 1974. The political language of the helping professions. *Politics & Society* 4 (3): 295–310.
Edwards, Richard L., ed. 1995. *Encyclopedia of social work*. 19th ed. Washington, D.C.: National Association of Social Workers.
Eisenhuth, Elizabeth. 1981. The theories of Heinz Kohut and clinical social work practice. *Clinical Social Work Journal* 9 (2): 80–90.
El Rasheed, Amany. 2001. Alexithymia in Egyptian substance abusers. *Substance Abuse* 22 (1): 11–21.
Emmett, Isobel, and D.H.J. Morgan. 1982. Max Gluckman and the Manchester shopfloor ethnographies. *Custom and conflict in British society*, ed. Ronald Frakenberg, 140–165. Manchester: Manchester University Press.
Eng, Eugenia, and Edith Parker. 1994. Measuring community competence in the Mississippi Delta: The interface between program evaluation and empowerment. *Health Education & Behavior* 21 (2): 199–220.
Enns, Carolyn Zerbe. 1997. *Feminist theories and feminist psychotherapies*. New York: Haworth.
Estroff, Sue E. 1981. *Making it crazy: An ethnography of psychiatric clients in an American community*. Berkeley: University of California Press.
Evans, Estella Norwood. 1992. Liberation Theology, empowerment theory and social work practice with the oppressed. *International Social Work* 35 (2): 135–147.
Evans, Kathy M., Elizabeth A. Kincade, Aretha F. Marbley, and Susan R. Seem. 2005. Feminism and feminist therapy: Lessons from the past and hopes for the future. *Journal of Counseling and Development* 83 (3): 269–277.
Fainzang, Sylvie. 1994. When alcoholics are not anonymous. *Medical Anthropology Quarterly* 8 (3): 336–345.
Fairbanks, Robert P. 2009. *How it works: Recovering citizens in post-welfare Philadelphia*. Chicago: University of Chicago Press.
Farquhar, Judith. 1994. *Knowing practice: The clinical encounter of Chinese medicine*. Boulder, Colo.: Westview.

Ferguson, Harry. 2008. Liquid social work: Welfare interventions as mobile practices. *British Journal of Social Work* 38(3): 561–579.
Ferrara, Kathleen. 1994. *Therapeutic ways with words.* New York: Oxford University Press.
Fewell, Christine H., and Leclair Bissell. 1978. The alcohol denial syndrome: An alcohol-focused approach. *Social Casework* 59:6–13.
Fine, Michelle A. 1992. Families in the United States: Their current status and future prospects. *Family Relations* 41 (4): 430–435.
Fine, Reuben. 1979. *A history of psychoanalysis.* New York: Columbia University Press.
Finkelstein, Norma. 1993. Treatment programming for alcohol and drug-dependent pregnant women. *International Journal of the Addictions* 28 (12): 1275–1309.
———. 1994. Treatment issues for alcohol-and drug-dependent pregnant and parenting women. *Health and Social Work* 19 (1): 7–15.
Finn, Janet L., and Lynne Underwood. 2000. The state, the clock, and the struggle: An inquiry into the discipline for welfare reform in Montana. *Social Text* 18 (1): 109–134.
Fischer, Constance T. 1994. *Individualizing psychological assessment.* New York: Routledge.
Fish, Vincent. 1993. Poststructuralism in family therapy: Interrogating the narrative/conversational mode. *Journal of Marital and Family Therapy* 19 (3): 221–234.
Fisher, Pamela J., and William R. Breakley. 1991. The epidemiology of alcohol, drug, and mental disorders among homeless persons. *American Psychologist* 46 (11): 1115–1128.
Fliegelman, Jay. 1993. *Declaring independence: Jefferson, natural language, and the culture of performance.* Stanford: Stanford University Press.
Floersch, Jerry Eugene. 2002. *Meds, money, and manners: The case management of severe mental illness.* New York: Columbia University Press.
———. 2000. Reading the case record: The oral and written narratives of social workers. *Social Service Review* 74 (2): 169–192.
———. 1999. Review of *Under the Cover of Kindness,* by Leslie Margolin. *American Journal of Sociology* 104 (4): 216–218.
Flores, Philip J. 1988. Psychoanalytic considerations of the etiology of compulsive drug use. In *Essential papers on addiction,* ed. Daniel Yalisove, 87–108. New York: New York University Press.
———. 2004. *Addiction as an attachment disorder.* New York: Jason Aronson.
Flynn, Patrick M., Robert L. Hubbard, James W. Luckey, Barbara H. Forsyth, Timothy K. Smith, Charles D. Phillips, Douglas L. Fountain, Jeffrey A. Hoffman, and Joseph J. Koman. 1995. Individual assessment profile (IAP): Standardizing the assessment of substance abusers. *Journal of Substance Abuse Treatment* 12 (3): 213–221.
Ford, Gary G. 1996. An existential model for promoting life change: Confronting the disease concept. *Journal of Substance Abuse Treatment* 13 (2): 151–158.
Fording, Richard, Sanford F. Schram, and Joe Soss. 2006. Devolution, discretion, and local variation in TANF sanctioning. University of Kentucky Poverty Research Discussion Paper Series 2006-4.

Forsberg, Hannele, and Åse Vagli. 2006. The social construction of emotions in child protection case-talk. *Qualitative Social Work* 5 (1): 9–31.

Foucault, Michel. 1978. *The history of sexuality.* Vol. 1, *An introduction.* New York: Random House.

———. 1984a. Nietzsche, genealogy, and history. In *The Foucault reader,* ed. Paul Rabinow, 76–100. New York: Pantheon.

———. 1984b. What is enlightenment? In *The Foucault reader,* ed. Paul Rabinow, 32–50. New York: Pantheon.

———. 1985. *The history of sexuality.* Vol. 2, *The uses of pleasure.* Translated by R. Hurley. New York: Vintage.

———. 1988. Technologies of the self. In *Technologies of the self: A seminar with Michel Foucault,* ed. Luther Martin, Huck Gutman, and Patrick Hutton, 16–50. Amherst: University of Massachusetts Press.

———. 1993. About the beginning of the hermeneutics of the self: Two lectures at Dartmouth. *Political Theory* 21 (2): 198–227.

———. 1999a. On the government of the living. In *Religion and culture,* ed. Jeremy Carrette, 154–157. New York: Routledge.

———. 1999b. Pastoral power and political reason. In *Religion and culture,* ed. Jeremy Carrette, 135–52. New York: Routledge.

Foytlin, Matt A., Clarise A. Nelson, Wali Rahman, and Jurgen Streeck. 1999. Casualties of lyrical combat. Paper read at Texas Linguistic Forum.

Fraser, Nancy, and Linda Gordon. 1994. A genealogy of dependency: Tracing a keyword of the U.S. welfare state. *Signs: Journal of Women in Culture and Society* 19 (2): 309–336.

Freire, Paulo. 1970. *Pedagogy of the oppressed.* New York: Herder and Herder.

———. 1973. *Education for critical consciousness.* New York: Seabury.

Freud, Anna. 1937. *The ego and the mechanisms of defense.* London: Hogarth.

Freud, Sigmund. 1938. An outline of psychoanalysis. In *The standard edition of the complete psychological works of Sigmund Freud, Volume 23,* 144–207. London: Hogarth Press.

———. 1955 [1939]. *Moses and monotheism.* New York: Vintage.

———. 1959 [1926]. Inhibitions, symptoms and anxiety. In *The standard edition of the complete psychological works of Sigmund Freud,* ed. James Strachey. London: Hogarth.

Friedman, Jennifer, and Marixa Alicea. 2001. *Surviving heroin: Interviews with women in methadone clinics.* Gainesville: University Press of Florida.

Friedmann, Peter D., Jeffrey A. Alexander, and Thomas A. D'Aunno. 1999. Organizational correlates of access to primary care and mental health services in drug abuse treatment units. *Journal of Substance Abuse Treatment* 16 (1): 71–80.

Freidson, Eliot. 1986. *Professional powers: A study of the institutionalization of formal knowledge.* Chicago: University of Chicago Press.

Fulkerson, Jayne A., Patricia A. Harrison, and Timothy J. Beebe. 1999. DSM-IV substance abuse and dependence: Are there really two dimensions of substance use disorders in adolescents? *Addiction* 94 (4): 495–506.

Gal, Susan. 1991. Between speech and silence: The problematics of research of language and gender. In *Gender at the crossroads of knowledge,* ed. Michaela DiLeonardo, 175–203. Berkeley: University of California Press.

---. 1992. Multiplicity and contestation among ideologies: A commentary. *Pragmatics* 2 (3): 445–449.

---. 1995a. Domination and the arts of resistance: Hidden transcripts (Book Review). *Cultural Anthropology* 10 (3): 407–424.

---. 1995b. Lost in a Slavic sea: Linguistic theories and expert knowledge in 19th century Hungary. *Pragmatics* 5:155–166.

---. 1998. Multiplicity and contention among language ideologies. In *Language ideologies: Practice and theory*, ed. Bambi B. Schieffelin, Kathryn Ann Woolard, and Paul V. Kroskrity, 317–322. New York: Mouton de Gruyter.

---. 2005. Language ideologies compared: Metaphors of public/private. *Journal of Linguistic Anthropology* 15 (1): 23–37.

Gal, Susan, and Judith T. Irvine. 1995. The boundaries of languages and disciplines: How ideologies construct difference. *Social Research* 62 (4): 967–1001.

Galanter, Marc, Linda Glickman, David Singer. 2007. An overview of outpatient treatment of adolescent substance abuse. *Substance Abuse* 28 (2): 51–58.

Gambrill, Eileen D. 1999. Evidence-based practice: An alternative to authority-based practice. *Families in Society* 80 (4): 341–350.

---. 2006. *Social work practice: A critical thinker's guide.* New York: Oxford University Press.

Garcia, Angela. 2008. The elegiac addict: History, chronicity, and the melancholic subject. *Cultural Anthropology* 23 (4): 718–746.

Garriott, William. 2008. A body on drugs: Methamphetamine and the making of a new criminal type in the rural United States. Ph.D. diss., Princeton University, Princeton, N.J.

Garrity, John. 2000. Jesus, peyote, and the holy people: Alcohol abuse and the ethos of power in Navajo healing. *Medical Anthropology Quarterly* 14 (4): 521–542.

General Definition of Homeless Individual, 42 U.S.C. §119 (2007).

Germain, Carel B., and A. Gitterman. 1980. *The life model of social work practice.* New York: Columbia University Press.

Gibbs, Leornard E., and Eileen D. Gambrill. 2002. Evidence-based practice: Counterarguments to objections. *Research on Social Work Practice* 12 (3): 452–476.

Gilbert, Neil. 1979. The design of community planning structures. *Social Service Review* 53 (4): 644–654.

Gilbert, Neil, and Harry Specht. 1976. *The emergence of social welfare and social work.* Itasca, Ill.: Peacock.

Gilbert, Neil, Harry Specht, and David A. Lindeman. 1981. Social service planning cycles: Ritualism or rationalism? *Social Service Review* 55 (3): 419–433.

Gilligan, Carol. 1982. *In a different voice: Psychological theory and women's development.* Cambridge, Mass.: Harvard University Press.

Gilyard, Keith. 1996. *Let's flip the script: An African American discourse on language, literature, and learning.* Detroit: Wayne State University Press.

Goffman, Erving. 1961. *Asylums: Essays on the social situation of mental patients and other inmates.* New York: Doubleday.

———. 1974. *Frame Analysis: An essay on the organization of experience.* New York: Harper and Row.

———. 1979. Footing. *Semiotica* 25:1–29.

———. 1981. *Forms of talk.* Philadelphia: University of Pennsylvania Press.

Goodwill Industries of Greater Detroit. Flip the Script. Available at http://www.goodwilldetroit.org/programs/flip-the-script.aspx (retrieved August 16, 2008).

Gordon, Linda. 1986a. Family violence, feminism, and social control. *Feminist Studies* 12 (3): 452–478.

———. 1988a. *Heroes of their own lives: The politics and history of family violence, Boston, 1880–1960.* Chicago: University of Illinois Press.

———. 1988b. What does welfare regulate? *Social Research* 55 (4): 609–630.

Gornick, Janet C., and David S. Meyer. 1998. Changing political opportunity: The anti-rape movement and public policy. *Journal of Policy History* 10 (4): 367–398.

Gorski, Terrence. 2000. *Denial Management Counseling professional guide: Advanced clinical skills* New York: Herald.

Gounis, Kostas. 1993. *The domestication of homelessness: The politics of space and time in New York City shelters.* New York: Columbia University Press.

Greenfield, Shelly F., and Grace Hennessy. 2004. Assessment of the patient. In *The American psychiatric publishing textbook of substance abuse treatment,* ed. Marc Galanter and Herbert D. Kleber. Arlington, Va.: American Psychiatric.

Greenspan, Miriam. 1983. *A new approach to women and therapy.* New York: Tab Books.

Gremillion, Helen. 2003. *Feeding anorexia: Gender and power at a treatment center.* Durham, N.C.: Duke University Press.

Grice, H. Paul. 1957. Meaning. *Philosophical Review* 66 (3): 377–388.

———. 1989. *Studies in the way of words.* Cambridge, Mass.: Harvard University Press.

Grosz, Elizabeth. 1995. *Space, time, and perversion: Essays on the politics of bodies.* New York: Routledge.

Gubrium, Jaber F., and James A. Holstein. 1997. *The new language of qualitative method.* New York: Oxford University Press.

Gulati, Padi. 1982. Consumer participation in administrative decision making. *Social Service Review* 56 (1): 72–84.

Gumperz, John J. 1982. *Discourse strategies.* New York: Cambridge University Press.

Gupta, Akhil, and James Ferguson. 1997. *Anthropological locations: Boundaries and grounds of a field science.* Berkeley: University of California Press.

Gutierrez, Lorraine M. 1990. Working with women of color: An empowerment perspective. *Social Work* 35 (2): 149–153.

———. 1994. Beyond coping: An empowerment perspective on stressful life events. *Journal of Sociology and Social Welfare* 21 (3): 201–219.

Gutierrez, Lorraine M., K. A. DeLois, and L. GlenMaye. 1995. Understanding empowerment practice: Building on practitioner-based knowledge. *Families in Society* 76 (9): 534–542.

Gutierrez, Lorraine M., Ruth J. Parsons, and Enil O. Cox. 1998. *Empowerment in social work practice. A sourcebook.* Pacific Grove, Calif.: Brooks/Cole.

Haaken, Janice. 1993. From Al-Anon to ACOA: Codependency and the reconstruction of caregiving. *Signs* 18 (2): 321–345.

———. 1998. *Pillar of salt: Gender, memory, and the perils of looking back.* New Brunswick, N.J.: Rutgers University Press.

Hacking, Ian. 1975. *Why does language matter to philosophy?* New York: Cambridge University Press.

———. 1991. The making and molding of child abuse. *Critical Inquiry* 17 (2): 253–288.

———. 1999. *The social construction of what?* Cambridge, Mass.: Harvard University Press.

Hall, Christoper, Stefaan Slembrouck, and Srikant Sarangi. 2006. *Language practices in social work: Categorisation and accountability in child welfare.* London: Routledge.

Hall, Christopher, Kirsi Juhila, Nigel Parton, Tarja Poso, eds. 2003. *Constructing clienthood in social work and human services.* London: Kingsley.

Hall, Joanne M. 1996. Pervasive effects of childhood sexual abuse in lesbians' recovery from alcohol problems. *Substance Use & Misuse* 31 (2): 225–239.

Hall, Joanne M., and Jill Powell. 2000. Dissociative experiences described by women survivors of childhood abuse. *Journal of Interpersonal Violence* 15 (2): 184–204.

Hall, Kira. 1995. Lip service on the fantasy lines. In *Gender articulated: Language and the socially constructed self*, ed. Kira Hall and Mary Bucholtz, 183–216. New York: Routledge.

Hanks, William F. 1987. Discourse genres in a theory of practice. *American Ethnologist* 14 (4): 668–692.

———. 1993. Metalanguage and the pragmatics of deixis. In *Reflexive language: Reported speech and metapragmatics*, ed. John Lucy, 127–158. New York: Cambridge University Press.

———. 1996a. *Language and communicative practices.* Boulder, Colo.: Westview.

———. 1996b. Exorcism and the description of participant roles. In *Natural histories of discourse*, ed. Michael Silverstein and Greg Urban, 160–202. Chicago: University of Chicago Press.

Haraway, Donna J. 1991. *Simians, cyborgs, and women: The reinvention of nature.* New York: Routledge.

Harrison, Patricia A., Norman G. Hoffmann, and Glenace E. Edwall. 1989. Sexual abuse correlates: Similarities between male and female adolescents in chemical dependency treatment. *Journal of Adolescent Research* 4 (3): 385–399.

Hartman, Ann. 1978. Diagrammatic assessment of family relationships. *Social Casework* 59 (8): 465–476.

———. 1988. Foreword. In *Paradigms of clinical social work*, ed. Rachelle A. Dorfman,vii–xi. New York: Brunner/Mazel.

Hasenfeld, Yeheskel. 1972. People processing organizations: An exchange approach. *American Sociological Review* 37(3): 256–263.

———. 1983. *Human service organizations.* Upper Saddle River, N.J.: Prentice Hall.

———. 1987. Power in social work practice. *Social Service Review* 10:41–56.
———. ed. 1992. *Human services as complex organizations*. Thousand Oaks, Calif.: Sage.
———. ed. 2009a. The attributes of human service organizations, In *Human services as complex organizations*, ed. Y. Hasenfeld, 9–32. Thousand Oaks, Calif.: Sage.
———. ed. 2009b. Worker-client relations: Social policy in practice. In *Human services as complex organizations*, ed. Y. Hasenfeld, 405–426. Thousand Oaks, Calif.: Sage.
Hasenfeld, Yeheskel, and Richard A. English, eds. 1974. *Human service organizations: A book of readings*. Ann Arbor: University of Michigan Press.
Hastings, Adi. 2008. Licked by the mother tongue: Imagining everyday Sanskrit at home and in the world. *Journal of Linguistic Anthropology* 18 (1): 24–45.
Hauser, Stuart T. 1986. Conceptual and empirical dilemmas in the assessment of defenses. In *Empirical studies of ego defenses*, ed. Dante Cicchetti and Donald J. Cohen, 89–99. Washington D.C.: American Psychiatric Press.
Hazelden Educational Materials Agency. 1975. *Dealing with denial*. Center City, Minn.: Hazelden.
Heath, Dwight, ed. 2000. *Drinking occasions: Comparative perspectives on alcohol and culture*. New York: Routledge.
Hepworth, Dean, Ronald Rooney, and Jo Ann Larsen. 2002. *Direct social work practice: Theory and skills*. 6th ed. Pacific Grove, Calif.: Brooks Cole.
Heron, Barbara. 2005. Self-reflection in critical social work practice: Subjectivity and the possibilities of resistance. *Reflective Practice* 6 (3): 341–351.
Hill, Jane H. 1995. The voices of Don Gabriel: Responsibility and self in a modern Mexicano narrative. In *The dialogic emergence of culture*, ed. Dennis Tedlock and Bruce Mannheim, 97–147. Urbana: University of Illinois Press.
———. 2000. "Read my article": Ideological complexity and the overdetermination of promising in American presidential politics. In *Regimes of language: Ideologies, polities, and identities*, ed. Paul V. Kroskrity, 259–291. Santa Fe, N.M.: School of American Research Press.
———. 2007. Mock Spanish: A site for the indexical reproduction of racism in American English. In *Race, ethnicity, and gender*, ed. Joseph H. Healey and Eileen O'Brien, 270–284. Los Angeles: Pine Forge.
Hollis, Florence. 1964. *Casework: A psychosocial therapy*. New York: Random House.
Hopper, Kim. 1987. The public response to homelessness in New York City—The last hundred years. In *On being homeless: Historical perspectives*, ed. Rick Beard, 88–101. New York: Schneidereith.
———. 1990. Research findings as testimony: A note on the ethnographer as expert witness. *Human Organization* 49 (2): 110–113.
———. 2003. *Reckoning with homelessness*. Ithaca, N.Y.: Cornell University Press.
Hopper, Kim, and Jim Baumohl. 1994. Held in abeyance: Rethinking homelessness and advocacy. *American Behavioral Scientist* 37 (4): 522–552.
Hunt, Leslie L. 1971. *25 Kites that fly*. New York: Dover.
Hurley, Dorothy L. 1991. Women, alcohol, and incest: An analytical review. *Journal of Studies on Alcohol* 52 (3): 253–268.

Inger, Ivan B. 1993. A dialogic perspective for family therapy: The contributions of Martin Buber and Gregory Bateson. *Journal of Family Therapy* 15 (3): 293–314.

Inoue, Miyako. 2006. *Vicarious language: Gender and linguistic modernity in Japan*. Berkeley: University of California Press.

Irvine, Judith T. 1982. Language and affect: Some cross-cultural issues. In *Contemporary perceptions of language: Interdisciplinary dimensions*, ed. H. Byrnes, 31–47. Washington, D.C.: Georgetown University Press.

———. 1989. When talk isn't cheap: Language and political economy. *American Ethnologist* 16 (2): 248–267.

———. 1990. Registering affect: Heteroglossia in the linguistic expression of emotion. In *Language and the politics of emotion*, ed. Catherine Lutz and Lila Abu-Lughod, 126–161. Cambridge: Cambridge University Press.

———. 1996. Shadow conversations: The indeterminacy of participant roles. In *Natural histories of discourse*, ed. Michael Silverstein and Greg Urban, 131–159. Chicago: University of Chicago Press.

Irvine, Judith T., and Susan Gal. 2000. Language ideology and linguistic differentiation. In *Regimes of language: Ideologies, polities, and identities*, ed. Paul V. Kroskrity, 35–83. Santa Fe, N.M.: School of American Research Press.

Jackson, John L. 2005. *Real black: Adventures in racial sincerity*. Chicago: University of Chicago Press.

Jakobson, Roman. 1980. *The framework of language*. Ann Arbor: University of Michigan Press.

Janis, Irving L. 1983. *Short-term counseling*. New Haven, Conn.: Yale University Press.

Jasinski, Jana L., Lina M. Williams, and Jane Siegel. 2000. Childhood physical and sexual abuse as risk factors for heavy drinking among African-American women: a prospective study. *Child Abuse & Neglect* 24 (8): 1061–1071.

Jenkins, Shirley, Beverly Diamond, Mark Flanzraich, J. Gibson, J. Hendricks, and Nabil Marshood. 1983. Ethnic differentials in foster care placements. *Social Work Research & Abstracts* 19 (4): 41–45.

Johnson, Vernon. 1980. *I'll quit tomorrow: A practical guide to alcoholism treatment*. New York: Harper and Row.

Kahn, Alfred J. 1976. Service delivery at the neighborhood level: Experience, theory, and fads. *Social Service Review* 50 (1): 23–56.

Kalb, Melvyn, and Morton S. Propper. 1976. The future of alcohology: Craft or science? *American Journal of Psychiatry* 133 (6): 641–645.

Kamerman, Sheila B. 1974. Participation, leadership, and experience: Imbalance or in balance? *Social Service Review* 48 (3): 403–411.

Kaminski, Michelle, Jeffrey S. Kaufman, Robin Graubarth, and Thomas G. Robins. 2000. How do people become empowered? A case study of union activists. *Human Relations* 53 (10): 1357–1382.

Kant, Immanuel. 1969. *Critique of pure reason*, trans. N. K. Smith. Edinburgh: MacMillan & Co.

Kaplan, Harold I., and Benjamin J. Sadock. 1981. *Modern synopsis of comprehensive textbook of psychiatry*. New York: Williams & Wilkins.

Karls, James M., and Karin Wendrei, E. 1994. *Person-In-Environment system:*

The PIE classification system for social functioning problems. Washington, D.C.: National Association of Social Workers.

Kaskutas, Lee Ann. 1989. Women for Sobriety: A qualitative analysis. *Contemporary Drug Problems* 16:177–200.

———. 1992. Beliefs on the source of sobriety: Interactions of membership of Women for Sobriety and Alcoholics Anonymous. *Contemporary Drug Problems* 19:631–48.

———. 1996. Pathways to self-help among Women for Sobriety. *American Journal of Drug and Alcohol Abuse* 22 (2): 259–280.

Katz, Michael B. 1983. *Poverty and policy in American history.* New York: Academic Press.

Kaufman, Edward R. 1994. *Psychotherapy of addicted persons.* New York: Guilford.

———. 1992. Countertransference and other mutually interactive aspects of psychotherapy with substance abusers. *American Journal on Addictions* 1 (3): 185–202.

Keane, Webb. 1997. *Signs of recognition: Powers and hazards of representation in an Indonesian society.* Berkeley: University of California Press.

———. 2002. Sincerity, "modernity," and the Protestants. *Cultural Anthropology* 17 (1): 65–92.

———. 2007. *Christian Moderns: Freedom and fetish in the mission encounter.* Berkeley: University of California Press.

Kearney, Robert J. 1996. *Within the wall of denial: Conquering addictive behaviors.* New York: Norton.

Keeney, Bradford P., and Jeffrey Ross. 1983. Learning to learn systemic therapies. *Journal of Strategic and Systemic Therapies* 2 (2): 22–30.

Keeney, Bradford P., and Douglas H. Sprenkle. 1982. Ecosystemic epistemology: Critical implications for the aesthetics and pragmatics of family therapy. *Family Process* 21 (1): 1–19.

Keller, Daniel S., Kathleen M. Carroll, Charla Nich, and Bruce J. Rounsaville. 1995. Alexithymia in cocaine abusers response to psychotherapy and pharmacotherapy. *American Journal on Addictions* 4 (3): 234–244.

Kemp, Susan P. 2001. Environment through a gendered lens: From person-in-environment to woman-in-environment. *Affilia* 16 (1): 7–30.

Kemp, Susan P., James K. Whittaker, and Elizabeth Tracy. 1997. *Person-environment practice: The social ecology of interpersonal helping.* New York: Aldine.

Keyes, Cheryl L. 1996. At the crossroads: Rap music and its African nexus. *Ethnomusicology* 40 (2): 223–248.

Kieffer, Charles. 1984. Citizen empowerment: A development perspective. In *Studies in empowerment: Steps toward understanding and action,* ed. Julian Rappaport, Carolyn Swift, and Robert Hess, 9–35. New York: Routledge.

Kockelman, Paul. 2007. Agency: The relationship between meaning, power, and knowledge. *Current Anthropology* 48 (3): 375–401.

Kondrat, Mary E. 1999. Who is the "self" in self-aware: Professional self-awareness from a critical theory perspective. *Social Service Review* 73 (4): 451–475.

Kramer, Ralph M. 1975. The organizational character of the voluntary service agency in Israel. *Social Service Review* 49 (3): 321–343.

Kroskrity, Paul V. 1998. Arizona Tewa Kiva speech as a manifestation of a dominant language ideology. In *Language ideologies: Practice and theory*, ed. Bambi Schieffelin, Kathryn A. Woolard, and Paul V. Kroskrity, 103–122. Oxford: Oxford University Press.

———. 2000. *Regimes of language: Ideologies, polities, and identities*. Santa Fe, N.M.: School of American Research Press.

Krystal, Henry. 1979. Alexithymia and psychotherapy. *American Journal of Psychotherapy* 33 (1): 17–31.

———. 1982–1983. Alexithymia and the effectiveness of psychoanalytic treatment. *International Journal of Psychoanalytic Psychotherapy* 9:353–378.

Krystal, Henry, and Herbert A. Raskin. 1970. *Drug dependence: Aspects of ego function*. Detroit: Wayne State University Press.

Kubler-Ross, Elizabeth. 1969. *On death and dying*. New York: Macmillan.

Kuipers, Joel C. 1989. "Medical discourse" in anthropological context: Views of language and power. *Medical Anthropology Quarterly* 3 (2): 99–123.

Kulick, Don. 2003a. Language and desire. In *The handbook of language and gender*, ed. Janet Holmes and Miriam Meyerhoff, 119–141. Malden, Mass.: Blackwell.

———. 2003b. Gay and lesbian language. *Annual Review of Anthropology*, 29: 243–285.

Kulick, Don, and Charles Klein. 2003. Scandalous acts: The politics of shame among Brazilian travesti prostitutes. In *Recognition struggles and social movements: Contested identities, agency, and power*, ed. Barbara Hobson, 215–238. New York: Cambridge University Press.

LabCorp, Inc. *Drugs of abuse reference guide*. 2007. http://www.labcorp.com/pdf/doa_reference_guide.pdf (retrieved August 19, 2007).

Labov, William. 1972a. *Language in the inner city: Studies in the Black English vernacular*. Philadelphia: University of Pennsylvania Press.

———. 1972b. Some principles of linguistic methodology. *Language in Society* 1 (1): 97–120.

Labov, William, and David Fanshel. 1977. *Therapeutic discourse: Psychotherapy as conversation*. New York: Academic Press.

Laird, Joan. 1994. "Thick description" revisited: Family therapist as anthropologist-constructivist. In *Qualitative research in social work*, ed. Edmund Sherman and William J. Reid, 175–189. New York: Academic Press.

Lakoff, Andrew. 2005. *Pharmaceutical reason: Knowledge and value in global psychiatry*. New York: Cambridge University Press.

Lamoreaux, Naomi R. 1986. Banks, kinship, and economic development: The New England case. *Journal of Economic History* 46 (3): 647–667.

Laplanche, Jean, and Jean-Bertrand Pontalis. 1973. *The language of psychoanalysis*. Translated by D. Nicholson-Smith. New York: Norton.

Latour, Bruno, and Peter Weibel. 2005. *Making things public: Atmospheres of democracy*. Cambridge, Mass.: MIT Press.

Latour, Bruno. http://www.bruno-latour.fr/ (retrieved August 16, 2008).

Lave, Jean, and Etienne Wenger. 1991. *Situated learning: Legitimate peripheral participation*. New York: Cambridge University Press.

Lazarus, Arnold A. 1989. Why I am an eclectic (not an integrationist). *British Journal of Guidance and Counseling* 17 (3): 248–258.

———. 1992. Multimodal therapy: Technical eclecticism with minimal integration. In *Handbook of psychotherapy integration*, ed. John C. Norcross and Marvin R. Goldfried, 231–263. New York: Basic Books.

———. 2006. *Brief but comprehensive psychotherapy: The multimodal way.* New York: Springer.

Lee, Benjamin. 1997. *Talking heads: Language, metalanguage, and the semiotics of subjectivity.* Durham, N.C.: Duke University Press.

Lemanski, Michael. 2001. *History of addiction and recovery in the United States.* Tucson, Ariz.: Sharp.

Leon, Anne M., and Elizabeth Marie Armantrout. 2007. Assessing families and other client systems in community-based programmes: Development of the CALF. *Child and Family Social Work* 12 (2): 123–132.

Lerman, Hannah. 1986. From Freud to feminist personality theory: Getting here from there. *Psychology of Women Quarterly* 10:1–18.

Levav, I., N. Zilber, E. Danielovich, E. Aisenberg, N. Turetsky. 1987. The etiology of schizophrenia: A replication test of the social selection vs. the social causation hypotheses. *Acta Psychiatrica Scandinavica* 75(2): 183–189.

Levine, Harry G. 1978. The discovery of addiction. *Journal of Studies on Alcohol* 39 (1): 143–174.

Lewis, Elizabeth. 1991. Social change and citizen action: A philosophical exploration for modern social group work. *Social Work with Groups* 14 (3/4): 23–34.

Lewis, Oscar. 1966. The culture of poverty. *Scientific American* 215 (4): 19–25.

Lieberman, Stuart. 1998. History containing systems *Journal of Family Therapy* 20 (2): 195–206.

Lima, Elvira S., and Marineusa Gazzetta. 1994. From lay teachers to university students: The path for empowerment through culturally based pedagogical action. *Anthropology and Education Quarterly* 25 (3): 236–249.

Linders, Annulla. 1998. Abortion as a social problem: The construction of opposite solutions in Sweden and the United States. *Social Problems* 45 (4): 488–509.

Lindsey, Duncan. 1994. *The welfare of children.* New York: Oxford University Press.

Linehan, Marsha M. 1993a. *Cognitive-behavioral treatment of borderline personality disorder.* New York: Guilford.

———. 1993b. *Skills training manual for treating borderline personality disorder* New York: Guilford.

Link, Brice G., and Joe C. Phelan. 1996. Understanding sociodemographic differences in health—the role of fundamental social causes. *American Journal of Public Health* 86 (4): 471–472.

Lipsky, Michael. 1980. *Street-level bureaucracy: Dilemmas of the individual in public services.* New York: Russell Sage Foundation.

Lipsky, Michael, and Stephen R. Smith. 1989. When social problems are treated as emergencies. *Social Service Review* 63 (1): 5–25.

Loseke, Donileen R. 1992. *The Battered woman and shelters: The social construction of wife abuse.* Albany: State University of New York Press.

Lovern, John D. 1991. *Pathways to reality: Erickson-inspired treatment approaches to chemical dependency.* Philadelphia: Brunner/Mazel.

Lowney, Kathleen S. 1999. *Baring our souls: TV talk shows and the religion of recovery.* New York: Aldine deGruyter.

Lucy, John A. 1993. Reflexive language and the human disciplines. In *Reflexive language: Reported speech and metapragmatics*, ed. John Lucy, 9–32. New York: Cambridge University Press.

Luhrmann, Tanya M. 2001. *Of two minds: The growing disorder in American psychiatry*. New York: Vintage.

Lutz, Catherine A. 1988. *Unnatural emotions: Everyday sentiments on a Micronesian atoll and their challenges to Western theory*. Chicago: University of Chicago Press.

Lutz, Catherine, and Lila Abu-Lughod, eds. 1990. *Language and the politics of emotion*. Cambridge: Cambridge University Press.

Lyons, Thomas. 2001. Ambiguous narratives. *Cultural Anthropology*, 16 (2): 183–201.

MacAndrew, Craig, and Robert Edgerton. 1969. Drunkeness as time out. In *Drunken comportment: A social explanation*, ed. Craig MacAndrew and Robert Edgerton, 83–99. New York: Aldine.

Malinowski, Bronislaw. 1950 [1922]. *Argonauts of the Western Pacific: An account of native enterprise and adventure in the archipelagoes of Melanesian New Guinea*. New York: Dutton.

Malysiak, Rosalyn. 1997. Exploring the theory and paradigm base for wraparound. *Journal of Child and Family Studies* 6 (4): 399–408.

———. 1998. Deciphering the tower of Babel: Examining the theory base for wraparound fidelity. *Journal of Child and Family Studies* 7 (1): 11–25.

Mancini, Michael A. 2007. Efficacy in recovery from serious psychiatric disabilities: A qualitative study with fifteen psychiatric survivors. *Qualitative Social Work* 6 (1): 49–74.

Mandell, Wallace, James Dahl, David S. Mandell, and Jennifer Butler. 2007. Prevalence of alexithymia among substance abuse clients in therapeutic community treatment. Paper read at American Public Health Annual Meeting, Washington, D.C.

Marcus, George E., and Michael M. J. Fischer. 1986. *Anthropology as cultural critique: An experimental moment in the human sciences*. Chicago: University of Chicago Press.

Marcus, Sharon. 2002. Fighting bodies, fighting words: A theory and politics of rape prevention. In *Gender struggles: Practical approaches to contemporary feminism*, ed. Constance L. Mui and Julian S. Murphy, 166–185. New York: Rowan and Littlefield.

Margolin, Leslie. 1997. *Under the cover of kindness: The invention of social work*. Charlottesville: University of Virginia Press.

Marsh, Jeanne C. 2002. Learning from clients. *Social Work* 47 (4): 341–344.

Marsh, Jeanne C., Dingcai Cao, and Thomas D'Aunno. 2004. Gender differences in the impact of comprehensive services in substance abuse treatment. *Journal of Substance Abuse Treatment* 27 (4): 289–300.

Marsh, Jeanne C., Thomas A. D'Aunno, and Brenda Smith. 2000. Increasing access and providing social services to improve drug treatment for women with children. *Addiction* 95 (8): 1237–1248.

Martin, Emily. 1987. *Woman in the body: A cultural analysis of reproduction*. Boston: Beacon.

———. 1994. *Flexible bodies.* Boston: Beacon.
Marvasti, Amir B. 2002. Constructing service worthy homeless through narrative editing. *Journal of Contemporary Ethnography* 31 (5): 615–651.
Masco, Joseph. 2006. *The nuclear borderlands: The Manhattan Project in post–cold war New Mexico.* Princeton, N.J.: Princeton University Press.
Maskovsky, Jeffrey. 2001. The other war at home: The geopolitics of U.S. poverty. *Urban Anthropology,* 30(2–3): 215–238.
Matoesian, Gregory M. 1993. *Reproducing rape: Domination through talk in the courtroom.* Chicago: University of Chicago Press.
———. 1999. The grammaticalization of participant roles in the constitution of expert identity. *Language in Society* 28 (4): 491–521.
———. 2001. *Law and the language of identity discourse in the William Kennedy Smith rape trial.* Oxford: Oxford University Press.
———. 2008. Role conflict as an interactional resource in the multimodal emergence of expert identity. *Semiotica* 171:15–49.
McCracken, Stanley, and Tina Rzepnicki. 2009. The role of theory in conducting evidence based clinical practice. In *The play and place of theory in social work practice,* ed. William Borden. New York: Columbia University Press.
McDowell, David M., and Henry I. Spitz. 1999. *Substance abuse: From principles to practice.* Philadelphia: Brunner/Mazel.
McElhinny Bonnie S. 1995. Challenging hegemonic masculinities: Female and male police officers handling domestic violence. In *Gender articulated: Language and the socially constructed self,* ed. Kira Hall and Mary Bucholtz, 217–242. New York: Routledge.
McGoldrick, Monica, and Randy Gerson. 1985. *Genograms in family assessment.* New York: Norton.
McGoldrick, Monica, Randy Gerson, and Sylvia Shellenberger. 1999. *Genograms: Assessment and intervention.* 2nd ed. New York: Norton.
McLeod, Jane D., and Ronald C. Kessler. 1990. Socioeconomic status differences in vulnerability to undesirable life events. *Journal of Health and Social Behavior* 31 (2): 162–172.
Mead, Margaret. 1972. *Blackberry winter: My earlier years.* New York: William Morrow.
Medrano, Martha A., William A. Zule, John Hatch, and David P. Desmond. 1999. Prevalence of childhood trauma in a community sample of substance-abusing women. *American Journal of Drug and Alcohol Abuse* 25 (3): 449–462.
Mehan, Hugh. 1996. The construction of an LD student: A case study in the politics of representation. In *Natural histories of discourse,* ed. Michael Silverstein and Greg Urban, 253–276. Chicago: University of Chicago Press.
Mercer-McFadden, Carolyn, and Robert E. Drake. 1992. *A review of outcome measures for assessing homeless populations with severe mental illness and co-occurring substance abuse.* New Ipswich, N.H.: New Hampshire–Dartmouth Psychiatric Research Center.
Mertz, Elizabeth. 1993. Learning what to ask: Metapragmatic factors and methodological reification. In *Reflexive language: Reported speech and metapragmatics,* ed. John A. Lucy, 159–174. New York: Cambridge University Press.

———. 1996. Recontextualization as socialization: Text and pragmatics in the law school classroom. In *Natural histories of discourse*, ed. Michael Silverstein and Greg Urban, 229–249. Chicago: University of Chicago Press.

———. 1998. *Linguistic ideology and praxis in U.S. law school classrooms*, ed. Bambi B. Schieffelin, Kathryn A. Woolard, and Paul V. Kroskrity, 149–162. New York: Oxford University Press.

———. 2007. *The language of law school: Learning to "think like a lawyer."* New York: Oxford University Press.

Meyer, Carol H. 1976. *Social work practice.* New York: Free Press.

———. ed. 1983a. *Clinical social work in the eco-systems perspective.* New York: Columbia University Press.

———. 1983b. Editorial: The power to define problems. *Social Work* 28:99.

———. 1995. Assessment. In *Encyclopedia of social work*, ed. Richard L. Edwards. Washington, D. C.: National Association of Social Workers.

Meyers, Marcia K., Bonnie Glaser, and Karin M. Donald. 1998. On the front lines of welfare delivery: Are workers implementing policy reforms? *Journal of Policy Analysis and Management* 17 (1): 1–22.

Meyers, Todd. 2009. Things under the tongue: Pharmacotherapy, its intersections and its afterlife in urban America. Ph.D. diss., Johns Hopkins University, Baltimore, Md.

Michels, Phillip J., N. Peter Johnson, Robert Mallin, J. T. Thornhill, Sunil Sharma, Harold Gonzales, and Robert Kellett. 1999. Coping strategies of alcoholic women. *Substance Abuse* 20 (4): 237–248.

Midanik, Lorraine T. 1989. Perspectives on the validity of self-reported alcohol use. *Addiction* 84 (12): 1419–1423.

Milby, Jesse B., Joseph E. Schumacher, Dennis Wallace, Michelle J. Freedman, and Rudy E. Vuchinich. 2005. To house or not to house: The effects of providing housing to homeless substance abusers in treatment. *American Journal of Public Health* 95 (7): 1259–1265.

Miller, Brenda A., William R. Downs, Dawn M. Gondoli, and Angeliki Keil. 1987. The role of childhood sexual abuse in the development of alcoholism in women. *Violence and Victimization* 2 (3): 157–172.

Miller, Jean Baker. 1976. *Toward a new psychology of women.* Boston: Beacon.

Miller, Judith L. 2002. The board as a monitor of organizational activity: The application of agency theory to nonprofit boards. *Nonprofit Management and Leadership* 12 (4): 429–450.

Miller, William R. 2003. Spirituality, treatment, and recovery. *Recent Developments in Alcoholism* 16:391–404

———. 2004. The phenomenon of quantum change. *Journal of Clinical Psychology* 60 (5): 453–460.

———. 2009. Conversation with William R. Miller. *Addiction* 104 (6): 883–893.

Miller, William R., and Kathleen M. Carroll. 2006. *Rethinking substance abuse: What the science shows, and what we should do about it.* New York: Guilford.

Miller, William R., and Janet C'de Baca. 2001. *Quantum change: When epiphanies and sudden insights transform ordinary lives.* New York: Guilford.

Miller, William R., and Stephen Rollnick. 1991. *Motivational interviewing: Preparing people to change addictive behavior.* New York: Guilford.

———. 2002. *Motivational interviewing: Preparing people for change.* New York: Guilford.
Miller, William, and J. Scott Tonigan. 1996. Assessing drinkers' motivation for change: The stages of change readiness and treatment eagerness scale. *Psychology of Addictive Behaviors* 10 (2): 81–89
Mitchell, Winifred L. 1994. Pragmatic literacy and empowerment: An Aymara example. *Anthropology and Education Quarterly* 25 (3): 226–235.
Mitchell-Kernan, Claudia. 1999. Signifying, loud-talking, and marking, in *Signifyin(g), sanctifyin', and slam dunking*, ed. Gena D. Caponi, 309–330. Amherst: University of Massachusetts Press.
Mohanty, Chandra. 1992. Feminist encounters: Locating the politics of experience. In *Destabilizing theory*, ed. Michelle Barret and Anne Phillips, 74–92. Cambridge: Polity.
Moore, Dawn. *Criminal artefacts: Governing drugs and users.* Vancouver: University of British Columbia Press.
———. 2007. Translating justice and therapy: The drug treatment court networks. *British Journal of Criminology* 47(1): 42–60.
Morgan, Gareth. 1986. *Images of organizations.* Newbury Park, Calif.: Sage.
Morgan, Marcyliena 1996. Conversational signifying: Grammar and indirectness among African American women. In *Interaction and grammar*, ed. Elinor Ochs, Emanuel A. Schegloff, and Sandra A. Thompson, 405–434. New York: Cambridge University Press.
———. 2002. *Language, discourse, and power in African American culture.* New York: Cambridge University Press.
Morgan, Thomas J. 2006. Behavioral treatment techniques for psychoactive substance abuse disorders. In *Treating substance abuse: Theory and technique*, ed. Jonathan Morgenstern and Frederick Rotgers, 190–216. New York: Guilford.
Morgenstern, Jon. 2000. Effective technology transfer in alcoholism treatment. *Substance Use & Misuse* 35(12): 1659–1678.
Mouffe, Chantal. 2005a. *The return of the political.* London: Verso.
———. 2005b. Some reflections on an agonistic approach to the public. In *Making things public*, ed. Bruno Latour and Peter Weibel, 804–807. Cambridge, Mass.: MIT Press.
Moynihan, Daniel Patrick. 1965. *The negro family: The case for national action*, ed. Department of Labor. Washington, D.C.: U.S. Government Printing Office.
Mullender, Audrey, and David Ward. 1991. Empowerment through social action group work: The "self-directed" approach. *Social Work with Groups* 14 (3–4): 125–139.
Mulvey, Kevin P., Susan Hubbard, and Susan Hayashi. 2003. A national study of the substance abuse treatment workforce. *Journal of Substance Abuse Treatment* 24 (1): 51–57.
Myers, Laura L., and Bruce A. Thyer. 1997. Should social work clients have the right to effective treatment? *Social Work* 42 (3): 288–299.
Myrick, Hugh, Scott Henderson, Bonnie Dansky, Christine Pelic, and Kathleen T. Brady. 2002. Clinical characteristics of under-reporters on urine drug screens in a cocaine treatment study. *American Journal on Addictions* 11 (4): 255–261.

National Association of Alcohol and Drug Abuse Counselors. 1995. *Ethical standards of alcohol and drug abuse counselors*. Arlington, Va.: Association for Addiction Professionals.

National Association of Social Workers. 1996. *Code of ethics of the National Association of Social Workers*. Washington, D.C.: National Association of Social Workers.

National Institute on Drug Abuse. 1997. About NIDA, Mission. http://www.nida.nih.gov/about/aboutnida.html (retrieved August 23, 2008).

National Institutes of Health. 1997. U.S. Department of Health and Human Services. Ninth Special Report to the U.S. Congress on Alcohol and Health. No. 97-4107.

Nelson, Barbara J. 1984. *Making an issue of child abuse: Political agenda setting for social problems*. Chicago: University of Chicago Press.

Nes, Janet A., and Peter Iadicola. 1989. Toward a definition of feminist social work: A comparison of liberal, radical, and socialist models. *Social Work* 34 (1): 12–21.

Newman, Michael. 2005. Rap as literacy: A genre analysis of hip-hop ciphers. *Text* 25 (3): 399–436.

Norcross, John C. 2005. A primer on psychotherapy integration. In *Handbook of psychotherapy integration*, ed. John C. Norcross and Marvin R. Goldfried, 3–23. New York: Oxford University Press.

Norcross, John C., Christie P. Karpiak, and Kelly M. Lister. 2005. What's an integrationist? A study of self-identified integrative and (occasionally) eclectic psychologists. *Journal of Clinical Psychology* 61 (12): 1587–1594.

Nye, Catherine H. 1994. Narrative interaction and the development of client autonomy in clinical practice. *Clinical Social Work Journal* 22 (1): 43–57.

O' Dwyer, Phillip. 2004. Treatment of alcohol problems. In *Clinical work with substance-abusing clients*, ed. Shulamith L. Straussner, 171–186. New York: Guilford.

O' Looney, John. 1993. Beyond privatization and service integration: Organizational models for service delivery. *Social Service Review* 67 (4): 501–534.

Ochs, Elinor, and Lisa Capps. 1996. Narrating the self. *Annual Review of Anthropology* 25:19–43.

———. 2002. *Living narrative: Creating lives in everyday storytelling*. Cambridge, Mass: Harvard University Press.

Ochs, Elinor, and Bambi Schiefflin. 1989. Language has a heart. *Text* 9 (1): 7–25.

Ortner, Sherry B. 1996. *Making gender: The politics and erotics of culture*. Boston: Beacon.

———. 1998. Is female to male as nature is to culture? In *Women in culture: A women's studies anthology*, ed. Lucinda J. Peach, 23–44. London: Wiley-Blackwell.

Ortner, Sherry B., and Harriet Whitehead. 1981. *Sexual meanings: The cultural construction of gender and sexuality*. New York: Cambridge University Press.

Ozminkowski, Ronald J., Tami Mark, Leo Cangianelli, J. Michael Walsh, Robert Davidson, Ron R. Flegel, and Ron Z. Goetzel. 2001. The cost of on-site versus off-site workplace urinalysis testing for illicit drug use. *Health Care Management* 20 (1): 59–69.

Padgett, Deborah K., Lelya Gulcur, and Sam Tsemberis. 2006. Housing First services for people who are homeless with co-occurring serious mental illness and substance abuse. *Research on Social Work Practice* 16 (1): 74–83.

Paley, Julia. 2001. The paradox of participation: Civil society and democracy in Chile. *Political and Legal Anthropology Review* 24:1–12.

Panksepp, Jaak, Christine Nocjar, Jeff Burgdorf, Jules B. Panksepp, and Robert Huber. 2004. The role of emotional systems in addiction: A neuroethological perspective. *Nebraska Symposium on Motivation* 50:85–126.

Paolino, Ronald M. 1991. Identifying, treating, and counseling drug abusers. In *Drug testing: Issues and options*, ed. Louis J. W. Robert H Coombs, 215–234. New York: Oxford University Press.

Park, Yoosun. 2005. Culture as deficit: A critical discourse analysis of the concept of culture in social work discourse. *Journal of Sociology and Social Welfare* 32 (3): 11–33.

Parsons, Ruth J. 1991. Empowerment: Purpose and practice principle. *Social Work with Groups* 14 (2): 7–21.

Patti, Rino J. 1974. Limitations and prospects of internal advocacy. *Social Casework* 55 (8): 537–545.

Paulhus, Delroy L. 1998. *The Paulhus deception scales: BIDR Version 7*. Toronto/Buffalo: Multi-Health Systems.

Pavetti, LaDonna, Michelle K. Derr, and Heather Hesketh. 2003. *Review of sanction policies and research studies: Final literature review*. Department of Health and Human Services. Available at http://aspe.hhs.gov/HSP/TANF-Sanctions03/full-report.pdf (retrieved October 24, 2008).

Peck, Edward. 1995. The performance of an NHS Trust Board: Actors' accounts, minutes and observation. *British Journal of Management* 6 (2): 135–156.

Peirce, Charles S. 1955. Logic as semiotic: The theory of signs. In *Philosophical writings of Peirce*, ed. J. Buchler 98–119. New York: Dover.

Perry, Marc D. 2004. Los Raperos: Rap, race, and social transformation in contemporary Cuba. Ph.D. dissertation, University of Texas at Austin.

Personal Responsibility and Work Opportunity Reconciliation Act of 1996 §§193, 104 U.S.C. §3734 (1996).

Peterson, Vincent, Bernard Nisenholz, and Gary Robinson. 2003. *A nation under the influence: America's addiction to alcohol*. Boston: Allyn and Bacon.

Petry, Nancy M. 2000. A comprehensive guide to the application of contingency management procedures in clinical settings. *Drug and Alcohol Dependence* 58 (1–2): 9–25.

——. 2002. Contingency management in addiction treatment. *Psychiatric Times* 19 (2).

Philips, Susan U. 1998. *Ideology in the language of judges: How judges practice law, politics, and courtroom control*. New York: Oxford University Press.

——. 2010. Semantic and interactional indirectness in Tongan lexical honorification. *Journal of Pragmatics* 42:317–336.

Pihel, Erik. 1996. A furified freestyle: Homer and hiphop. *Oral Tradition* 11 (2): 249–269.

Pine, Jason. 2007. Economy of speed: The new narco-capitalism. *Public Culture* 19 (2): 357–366.

Pollack, Harold A., and Thomas A. D'Aunno. 2008. Dosage patterns in methadone treatment: Results from a national survey, 1988–2005. *Health Services Research* 43 (6): 2143–2163.

Polusny, Melissa A., and Victoria M. Follette. 1995. Long-term correlates of child sexual abuse: Theory and review of the empirical literature. *Applied and Preventive Psychology* 4 (3): 143–166.

Pomeroy, Elizabeth C., Rebecca J. Walker, and John S. McNeil. 1996. Psychoeducational model for caregivers of persons with AIDS. *Journal of Family Social Work* 1 (4): 19–37.

Potter-Efron, Ronald T. 2002. *Shame, guilt, and alcoholism: Treatment issues in clinical practice*. New York: Haworth.

Prochaska, James O., Carlo C. DiClemente, and John C. Norcross. 1992. In search of how people change: Applications to addictive behaviors. *American Psychologist* 47 (9): 1102–1114.

Quinn, James F., Eugenia Bodenhamer-Davis, D. Shane Koch. 2004. Ideology and the stagnation of AODA treatment modalities in America. *Deviant Behavior* 25 (2): 109–131.

Quirk, Stuart. 2001. Emotion concepts in models of substance abuse. *Drug and Alcohol Review* 20 (1): 95–104.

Raikhel, Eugene. 2009. Institutional encounters: Identification and anonymity in Russian addiction treatment (and ethnography). In *Being there: The fieldwork encounter and the making of truth*, ed. John Borneman and Abdellah Hamoudi, 201–206. Berkeley: University of California Press.

Rapp, Rayna. 1988. Chromosomes and communication: The discourse of genetic counseling. *Medical Anthropology Quarterly* 2 (2):143–157.

Rappaport, Julian. 1981. In praise of paradox: A social policy of empowerment over prevention. *American Journal of Community Psychology* 9 (1): 1–25.

———. 1984. Studies in empowerment: Introduction to the issue. In *Studies in empowerment: Steps toward understanding and action*, ed. Julian Rappaport and Robert Hess, 1–8. New York: Haworth.

———. 1995. Empowerment meets narrative: Listening to stories and creating settings. *American Journal of Community Psychology* 23 (5): 795–807.

Rapping, Elayne. 1996. *The culture of recovery: Making sense of the self-help movement in women's lives*. Boston: Beacon.

Rascal, Dizzee. 2008. The world outside. *Maths and English*. New York: Definitive Jux/2008 XL Recordings. Album.

Rasmussen, Sandra. 2000. *Addiction treatment: Theory and practice*. Thousand Oaks, Calif.: Sage.

Rawls, John. 1971. *A theory of justice*. Vol. 1. Cambridge, Mass.: Harvard University Press.

Ray, Oakley, and Charles Ksir. 1999. *Drugs, society, and human behavior*. Burr Ridge, Ill.: WCB/McGraw Hill.

Razlog, O., S. Longbottom, L. Marcoci, F. Seidel, and I. Razlog. 2007. Alexithymia in patients with substance addiction being treated by cognitive-behavioural psychotherapy within Minnesota model treatment. *European Psychiatry* 22:197.

Reddy, William. 2001. *The navigation of feelings: A framework for the history of emotions.* New York: Cambridge University Press.

Reed, Beth Glover. 1982. *Treatment services for drug dependent women, Volume II.* Rockville, Md.: National Institute on Drug Abuse: U.S. Department of Health and Human Services, Public Health Service, Alcohol, Drug Abuse, and Mental Health Administration.

———. 1985. Drug misuse and dependency in women: The meaning and implications of being considered a special population or minority group. *Substance Use & Misuse* 20 (1): 13–62.

———. 1987. Developing women-sensitive drug dependence treatment services: Why so difficult? *Journal of Psychoactive Drugs* 19 (2): 151–164.

Reinarman, Craig. 2005. Addiction as accomplishment: The discursive construction of disease. *Addiction Research and Theory* 13 (4): 307–320.

Rich, Adrienne. 1977. *Of woman born.* New York: Bantam.

Richards, Henry J., and Shilpa M. Pai. 2003. Deception in prison assessment of substance abuse. *Journal of Substance Abuse Treatment* 24 (2): 121–128.

Riessman, Catherine. 2003. Performing identities in illness narrative: Masculinity and multiple sclerosis. *Qualitative Research* 3 (1): 5–34.

———. 1990. *Divorce talk.* New Brunswick, N.J.: Rutgers University Press.

———. 1992. Making sense of marital violence: One woman's narrative. In *Storied lives: The cultural politics of self-understanding,* ed. George C. Rosenwald and Richard L. Ochberg, 231–249. New Haven, Conn.: Yale University Press.

Rinn, William, Nitigna Desai, Harold Rosenblatt, and David R. Gastfriend. 2002. Addiction denial and cognitive dysfunction: A preliminary investigation. *Neuropsychiatry Clinical Neuroscience* 14 (1): 52–57.

Robertson, Jennifer E. 1992. The politics of androgyny in Japan: Sexuality and subversion in the theater and beyond. *American Ethnologist* 19 (3): 419–442.

———. 1998. *Takarazuka: Sexual politics and popular culture in modern Japan.* Berkeley: University of California Press.

Robins, Lee N., and Thomas R. Przybeck. 1985. Age of onset of drug use as a factor in drug and other disorders. *Etiology of drug abuse: Implications for prevention.* NIDA Research Monograph Series 56:178–192.

Rodriguez, Ned, Susan W. Ryan, Anderson B. Rowan, and David W. Foy. 1996. Posttraumatic stress disorder in a clinical sample of adult survivors of childhood sexual abuse. *Child Abuse and Neglect* 20 (10): 943–952.

Rogers, Doug. 2005. Moonshine, money, and the politics of liquidity in rural Russia. *American Ethnologist* 32 (1): 63–81.

Rogers, Gerald T. 1983. *How to sabotage your treatment.* (Screenplay by Nancy Hull-Adamski). Skokie, Ill.: Gerald T. Rogers Productions.

Rogler, Lloyd H. 1996. Increasing socioeconomic inequalities and the mental health of the poor. *Journal of Nervous and Mental Disease* 184 (12): 719–722.

Rohsenow, Damaris J., Richard Corbett, and Donald Devine. 1988. Molested as children: A hidden contribution to substance abuse? *Journal of Substance Abuse Treatment* 5 (1): 13–18.

Rosaldo, Michelle Z. 1980. *Knowledge and passion: Ilongot notions of self and social life.* New York: Cambridge University Press.

———. 1982. The things we do with words: Illongot speech acts and speech act theory in philosophy. *Language in Society* 11 (2): 203–237.
Rose, Nikolas. 1990. *Governing the soul: The shaping of the private self.* London: Routledge.
———. 1996. *Inventing our selves: Psychology, power, and personhood.* Cambridge: Cambridge University Press.
Rose, Stephen M. 1990. Advocacy/empowerment: An approach to clinical practice for social work. *Journal of Sociology and Social Welfare* 17 (2): 41–51.
Rose, Stephen M., and Bruce L. Black. 1985. *Advocacy and empowerment: Mental health care in the community.* New York: Routledge.
Rosenfeld, Joseph. 1994. Denial: Reports of its death are premature (Editorial). *Behavioral Health Management,* September 1.
Rosenthal, M. Zachary, Thomas R. Lynch, and Marsha M. Linehan. 2005. Dialectical behavior therapy for individuals with borderline personality disorder and substance use disorders. In *Clinical textbook of addictive disorders,* 3rd ed., ed. Richard J. Frances, Sheldon Miller, and Avram H. Mack, 615–636. New York: Guilford.
Rothschild, Debra. 1995. Working with addicts in private practice: Overcoming initial resistance. In *Psychotherapy and substance abuse: A practitioner's handbook,* ed. Arnold M. Washton, 192–203. New York: Guilford.
Rush, Benjamin. 1805. *Inquiry into the effects of ardent spirits upon the human body and Mind.* Philadelphia: Bartam.
Saari, Carolyn. 1986. *Clinical social work treatment: How does it work?* New York: Gardner.
———. 2004. Editorial: Culture and psychoanalytic theory. *Clinical Social Work Journal* 32 (1): 3–6.
Sackett, David L., W. Scott Richardson, William Rosenberg, and R. Brian Haynes. 1997. Is this evidence about a diagnostic test important? In *Evidence-based medicine: How to practice and teach EBM,* ed. David L. Sackett, W. Scott Richardson, William Rosenberg, and R. Brian Haynes, 118–128. London: Churchill Livingstone.
Sacks, Stanley, George De Leon, JoAnn Y. Sacks, Karen McKendrick, and Barry S. Brown. 2003. TC-oriented supported housing for homeless MICAs. *Journal of Psychoactive Drugs* 35 (3): 355–366.
Saleebey, Dennis. 1992. *The strengths approach in social work practice.* New York: Longman.
———. 1994. Culture, theory, and narrative: The intersection of meanings in practice. *Social Work* 39 (4): 351–359.
———. 2002. *The strengths perspective in social work practice.* 2nd ed. White Plains, N.Y.: Longman.
Sands, Roberta G. 1996. The elusiveness of identity in social work practice with women: A postmodern perspective. *Clinical Social Work Journal* 24 (2): 167–186.
Sandfort, Jodi. 2009. Human service organizational technology: Improving understanding and advancing research. In *Human services as complex organizations,* ed. Y. Hasenfeld, 269–290. Thousand Oaks, Calif.: Sage.

Santiago-Irizarry, Vilma. 1996. Culture as cure. *Cultural Anthropology* 11 (1): 3–24.

———. 2001. *Medicalizing ethnicity: The construction of Latino identity in a psychiatric setting.* Ithaca, N.Y.: Cornell University Press.

Saris, A. Jamie. 2008. An uncertain dominion: Irish psychiatry, methadone, and the treatment of opiate abuse. *Culture, Medicine, and Psychiatry* 32 (2): 259–277.

Saunders, Barry F. 2009. *CT suite: The work of diagnosis in the age of noninvasive cutting.* Durham, N.C.: Duke University Press.

Schroedel, Jean Reith, and Pamela Fiber. 2001. Punitive versus public health oriented responses to drug use by pregnant women. *Yale Journal of Health Policy, Law, and Ethics* 1:217–235.

Schull, Natasha D. 2006. Machines, medication, modulation: Circuits of dependency and self-care in Las Vegas. *Culture, Medicine, and Psychiatry* 30 (2): 223–247.

Schumacher, Joseph E., Stuart Usdan, Jesse B. Milby, Dennis Wallace, and Cecelia McNamara. 2000. Abstinent-contingent housing and treatment retention among crack-cocaine-dependent homeless persons. *Journal of Substance Abuse Treatment* 19 (1): 81–88.

Schwartzman, Helen B. 1989. *The meeting: Gatherings in organizations and communities.* New York: Plenum.

Scott, Cynthia G. 2000. Ethical issues in addiction counseling. *Rehabilitation Counseling Bulletin* 43 (4): 209–214.

Scott, James C. 1987. *Weapons of the weak: Everyday forms of peasant resistance.* New Haven, Conn.: Yale University Press.

———. 1992. *Domination and the arts of resistance: Hidden transcripts.* New Haven: Yale University Press.

Scott, Joan W. 1991. The evidence of experience. *Critical Inquiry* 17(4): 773–797.

Searle, John R. 1969. *Speech acts: An essay in the philosophy of language.* New York: Cambridge University Press.

———. 1983. *Intentionality: An essay in the philosophy of mind.* Cambridge: Cambridge University Press.

Sedgwick, Eve K., and Adam Frank. 1995. Shame in the cybernetic fold: Reading Silvan Tomkins. In *Shame and its sisters: A Silvan Tomkins reader*, ed. Eve K. Sedgwick and Adam Frank, 1–28. Durham, N.C.: Duke University Press.

Shethar, Alissa. 1993. Literacy and "empowerment'? A case study of literacy behind bars. *Anthropology and Education Quarterly* 24 (4): 357–372.

Shoaps, Robin A. 2002. "Pray earnestly": The textual construction of personal involvement in Pentecostal prayer and song. *Journal of Linguistic Anthropology* 12 (1): 34–71.

Sifneos, Peter E. 1996. Alexithymia: Past and present. *American Journal of Psychiatry* 153 (7 Suppl.): 137–142.

Silverstein, Michael. 1976. Shifters, linguistic categories, and cultural description. In *Meaning in anthropology*, ed. Keith Basso and Henry Selby, 11–55. Albuquerque: University of New Mexico Press.

———. 1979. Language structure and linguistic ideology. In *The elements: A parasession on linguistic units and levels*, ed. Paul Clyne, William Hanks, and Carol Hofbauer, 193–247. Chicago: Chicago Linguistics Society.

——. 1985. Language and the culture of gender: At the intersection of structure, usage, and ideology. In *Semiotic mediation: Sociocultural and psychological perspectives*, ed. Elizabeth Mertz and Richard J. Parmentier, 219–259. Orlando, Fla.: Academic Press.

——. 1993. Metapragmatic discourse and metapragmatic function. In *Reflexive language: Reported speech and metapragmatics*, ed. John Lucy, 33–58. New York: Cambridge University Press.

——. 1996. Monoglot "standard" in America: Standardization and metaphors of linguistic hegemony. In *The matrix of language: Contemporary linguistic anthropology*, ed. Donald Brenneis and Ronald K. S. Macauly, 284–306. Boulder, Colo.: Westview.

——. 1998. The improvisational performance of culture in realtime discursive practice. In *Creativity in Performance*, ed. K. Sawyer, 265–312. Greenwich, Conn.: Ablex.

——. 2001. The limits of awareness. In *Linguistic anthropology: A reader*, ed. A. Duranti, 382–401. New York: Blackwell.

——. 2003a. *Talking politics*. Chicago: Prickly Paradigm.

——. 2003b. Indexical order and the dialectics of sociolinguistic life. *Language and Communication* 23 (3–4): 193–229.

——. 2004. "Cultural" concepts and the language-culture nexus. *Current Anthropology* 45 (5): 621–652.

——. 2005. Axes of evals. *Journal of Linguistic Anthropology* 15 (1): 6–22.

——. 2006. Old wine, new ethnographic lexicography. *Annual Review of Anthropology* 35:481–496.

Silverstein, Michael, and Greg Urban. 1996. The natural history of discourse. In *Natural histories of discourse*, ed. M. Silverstein and G. Urlan, 1–20. Chicago: University of Chicago Press.

Simon, Barbara L. 1994. *The empowerment tradition in American social work: A history*. New York: Columbia University Press.

Simpson, D. Dwyane, and Kevin Knight. 1998. *TCU data collection forms for correctional residential treatment*. Fort Worth: Texas Christian University, Institute of Behavioral Research.

Skoll, Geoffrey. 1992. *Walk the walk and talk the talk: An ethnography of a drug abuse treatment facility*. Philadelphia: Temple University Press.

Smith, Benjamin. 2005. Ideologies of the speaking subject in the psychotherapeutic theory and practice of Carl Rogers. *Journal of Linguistic Anthropology* 15 (2): 258–272.

Smith, Brenda D., and Stella E. F. Donovan. 2003. Child welfare practice in organizational and institutional context. *Social Service Review* 77 (4): 541–563.

Smith, Brenda D., and Jeanne C. Marsh. 2002. Client-service matching in substance abuse treatment for women with children. *Journal of Substance Abuse Treatment* 22 (3): 161–168.

Smith, Stephen Rathgeb. 2009. The political economy of contracting and competition. In *Human services as complex organizations*, ed. Y. Hasenfeld, 139–160. Thousand Oaks, Calif.: Sage.

Sohng, Sung Sil L. 1998. Research as an empowerment strategy. In *Empowerment in social work practice: A sourcebook*, ed. Lorraine Gutierrez, Ruth Parsons, and Enid O. Cox, 187–200. New York: Wadsworth.

Solomon, Barbara B. 1976. *Black empowerment: Social work in oppressed communities*. New York: Columbia University Press.
Soriano, Fernando I. 1995. *Conducting needs assessments: A multidisciplinary approach*. Thousand Oaks, Calif.: Sage.
Sosin, Michael R. 1986. *Private benefits: Material assistance in the private sector*. San Diego, Calif.: Academic Press.
———. 2002. Negotiating case decisions in substance abuse managed care. *Journal of Health and Social Behavior* 43 (3): 277–295.
———. 2005. The administrative control system of substance abuse managed care. *Health Services Research* 40 (1): 157–176.
———. 2009. Discretion in human service organizations: Traditional and institutional perspectives. In *Human services as complex organizations*, ed. Y. Hasenfeld, 381–402. Thousand Oaks, Calif.: Sage.
Sosin, Michael R., and Jane Yamaguchi. 1995. Case management routines and discretion in a program addressing homelessness and substance abuse. *Contemporary Drug Problems* 22 (2): 317–342.
Specht, Harry, and Mark E. Courtney. 1993. *Unfaithful angels: How social work has abandoned its mission*. New York: Free Press.
Spector, Malcolm, and John I. Kitsuse. 1987. *Constructing social problems*. New Brunswick, N.J.: Transaction.
Spencer, J. William, and Jennifer L. McKinney. 1997. We don't pay for bus tickets, but we can help you find work: The micropolitics of trouble in human service encounters. *Sociological Quarterly* 38 (1): 185–204.
Speranza, Mario, Maurice Corcos, Phillipe Stéphan, Gwenole Loas, Fernando Pérez-Diaz, Francois Lang, Jen Luc Venisse, Paul Bizouard, Matine Flament, Oliver Halfon, and Phillipe Jeammet. 2004. Alexithymia, depressive experiences, and dependency in addictive disorders. *Substance Use & Misuse* 39 (4): 551–580.
Sperling, Samuel J. 1958. On denial and the essential nature of defence. *International Journal of Psycho-Analysis* 39:25–38.
Spicer, Jerry. 1993. *The Minnesota Model: The evolution of the multidisciplinary approach to addiction recovery*. Center City, Minn.: Hazelden.
Spicer, Paul. 2001. Culture and the restoration of self among former American Indian drinkers. *Social Science and Medicine* 53 (2): 227–240.
Spiegel, Betsy R., and Chirstine H. Fewell. 2004. 12-step programs as a treatment modality. In *Clinical work with substance abusing clients*, ed. Shulamith L. A. Straussner, 125–145. New York: Guilford.
Spivak, Gayatri Chakravorty. 1988. Can the subaltern speak? In *Marxism and the interpretation of culture*, ed. Cary Nelson and Lawrence Grossberg, 271–316. Urbana: University of Illinois Press.
Staples, Lee. 1990. Powerful ideas about empowerment. *Administration in Social Work* 14 (2): 29–42.
Stein, J. A., J. M. Golding, J. M. Siegel, M. A. Burnam, and S. B. Sorenson. 1988. Long-term psychological sequelae of child sexual abuse. In *Lasting effects of child sexual abuse: Implications for child development and psychopathology*, ed. Gail E. Wyatt and Gloria J. Powell, 135–154. Thousand Oaks, Calif.: Sage.

Stinchcombe, Arthur L. 1965. Social structure and organizations. In *Handbook of organizations*, ed. James G. March, 229–259. Chicago: Rand McNally.

Strathern, Marilyn. 1988. *The gender of the gift: Problems with women and problems with society in Melanesia*. Berkeley: University of California Press.

Strauss, Anslem, Leonard Schatzman, Danuta Erlich, Rue Bucher, and Mel Sabshin. 1963. The hospital and its negotiated order. In *The hospital in modern society*, ed. Eliot Friedson, 147–169. New York: MacMillan.

Strom-Gottfried, Kim. 1999. Professional boundaries: An analysis of violations by social workers. *Families in Society* 80 (5): 439–449.

Sullivan, William, David J. Hartmann, and James L. Wolk. 1994. Implementing case management in alcohol and drug treatment. *Families in Society* 75 (2): 67–73.

Sun, An-Pyng. 2007. Relapse among substance-abusing women: Components and processes. *Substance Use & Misuse* 42 (1): 1–21.

Susser, Ida. 1996. The construction of poverty and homelessness in U. S cities. *Annual Review of Anthropology* 25:411–435.

Swora, Maria G. 2001. Narrating community: The creation of social structure in Alcoholics Anonymous through the performance of autobiography. *Narrative Inquiry* 11 (2): 363–384.

Taleff, Michael J. 1997. Solution-oriented and traditional approaches to alcohol and other drug treatment: Similarities and differences. *Alcoholism Treatment Quarterly* 15 (1):65–74.

———. 2006. *Critical thinking for addiction professionals*. New York: Springer.

Tarter, Ralph G., Arthur I. Alterman, and Kathleen I. Edwards. 1984. Alcoholic denial: A biopsychosocial interpretation. *Journal of Studies on Alcohol* 45 (3): 214–218.

Taylor, Carolyn, and Susan White. 2001. *Practising reflexivity in health and welfare: Making knowledge*. Buckingham, U.K.: Open University Press.

Taylor, Graeme J., James D. Parker, and R. Michael Bagby. 1990. A preliminary investigation of alexithymia in men with psychoactive substance dependence. *American Journal of Psychiatry* 147 (9): 1228–1230.

Taussig, Michael. 1986. *Shamanism, colonialism, and the wild man*. Chicago: University of Chicago Press.

———. 2004. *My cocaine museum*. Chicago: University of Chicago Press.

Tedlock, Dennis, and Bruce Mannheim. 1995. *The dialogic emergence of culture*. Urbana: University of Illinois Press.

Thyer, Bruce A., and Laura L. Myers. 1999. On science, antiscience, and the client's right to effective treatment. *Social Work* 44 (5): 501–504.

Tice, Karen W. 1998. *Tales of wayward girls and immoral women: Case records and the professionalization of social work*. Urbana: University of Illinois Press.

Tiebout, Harry M. 1953. Surrender versus compliance in therapy, with special reference to alcoholism. *Quarterly Journal of Studies on Alcohol* 14 (1): 58–68.

Tomilson, Matt. 2004. Perpetual lament: Kava drinking, Christianity, and sensations of historical decline in Fiji. *Journal of the Royal Anthropological Institute* 10 (3): 653–673.

Tomison, Adam M. 1996. *Child maltreatment and substance abuse*. Melbourne: National Child Protection Clearing House.

Tomkins, Silvan S. 1963. *Affect, imagery, consciousness.* New York: Springer.

Tomlin, Kathyleen M., and Helen Richardson. 2004. *Motivational Interviewing and stages of change: Integrating best practices for substance abuse professionals.* Center City, Minn.: Hazelden.

Tracy, Karen, and Heidi Muller. 2001. Diagnosing a school board's interactional trouble: Theorizing problem formulation. *Communication Theory* 11 (1): 84–104.

Troisi, Alfonos, Augusto Pasini, Michele Saracco, and Gianfranco Spalletta. 1998. Psychiatric symptoms in male cannabis users not using other illicit drugs. *Addiction* 93 (4): 487–492.

Trunnell, Eugene E., and William E. Holt. 1974. The concept of denial or disavowal. *Journal of the American Psychoanalytic Association* 22:769–784.

Tsemberis, Sam, Leyla Gulcur, and Maria Nakae. 2004. *Housing first, consumer choice, and harm reduction for homeless individuals with a dual diagnosis.* Washington, D.C.: American Public Health Association.

Urban, Gregory. 1989. The "I" of discourse. In *Semiotics, self, and society,* ed. Benjamin Lee and Greg Urban, 27–52. New York: Mouton de Gruyter.

———. 1992. Two faces of culture. *Working Papers and Proceedings of the Center for Psychosocial Studies No. 49.* Chicago: Center for Psychological Studies.

———. 1996. Entextualization, replication, power. In *Natural histories of discourse,* ed. Micahel Silverstein and Greg Urban, 21–44. Chicago: University of Chicago Press.

United States Census Bureau. 1990. *Profile of selected social characteristics.* http://quickfacts.census.gov (retrieved June 15, 2008).

United States Sentencing Commission. 2006. Public hearing on cocaine sentencing policy, Washington, D.C., November 14.

Vaillant, George E. 1971. Theoretical hierarchy of adaptive ego mechanisms. *Archives of General Psychiatry* 24:107–118.

Valverde, Marianna. 1998. *Diseases of the will: Alcohol and the dilemmas of freedom.* New York: Cambridge University Press.

Van Den Bergh, Nan, and Lynn B. Cooper. 1986. Introduction to feminist visions for social work. In *Feminist visions for social work,* ed. Nancy Van Den Bergh and Lynn B. Cooper, 74–93. Silver Springs, Md.: National Association of Social Workers.

Van Wetering, Inkeke and Paul van Gelder. 2000. Vital force, avenging spirits, and zombies: Discourses on drug addiction among Surinamese Creole migrants in Amsterdam. In *Anthropology, development, and modernities: Explaining discourses, counter-tendencies, and violence,* ed. Alberto Arce and Norman Lang, 141–158. London: Routledge.

Veach, Laura J., Theodore P. Remley, Sola M. Kippers, James D. Sorg. 2000. Retention predictors related to intensive outpatient programs for substance use disorders. *American Journal of Drug and Alcohol Abuse* 26 (3): 417–428.

Verdejo-García, Anotnio, Antoine Bechara, Emily C. Recknor, and Miguel Perez-Garcia. 2006. Executive dysfunction in substance dependent individuals during drug use and abstinence: An examination of the behavioral, cognitive and emotional correlates of addiction. *Journal of the International Neuropsychological Society* 12 (3): 405–415.

Visher, Emily B., and John S. Visher. 1988. *Old loyalties, new ties: Therapeutic strategies with stepfamilies*. New York: Psychology Press.
Volosinov, Valentin N. 1973. *Marxism and the philosophy of language*. Translated by Ladislav Matejka and I. R. Titunik. New York: Seminar.
Waelder, Robert. 1951. The structure of paranoid ideas—A critical survey of various theories. *International Journal of Psycho-Analysis* 32:167–177.
Wahlstrom, Jarls. 2006. Narrative transformations and externalizing talk in a reflecting team consultation. *Qualitative Social Work* 5 (3): 313–332.
Wakefield, Jerome C. 1988a. Psychotherapy, distributive justice, and social work. Part 1: Distributive justice as a conceptual framework for social work. *Social Service Review* 62 (2): 187–210.
———. 1988b. Psychotherapy, distributive justice, and social work. Part 2: Psychotherapy and the pursuit of justice. *Social Service Review* 62 (3): 353–382.
———. 1998. Foucauldian fallacies: An essay review of Leslie Margolin's *Under the Cover of Kindness*. *Social Service Review* 72 (4): 545–587.
Wallace, John. 1978. Working with the preferred defense structure of the recovering alcoholic. In *Practical approaches to alcoholism psychotherapy*, ed. Sheldon Zimberg, John Wallace, and Shelia B. Blume, 19–29. New York: Springer.
Wallen, Jacqueline, and Kate Berman. 1992. A comparison of male and female clients in substance abuse treatment. *Journal of Substance Abuse Treatment* 9 (3): 243–248.
Wallerstein, Nina, and Edward Bernstein. 1988. Empowerment education: Freire's ideas adapted to health education. *Health Education and Behavior* 15 (4): 379–394.
Walters, Glenn D. 1994. *Escaping the journey to nowhere: The psychology of alcohol and other drugs*. Bristol, Pa.: Taylor & Francis.
Weber, Max. 1958 [1904]. *The Protestant ethic and the spirit of capitalism*. Translated by Talcott Parsons. New York: Scribner's.
Weick, Ann. 1981. Reframing the person-in-environment perspective. *Social Work* 26 (2): 140–143.
Weiler, Kathleen. 1991. Friere and a feminist pedagogy of difference. *Harvard Educational Review* 61 (4): 449–474.
Weinberg, Darin. 2005. *Of others inside: Insanity, addiction, and belonging in America*. Philadelphia: Temple University Press.
Weiner, Annette B. 1976. *Women of value, men of renown: New perspectives in Trobriand exchange*. Austin: University of Texas Press.
Weisner, Constance, and Laura Schmidt. 1993. Alcohol and drug problems among diverse health and social service populations. *American Journal of Public Health* 83 (6): 824–829.
Weiss, Roger D., Steven M. Mirin, and Roxanne L. Bartel. 1994. *Cocaine*. Washington, D.C.: American Psychiatric Press.
West, David. 1990. *Authenticity and empowerment: A theory of liberation*. London: Harvester Wheatsheaf.
Westermeyer, Joseph. 1979. "The drunken Indian": Myths and realities. In *Beliefs, behaviors, and alcoholic beverages: A cross-cultural survey*, ed. Mac Marshall, 110–115. Ann Arbor: University of Michigan Press.

Weyerer, Siegfried. 1994. Social risk factors in schizophrenia. *Psychological Reports* 74 (3): 795–800.
White, Michael, and David Epston. 1990. *Narrative means to therapeutic ends.* New York: Norton.
White, William L. 1993. *Critical incidents: Ethical issues in substance abuse prevention and treatment.* Bloomington, Ind.: Lighthouse Training Institute.
———. 1996. *Pathways from the culture of addiction to the culture of recovery: A travel guide for addiction professionals.* Center City, Minn.: Hazelden.
———. 1998. *Slaying the dragon: The history of addiction treatment and recovery in America.* Bloomington, Ill: Chesnut Health Systems.
———. 2002. An addiction recovery glossary: The languages of American communities of recovery. Available at http://www.facesandvoicesofrecovery.org/pdf/White/white_add-rec-glossary.pdf (retrieved October 5, 2008).
Wilce, James M. 1998. The pragmatics of "madness": Performance analysis of a Bangladeshi woman's "aberrant" lament. *Culture, Medicine, and Psychiatry* 22 (1): 1–54.
———. 2003. *Eloquence in trouble: The poetics and politics of complaint in rural Bangladesh.* New York: Oxford University Press.
———. 2008. *Crying shame: Metaculture, modernity, and the exaggerated death of lament.* Malden, Mass.: Wiley-Blackwell.
Wilcox, Danny M. 1998. *Alcoholic thinking: Language, culture, and belief in Alcoholics Anonymous.* Westport, Conn.: Praeger/Greenwood.
Williams, Jill, and Marvin Swartz. 1998. Treatment boundaries in the case management relationship: A clinical case and discussion. *Community Mental Health Journal* 34 (3): 299–311.
Williams, Raymond. 1983. *Keywords: A vocabulary of culture and society.* New York: Oxford University Press.
Wills, Thomas A., Donato Vaccaro, Grace McNamara, and A. Elizabeth Hirky. 1996. Escalated substance use: A longitudinal grouping analysis from early to middle adolescence. *Journal of Abnormal Psychology* 105 (2): 166–180.
Wilsnack, Sharon C., Nancy D. Vogeltanz, Albert D. Klassen, and T. Robert Harris. 1997. Childhood sexual abuse and women's substance abuse: National survey findings. *Journal of Studies on Alcohol* 58 (3): 264–271.
Winick, Charles, Arlene Levine, and William A. Stone. 1992. An incest survivors' therapy group. *Journal of Substance Abuse Treatment* 9 (4): 311–318.
Wolock, Isabel. 1982. Community characteristics and staff judgments in child abuse and neglect cases. *Social Work Research and Abstracts* 18 (2): 9–15.
Woolard, Kathryn A. 1998. Introduction: Language ideology as a field of inquiry. In *Language ideologies: Practice and theory,* ed. Bambi B. Schieffelin, Kathyrn A. Woolard, and Paul V. Kroskrity, 3–47. Oxford: Oxford University Press.
Woolard, Kathryn A., and Bambi B. Schieffelin. 1994. Language ideology. *Annual Reviews in Anthropology* 23 (1): 55–82.
Wright, Susan. 1994. Culture in anthropology and organizational studies. In *Anthropology of organizations,* ed. Susan Wright, 1–34. London: Routledge.
Wurmser, Leon. 1974. Psychoanalytic considerations of the etiology of compulsive drug use. *Journal of the American Psychoanalytic Association* 22:820–843.
———. *The mask of shame.* Baltimore, Md.: Johns Hopkins University Press.

———. 1985. Denial and split identity: The issues in the psychoanalytic psychotherapy of compulsive drug users. *Journal of Substance Abuse Treatment* 2: 89–96.

———. 1992. Psychology of compulsive drug use. In *The chemically dependent: Phases of treatment and recovery*, ed. Barbara Wallace, 92–114. New York: Brunner/Mazel.

———. 1995. *The hidden dimension: Psychodynamics in compulsive drug use.* New York: Aronson.

Yeo, Michael. 1993. Toward an ethic of empowerment for health promotion. *Health Promotion International* 8 (3): 225–235.

Young, Allan. 1995. *The harmony of illusions: Inventing post-traumatic stress disorder.* Princeton, N.J.: Princeton University Press.

———. 1999. An alternative history of traumatic stress. In *Handbook of human responses to trauma*, ed. A. Y. Shalev, Alexander C. McFarlane, and Rachel Yehuda, 51–66. New York: Springer.

———. 2001. On traumatic neurosis and its brain. *Science in Context* 14 (4): 661–683.

Young, Ed. 1989. On the naming of the rose: Interests and multiple meanings as elements of organizational culture. *Organization Studies* 10 (2): 187–206.

Young, Iris Marion. 1994. Punishment, treatment, empowerment: Three approaches to policy for pregnant addicts. *Feminist Studies* 20 (1): 33–57.

Yule, G. Udny. 1904. On a convenient means of drawing curves to various scales. *Biometrika Trust* 3 (4): 469–471.

Zacharakis-Jutz, Jeff. 1988. Post-Freirean adult education: A question of empowerment and power. *Adult Education Quarterly* 39 (1): 41–47.

Ziefert, Majorie, and Karen S. Brown. 1991. Skill building for effective intervention with homeless families. *Families in Society* 72 (4): 212–219.

Zierler, Stevens, Lisa Feingold, Deborah Laufer, Priscilla Velentgas, Ira Kantrowitz-Gordon, and Kenneth Mayer. 1991. Adult survivors of childhood sexual abuse and subsequent risk of HIV infection. *American Journal of Public Health* 81 (5): 572–575.

Zippay, Allison. 1995. The politics of empowerment. *Social Work* 40 (2): 263–267.

Index

AA (Alcoholics Anonymous), 12–14, 79, 121–4, 130, 202–9, 240n6, 244n22, 262n1, 265n20, 273n15; and "90/90s," 14, 202–3, 206; and the Big Book, 86; and disease model of addiction, 12–4, 86, 123, 240n6, 242n14; and the Minnesota Model, 12, 123, 262n2; and the Twelve Steps, 123, 262n3. *See also* NA; Twelve Steps; WFS

act-performing consciousness, 190–6, 223, 277n27. *See also* ethics

Addams, Jane, 227–8, 232

addiction, 1–5, 9, 13, 41–2, 48, 82–3, 85–7, 95, 107, 120, 137, 171, 174, 232–3, 241n12, 248n17, 256n1, 258n18, 264n10; and assessment, 82–3, 96–8, 98–101; Bateson on, 90, 257n5; and chronicity, 104–5, 123; and denial, 11–4, 84–96, 100–9, 119–20, 131–2, 167–9, 197, 235–7, 256n2, and 3, 257n6, 257nn9, and 11; Derrida on, 85–6, 89, 120, 256n1; as disease, 1–2, 11–3, 72, 86, 89, 90, 104–5, 123, 240n6, 242n14, 244n22, 262n2, 262n36, 262n37; DSM-IV definition of, 99–101, 258n18; and gender, 31, 106, 112–8, 138–41; and insight, 12–3, 82–3, 90–5, 104, 112, 123, 186, 197, 243n19, 262n37; science of, 95–8; and secrets, 14, 264n15; and structure, 4, 26, 27–48, 53, 93, 97, 120, 124, 210–1; and subjectivity, 13, 92–5, 120, 123, 180, 233, 248n1; theories of, 4, 11–3, 86, 107–8, 123; and will, 90–1, 240n5, 243n19, 256n4, 262n37. *See also* addiction treatment; alcoholism; dependency; drugs; sobriety

addiction treatment, 1–5, 6–8, 10–3, 15, 18, 22, 31, 79, 86, 88, 93, 95–8, 107, 112–3, 120, 123, 150, 194, 210, 224, 226, 232–7; and coercion, 167–9; and confrontation, 104, 235, 244n22, 259n22; and Contingency Management (CM), 247n15; and discharge, 253n23; and inpatient services/IOPs (Intensive Outpatient Programs), 77, 79, 240n8; and language, 1–2, 22, 93, 108–11, 119–20, 121–6; mainstream, 4–5, 13–18, 194, 240n6; and outpatient services, 9, 79, 243n20; phases of, 43–4, 105, 210, 170–5; stakes of, 18–9, 32, 69–70, 77–9, 80–2, 199–201; and treatment contract, 10, 77, 167–9, 202–3, 246n10, 269n21. *See also* clinography; MI; Minnesota Model; therapy

AFDC (Aid to Families with Dependent Children), 23, 79, 243n16. *See also* welfare

agency, 5–6, 18–20, 154, 226; and addiction, 168; and gender, 117–8, 262n36; linguistic agency, 132, 170, 198, 221, 273n10. *See also* identity

Agha, Asif, 207, 242n15, 251n13

alcoholism, 89, 100, 243n19, 258n12. *See also* addiction

alexithymia, 108

Althusser, Louis, 16, 153, 180, 251n13

analogy, 26, 34–9, 48, 53, 269n22. *See also* icon; Peirce; Silverstein

anger, 13, 93–5, 106–12, 116, 119–20, 129, 134, 139–40, 215–6

anthropology, 22, 58, 154, 218, 232, 245n26, 250n11; of social work, 262n1, 264n10; of the US, 20. *See also* ethnography; linguistic anthropology

assessment, 3–4, 11, 42–3, 51–7, 60–77, 79, 80–4, 95–106, 158, 196, 229–30, 249n3, 254n26, 258nn14, and 17; and assessment instruments, 96–7, 250nn10, and 11, 252n15, 258nn13, and 15; and drug testing, 66–9, 70–2, 72–5, 101, 254nn24, and 28; and people processing, 53–7, 249n6; and stories, 51–7, 60–5, 66, 71, 76, 83–4; as text, 11, 51–5, 64–6, 75–6; travels of, 10–1, 52–5, 65, 75–9, 229–20. *See also* case; diagnosis; evaluation; intake interview; storytelling

Augustine, 13, 244n23, 257n9, 261n32

318 • Index

Austin, John L., 4, 17, 103, 158–9, 192, 267n12
authority, 76, 81, 89, 126, 154, 156, 159, 224, 266n4. *See also* institution

Bakhtin, M. M., 190, 193–4; and double voicing, 106, 191, 260n25
Bateson, Gregory: on addiction, 90, 257n5; the genogram of, 61,250n11; and metacommunication, 159; and systems therapies, 250n11
Bauman, Richard, 5, 54, 159, 184, 192
Benveniste, Emile, 108, 141
body, 67, 260n28; Butler on, 201; and drug testing, 67, 69, 101, 143, 201–2; and language, 69, 101, 201, 209; as text, 201–2
boundaries, 32–3, 42, 44, 47, 246n11, 248n19, 265n18; and "boundary lapses," 46–7, 248n19; institutional, 266n5; professional, 32–3, 44, 46–7, 145
Briggs, Charles, 5, 54, 75, 82, 272n5
Brodwin, Paul, 212, 268n13, 274n18
Bronfenbrenner, Urie, 58, 228, 277n5; and the ecological model, 60, 228–9
Bush, George W., 23, 243n17
Butler, Judith, 16, 153, 201, 266n3, 271n33, 273n10

case: and case conference, 4, 10; and "case coordination," 33, 36; and case file, 11, 52–3, 249n4. *See also* assessment
case management, 10–1, 42–3, 57, 79, 83–4, 160–4, 196, 212, 239n1, 250n10; and case managers' conflict with therapists, 33–7, 42, 46, 152, 155–6, 160–5, 215
CD (chemical dependency). *See* dependency
Chenot, David, 252n16
child abuse/ neglect, 60, 63, 68, 255n32; and duty to report, 77–9, 147, 253n21, 255n29, 272n8. *See also* Child Protective Services
child care, 10, 38–40, 176, 181–2, 278n12
Child Protective Services (CPS), 77–80, 200, 253n21, 265n22
childhood sexual abuse, 52, 112–117; and drug use, 113–5, 261n31; and shame, 114, 117, 216, 234–5, 261n35
client: as ethnographer, 19, 191, 193, 223, 231; and processing, 53–4, 55–7, 75–6, 249n6. *See also* consumer

Client Advisory Committee, 15–6, 170–83
client representatives, 16–7, 151–3, 170–89
clinography, 11–3, 85, 93, 106, 107–12, 114, 119–120, 214; and subjectivity, 13, 84, 86, 92–95, 107, 110, 120. *See also* addiction treatment; anger; denial; shame
Clinton, Bill: and empowerment, 245n5; and welfare, 8–9, 23–4, 39–41, 165, 245n1, 245nn2, 3, and 4
community, 7, 166, 170–6; as market, 37–8; and participation, 38, 170–6
compliance, 89, 130–2, 264n9, 268n14; as denial, 89, 132. *See also* expertise; flipping the script
confession, 84, 93, 125, 179–82, 265n20; Augustine on, 261n32; and boardroom, 16, 180–2, 202, 232; Foucault on 124, 180
confidentiality, 143–7; and "Rights and Responsibilities," 145, 269n21. *See also* privacy
consumer, 10, 28, 43, 46, 158, 160, 170–6, 243n18, 246n10, 269n24, 271n32; and consumer choice, 77, 160–2, 171, 219; and consumer participation, 28–32, 152–8, 170–7, 269n25; and consumerism, 164, 171, 269n25. *See also* client; empowerment; participation
contextualization, 54, 75–6, and contextualization cues, 193, 195, 199. *See also* index; text
crisis: evidentiary, 19, 68, 195, 226; realist/ nominalist/ metapragmatic, 158–60
critique, 208, 215–7; feminist, 204–8; institutional, 5, 137, 148, 150, 176, 181–3, 189, 207–8; and institutional insulation, 15, 126, 142, 205. *See also* boundaries; flipping the script
Cruikshank, Barbara, 166
culture, 1–5, 20–22, 224, 232–3, 260n28; American, 3–4, 122, 125–6, 150, 224–6, 237, 240n5, 248n1; as "deficit," 242n14; and language, 4, 10, 13–15, 22, 124–6, 150; "new culture of welfare," 270n30; and politics, 22, 228–9. *See also* anthropology; gender; language; race; sensitivity

de Certeau, Michel, 221, 275n26
deixis, 141–2; and rules of use, 141–2. *See also* index; metapragmatics

Index • 319

denial, 4, 11, 13, 82–4, 86–95, 100–7, 119–20, 131–2, 235–7, 256n2, 257nn6, 9, and 11; and death, 104–6; as defense; S, 87–9, 92, 107, 131–2; A. Freud on, 87–8; S. Freud on, 87; T. Gorski on, 86, 89; and lying, 14, 102–3, 132; and repression, 88; topographical metaphors of, 13, 92–4, 107, 111, 119

dependency: chemical (CD); 10, 23–7, 53, 79, 99–100; discourses of, 8–9, 23–7, 37–41, 46–8, 243n17, 269n24; and DSM-IV, 99–100, 259n19; economic, 8–9, 11, 23–7, 45, 46–8, 243n17; Fraser and Gordon on, 9, 24–5; "welfare dependency," 8–9, 25, 41. *See also* addiction; self-sufficiency; welfare

Derrida, Jacques, 85–6, 89, 120, 256n1

Desjarlais, Robert, 124, 221–2

diagnosis, 66, 79, 87, 89, 95–101, 244nn21, and 24. *See also* assessment

distillation, 4, 13, 122–6, 148–50, 224–37; and impurities of language, 137, 150; institutional practice as, 126; and quality control, 144; stations of, 126. *See also* HOW; metalinguistic labor; semiotic process

domestic violence, 7, 57, 63–4, 72, 79, 239n1, 241n10, 251n14

Douglas, Mary, 34, 41. *See also* icon, institution

drug testing, 28, 66–9, 70–2, 72–5, 79, 101, 211–7, 229, 252n18, 254nn24, and 28, 272n8; and assessment, 66–75, 101, 254n28; and discharge, 78–9, 271n31; and evidence, 101; and "faking positive," 75, 80–2, 254n28; and monitored urinalysis, 215–7; and retraumatization, 66, 72, 211; and trumping, 212, 253n20. *See also* body; flipping the script

drugs, 3, 66, 72–5, 117, 127, 232–5, 252n17, 253n19. *See also* addiction

DSM-IV (*Diagnostic and Statistical Manual of Mental Disorders*), 99–101, 259nn19, and 20

Duranti, Alessandro, 239n4, 272n6

duty to report, 77–9, 147, 255n29. *See also* child abuse/neglect; Child Protective Services

EBP (Evidence-Based Practice), 206–7, 274n16, 276n4

empowerment, 7, 160–70, 188–9, 208, 210–1, 230, 268nn16, 17, and 20; and Freire, 165; and "citizen empowerment," 166; and Clinton on "empowerment zones," 165–6; and neoconservatives on "personal empowerment," 165; as politcotherapeutic discourse, 152; and privatization, 166. *See also* enablement

enablement, 152, 160–4, 230; definition of, 268n14

entextualization, 54, 76, 266n4. *See also* assessment, text

epistemology: Bateson on 90; and denial, 90, 101; and expertise, 207–9; and language,115, 135, 208; and truth, 102, 120, 207–9

erasure, 40, 47, 69–70, 107, 140; Irvine and Gal on, 265n17. *See also* icon; indexical iconization

ethics, 223, 240n5, 244n23, 252n16; Brodwin on, 268n13, 274n18; professional, 47. *See also* act-performing consciousness

ethnography, 4–5, 20, 159, 195–6, 232–3, 267n6; and flipping the script, 19, 191, 223, 231; social work as, 226, 232; Strathern on, 22, 231

euphemism, 156, 169, 269n22

evaluation, 1, 94, 218, 229, 231, 249n6; and distribution, 3, 196, 209, 218, 229; and language, 4, 26–7, 126, 144, 150, 195. *See also* assessment; labor

evidence, 11, 19, 67–9, 73, 101, 149–50, 194–5, 208, 226. *See also* epistemology; flipping the script; signs

expertise, 94–101, 119–20, 127–32, 148–149, 211–2, 225–6, 276n2; and drug testing, 132; and flipping the script, 19, 211–2, 225–6

feelings, 4–5, 107–11, 129, 137–43, 176–81; and addiction, 107. *See also* anger; clinography; shame

feminism, 201–7, 262n26; and addiction treatment, 112–3, 273n13; and critique of therapy, 204–8; and feminist therapy; 242n13, 260n29; and "the personal is political," 112, 277n6. *See also* gender

Fliegelman, Jay, 240n5, 248n1

flipping the script, 17–20, 21, 182–3, 190–223, 247n4, 271n1; and act-

flipping the script *(continued)*
  performing consciousness, 193, 196, 223, 277n27; as collective practice, 202, 216, 273n11; and compliance, 130; definition of; 3, 190–1; and drug testing, 199–202, 213–7; and evidentiary crises; 19, 195, 209, 226, 245n26; and expertise, 19, 211–2, 225; and framing, 210, 213–5, 218–9; and freestyle hip-hop; 219–20, 274nn20, and 21; and metalinguistic awareness, 19, 150, 193–4, 195–7, 230; as politics, 186, 189, 196–7, 204, 214–33, 226; and race, 194, 219–21; 275n22; 277n27; and situated practice, 194, 199, 225, 231; and "talking the talk," 130–1, 190, 195. *See also* compliance; evaluation; expertise; metalinguistics; script; truth
Flores, Phillip, 95–6, 104
Foucault, Michel, 25, 124–5, 180, 226, 246n8, 276n3
framing, 158–64, 210–6; and flipping the script, 210, 213–5 218–9; in policy process, 214–5. *See also* wordsmithing
Freud, Sigmund, 87–8, 257n9

Gal, Susan, 5, 78, 126, 152, 265n17
gender, 106, 112–8, 137–42, 205–8, 271n2, 278n12; and gender sensitivity, 8, 31, 234–5, 242n13; and gender-specific addiction treatment, 6, 112–113, 234, 278n11. *See also* culture; feminism; race; sexuality; shame; WFS
genograms, 59–62, 240n11, 251n12; and assessment, 250n10; and GenoPro, 62; and PIE, 59–60
Goffman, Erving: and asylums, 222, 250n8; and framing, 159; and institutions, 47; and participation framework, 192
group therapy, 90–2, 107–9, 133–7, 158, 193, 259n21, 264n15; and confidentiality, 143–8; and group therapy room, 11–3; and rules of speaking, 14, 152–8

Hasenfeld, Yeheskel, 34, 249n6
Hill, Jane, 239n3, 254n26
homelessness, 6–11, 51, 56–7, 241nn11, and 12, 247n16, 255n32; definitions of, 241n10; and dependency, 9–11; and social drift vs. social causation, 42, 241n12. *See also* housing

honesty, 1, 133–50, 183, 191, 198, 205, 208–10, 213–4, 259n21. *See also* HOW
housing, 79; and "the hook," 32, 77; and housing-first, 233, 277nn8, and 9; and Section Eight, 33, 247n13. *See also* homelessness
HOW (honesty, openness, and willingness), 1, 133–50, 191, 205, 213–214; and rules of speaking, 143–4. *See also* distillation; honesty; openness; willingness

icon, 26–48; and client icon, 38–41, 47–8; Fraser and Gordon on, 25; Peirce on, 26. *See also* analogy; indexical iconization
identity, 34–8, 57, 250n8, 276n27; and addict identity, 180–2; institutional, 154, 189. *See also* icon; interpellation; role
ideology. *See* language ideology
index, 138, 140, 142; and deixis,141–2; and erasure, 106–7; Peirce on, 26; and selective indexing 78–9. *See also* deixis; indexical iconization; signs
indexical iconization, 106–7, 115–6, 126, 129, 135–6, 138–42, 265n17; and distillation, 142
inner reference, 4, 11–9, 94, 119–20, 122–6, 129–31, 133–50, 158, 180–2, 191–5, 197–202, 213–4, 218–23, 224–37, 239n3; and personalist ideologies, 239n4. *See also* HOW; language ideology
insight, 12–3, 82–3, 90–5, 104, 112, 115–116, 123, 133, 186, 197, 243n19, 262n37; and confrontation, 104. *See also* addiction; will
institution, 2–20, 38, 40, 43–8, 62, 78, 122–6, 149–50, 153–4, 170, 188–9, 194, 220–3, 224–6, 237, 246n9, 266n5, 276n2; and accountability, 269n21; and authority, 89, 106, 126, 156; and conflict, 33–37, 42, 46, 152; 155–6; 160–165, 215; and identity, 154, 189; and institutional insulation, 15, 126, 142, 229; and naturalization, 34, 206; and power, 154, 180. *See also* authority; role
intake, *See* assessment
intentionality, 103, 267n12; and truth, 101, 106. *See also* sincerity
interpellation: Althusser on 181–2, 251n13; and anticipatory interpellation, 16, 153–4, 160, 170, 182, 187, 191, 230; Butler on, 271n33

intervention, the: and V. Johnson, 259n22; as popular discourse, 104
interview: Briggs on, 54, 75, 82; clinical/social work, 51–6, 66–5, 76, 82, 83, 97, 101, 196, 230, 249n4, 250n9; social scientific, 13, 17–9, 75, 82, 195–6, 245n26, 272n5. *See also* assessment; MI
inventory, 56, 93–6, 107–15, 119–20; and expertise, 120. *See also* clinography
Irvine, Judith, 265n17, 274n17

Jakobson, Roman, 272n6

Kaufman, Edward, 88–9
Keane, Webb, 124, 224
kinship, 250n11; as 'environment', 58. *See also* genograms

labor: evaluative and distributive, 196, 209, 229; and indexical iconization, 142. *See also* metalinguistic labor
language: functions of, 3–4, 124–6, 193–4, 218, 224; and talking cure, 3, 13, 244n21; and ways of speaking, 2–3, 151–4, 222. *See also* inner reference; language ideology; metalinguistic labor; metalinguistics; performance; reference; signs; therapy
language ideology, 54–5, 188–9, 196, 233, 265n17, 260n28; African American, 220, 275n24; and American culture, 3–5, 15, 124, 224, 248n1; and inner reference, 4, 124–5, 190, 220, 224; and logocentrism, 85, 120; and personalist ideologies, 239n4; and semiotic ideology, 5, 189, 191, 226, 236, 272n4
Latour, Bruno, 151, 188–9, 266nn1, and 2
linguistic anthropology, 124, 153, 159, 246n8, 272n6; and emotion, 260n28, 275n25; and institution, 9, 36, 62, 126, 170, 251n13; and interview, 54; and gender, 152; and metapragmatic awareness, 193–6; and performativity, 159, 192–4. *See also* language ideology; metalinguistics; semiotic processes
Lipsky, Michael, 25, 173

Malinowski, Bronislow, 1–2, 20
meetings, 151–8, 173–9; and framing, 162–5; and meeting minutes, 121, 156–7, 230, 267nn8, and 11, 268n15;

and representation, 156, 158, 268n15, 270n28
memory, 111–113; Augustine on 244n23, 257n9, 261n32; and drugs, 117; traumatic, 114, 125. *See also* Young
metalinguistics, 13–5, 19, 51, 55, 69, 76, 119–20, 121–6, 127–9, 133–5, 139–50, 158, 168, 170, 185, 189, 191–7, 199, 205, 207–8, 224–5, 235, 242n15, 266n1, 269n22, 272n6; and flipping the script, 195–6; and metacommunication, 159; 162. *See also* language ideology; metalinguistic awareness; metalinguistic labor; metapragmatics
metalinguistic awareness, 19, 150, 193–7, 220–1, 225, 230
metalinguistic labor, 15, 22, 40, 48, 93, 120, 121–6, 133, 140–50, 152, 158, 180, 184, 197, 224
metapragmatics, 158–9, 197–8, 207–8, 225, 272n6; and metapragmatic crisis, 158–9
methodology: and flipping the script, 195–6, 245n26; and metapragmatics, 195–6
Miller, William, 235–6, 256n2. *See also* Motivational Interviewing (MI)
mimesis, 191, 221–2, 226; Bakhtin on, 194. *See also* flipping the script
Minnesota Model, 12, 123, 240n6, 244n22, 262n2. *See also* AA
Motivational Interviewing (MI), 12, 123, 235–7, 256n2, 258n16, 259n22, 278n14
Mouffe, Chantal, 218, 274n19

NA (Narcotics Anonymous), 12, 272n15. *See also* AA; Twelve Steps; WFS
narrative, 1–3, 4–5, 11–2, 18, 37–9, 138, 147, 218, 235, 250nn7, and 9, 258n17, 261n33; and assessment, 51–7, 64–5, 69; and narrative therapy, 122; and "recovery narratives," 3, 11–2, 56, 60, 115, 129, 235. *See also* script; storytelling
naturalization, 15, 22, 40, 125, 224
neoliberalism, 8–9, 38, 166–7, 259n20, 269n23. *See also* consumer; welfare
NIAAA (National Institute for Alcohol Abuse and Alcoholism), 96, 258n12
NIDA (National Institute on Drug Abuse), 96, 258n12
NIH (National Institutes of Health), 258n12

openness, 1, 133–7, 139–41, 147–50, 183, 191, 198, 205, 208–10, 213–4; as evidence of honesty, 134. *See also* HOW

participation, 21–22, 170–7, 268n18; consumer, 28–32, 152, 189, 269n25; and empowerment 166, 174; and program governance, 21–9, 171–3; and rationales for non-participation, 173–89
Peirce, Charles S., 26–7
people processing, 34, 249n6
performance, 19, 130, 152, 191–3, 214; illocutionary and perlocutionary force, 123, 130, 221; and performatives, 4, 17, 123, 158–9, 192; and reference, 19, 192–4, 272n4, 240n7
personhood: ethics of, 223; ideologies of, 3, 41, 55, 220, 224, 246n11, 248n1; policies of, 25, 40. *See also* subjectivity
PIE (Person-In-Environment), 57–8, 252n15
policy, 159, 173, 214–8; institutional, 26, 159, 216; of personhood, 25, 40
politics, 151, 188–9, 271n34; and culture, 22, 228–9, 266n4; definition of, 218–20, 266n4; and flipping the script, 196–7, 182–3, 218; institutional, 151, 226; of language, 1–22, 26, 36, 48, 266n4, 274n24; and politico-therapeutic discourse, 9, 152, 153; and representation, 151–3, 188–9; of therapy, 10, 126, 148, 229–30, 249n4, 260n28
poverty, 23–4, 241n9, 241n12, 255n32
power: and assessment, 51, 69; and coercion, 168–70; institutional, 154, 180, 226; and therapy, 148; and resistance, 226, 275n25, 276n3
privacy, 51, 137–42, 146, 248n1, 264n16. *See also* confidentiality; personhood

race, 219–20, 276n27; and African American verbal repertoires, 220, 275n24; and flipping the script, 194, 219–20; and gender, 26; and institutional racism, 26, 220–1
Raymond, Williams, 24
Reddy, William, 260n28
Reed, Beth Glover, 112
reference, 3–4, 129, 140–1; and performance, 19, 192–4, 272n4, 240n7. *See also* inner reference; language ideology

reflexivity, 230–1. *See also* metalinguistic awareness
register, 242n15, 247n14
representation, 151–8, 161–4, 182–9, 266n1, 268n15; and *Dingpolitik*, 151, 266n2; and evaluation, 53, 229; and semiotic economy, 224
ritual, 1–2, 5, 264n10; assessment as, 53; of discourse, 180; and group therapy, 11
role, 17, 19; inhabitation, 179–80, 224–5; recruitment, 62, 220, 251n13. *See also* institution; interpellation
Rosaldo, Michelle, 239n3, 267n12
Rose, Nicholas, 166

safety, 78, 134; and group therapy, 44–5, 102–4, 145–8, 202–5. *See also* Child Protective Services; therapy
script, 1–6, 13, 17, 23, 189, 192–5, 199, 225, 226, 231–2, 272n3; feminist, 19, 205–8; urinalysis as, 201–2, 210–4. *See also* flipping the script, narrative, storytelling
secrets: and denial, 14, 132; and "hidden agendas," 197–9; and "secrets keep you sick," 14, 132, 138–9
self-awareness. *See also* insight
self-help, 14, 124, 171, 242n13, 265n20, 277n6; ideology of, 164, 189; and the Twelve Steps, 203. *See also* welfare
self-sufficiency, 3, 8, 10–1, 30, 33–4, 38, 44–7, 149, 166, 217. *See also* dependency, empowerment, sobriety.
semiotic process, 3, 9, 15, 25, 36, 53, 126, 140–2, 240n7, 251n13, 265n17; Peirce on, 26. *See also* erasure; indexical iconization; language ideologies; signs
sensitivity, 8, 31, 46, 106–7, 113, 203, 208, 234, 242n13; to addiction, 163–4; cultural, 242n14. *See also* gender
sexuality, 124, 138–41, 264n16
shame, 13, 93–5, 112, 118–20, 138–42, 214–6; and sexual abuse 112–7, 261n35; and women, 116–8, 215, 234. *See also* clinography
signs, 4, 15, 26, 94, 119–20, 125, 133, 141, 163, 194, 232, 258n17, 261n32; urinalysis as procurement of, 210–1. *See also* evidence; icon; index; reference; semiotic process

Silverstein, Michael, 36, 38, 54, 126, 141–2, 193–4, 240n7, 251n13, 266n4, 267n6, 272nn6, and 9
sincerity, 124, 195, 274n17, 276n27
sobriety, 2–4, 8, 10–5, 30, 33–4, 38, 44–50, 90–5, 109, 120, 149, 194, 202, 217, 237; and distillation, 120, 124, 127; and language, 4, 15, 120, 124, 127, 133–50, 224–6; Weber on 13, 240n5, 244n23. *See also* addiction, dependency, self-sufficiency
social services, 2–8, 14, 153, 226, 229, 234, 239n1, 249n6, 277n6; individualization of, 7; transportation, 31–2; "wrap-around" service delivery, 7. *See also* child care; housing
social work, 2–3, 22, 57, 65, 165, 196, 226–237; and MSW (Master's degree in Social Work), 239n1; and National Association of Social Workers Code of Ethics, 255n29; and social worker as ethnographer, 227–230
storytelling, 49–57, 62–72, 82–4, 265n20; and (auto)biography, 36, 51, 57, 250n9; and "social histories," 51, 60, 65–6, 129; travel of, 75–9; and "War stories," 49, 52, 129. *See also* assessment, narrative
strategy, 19, 22, 68, 74, 82, 157–8, 187, 221–2; de Certeau on, 221, 275n26; Desjarlais on, 221–2; linguistic, 17, 202, 82, 95, 107, 140, 145, 153, 157–8, 182, 189, 196, 198, 202, 208, 221–2, 245n26, 260n25, 263n6, 266n4
Strathern, Marilyn, 22, 231
structure, 27–35, 46–8, 97, 105; in addiction treatment, 43–6; institutional, 37–41; personal, 41–3; and practice, 30–35; 46
subjectivity, 85, 180, 248n1; addicted subjectivity, 13, 85–7, 92–5, 107, 120, 233; and language, 123, 248n1; topographical model of, 92–4, 110, 122–3, 257n9. *See also* personhood; privacy

text: assessment as, 11, 51–5, 64–6, 75–6; the body as, 202; and contextualization and entextualization, 54, 75–6, 266n4; and meeting minutes, 121, 156–7, 230, 267nn8, and 11, 268n15; and text-artifacts, 21, 192. *See also* context
therapy: approaches to, 233–7; and hybridity, 14; individual, 129, 198; (mate)language of, 1–5, 15, 21–2, 121–2, 127–33, 133–5, 135–7, 137–42, 143–150, 179; narrative, 122; and politics 9–10, 126, 152–3, 224, 229–30; and safety, 102–3, 146; and time, 43–6. *See also* addiction treatment; group therapy
trauma, 60, 62–5, 112–4, 235, 260n30; Young on, 125, 264n15. *See also* childhood sexual abuse
truth: and addiction, 82, 85–9, 101–2, 108–9; and evidence, 72–3, 82–4, 213; and flipping the script, 207–9; and inner reference, 92–5, 109–20, 133, 137–42; and representation, 151–2
Twelve Steps, 123, 262n3; and prohibition of cross-talk, 265n20. *See also* AA, NA, WFS

urinalysis. *See* drug testing

voice: Bakhtin on, 191, 260n25; and the body, 201; and "having a voice," 269n25

Weber, Max, 13, 244n23
welfare: and "the end of welfare as we know it," 23, 65; and paternalism, 165; and "personal responsibility," 24, 39, 176, 181, 227; and PRWORA (Personal Responsibility and Work Opportunity Reconciliation Act), 24, 40, 243n16, 246n6; and retrenchment 2, 24, 38, 40–1, 65, 153, 164, 174, 227; and "welfare dependency," 8–9, 25, 41, 243n17; and welfare reform, 26, 40, 48, 64–5, 269n25; and welfare state, 14, 165–6, 259n20.
will, 90–2, 256n4; and insight, 243n19, 262n37; and sobriety, 240n5. *See also* addiction
willingness, 1, 133–7, 137–40, 144, 147–50, 183, 191, 198, 205, 208–10, 213–4; *See also* HOW
Women for Sobriety (WFS), 13–14, 203–10, 265n20, 273n13; and Thirteen Affirmations, 14. *See also* AA; gender, NA
wordsmithing, 152–3, 164, 165–70, 183–9, 225–6; *See also* framing
Wurmser, Leon, 88, 260n27, 261n35

Young, Allan, 125, 264n15